A Theory of Political Obligation

CW00392712

Margaret Gilbert offers an incisive new approach to a classic problem of political philosophy: when and why should I do what the laws of my country tell me to do? Beginning with carefully argued accounts of social groups in general and political societies in particular, the author argues that in central, standard senses of the relevant terms membership in a political society in and of itself obligates one to support that society's political institutions. The obligations in question are not moral requirements derived from general moral principles, but a matter of one's participation in a special kind of commitment: joint commitment. An agreement is sufficient but not necessary to generate such a commitment. Gilbert uses the phrase 'plural subject' to refer to all of those who are jointly committed in some way. She therefore labels the theory offered in this book the plural subject theory of political obligation.

The author concentrates on the exposition of this theory, carefully explaining how and in what sense joint commitments obligate. She also explores a classic theory of political obligation—actual contract theory—according to which one is obligated to conform to the laws of one's country because one agreed to do so. She offers a new interpretation of this theory in light of a plural subject theory of agreements. She argues that actual contract theory has more merit than has been thought, though the more general plural subject theory is to be preferred. She compares and contrasts plural subject theory with identification theory, relationship theory, and the theory of fair play. She brings it to bear on some classic situations of crisis, and, in the concluding chapter, suggests a number of avenues for related empirical and moral inquiry.

Clearly and compellingly written, *A Theory of Political Obligation* will be essential reading for political philosophers and theorists.

Margaret Gilbert holds the Melden Chair in Moral Philosophy at the University of California, Irvine.

A Theory of Political Obligation

Membership, Commitment, and the Bonds of Society

Margaret Gilbert

CLARENDON PRESS · OXFORD

OXFORD
UNIVERSITY PRESS

Great Clarendon Street, Oxford OX2 6DP

Oxford University Press is a department of the University of Oxford.
It furthers the University's objective of excellence in research, scholarship,
and education by publishing worldwide in

Oxford New York

Auckland Cape Town Dar es Salaam Hong Kong Karachi
Kuala Lumpur Madrid Melbourne Mexico City Nairobi
New Delhi Shanghai Taipei Toronto

With offices in

Argentina Austria Brazil Chile Czech Republic France Greece
Guatemala Hungary Italy Japan Poland Portugal Singapore
South Korea Switzerland Thailand Turkey Ukraine Vietnam

Oxford is a registered trademark of Oxford University Press
in the UK and in certain other countries

Published in the United States
by Oxford University Press Inc., New York

British Library Cataloguing in Publication Data

Data available

Library of Congress Cataloging in Publication Data

Gilbert, Margaret.
  A theory of political obligation : membership, commitment, and the
bonds of society / Margaret Gilbert.
      p. cm.
  Includes bibliographical references and index.
  ISBN-13: 978-0-19-927495-6 (alk. paper)
  ISBN-10: 0-19-927495-9 (alk. paper)
  1. Political obligation.   I.   Title.
  JC329.5.G55 2006
  306.2—dc22

                                                    2006008586

Typeset by Laserwords Private Limited, Chennai, India
Printed in Great Britain
on acid-free paper by
Biddles Ltd., King's Lynn, Norfolk

ISBN 978-0-19-927495-6 (Hbk.)   978-0-19-954395-3 (Pbk.)

10 9 8 7 6 5 4 3 2 1

For
Miriam Gilbert
1911–2000
In loving memory

Preface

This book expounds and defends a novel approach to a long-standing problem in political philosophy—the problem of political obligation. A central version of this problem may be put as follows: 'Does membership in a political society obligate one to uphold the political institutions of that society?' I refer to this as *the membership problem*. Many have been inclined to give a positive answer, but no argument to that effect has found general acceptance.

My solution to the membership problem appeals to a particular conception of a political society. According to this conception, the members of a political society are jointly committed to uphold its political institutions. From this it can be argued that they are obligated to uphold them. A large part of the novelty of this solution is its invocation of joint commitment as a source of obligation.

I first argued for the central role of joint commitment in human behaviour in my 1989 book *On Social Facts*. I continue to refine my understanding of this fundamental idea. I refer to those who are jointly committed in some way as *plural subjects*, and thus refer to my solution to the membership problem as *the plural subject theory of political obligation*.

In order not to complicate the exposition of this theory, I focus on the explanation of my own ideas. Of the other positions I discuss, I spend most time on *actual contract theory*. This holds that political societies are constituted by agreements that obligate their members to uphold their political institutions. It has been on the philosophical menu for more than two thousand years in one form or another and is probably the best-known theory of political obligation. It has significant attractions, but has fallen out of favour in light of two standard objections. As I explain, actual contract theory can be understood as a special case of plural subject theory. So understood, it can be defended against one, but not both, of the standard objections. The more general theory is proof against both.

I first envisioned this theory when completing *On Social Facts*. Since then, I have given many related presentations in Europe and the United States and have published a number of articles that explore pertinent issues. This book pulls together different threads, addresses a number of central questions for the first time, and explores others in greater depth. Inevitably, it touches on many issues that call for further discussion.

The book is divided into three parts, each of which is outlined before the chapter that opens it. Each chapter is preceded by a short summary. Where I think it may be helpful, I have marked significant new themes and points by the introduction of a subheading. In many cases comments and references to the work of other authors have been confined to the footnotes so as not to distract the reader from the main flow of the argument.

I am grateful to all of those who have discussed this material with me. They have often forced me to clarify and deepen central points in the argument, and helped me better to understand its scope and its limits. Particular thanks go to Virginia Held, Arthur Kuflik, and Jonathan Wolff, official commentators on various occasions when I gave talks on these ideas, and to those who have published comments on my work in this area including Ulrich Balzer, Richard Dagger, and John Simmons.

John Horton read the penultimate version of the manuscript and made many helpful comments. I am most grateful to him and to two anonymous readers for the Press. Special thanks also to Paul Bloomfield, Richard Hine, David Slutsky, and John Troyer for reading and commenting on parts of the manuscript, and to John Simmons—whose work on political obligation has been an important stimulus—for encouraging me to write this book.

Discussions with the students in my classes on political obligation and related topics at the University of Connecticut, King's College London, and the Technical University of Dresden, have been stimulating and helpful. Colin Caret provided substantial help with the Bibliography and in preparation of the text. My thanks to all of these and, as always, to Shelly Burelle.

In the years since its inception this project has greatly benefited from the financial support of the University of Connecticut, Storrs; the American Council of Learned Societies (research fellowship 1989–90); the National Endowment for the Humanities (summer stipend, 1999); and the Swedish Collegium for Advanced Study in the Social Sciences (visiting fellowship, spring 2004).

Throughout the time I have been working on this book, my friends and family have been kind and patient with one who was unable to socialize as much as they (and she) would have liked. My warm appreciation goes to all of them. My mother, Miriam Gilbert, deserves the greatest thanks in this respect. I dedicate this book to her memory with gratitude and love.

Three friends, now greatly missed, contributed in different, important ways to this book at different stages on its way. Thanks always to Margaret Dauler Wilson, Lucille Nahemow, and Gregory Nolder.

The paperback printing includes a few clarifying changes to the original text and some amplification of the index that do not affect the pagination of the book.

Contents

PART I

A Central Problem of Political Obligation

This part introduces the problem addressed in this book and distinguishes it from a number of others that have been referred to as 'the problem of political obligation'. The focal problem here is the membership problem: Does membership in a political society obligate one to uphold the political institutions of that society? For short: Are there political obligations?

I offer an initial clarification of the nature of obligation and outline my understanding of what a maximally satisfactory solution to the membership problem would achieve. I then spend some time on a famous solution to the membership problem: actual contract theory.

Though it has had some formidable proponents, this is now generally dismissed by reference to two standard objections. At the same time people often allow that aspects of the theory make it particularly attractive as a solution to the membership problem. I explain these and review the two standard objections. It is clear that in spite of its merits, actual contract theory falls short of the standards of success proposed.

Some authors have recently opted for alternatives to actual contract theory in terms of subjective identification or the existence of relationships. I argue that though these suggestions have some plausibility, inquiry cannot stop with them. As will emerge in the course of the book, all of the theories discussed in this part have something in common with my own solution to the membership problem.

1
The Membership Problem

This chapter introduces the problem that is the focus of this book. It divides into two main sections. The first offers an initial clarification of some critical terms. The second distinguishes the problem at hand from a number of others that have been discussed in the literature of political philosophy.

1.1 The Problem

The Laws' Idea

More than two thousand years ago, the philosopher Socrates was condemned to death in the Athenian courts. After his death, his pupil Plato wrote an imaginary dialogue depicting the situation before Socrates' death sentence was carried out. Socrates' friend Crito, who believes he is innocent, is trying to persuade him to flee Athens to escape death. Socrates describes what he thinks the laws of Athens would say in opposition to Crito's urgings. The following quotation is from the speech he imagines:

> if you cannot persuade your country, you must do whatever it orders, and patiently submit to any punishment that it imposes... And if it leads you out to war, to be wounded, or killed, you must comply, and it is right that you should do so.[1]

Are the laws right? Is it the case that one must do whatever one's country orders? Must one do so even if one is likely to be maimed or killed as a result? Is it the case that one must take whatever punishment one's country has meted out? Must one do this even if one's death is a certain or near-certain consequence?

The question is not, it should be said, a question of what one can get away with. As Socrates' friend Crito makes clear in the course of the dialogue, it

---

[1] Plato (1978a: 51c). I shall cite only margin numbers for Plato's texts.

would be easy enough for him to flee from Athens to another jurisdiction where he could live out the rest of his days.

Clarifying the Issue

The question needs, in fact, a fair amount of clarification. Let me focus, first, on the fact that the laws refer to 'orders'.[2]

I take it that to speak of orders or commands *presupposes* that it is in some sense incumbent on the recipient of the orders to do what he (or she or it) is ordered to do.[3] For to issue a genuine order one needs the authority or standing to do so. One must, that is, have the right to be obeyed. This right entails an obligation to conform to the order on the part of its recipient. Thus, there is a sense in which he *must* conform. This may suggest putting the question as follows: does one's country have the authority to give one orders? I shall adopt a different procedure, which is not to say that I shall ignore the topic of authority in this book.[4]

I understand the question in terms not of authoritative orders—if you like, genuine orders—but purported ones. A purported order may be an order proper, but it need not be. What is necessary for there to be a purported order is only the stance of the one who issues it. He must presume or, in effect, propose that he is issuing an order proper.

Carefully put, then, the question is this: must one act in accordance with one's country's purported orders—whatever they are? Should one fail to do so, must one then submit to whatever painful process one's country metes out in response—even one's death?

I do not write of *obedience* here, since obedience strictly speaking implies the existence of a genuine and not merely purported order. One can act in accordance with a merely purported order, comply with it, do what it says, and so on (these things all being more or less the same). One cannot, however, *obey* it. I take this to be a purely logical point. Both 'order' and 'obedience' are terms that, strictly speaking, presuppose authority.

I say 'strictly speaking' since there is no need to deny that these terms are sometimes used in a relatively loose way. Thus in describing an encounter with a gunman someone might say: 'He ordered me to hand over my wallet.'

---

[2] The Greek verb for what is reasonably translated as 'orders' in the quotation is (in transliteration) *keleuein*.

[3] For the sake of brevity I shall generally use the generic 'he'. In the case of the generic recipient of orders I have here used the alternative 'he or she or it' rather than the conventional 'he or she' since orders can be given to collectives—as in 'The government ordered the company to provide better health insurance for its employees'.

[4] It is mostly addressed in Ch. 11, below, after the main theses of the book have been elaborated.

I take this to be a loose way of speaking. Be that as it may, it is a different way of speaking, assuming that the person who says this would not allow that the gunman had any kind of right to be obeyed.

I take punishment, strictly speaking, to be a matter of authority also. Someone who responds in a hostile fashion to one who fails to conform to a purported order of his own may describe himself as 'punishing' the nonconformist. Unless he has authority to punish, however, this is merely purported punishment—strictly speaking.

'Punishment', too, is a term that is sometimes used in what looks like a different way, one that does not presuppose authority. That such a different use exists would not be surprising given that the idea of punishment, strictly speaking, is a relatively rich one. It involves at least two things: some kind of negative treatment in response to an action of the person so treated, and the standing to impose such treatment in this case. It would not be surprising that a weaker notion involving only one of these things should coexist with the stronger notion. Similar things can be said with respect to those weaker notions of 'order', 'obedience', and so on that lack the presupposition of authority. For present purposes it is enough that a standard construal of these terms—which is the construal I adopt here—is indeed authority-presupposing. This means that one must exercise a special caution in using them in the present context.

The question I put here is not a better question than the one about authority. It is simply a different question, one that has much interested philosophers.

It will be awkward, in what follows, to use the rather cumbersome phrase 'purported orders'. So I will mostly write of 'orders', simply. That purported orders are in question should be understood. The same goes for the other terms just mentioned, and any others that fall into the same category.

The laws address Socrates in particular. At one point in their oration they note that his circumstances are somewhat special. They are such that he, if anyone, should comply with their orders. They suggest, too, that Athens is somewhat special, being a well-governed state. They also emphasize that Athenian citizens can emigrate if they choose, something that might not have been the case. It is not clear precisely why they make note of these special features. For the quoted passage strongly suggests the following simple idea: one must conform to the commands of one's country, and pay the ensuing penalty if one does not, *by virtue of the fact that the country in question is one's own.* Without meaning to imply exegetical accuracy, I shall now refer to this as *the laws' idea.*

The Laws' Allies

The laws' idea is not unique to them. Others have either expressed or reported on similar views. Thus in his now classic work, *Moral Principles and Political Obligations*, A. John Simmons writes:

Many people feel, I think, that they are tied in a special way to their government... While they complain loudly and often, and not without justification, of the short-comings of government, they feel that they are nonetheless bound to support their country's political institutions... in ways that they are not bound to the corresponding institutions in *other* countries.[5]

In his classic work *In Defense of Anarchism*, Robert Paul Wolff writes in a more personal vein:

When I take a vacation in Great Britain, I obey its laws, both because of prudential self-interest and because of the obvious moral considerations concerning the value of order,... and so forth. On my return to the United States, I have a sense of re-entering *my* country, and if I think about the matter at all, I imagine myself to stand in a different and more intimate relationship to American laws. They have been promulgated by *my* government, and I therefore have a special obligation to obey them.[6]

Whatever the precise extent of this sense of things, it is clearly part of the experience of many.[7]

Wolff, like Simmons, found it hard to justify. Indeed, each of these philosophers argued, in his own way, that it was illusory. In contrast, a number of philosophers have maintained that it is incontrovertible.

Thomas McPherson is one of the authors in question.[8] He writes:

Belonging in society involves... rights and obligations. Understanding what it is to be social would be impossible unless we understood what it is to have rights and obligations—and vice versa... That social man has obligations is an analytic, not a synthetic, proposition... 'Why should I obey the government?' is an absurd question. We have not understood what it means to be a member of political society if we

---

[5] Simmons (1979: 3–4). He later (1979: 34 n. *h*) cites the observation by Ewing (1947: 213) that it is 'almost universally held' that we have some special obligation to *our* country. The conclusion of Simmons's book is that the feeling in question is (mostly) misguided. I discuss aspects of Simmons's discussion at various points in the text and notes below.

[6] R. P. Wolff (1970: 18–19). Note the 'therefore' in the last sentence. Wolff's philosophical conclusion—as opposed to his pre-theoretical thoughts—on this matter is similar to that of Simmons. Both have been referred to as 'philosophical anarchists'. See Horton (1992: 123–36).

[7] Its precise extent is of course an empirical matter about which there may yet be insufficient data. Cf. Green (1996) repr. in Edmunson ed. (1999).

[8] Others include Pitkin (1966), discussed by Simmons (1979: 39); and MacDonald (1951), discussed by Horton (1992: 138–41). Horton himself develops what he sees as an argument of roughly this kind. I say more about his view later in the text.

suppose that political obligation is something that we might not have had and that therefore needs to be justified . . .'[9]

Analytic Membership Arguments

McPherson here invokes a distinction from the philosophy of language, the analytic-synthetic distinction. I take his point to be roughly as follows. To say that the members of a political society are obligated to obey its laws is to say something that is true by virtue of the meanings of the terms involved. It is, in other words, analytic. Given the meanings of its terms, it cannot be false. It is true as a conceptual matter or as 'a matter of logic'. It cannot be refuted by an appeal to experience. So it makes no sense to doubt it.

Something like the analytic-synthetic distinction goes back a long way. In the contemporary philosophical literature it has been famously criticized and defended.[10] Discussions of this matter can go right to the heart of the philosophy of language and there is no possibility of engaging with them here. I take the debate to continue and shall allow that for purposes of this discussion a distinction along these lines is legitimate.[11]

I shall refer to arguments like McPherson's as *analytic membership arguments*.[12] Such arguments vary enormously in terms of their content, clarity, and sophistication. They may amount to little more than bare assertion. When that is the case I shall say that we are being offered a *general* analytic membership argument. When some argument is given, in particular when the connection between belonging in society and obligations is to some extent explained, however roughly, I shall say that the author proposes a *special* analytic membership argument.

Clearly, the sense of things expressed by proponents of analytic membership arguments accords with the laws' idea. Like the people to whom Simmons refers, and Wolff in his pre-theoretical stance, they can be counted among the laws' allies.

Before continuing I should make two terminological points. First, I originally couched the laws' idea in terms of what one 'must' do (where this was not just a matter of what one could not get away with). Like McPherson, many contemporary authors write of 'obligations' in the present context. I take it

---

[9] McPherson (1967: 64; see also 65).

[10] The distinction was famously criticized by Quine (1951); and defended by Grice and Strawson (1956) among others.

[11] Cf. Gilbert (1989: 11).

[12] Pateman (1979) refers to 'the conceptual argument'. Simmons (1979) writes of 'the linguistic argument'. I used the label 'analytic membership argument' in Gilbert (1993c). The inclusion of 'membership' indicates what I take to be the central term or concept in the argument—at least in the version with which I was, and am, most concerned.

that if I have an obligation to do something then in some sense I 'must' do it. I recur to the topic of obligations at length later. For now I continue to write of 'obligations' without further comment.

Second, another 'slide' in the text here is from the reference to a person's 'country' to references (as in the quote from McPherson) to a 'political society'. Suffice it to say, for now, that the equation of one's country with the political society of which one is a member appears to be a natural one. The situation appears to be different with the term 'nation'. Sometimes this is used more as a synonym of 'people', where a people may not yet be organized into a political society. Sometimes it means something closer to 'country'. Sometimes, again, it is used in a context where, roughly, some person or body has control of a territory and engages in relations with other such persons. In such situations, too, there may be no political society.[13]

There have also been references in this section not just to orders but also to laws, governments, and political institutions. For purposes of this section I shall suppose that (purported) orders of some kind are at issue in all of these cases.

In a brief consideration of general analytic membership arguments, Simmons proposes that even if one accepts that a member of a political society, as such, has the relevant obligations one can still quite reasonably ask 'Why do members of a political society have these obligations?' 'On what are these obligations based?'[14]

Whether or not the supposed analytical connections exist depends, of course, on the notion of membership in a political society that is at issue. This brings up an important point. It is not necessary to suppose that there is a single 'correct' understanding of what membership in a political society is. There may be one plausible way of understanding this, given standard meanings of the relevant terms, or there may be several. A theorist may or may not be concerned with standard meanings. He may wish, rather, to stipulate a definition that is intended to capture an important phenomenon he takes to be worthy of the name.

Each theorist therefore needs to say something about his own understanding of what membership in a political society amounts to. It may be that one can make an analytic membership argument for the construal he has in mind, but not for others.

In mounting his arguments against the laws' idea, Simmons is not explicit on this matter. Evidently he is mostly operating with quite a broad notion of membership in a political society. On one occasion he allows that there is a narrower notion in relation to which there is a tight, if not analytic, relationship

---

[13]　Compare Walzer (1977: 54).　　[14]　Simmons (1979: 42).

between membership and obligation.[15] He refers, here, to membership 'in the full sense of the word'. Given his overall argument and negative conclusion, however, he clearly has another sense of the word in mind most of the time.

I take Simmons to be correct in suggesting that general analytic membership arguments raise at least the following two issues. First, is there indeed some conceptual connection between membership in a political society—under some natural construal—and obligation? Second: what is the ground of the obligation? Can it be given an articulate basis?

Some Immediate Concerns

i. Is there Some Confusion? One may think that there is a serious problem for all analytic membership arguments. For one may think, in somewhat vague and general terms, that whether or not someone is a member of a particular political society is a matter of natural fact, whereas whether or not he must do such-and-such or has obligations is not a fact of this kind. It is, if you like, a non-natural fact.[16] One may then infer that any analytical membership argument must be confused. How can 'I am a member of a political society'—a natural fact—logically imply 'I have obligations'—a non-natural fact? In pursuit of this line of thought, one might wonder whether some non-natural premiss—some moral claim, perhaps—is being slipped into the argument.

ii. Morally Unacceptable Institutions It could be wrong, of course, to think someone's being a member of a particular political society is a matter of 'natural' fact—depending on what that comes down to. On the other hand, some 'non-natural' premisses may look implausible from the start.

Thus one might suspect that the argument depends on a definition of 'political society' such that a political society cannot be evil. Without entering into the question yet as to what a political society is, it may seem implausible to deny that there can be an evil political society. Someone who is of this opinion may voice the following concern in relation to analytic membership arguments. Given the possibility of evil political societies, how can it be that the members of *all* political societies are obligated in the way suggested? That is, after all, what those who put forward analytic membership arguments claim. They do not refer to membership in *good* political societies, but to membership in political societies, full stop.

---

[15] Simmons (1979: 140).

[16] Compare G. E. Moore's allusion to the 'non-natural' property of goodness. He contrasted goodness with yellowness, which he deemed a 'natural' property in Moore (1968).

Some may not be comfortable using the epithet 'evil', generally or in this context. The question at issue does not depend on its use. It is surely pertinent to at least some morally flawed societies that do not count precisely as evil.[17]

A related issue is this. What if, in the midst of an otherwise good set of orders, a morally wicked order appears? The idea that one could be obligated to conform to such an order may seem preposterous—or at least to stand in need of explanation.

As to punishment, what if a court's judgement is on a given occasion erroneous or the penalty it imposes excessive? Many would argue that the case of the historical Socrates involved both of the last. They would argue that he was not a malign influence on the youth of Athens, as he was alleged to have been. They would argue, further, that even had he been such an influence, the death penalty was too great for such a crime, if it is acceptable for any. Was he obligated to submit to this penalty? Was there any sense in which he *must* do so?

iii. What Kind of 'must' and How Significant?   One might indeed wonder exactly what it can mean to say that one *must* obey one's country's orders. Here I revert to the language in terms of which I first formulated the laws' idea. The same worries may arise if the idea is couched in terms of obligation.[18] Can doing something contrary to what one's country orders never be justified? Perhaps if one drives without stopping at a stop sign on the road one can avoid being killed by a rogue driver. Surely it cannot sanely be argued that one must abide by the law on that occasion?

Again, must one—in some sense—conform to absolutely all of one's country's commands? What if one is driving towards a stop sign in an empty desert? In what sense must one stop? Is there such a sense?[19] How, if so, can this 'must' be the same as that in the laws' claim, which appears to discount one's interest in not dying? The laws do say, after all, 'if it leads you out to war, to be wounded or killed, you must comply'.

These are all good questions and they all press on the question: of what kind is the 'must' at issue? What intelligible role can it play in persuading Socrates to drink hemlock and die as the laws command? They also make clear something I take to be central to the laws' idea, a point worth amplifying here.

One's country's commands are likely to be many, and they will probably vary along several dimensions. Consider, for instance, the personal effort needed

[17] Compare Dagger (2000).
[18] Later I focus on the latter formulation.
[19] See Smith (1973).

for compliance. Conforming to some—participating in military operations, say—will be extremely demanding in terms of personal effort. Conforming to others—for instance, stopping one's car at a red light—will rarely be at all demanding. Similarly, the personal risks involved will vary enormously.

Again, one's country's commands may vary greatly with respect to the likely harm—in the sense, roughly, of pain and suffering—caused by a given person's nonconformity. In some cases one person's nonconformity will inevitably cause serious harm. For example, one person's contravening a law against violent assault will doubtless involve both mental and physical harm to those who are assaulted. In others nonconformity is unlikely to be a grave matter.[20] A given person's failure to buy a dog licence will generally not harm anyone seriously. True, the public coffers will be out a pound or two. That is nothing compared to the loss of a life or a limb.

In yet other cases, indeed, nonconformity will be the *least* harmful option. Conformity may harm the person conforming, it may harm others, or that person and others as well. This may mostly be the case when the command is clearly a morally unacceptable one. It can also happen as a result of unforeseen consequences of an apparently reasonable order, as the example of the need to run a stop sign in order to avoid death at the hands of a rogue driver shows.

In the case of some commands the default of many will cause serious problems for the country by virtue of the nature of the law in question. In the case of others, it will not. Rampant violence would clearly be a serious problem, not only for those directly hurt by it, but for those involved in law enforcement and in aiding the victims of violence, and those whose sense of personal security from violence is threatened.[21] Rampant driving above an unnecessarily low speed limit is different. Overall, it may do more good than harm, insofar as people get where they are going sooner. And if all drive at the same speed there will be less risk of collision.

Nonconformity with one and the same general command may vary enormously in its consequences depending on the context. Suppose that in your country the signal to traffic to stop is a particular type of red sign. Not stopping at such a red sign at a busy intersection could directly result in grievous harm to many people; not stopping at such a sign in an empty desert is unlikely to harm anyone.

The point to be made here is this. The laws' idea does not discriminate among the commands and contexts mentioned. According to the laws' idea, if one's

---

[20] It may always be somewhat problematic for the society as a whole. See Ch. 11, below.

[21] J. S. Mill (1979: Ch. 5), urges with undoubted perspicacity that a sense of security is necessary to human happiness.

country has issued the relevant commands then for that reason—irrespective of any others—there is a sense in which one must obey them.[22] Can something be made of this idea? Evidently this 'something' should satisfy at least the following conditions. It should deal plausibly with the case of morally unacceptable laws and legal systems. It should explain how otherwise pointless conformity can in some sense be mandatory. And it should show how this explanation relates to the case where my conformity is liable gravely to disadvantage me or others that I care about.

The Problem Restated

Must one obey the commands of one's country simply because it is one's country? This is a version of what has become known in philosophy as *the problem of political obligation*. In what follows I rephrase the question precisely in terms of obligations: is one obligated to obey the commands of one's country simply because it is one's country? As noted earlier, putting the question this way follows a standard contemporary practice.[23] The answer depends, clearly, on what an obligation is and on what it is for a country to be one's country. More will be said on both counts in due course.

The laws of Athens refer to doing whatever one's country orders or commands. What should one think of as included in these orders? Of course one's country's laws go in—if it has laws.[24] It is common, indeed, to put the question associated with the laws' idea as follows: 'Is there a special obligation to obey the laws of one's own country?' This is certainly an important if not central part of the question. It is, one might say, emblematic of the problem as a whole. Nonetheless one can usefully frame the question in broader terms. There is more than one reason to do so.

One has just been indicated: a country may not have laws according to reasonable accounts of what a law is. I have not yet said what I take a country to be, but the point can be made in advance of any such statement. The question 'what is a law?' has been much debated.[25] The narrower one's account of laws, the more likely it is that there are countries which, though not 'lawless', are without laws strictly speaking. For example, various rules may gradually become established in a society without being the product of any formally constituted legislature or lawgiver.[26] Some such rules have, indeed,

---

[22] Compare Klosko (1992: 3).

[23] Though not a universal one. Another common phrasing refers to 'duty'. For more on these terms see Ch. 2, below.

[24] '. . . if it has laws'. See the text below.

[25] Classic texts include Hart (1961); Dworkin (1977).

[26] See Ch. 9, below, for an extended discussion of the nature of such 'informal' rules.

been referred to as constituting 'customary law'. Suppose, however, that one's preferred account of a law for some reason excludes such rules. It seems one should allow, in spite of this, that the laws' question was relevant to countries without laws proper.[27]

Even given a relatively narrow account of a law, there are important distinctions to be made among laws, and speaking of an obligation to obey the law may tend to focus attention on one particular type of law at the expense of other types. Thus, speaking of laws may tend to conjure up those relatively mutable laws that are not part of a constitution. By a constitution I mean something like this: a framework of laws in accordance with which other laws are made and unmade, a framework of laws which, though they may themselves be mutable to some extent, are understood to be more basic and less mutable than are other non-constitutional laws.[28] In their speech, the laws of Athens do not distinguish between constitutional and other laws, and this seems to be the right approach. It is standard, after all, to consider the constitution together with the other laws of a country as a kind of unity, a legal system.

Speaking of laws may also lead one to overlook that class of laws that deals with non-compliance to other laws and, importantly, the question of punishment. These will include laws about who may intervene in behaviour perceived to be non-compliant, how the reality of non-compliance is to be determined, who is to decide on punishment, and which punishments are applicable for a given type of delict. The laws of Athens suggest, reasonably, that submitting to punishments that are imposed through due process of law is a way of obeying one's country's orders. They implicitly distinguish the laws regulating the process of punishment from others, and this too seems reasonable. Their inclusion in the class of one's country's orders, however, is not in doubt.

The laws' idea seems naturally to extend to matters other than conformity with rules and laws of whatever kind. Suppose, for instance, that one's country, A, embarks on a defensive war against another country, B. It is consonant with the laws' idea that one has some obligations in this regard, by virtue of the fact that country A is one's own country. Irrespective of any laws to that effect, one is presumably obligated not to give country A's military secrets to B, thus undermining A's war effort.[29]

---

[27] There is more on behalf of this point in Ch. 9, below.

[28] Thus an amendment to the so-named US Constitution can only be made under conditions different from and stricter than those of amendments to laws not part of the Constitution. By a 'non-constitutional' law I do not of course mean an 'unconstitutional' law.

[29] Cf. Simmons (1979: 5).

To get around such problems, I shall not formulate the question of this book in terms of conformity to laws. Rather, following a somewhat established tradition, I shall formulate it in terms of supporting or upholding political institutions.[30] I take a country's *political institutions* to be those of its institutions that pertain to its governance. I understand these to include both certain relatively 'free-standing' social rules and complex legal systems, both particular rulers and established procedures for arriving at a ruling body. It may seem odd to think of a particular king, say, as a political institution. This may seem less odd when one is clear that it is that person's rule or that person as ruler rather than that person himself or as an individual that is at issue. *Supporting* or *upholding* political institutions will be understood to include but not be limited to conformity to those political institutions, such as laws and commands, in relation to which the notion of conformity makes the best sense. In all of this the earlier caveat about authority holds. Insofar as government or 'rule' in all its forms implies the authority to rule, the question concerns purported rule, something that would, *given* the right authority, be rule proper.

The question at issue in this book can now be formulated as follows. Is one obligated to uphold the political institutions of one's country, simply because it is one's country? It could sometimes be unclear how one is to fulfil a *general* obligation to uphold one's country's political institutions. Perhaps there is a conflict between different elements of the relevant set of political institutions so that in complying with one law, say, one thereby violates another. If there is no clear answer as to which law takes precedence, then what one should do to accord with one's general obligation will be moot. For the sake of the discussion here I shall assume it is often clear enough.

Political Obligation Defined

As should now be clear, this book is concerned with a general obligation that conforms to a complex specification. It has both a particular source and a particular content. As to its content, it is an obligation to uphold the political institutions of one's country, whatever precisely these are. As to its source, it is an obligation one has by virtue of the fact that the country in question is one's country.

Unless the context indicates otherwise, the phrase 'political obligation' will be used in what follows to refer to the general obligation just specified—if such there be. If there is no such general obligation then there is no political obligation in the sense in question.

---

[30] Cf. ibid. Walzer (1970: p. xiii) writes rather of a 'political system' that is a matter of 'rules'.

Similarly, the phrase 'political obligations' will be used to refer to whatever specific obligations fall under this general obligation. Thus Jane's political obligations will be all the specific obligations Jane has, given her general political obligation. They may range from obtaining a dog licence, say, to joining the army. The details will depend on the particular political institutions of her country. Once again, it could be that there are no political obligations.

It is important to understand that the foregoing definitions are stipulative. The phrases 'political obligation' and 'political obligations' are hardly part of vernacular usage, so each theorist needs to make clear how he is construing them. Others have used the phrase in ways other than mine. There is nothing wrong with these ways, but confusion could result if the possibility of divergence is not understood.

Given the foregoing definitions, the question of this book can now be put compactly thus. Are there political obligations? As I now explain, this question can be construed as relating to membership in a particular type of social group. Thus the problem of political obligation meets the theory of social groups.

The Membership Problem

Are there political obligations? Given the preceding definition of such obligations this clearly depends on what a country, and more particularly one's own country, is. The term 'country' has had a full life in vernacular usage. Doubtless different people, theorists included, use it in somewhat different ways. For present purposes I adopt a standard construal mentioned earlier: I take a country to be a type of political society. I take a political society, in its turn, to be a society with a set of political institutions and I take a society to be a type of social group.

I later argue in detail for a particular account of such groups. For now I restrict myself to some brief preliminary remarks on the relatively narrow sense of 'social group' I have in mind. Merely having a distinguishing feature in common, however significant that feature, is not enough to make the members of a given population into a social group in this sense. The population consisting of all human males, for instance, does not as such constitute a social group in the sense in question. To point the contrast, such a population may be referred to, in an echo of Rousseau, as a (mere) aggregate of human individuals—albeit in this case an aggregate of human beings differentiated from others by the possession of a significant common feature.[31] The same goes for the smaller population consisting of all men with a particular sexual orientation, for

---

[31] In Ch. 5 of the *Social Contract*, Rousseau (1983: 23) contrasts an 'aggregation' with an 'association'.

instance. Its members will not count as members of a social group simply by virtue of their possession of this common feature. Nor will people all of whom hold a particular belief or set of beliefs count as a social group merely by virtue of that fact. The point is not that there is no viable notion of social group that would include some or all of these populations, but rather that the notion with which I am concerned here is a narrower one.

A brief informal list of examples of social groups of the type I have in mind might include discussion groups, families, trade unions, sports teams, terrorist cells, and armies. Of course, there are important differences between these groups, but to many they seem at one level to be 'all of a kind'. Among other things, they are not mere aggregates. I shall in due course carefully pursue the question of what, at the most general level, distinguishes them from such aggregates. A given aggregate could, of course, develop into such a group. The question is: when and how has that transition occurred?

When is a social group a society? A variety of social groups have been referred to as 'societies'. They tend to be large. They can, however, be very small. Indeed, John Locke said that the first society was that between man and wife.[32] And there are secret societies, and so on, that may be quite small. As to political societies, even very small groups may have political institutions as I understand these. That is, such a group may have institutions relating to its governance. For example, in a particular marriage it may be established that, as it is sometimes put, one spouse's 'word is law'. This marital couple, then, will count as a political society in the broad sense just defined. People would not normally refer to all 'political societies' in this sense as 'countries', which is why I said that I take a country to be but a type of political society. It is not the only type of political society. What differentiates a country from political societies of other types? Briefly put, some central points are as follows.

First, a country generally, if not by definition, has a relatively definite, relatively permanent location—it persistently occupies a certain geographical area or land mass. The precise boundaries of this area may or may not be in dispute with other countries. It may or may not increase or decrease in size over the years. Second, this geographical area, or territory, is typically quite large. That is not to say that different countries may not occupy territories of widely differing sizes, some being tiny in relation to others. Once more relating to size, countries tend to be relatively large political societies in terms of the number of their members. That is not to say, again, that they cannot vary widely in this respect. Size of membership and size of territory may tend

---

[32] Locke (1980: Ch. 7, sect. 66, p. 42).

to be correlated, but a country that is territorially vast may have a smaller population than a country with a considerably smaller territory.

Given its relatively large size, the next point is not surprising. A country is a political society of a type that is likely to include within it other, smaller societies including political societies. Thus in *The Rules of Sociological Method* the sociologist Émile Durkheim contrasted the wider society with the smaller societies that it encloses, societies such as trade unions and literary societies.[33] Consider also philosopher John Rawls's reference to a 'social union of social unions' in *The Theory of Justice*.[34] To some extent this is true of all societies of more than two people. Thus family therapists often point out that there may, for instance, be a coalition of mother and son within the family of father, mother, and son. One would suppose, however, that the larger the group, the more likely its inclusion of smaller groups within it.[35]

Finally, and relating to all of the previous points, a country is a political society of a type within whose territorial boundaries its members can live 'whole lives'. They may be born, socialized, educated, employed, married, and buried there. Though many people leave their countries of origin permanently for one reason or another, many do not, and do not feel the need to. They are therefore likely to have some familiarity with the society's history and to be skilled participants in a relatively rich set of local practices and conventions that have developed over an extended period of time—perhaps over many generations.

Given only these points one can already see why someone's country is liable to arouse those sentiments referred to as patriotic. *Patria*, of course, is the Latin word for *country*, and is linked in its turn to *pater*, father.

As I shall understand it in this book a country is the country of a particular person if and only if that person is a member of the political society that constitutes the country in question. The country I call 'mine' in the relevant sense can at the same time be referred to as 'our' country by me and its other members. The same goes for the political institutions of the society: they will be *our* political institutions, in that we are all members of the society whose institutions they are. The legal system—if there is one—will be ours; the ruler—if there is one—will be our ruler. As the last sentence indicates, I see no reason to limit the idea of a country to any particular form of political organization.

It may be that membership in any social group involves obligations. If so, political obligations may constitute the political society version of these

---

[33] Durkheim (1982: 52).

[34] Rawls (1971: 527).

[35] I say more on the nature of such inclusion in Ch. 8, below.

obligations of membership. That there are obligations of membership in general is an important part of what I shall argue.

I refer to the question on which I focus as *the membership problem*. One way of putting it is as follows. Does membership in a political society in and of itself involve obligations to uphold the relevant political institutions? Alternatively: are there plausible senses of the relevant terms such that membership in a political society obligates one to uphold its political institutions?

The second formulation makes it clear that several of the significant terms involved—including 'political society', 'member of a political society', and 'obligations'—are susceptible of different interpretations, and that it will be incumbent upon one who gives a satisfactory answer to clarify the interpretations in question. The first formulation may be called *the material formulation*; the second, *the conceptual formulation*. The material formulation is less cumbersome, and I shall often use it. At the same time, I consider the conceptual formulation primary.

1.2 Four Distinct Questions

The membership problem is distinct from a number of similar questions that have been referred to in the literature as 'the problem of political obligation'. In this section I focus on four such questions. They are all significant and interesting. It is important to distinguish them from the membership problem. Though they are not the focus of the present work, it bears on all of them.

Questions about Residents

Suppose someone says, 'Do this!' or 'Don't do that!'—addressing a purported order to another person or to a number of other people. Under what circumstances, and why, are they obligated to comply? More briefly, when and why is anyone obligated to do what he is told?[36]

In the literature of political philosophy less basic versions of this question are common. These refer to a situation in which there is a 'government', 'state', or 'country', terms all of which may be variously construed and need to be elucidated if one is to be clear about the general situation that is supposed to be at issue.

In order to give the flavour of these versions and to generalize from a variety of texts, I first introduce some relatively technical terms. I shall use the

---

[36] See Klosko (1992: 1).

term 'imperator' for a person or collective body which addresses (purported) orders to everyone who resides in a certain geographical area or territory.[37] An example of such an order is, 'Everyone living on this island, drive on the right!' A broader notion of an imperator would involve orders intended to apply to all who fell under a certain description, which might or might not relate to the matter of where they resided. For instance, it might be addressed to all who wished to be considered faithful followers of a particular person or deity, or to the descendants of a particular person. The narrower sense will suffice for my purposes here.

An imperator in my technical sense may or may not issue credible threats to punish those who do not comply with its directives, and it may or may not be generally complied with by the residents of the territory in question. Such an imperator contrasts, then, with the richer image of one whose commands backed by threats are accompanied by a habit of obedience among those who do as he commands them to do.[38] The same goes for other contexts in which an imperator in this sense may operate. I shall refer to the geographical area targeted by a given imperator's imperatives as 'an imperator's territory' and to those who reside in an imperator's territory as 'residents in an imperator's territory' or 'residents' for short.

One common 'problem of political obligation' is roughly this. Under what conditions are residents obligated to comply with the imperatives of the relevant imperator? Thus Gregory Kavka writes:

What moral reasons, grounds, or considerations, if any, imply that individuals residing within the territory of a State (or a State of a certain kind) ought to obey the laws and directives of the officials of that State? This, in broad terms, is the problem of political obligation, which concerns whether and when there is a moral justification of political obedience.[39]

Note, in particular, that Kavka asks whether 'individuals residing within the territory of a State . . . ought to obey the laws and directives of the officials of that State . . . '.

What Kavka describes as the problem of political obligation differs from the membership problem in at least four ways. The first difference is the most significant for the purpose of this subsection. It does not put the nature of

---

[37] It would be hard to use any word in this context that did not have some connotations going beyond the mere issuance of imperatives. For most English speakers, though, this Latin word will be less familiar than many that could be used.

[38] This image is familiar to many through Hart (1961: 18–19), referring to the jurist John Austin's conception of law.

[39] Kavka (1986: 385).

membership in a political society at its core. It does not preclude membership in a political society from being part of the answer, but it leaves open the possibility of answers that do not appeal to such membership, nor, indeed, to residence as such. Such answers might refer, for instance, to the quality of the orders (such as their utility) or of the imperator (such as its wisdom, justice, or efficiency).

Second, and relatedly, Kavka explicitly envisages the possibility of a variety of grounds for obedience. In contrast, the membership problem is concerned with only one such ground—membership as such. It is true that there could be different forms of membership, and different grounds of obligation for different forms of membership.[40] On the face of it, then, the membership problem might receive a conjunctive rather than a simple answer. I say more later about how one might decide between several otherwise plausible solutions that invoke different forms of membership. Kavka's concerns are still in principle less restricted than those of the membership problem, which is only concerned with a specific type of ground of obligation or, more broadly, reason for compliance, namely, membership in some intuitive or everyday sense.

A third difference between Kavka's problem of political obligation and the membership problem as I have stated it is this. In explaining his problem Kavka refers not to obligations but to 'reasons, grounds, or considerations'.[41] I focus on this way of formulating the problem shortly. I shall also focus shortly on the fourth difference, which is that Kavka qualifies the kinds of reasons he is interested in as 'moral' ones.

In the statement of the problem quoted above Kavka suggests, in parentheses, that it is possible that only residence in the territory of a certain *kind* of State will involve obligations. This is a common idea in discussions of the problem of political obligation. Indeed, many make it clear at the outset that they are interested only in the case of political societies much like their own.[42] Suffice it to say, for now, that the membership problem alludes to no analogous distinction among kinds of political society. The issue concerns political societies in general, whether or not they can be properly referred to as democratic, liberal, relatively just, or whatever. I say more, shortly, about the appropriateness of leaving things open in this way.

I return now, to the first difference between Kavka's problem of political obligation and the membership problem. The point to be made here—in terms of obligations—is this. One must distinguish two questions. The first concerns the conditions under which residents have obligations with respect

---

[40] Cf. Locke (1980); Tussman (1960).
[41] See also Kavka (1986: 308 n. 39).
[42] See e.g. Klosko (1992: 122–3).

to the purported orders of the relevant imperator, or similar matters. This may be termed, for short, *the residence problem*. The second—the membership problem—is posed in terms of membership and concerns the obligations of members of a political society as such.

Though distinct, these problems are not unrelated. Certainly the membership problem bears on the residence problem. Suppose one has successfully argued for obligations of membership in a political society, obligations to uphold the political institutions of the society. Suppose that according to one's understanding of such membership, plausibly, it is not simply equivalent to residence in the territory of an imperator.[43] In spite of that, the residence problem will then be at least partially solved. For suppose that the residents in the territory of a given imperator are also members of a political society, and the ruler of that society is the imperator in question. His rule, that is, is one of the political institutions of the society in question. The argument will have shown that residents of this kind, at least, are obligated to comply with the orders of the imperator insofar as he is indeed their ruler.

In discussing the membership problem one might, less plausibly, operate with a broad notion of membership in a political society that was more or less equivalent to that of residence in the territory of an imperator. One would then ask whether membership in this broad sense was itself a ground of obligation. If the result were positive, this would of course provide a positive answer to both the residence problem and the membership problem: at least one kind of membership would be obligating, as would residence. If the result were negative that would not conclude discussion of the membership problem, however, insofar as narrower notions of membership remained to be investigated. Nor would it conclude discussion of the residence problem, insofar as membership in whatever sense is not the only possible ground of obligation of residents in the territory of an imperator.

Questions about Obligations Characterized as 'Moral'

A preponderance of writers concerned with a 'problem of political obligation' assumes that a particular species of obligation is at issue, namely, moral obligation.[44] This goes both for those who are concerned with the

---

[43] The idea that membership is equivalent to residence is not intuitive. Nor are several more qualified notions that might be derived from versions of the residence problem. For instance, the benevolence of a given imperator or his ability to back up his edicts with considerable force would not, in and of itself, seem to make residence in the relevant territory a form of societal membership.

[44] Thus e.g. Singer (1973: 3) 'If there is any obligation to obey the law it must, ultimately, be a moral obligation'; Horton (1992: 13) 'Political obligation concerns the moral or ethical bonds between individuals and their political community'. See also, among others, Sesonske (1964); Honderich (1976); Simmons (1979); Kavka (1986).

residence problem, discussed above, and those who are concerned with the membership problem.

Though it has been mooted, the claim that 'political obligations' are not moral obligations has not been found convincing. Several authors cite McPherson as one who has claimed that political obligations are not moral ones. Simmons observes that McPherson is 'not particularly clear about the status or character of his "nonmoralized political obligations" '.[45]

Among those who say that moral obligation is at issue, many leave it at that, without attempting to say what moral obligation is. One writer offers a characterization of 'moral' considerations but allows that there is room for disagreement on the matter and suggests that readers will do best to rely on their intuitive or pre-theoretical understanding.[46]

Sometimes an author appears to be assuming a residual definition of 'moral obligation'. That is, moral obligations are defined, explicitly or implicitly, as whatever obligations are not obligations of another, given sort. For instance, moral obligations are often residually defined—at least implicitly—as those obligations that are not legal obligations. This is a legitimate procedure. One problem with it, however, is that without some anchoring of the non-residual category the domain of the residual one may be left obscure. Another difficulty is that the residually defined category may be so broad as to include so-called obligations of significantly different types. I should emphasize that I use the term 'so-called' here, and in other contexts, without intending anything pejorative. 'So-called' obligations are those things, whatever they are, that have been referred to with some regularity as 'obligations' by speakers of English.[47]

Many philosophers who write of moral obligations appear to be operating with an intuitive, substantive conception of morality in mind. It is not an easy task to say precisely what this conception amounts to.[48] Nor is it easy to demarcate its contours. This demarcation problem is, indeed, surprisingly rarely a focus among those whose explicit concern is moral theory. It is therefore

---

[45] Simmons (1979: 4) citing McPherson (1967). See also Singer (1973). For a relatively extended critical discussion of McPherson, see Horton (1992). R. M. Hare (1989: 8–9) fears that claiming political obligations are not moral ones could lead people to ignore moral issues when confronted with political obligations. That depends, of course, on precisely what political obligations are understood to be.

[46] Singer (1973: 4–5): 'That is all I shall say about the meaning of "morality". If the reader disagrees, or is puzzled by what I have said, he will probably do better to read on. . . . I do not think that the way I use the term "moral" in the remainder of this book will cause much difficulty.'

[47] I understand that there are languages that have no exact equivalents of this term, something that is not surprising given the range of things that the English term has come to cover. It is to be hoped that, nonetheless, the discussion will be pertinent to the concerns of those whose main language is other than English. After all, my ultimate concern here is with a thing or things—obligation—rather than a word. The same goes for the other terms and phrases on which I focus in this book.

[48] It may be a mixture of separable conceptions. See e.g. Scanlon (1995).

understandable if, as is generally the case, the conception in question receives little explication in discussions outside that discipline.

Theorists of political obligation may, of course, stipulatively define 'morality' and 'moral obligation' however they wish. Confusion is likely to result, however, the further removed their stipulation is from the intuitive notion just referred to, unclear though its boundaries are.

The closer to that notion their usage is, meanwhile, the greater the danger that insisting that political obligations are moral obligations risks putting an important class of obligations beyond their purview. At least on the face of it, there could be obligations that are genuine in an important sense, though they do not count as moral obligations according to the intuitive notion in question. The sense I have in mind is this: if one has *a genuine obligation* to do a certain thing, one then has sufficient reason to do that thing. I say what I take this to mean in the next chapter. This characterization makes no attempt to specify what an *obligation* is: it only has to do with what I am calling the genuineness of an obligation.[49] As I explain in the next chapter, some so-called obligations are not genuine in this sense.

Compare, in this connection, the matter of moral *reasons*. According to a standard intuitive conception there are reasons for acting that are not moral ones. Thus the philosopher Thomas Scanlon writes: 'when one concludes that an action is [sc. morally] wrong, this entails the recognition of a *particular kind of reason* not to do it' (my emphasis).[50] To invoke another, quite popular term, the *normative* realm is generally considered to have a broader purview than the moral realm. A theorist who stipulated that all reasons were moral reasons on his definition of 'moral', or that the normative realm was coextensive with the moral realm, would thus be blurring intuitive distinctions. The point just made may help to make palatable the idea that genuine obligations need not always be moral ones.

In formulating the membership problem I have not restricted its concern to obligations characterized as moral. I do, however, take its focus to be what I have just referred to as genuine obligations.

Here is one reason for leaving things open. Suppose, first, that those who are members of a political society have what are, intuitively, genuine obligations to uphold the political institutions of that society. Suppose, second, that these obligations are *not* moral obligations in an intuitive sense or, for that matter, according to a given theoretical account of morality. It would clearly be

---

[49] Perhaps 'effectiveness' would be a better term, since I have in mind a positive relation to reason, in other words, a particular kind of normativity. As long as the definition is clear the particular label should not matter.

[50] Scanlon (2003: 283).

unfortunate if, having explored the moral question and reached the conclusion that membership does not involve *moral* obligations, one abandoned the topic and failed to discover that there are in the appropriate sense non-moral but genuine obligations of membership.

This is not, of course, to deny that we want to know what our intuitively moral obligations are with respect to the political realm. It is only to say that if there are genuine political obligations of another sort, we should want to know about them and understand their nature also.

Some theorists argue that morality is a chimera. It has been argued, for instance, that our everyday moral discourse involves erroneous pre-suppositions.[51] These theorists would presumably deny without reflection the existence of political obligations conceived of as moral obligations. On the face of it, they could still contemplate the existence of political obligations *not* characterized as moral. Thus an inquiry couched in more neutral terms is likely to attract more followers and to avoid that kind of rejection at the outset.

The main purpose of this section has been to make the following clear. In asking after the existence of political obligations in the sense of this book I am asking precisely whether and how people have *genuine* obligations in the sense defined with the source and content at issue. Whether these qualify as moral on one or another conception is not my primary concern.

As to the conception of morality at issue in this book when references to something qualified as 'moral' occur in passing, I take myself, like many others, to be operating with a substantive notion of morality. Precisely how this notion might be explicated is not important for present purposes.[52]

Questions that do not Relate Specifically to Obligations

In a passage quoted earlier, when explaining the problem he characterizes as 'the problem of political obligation', Gregory Kavka refers not to obligations but rather to (moral) 'reasons, grounds, or considerations'. There is something a little puzzling, perhaps, in calling something 'the problem of political obligation' while setting it out in other terms. Clearly, though, many of those who write on a problem they characterize as a problem of 'political obligation' are relatively unconcerned with whether what they are talking about naturally attracts the label 'obligations' as opposed, say, to 'duties' or 'requirements', or, indeed, 'reasons' or 'grounds'.[53]

---

[51] See esp. Mackie (1977). [52] Cf. Singer (1973: 5).

[53] This may be because they do not believe there is an affirmative solution in terms of obligations as opposed to reasons. See e.g. Lacey (1988: 121-2).

In contrast, the problem I focus on here—the membership problem—is a question about obligations specifically. I believe this question can be given a positive answer, an answer that will be developed in this course of this book. This will at the same time explain how membership in a political society, understood in a certain way, is a source of what might also be labelled 'duties', 'requirements', 'reasons', and 'grounds' for obedience—depending precisely on how these terms are construed.

I do not mean to imply that inquiries that fail to focus on obligations are in any way unworthy. I wish simply to emphasize that 'obligation' is a key term in this particular inquiry. In the next chapter, I give a partial characterization of obligations in terms of certain salient conditions. What I shall eventually argue is this: there are obligations inherent in a fundamental form of membership in a political society that fit both these broad conditions and further important specifications.

Questions about Liberal Democracies or other Particular Kinds of Polity

Many theorists who discuss a 'problem of political obligation' make it clear at the outset that they are only interested in a particular, preferred kind of political society. Often this is referred to as a liberal democracy.[54]

That one currently resides in such a society may be part of what enables one to raise and freely discuss this kind of question. However precisely its details and its animating ideas are spelled out, such a society may indeed be far preferable to any other kind. That does not mean that one should ignore the situation of those whose situations differ strongly from one's own. History and, indeed, contemporary life are full of kings and tyrants, of societies in which there are few freedoms, of societies that are not democracies in any standard sense.

To ignore such situations, is not only to exhibit a degree of parochialism. Such parochialism, though hardly a virtue, is not exactly a vice. A desire to limit one's concerns to one's own situation is understandable enough. So limiting one's concerns, however, risks failing to discover such obligations as may be found in political societies of all stripes, including one's own. Thus, however parochial our interests we stand to lose something important to our concerns if we fail to look beyond our own situation. The membership problem as I understand it concerns political societies generally—not societies of a particular type.

---

[54] As in Klosko (1992).

2

Obligations: Preliminary Points

This chapter begins with a general characterization of the broad class of obligations with which this book is concerned. The practical importance of political obligations given only this characterization is noted. An important species of such obligations is then discussed: these are sometimes referred to as 'directed' obligations. Finally, attention is paid to a kind of obligation that is not of the broad general kind specified at the outset. Obligations of this kind will be referred to as 'imputed obligations'. It is important to have these points in place before proceeding further with the membership problem.[1]

2.1 The Variety of Obligations

What are obligations? To some extent, the answer to this question depends on the person to whom you are talking. The use of the English term 'obligation' has broadened over time, and people speak of 'obligations' in a variety of contexts.[2] A familiar context for talk of obligation is the context of an agreement or a promise. Yet people also speak of obligations where no promise or agreement appears to be at issue. Thus Jane may be said to be obligated to save a child from drowning, if she can do so without endangering her own life, irrespective of her prior relationship to the child. Claire may be said to be under an obligation to reciprocate a benefit though her acceptance of the benefit implied no agreement with respect to such reciprocation. Someone may refer to Joe's obligations according to British law, meaning to refer, essentially, to what those laws have to say about people in his situation.

I shall not insist on a restrictive use of the term 'obligation' as its proper use.[3] Nor shall I offer a complete account of obligation that encompasses all of the

---

[1] One who is keen to forge ahead could read Sect. 2.1, the summary of Sect. 2.2, and Sects. 2.3 and 2.4, returning as necessary later.

[2] See the very useful discussion in Brandt (1964) for an extended illustration of this point.

[3] The opposite approach is taken in Hart (1955), whose position is discussed in Sect. 2.2, below.

different uses mentioned. It may well be that no useful account can be given. For, whatever their commonalities, it is evident from the above examples that so-called obligations are of significantly different types.

I noted in the last chapter that those who discuss problems of political obligation do not always focus on something they characterize specifically as obligation. Or they may focus on a specific type of obligation that they refer to as moral obligation. It is relatively rare to say, as I have done, that one is concerned with obligation, without insisting that the obligation in question is moral obligation. Nonetheless, I take there to be considerable common ground between myself and these other theorists. This can be made clear by reference to certain features that all would agree characterize the object of their concern. I enumerate these features below. I list them as features of obligations *simpliciter*. I should be understood to be referring only to obligations of the general kind with which I am concerned here.

In the discussion that follows I make use of some key terms I shall not attempt fully to explicate. I have in mind in particular rationality, and what rationality or reason requires. I take myself to be operating with an intuitive notion that relates to considerations of a variety of kinds. The breadth of this conception will emerge as the discussion progresses. At times I introduce a related technical term. The mathematical theory of games uses a technical notion of rationality such that it is a matter of maximizing utility according to one's personal 'utility function'. It is worth emphasizing at the outset that this is not the conception of rationality at issue here.[4]

2.2 Initial Assumptions about Obligation

To have an Obligation is to have Sufficient Reason to Act

Obligations of the type in question here are *genuine* in the sense adumbrated in the previous chapter: if one has a genuine obligation to do a certain thing, one then has sufficient reason to do that thing. This brings in the complex notion of having sufficient reason.

Breaking this down, I start with some amplification of the point that one who has an obligation of the type at issue *has reason* to act in such a way that the obligation is fulfilled. This is not to say that if you have reason to act in a certain way you have an obligation to act in this way. One may have reason to act in a certain way without having an obligation so to act, but not vice versa.

---

[4] For some pertinent discussion see Hollis and Sugden (1993).

The notion of having reason to act, as I am construing it here, is a relatively broad one. Its breadth may be demonstrated by reference to the following schema.

Person X *has reason* to perform action A if and only if, there is some consideration C such that C speaks in favour of X's performing A.

As I understand this, relevant considerations may vary significantly in type. In particular, the consideration in question may, but need not, be a matter of the character or consequences of act A.

Thus suppose, first, that some act Sue might perform would be an act of charity or kindness. I take it that its being of this kind speaks in favour of doing it. If so, Sue has reason to perform that action, by virtue of A's character. Suppose, second, that Sue decided two weeks ago to perform some action, and has not changed her mind. I take it that this consideration speaks in favour of her performing that action today, though in a different way. If so, Sue has reason to perform the act she decided upon. Her decision speaks in favour of the act, I take it, by virtue of what a decision is, not by virtue of the character of the act or of the consequences that are likely to flow from it, given the way it is in itself. One may, then, have reason to act in a certain way by virtue of the character or consequences of that act. One may also have reason to act in a certain way by virtue of other considerations.

I have deliberately couched this point about obligation in terms of '*having reason* to act' as opposed to '*having a reason* to act'. Philosophers tend to think of *a* reason for acting in a certain way as something that is securely attached to the nature or consequences of the act itself.[5] This may accord with the way people tend to talk of *reasons*, and marks, of course, an important *type* of consideration.

If someone asks why you are doing something, he may well have such a consideration in mind. Thus suppose someone asks Jane why she is going to vote for a particular candidate in today's election. Should she reply, 'Because I decided to do so some while back,' this would quite likely provoke the response 'Yes, but why did you so *decide*?' What the questioner wants is a statement about what is good about Jane's voting for that candidate, either in itself or in terms of its consequences.

Nonetheless, it is hard not to think of one's prior decision, in and of itself, as in some way speaking in favour of one's performing the act decided upon. Suppose Mike decides to post his tax return this afternoon. Night falls,

---

[5] Thus Raz (2001: 2), 'the only reason for any action is that the action, in itself or in its consequences, has good-making properties, has features which make it, *pro tanto*, good'. On *pro tanto*, see n. 12, below.

however, and he has not posted the return. He had become absorbed in his work and it was too late to post the return when he stopped for a rest. Remembering his decision, he is likely to feel things have gone off course. With this implication he may say to himself, 'Oh, I meant to post my tax return this afternoon!' This would not be the case if, in his estimation, his decision in no way spoke in favour of his acting as he had decided. Mike's likely reaction to his failure to do what he decided to do suggests that a decision does not only give one reason (in my sense) to do what one decided to do. It also gives one what I refer to as sufficient reason to do it.[6]

I say that

> X has *sufficient reason* for performing A if and only if a consideration C that speaks in favour of X's doing A is such that, all else being equal, rationality requires that X do A, given C.

In relation to this formula, *all else is equal* if and only if there are no considerations against doing A that make it the case that, in spite of C, rationality does not require X to do A.[7] One may, then, have sufficient reason to do something though countervailing considerations are such that one is rationally required *not* to do it. Or, countervailing considerations may be such that rationality *permits* one not to do it, without requiring that one not do it.

I shall regard an unqualified reference to what one 'ought' to do, or 'should' do in a given situation as equivalent to a reference to what is rationally required of one in the broad sense at issue here. I distinguish, therefore, what one 'ought' to do from what one is obligated to do. This accords with common assumptions. My unqualified 'oughts' and 'shoulds' should be understood accordingly in what follows.

In my terminology, it is common ground between myself and others who write on problems of political obligation that what is at issue in our discussions is a circumstance—call it 'obligation' or not—such that someone in that circumstance *has sufficient reason*, in the sense just characterized, to act in relevant ways. In other words, a positive solution to the problem at hand will demonstrate at least this: certain people in certain contexts have sufficient reason to support and comply with certain political institutions.

To say that one with an obligation has sufficient reason to act in a certain way is not to say that to have sufficient reason to act in some way is, in and of itself, to have an obligation. This is only a partial characterization of obligation.

---

[6] For further discussion of decisions see esp. Ch. 7, below.

[7] X will act *irrationally* in not doing A if X believes he has sufficient reason to do A, and that all else is equal, and yet does not do A.

Again, to say that to have an obligation is to have sufficient reason to act in a certain way leaves open the possibility that there are radically different kinds of obligation, as I believe there are.[8] The same goes for the following further partial characterization of obligations.

Obligations are Independent of Personal Inclinations and Self-interest

A salient aspect of obligations is that they may run contrary to the particular personal feelings, urges, and (more mildly) inclinations of the person with the obligation—contrary to that person's *inclinations*, for short. This shows that obligations are independent of inclinations, in the sense that one can have an obligation to do a certain thing without at all being inclined to do it, and vice versa.[9]

Obligations are in the same sense independent of the obligated person's self-interest narrowly construed. That is, they do not necessarily correspond to what is good for a person in terms of his health, wealth, contentment, and so on.[10] When I refer to a person's 'self-interest' in what follows this is how it should be understood.

The latter point connects with a well-known contrast made by H. L. A. Hart between being obligated, on the one hand, and being obliged, on the other.[11] One can properly say, 'I was obliged to do it' without implying that one had an obligation to do it. One's 'being obliged' might be a matter of self-interest. It could be a matter of obligation, but it need not. In illustration of this, consider the case of residents of an imperator's territory where agents of the imperator are known to track down anyone who contravenes the imperator's directives and punish them severely. One might appropriately say that these residents are obliged to obey the imperator's directives. Whatever precisely this means, one can say it without implying that these residents have any *obligation* to obey. Many actual residents, including the members of liberal, democratic societies are obliged in this sense to follow an imperator's directives or an important subset of such directives. Some may be more obliged (in this sense) than others.

If one conforms to this distinction, it appears that there will not be specifically prudential obligations. Prudence may *oblige* one to do something, but will not

---

[8] This does not preclude the possibility—discussed in the text below—that one of these kinds is fit to be called 'obligation proper'.

[9] Cf. Simmons (1979: 6), 'obligations . . . are independent of our desires to perform or not'.

[10] What is in one's self-interest, so construed, is often contrasted with the morally right thing to do, or the best thing to do overall. It is also commonly contrasted with obligation. See e.g. Horton (1992: 13–14). The thought is that these may coincide with self-interest but need not.

[11] Hart (1961: 80).

in and of itself support an *obligation* to do it. That seems to accord with the way the term 'obligation' is used.

Sufficiency Versus Conclusiveness

i. *Absolutely Conclusive Reasons*   I shall say that

> X has an *absolutely conclusive* reason for performing some action, A, if and only if a consideration C that speaks in favour of A is such that given C, rationality requires that X do A, *whatever else is true*.[12]

I introduce this notion here largely to make the point that to have sufficient reason to do something is *not* in and of itself to have an absolutely conclusive reason for doing it. Thus, the assumption that you cannot have an obligation to do something without having sufficient reason to do it does not entail that to have an obligation is to have an absolutely conclusive reason to do something. Nor shall I make the independent assumption that this is true.

This accords with the judgement of many writers on political obligation. They do not assume that to recognize an obligation is to identify an absolutely conclusive reason for action.[13] It also accords with standard judgements on the obligations associated with agreements and promises. Thus Tess may judge herself to be required to break her promise to Guido that she will attend the protest rally, when it turns out that this is the only way that a third person's life can be saved. She may then say to herself, 'I can't go to the rally now.' 'Breaking a promise' could simply be a matter of not doing what you said you would do. This standard phrase, however, suggests something that accords with a common judgement: breaking one's promise involves not just failing to do what one promised to do, but defaulting on a standing obligation to do what one promised.[14]

It is also common to judge that obligations can conflict. Once again, allusions to promises and agreements are often made in this connection. Suppose that Roz has made two promises such that keeping one entails breaking the other. For instance, she has promised to attend Frieda's graduation and also to help Betty with her house move in another state. Betty's move turns out to be taking place at the same time as the graduation ceremony. It is standard to

---

[12] Other qualifiers that have been used in this connection are 'absolute' (Raz 1975: 27), 'indefeasible' (Beran 1987: 13), and 'decisive' (Kagan 1989: 49). Kagan contrasts decisive reasons with those that are *pro tanto* by which he means a reason that 'always has force, but this force can be countered and overridden in various ways; a given act can be supported by a PTR even though that act is not morally required'.

[13] Here I echo Horton (1992: 14). See also, among others, Simmons (1979: 7–11).

[14] See e.g. Simmons (1979: 8).

take it that her two promises have given Roz conflicting obligations.[15] If one agrees with this, one cannot then argue that the obligation of a promise is an absolutely conclusive reason for conforming to the promise. Considerations such as this have led people to conclude that to have an obligation is not necessarily to have an absolutely conclusive reason. Some have concluded, indeed, that obligations are never absolutely conclusive reasons.[16]

I do not say that there is no way of arguing that the obligation of one who has made a promise is, after all, an absolutely conclusive reason. My point is only that common judgements suggest that it is not. Perhaps some obligations are such that the obligated person has an absolutely conclusive reason for fulfilling them, and others are not.

ii. Relative Conclusiveness Is an obligation always conclusive when the only countervailing consideration is a personal inclination that runs counter to the obligation? That is, do obligations always 'trump' inclinations, at least, with respect to what rationality requires? Some writers on political obligation have asserted that they do. Thus A. John Simmons: 'Obligations ... must be discharged regardless of our inclinations.'[17] Probably most such writers take their quarry to have this feature.

Certainly people often justify acting against their personal inclinations in terms of countervailing obligations. Promissory obligation is a case in point. Someone might very plausibly say: 'I don't want to leave now, but I must. I promised to be back by six.' This suggests that promissory obligation, at least, 'trumps' inclinations with respect to what rationality requires of the promisor, all things considered. In other words, if in a given situation one wants to do a certain thing, but has a promissory obligation not to do that thing, then rationality requires that one do what one is obligated to do. Similar things can be said in relation to self-interest. Thus, in a slight variant on the previous example, someone might very plausibly say 'This is not going to help me personally, but I promised her long ago that I would do it.'

One can, of course, break a promise, and one may decide to do so on grounds either of contrary inclination or self-interest: 'I can't bear the thought of spending even an hour with her. I know I said I'd go to lunch, but I won't.' That one may think this and act accordingly does not show that one's action is consonant with the dictates of rationality. The imagined utterance can be construed as an avowal that one is determined to act contrary to these dictates on this occasion, because one cannot bring oneself to conform to them.

---

[15] Thus I take the position of Simmons (1979: 8) to be typical.
[16] See Simmons (1979: 10).
[17] Simmons (1979: 7)

Clearly, if obligations in general trump both inclinations and self-interest, as such, from the point of view of what rationality requires they will be forceful factors in the direction of those susceptible to such requirements. For now, I simply note that it is common to regard obligations as relatively conclusive in this way.

The Practical Significance of Political Obligations Simply as Sufficient Reason

Irrespective of the precise relationship of obligations to inclinations and self-interest, the simple fact that they provide one with sufficient reason for action already gives obligations a high degree of practical importance. One can see this if one considers a situation where one has a particular obligation to do something and must make an otherwise arbitrary choice. If obligations are (merely) sufficient reasons, rationality requires one to act in accordance with one's obligation.

This is hardly a trivial point. One way to make that clear is by reference to cases like the following. Suppose that, within the confines of one's country, one has to choose whether to drive on the left or on the right. One has no reason to choose one option rather than the other. In particular, one has no expectations, either way, about the likely action of other drivers. Suppose, further, that one takes oneself to have sufficient reason to do what the laws of one's country say one is to do. One then discovers that according to the laws one is to drive on the left. If one is disposed to act rationally, one will then drive on the left. If other drivers are in the same position, so will they. Much harm will thus be avoided. The situation of the drivers before their knowledge of the applicable law is what has come to be known as a *coordination problem*.[18] There is little doubt that life in human societies is rife with such problems.[19] Some are relatively trivial, some are of enormous importance.[20]

It is hardly trivial, then, to claim that membership in a political society in and of itself gives one sufficient reason to support its political institutions. Thus the partial account of obligation given in this section already shows clearly the practical significance of a positive answer to the membership problem. The full import of such an answer will of course depend on a better understanding of the kind of obligation at issue.

---

[18] Schelling (1960) writes of 'coordination games'. Lewis (1969) writes of 'coordination problems'. Gilbert (1981) critically discusses Lewis's game-theoretical definition of 'coordination problem'. I forbear from attempting a precise definition of such problems here.

[19] Lewis (1969) gives a dozen or so examples.

[20] For more on coordination problems see Ch. 9, below.

Recalcitrance to the Obligated Person's Will

A further point may be added to these preliminary observations. If we consider two standard contexts in which people talk of obligations, we find that the obligated person is generally not in a position to remove the obligation, prior to fulfilling it, with no more than a mental act of his own.

In the case of a promise, for instance, the promisor cannot simply decide that 'the promise is off' and hence free himself of his obligation to fulfil the promise. Rather, as it is often put, he must wait upon release by the promisee. He can of course break the promise if he so decides, but then he has defaulted on an existing obligation. In the case of an obligation not dependent on a promise, such as the obligation to save a drowning child if one can do so without danger to oneself, one might be able to remove the obligation by changing one's circumstances—one might perhaps alert a better swimmer to a drowning child's predicament—but generally speaking one cannot do this simply by a mental act alone.

If obligations generally are recalcitrant to the obligated person's will, then personal decisions do not give rise to obligations, since they can be done away with by a simple change of mind.[21] This accords with everyday usage: decisions may be in some sense 'binding', yet they are not generally said to give rise to obligations.[22]

Given that obligations are recalcitrant to one's will, it is easy to see why people may feel trapped by them. Decisions give one sufficient reason to act but one can change this by a simple change of mind. Obligations give one sufficient reason to act, and one *cannot* change this by a simple change of mind. Thus suppose one has to decide between two equally attractive alternatives, A and B. One realizes that one is obligated to choose alternative A. At this point rationality requires one to choose A. Some may find it comforting to know what must be done. Others may find it confining.

Summary of the Discussion So Far

Given the type of obligation with which I am concerned there are several points of contact between my concerns and those of other theorists of political obligation. Perhaps the most important is that if I am obligated to do something I am rationally required to do it, all else being equal. Equivalently, in my terms, one has sufficient reason to do it. That I have an obligation to do something,

---

[21] Some people may be particularly averse to changing their minds in whatever circumstance. Some may be incapable of doing so as the result of some kinds of brain damage. In principle, however, a decision is open to reversal by the one who made it.

[22] On the senses in which a decision binds, and its relation to obligation, see Ch. 7, below.

in a given situation, does not close the question of what reason requires me to do. There may be a species of obligation that does close the question. I am not assuming this to be a feature of obligations in general, something on which many theorists concur.

These points are intended to provide no more than a partial description of those obligations with which I am concerned in this book. As will emerge, some so-called obligations do not all have the features listed. All that do are of considerable practical significance.

2.3 Directed Obligations

Hart's Proposal

The obligations of promises and agreements are generally considered paradigmatic. They have also proved recalcitrant to philosophical explanation. Theories as to how precisely promises obligate have proliferated, without any one being generally judged to be sufficient.[23] The type of obligation in question has certain quite striking features that were emphasized by the distinguished philosopher of law H. L. A. Hart in a well-known article. Hart proposed, in fact, that the term 'obligation' should be reserved for something with the features in question, contrary to the usage he observed among philosophers.

He wrote:

Most important are the points that (1) that obligations may be voluntarily incurred or created, (2) that they are *owed* to special persons (who have rights), (3) that they do not arise out of the character of the actions which are obligatory but out of the relationship of the parties.[24]

Later Hart amplifies point (3), referring to 'special transactions between individuals . . . or some special relationship in which they stand to each other', and to 'previous transactions and relations between individuals'.[25] There is much that could be discussed in relation to the details of the quoted characterization of obligations, which is given in a footnote. For now I leave it as it stands.

Hart discusses a number of cases that give rise to obligations according to his criteria.[26] What he sees as 'the most obvious case' is that of promises.[27]

---

[23] Vitek (1993) critically surveys a number of the options on offer. For my own perspective on the obligations of agreements and promises see Ch. 9, below.

[24] Hart (1955: 179 n. 7).   [25] Hart (1955: 183 and 190).

[26] Hart (1955: 183 ff.). He focuses on the 'special rights' he takes to be correlative with obligations.

[27] Hart (1955: 183).

Presumably he would be happy to put agreements under this heading also.[28] Hart distinguishes obligations from *duties*. Obligations as opposed to duties arise only on the basis of transactions or relationships between particular people. One properly speaks of an obligation to keep a promise; one speaks rather of a duty to rescue a stranger. One has an obligation to do what one agreed to do, but a duty to support just institutions in general.

The suggestion that we think of obligation proper along the lines Hart proposed has a long history. Thus, in his *Treatise on Obligation,* first published in 1791, the great French jurist Robert Joseph Pothier distinguished between two senses of the term 'obligation'. In the third chapter he writes: 'The term Obligation has two significations. In its most extensive signification . . . it is synonymous with the term *duty,* and comprehends imperfect as well as perfect obligations. We call imperfect obligations, the obligations for which we are accountable to God alone.'[29] An example he gives is that of obligations or duties of gratitude: 'He, who has received a signal benefit, is bound to render his benefactor all the services of which he is capable . . . Yet his benefactor has no right of requiring those services from him . . . '.[30] He then turns to the second signification:

The term obligation, in a sense more proper and less extensive, comprehends only perfect obligations, which are called also personal engagements, giving him, with whom they are contracted, the right of requiring performance of them.[31]

Hart's latter-day proposal concerning how we should conceive of obligation proper has been taken up by a fair number of those who write on problems of political obligation.[32] Interestingly enough, having made reference to something like Hart's narrow sense of obligation at the outset, and allowed this to be obligation proper, several theorists of political obligation go on to say that they will not—after all—limit their focus to obligation in this sense.[33]

---

[28] Many assume that an agreement is an exchange of promises and thus a complex of which promises are the elements. I critically discuss this idea in Ch. 9, below.

[29] Pothier (1802: 2).

[30] Ibid.

[31] Ibid. Pothier goes on to say that jurists define perfect obligations as involving 'a bond of right, binding us to another, to give, do or refrain from doing something'. Note that he allows that there are two legitimate senses of 'obligation', though one is the 'more proper' sense.

[32] e.g. Rawls (1971); Simmons (1979); Pateman (1979); Klosko (1992).

[33] Simmons (1979) spends some time spelling out a narrower use he culls from the writings of Hart and Rawls. He allows that there is a broader use of 'obligation' and says he will consider both obligations in the narrow sense and duties with respect to his problem of political obligation. Klosko (1992) also spells out a narrower use and then says he will not limit his inquiries to obligations in this narrow sense.

Thus they align themselves with authors who do not spend time elaborating a narrower notion.[34]

Hart himself proposes what can be taken as a solution to the membership problem in terms of obligations in the narrow sense he favours. His proposal, sometimes referred to as the 'fair play argument', has been elaborated in various ways by others. I discuss it later in this book.[35]

A relatively narrow use of the term 'obligation', where it is tied to something arising from transactions between persons such as those involved in promises and agreements, may indeed be close to the original meaning of the English term. By now, however, everyday usage allows for talk of 'obligations' in all of the above contexts.[36] As Hart, in effect, suggests, this broad use may indeed obscure important differences. That is quite likely if there has been an expansion outwards from an original meaning that took account of a particular, relatively distinctive class of things. The outward expansion will then cover things of significantly different types, notwithstanding the presence of similarities to the original class.

In relation to the membership problem, and without any particular type of solution in mind, there are respectable reasons for not reining things in, at the outset, beyond a characterization of obligation such as I have given. This reflects central and relatively indisputable aspects of the prevailing broad use of the term 'obligation'. It may, indeed, say the most that can be said without moving to a characterization of specific, differing *types* of obligation.

Caution is particularly in order with respect to certain aspects of Hart's and others' more restrictive conceptions. Hart would not hesitate to characterize his topic in the above quotation—obligation in his narrow sense—as moral obligation, where this is understood as other than legal obligation, and perhaps as having further, positive features as well.[37] For reasons given earlier I prefer not to qualify the obligation at issue in the membership problem in this way.

Again, though Hart specifically says that obligations *may be* 'voluntarily incurred or created', some later writers suppose that obligations, in the proper narrow sense, *must* be voluntarily incurred. In other words, it is logically impossible to have an obligation—in the sense at issue—that you did not

---

[34] Such as Horton (1992: 14). His account of obligations in the broad sense he works with is much like the partial account just presented here, except that he says obligations are moral reasons for acting. Depending on the breadth of his understanding of 'moral', there may be no difference between us.

[35] Ch. 11, below.

[36] See Brandt (1964) on both points.

[37] The relevant article focuses on rights, rights he characterizes, without definition of the qualifying term, as 'moral'.

incur by some voluntary act. Now the term 'voluntary' can be variously interpreted. In a standard interpretation, however, a fully *intentional* action—as opposed to an automatic response like a knee-jerk in reaction to a tap on the knee—may yet not be *voluntary*. Coercion or, indeed, circumstances of strong external pressure, are understood to make an act less than fully voluntary.[38] It is best in the present context not to assume that all obligations are incurred voluntarily, in this standard sense, or to limit one's focus to obligations so incurred. Though one might expect that any obligations resulting from membership in a social group are in some way founded on a relationship between persons, it is not obvious that the relationship will be voluntary in the sense just discussed.

Leaving aside relationships that are entered *unintentionally*, one must allow that relationships generally may be entered in circumstances of strong pressure, or where the alternatives are so unattractive as to be unthinkable. This is the situation of many immigrants who come to their new country as refugees from another. They come to the new country because living in the other has become intolerable and the new country is for some reason the most feasible alternative option.

There is a related danger that initially restricting attention to a narrowly specified kind of obligation—particularly if it is qualified as 'moral' and required to be based on a strongly voluntary transaction—will prevent a proper understanding of the obligating character of agreements, promises, and whatever else may obligate in a similar way. Though consideration of promises in particular evidently played a large role in prompting the formulation of the restrictions Hart originally proposed, the way in which they obligate—either the ground of the obligation or its nature—may yet have been misunderstood.

Understanding agreements is important in relation to the membership problem since perhaps the most famous solution to it alludes to them. I devote some time to this solution—actual contract theory—in this book.[39] I argue that one central objection to it derives from a misunderstanding of agreements and the type of obligation they involve.

Obligation and Owing

In spite of the reasonableness of concerns about focusing initially on obligations as specified by Hart, or in elaborations of his specification, I shall suggest in

---

[38] See e.g. Simmons (1979: 14). He later implies an interpretation of voluntariness as involving a lack of coercion (1979: 82). See Scheffler (1997: 193) for what looks like a broader usage: one must simply *do* something to perform a 'voluntary act'.

[39] In Chs. 4, 5, and 10, below.

the next chapter that the most satisfying solution to the membership problem will show that members of political societies have obligations in a sense close to Hart's.[40] In this section I specify that sense.

I shall abjure Hart's willingness to qualify the obligations in question as moral, and I shall not take on his assumption concerning the grounds of these obligations in interpersonal relationships or transactions. I shall for now leave that matter open. Finally, I shall assume neither that these obligations *can* be voluntarily created nor that they *cannot*. Evidently, I shall not assume that these obligations can *only* be incurred voluntarily—in any sense of the term.

Taking from Hart's account any qualification about morality, any specification of grounds, and any reference to the possibility of voluntary creation, something extremely significant remains. This comes in Hart's second clause: obligations of the type in question are 'owed to special persons (who have rights)'. Perhaps 'special persons' would better be replaced by 'specific persons' in the sense that if an obligation is owed, it has to be owed *to* someone. There need be nothing 'special' about these persons in the sense that they have any particular personal qualities. 'Specific persons', however, should not be understood as ruling out *all* persons as those to whom the obligation is owed. What is key here is the reference to 'owing', owing to one or more persons.

One might say, as Hart does, that an *obligation* is owed. Or one might say, perhaps more perspicuously, that one has an obligation of the kind in question if and only if *one owes someone a particular action*. Performing that action is the fulfilment of the obligation. The question of how one might come to owe someone an action will be set aside for now.[41]

The person to whom one owes the action is said to have a *right* to it. Thus rights are 'correlated', in a strong sense, with obligations of this type: for X to owe Y action A *is* for Y to have a right against X to X's performance of A, and vice versa.[42]

There is no need to worry about whether we are talking here about obligations proper, as opposed to a central class of obligations—perhaps the original class in terms of a gradual widening of the extension of the term. What is important is not the proper use of a word, but rather the nature of, in a broad sense, a 'thing'. Namely, an obligation of the type in question.

---

[40] Cf. Klosko (1992: 11), who says, without explanation, that a positive account of political obligation in terms of obligations in such a narrow sense would be most satisfactory (though he will not provide one).

[41] It is taken up in Ch. 7, below.

[42] For discussion see Upton (2000).

Some authors simply say that an obligation of the type with which they are concerned is an obligation 'to' or 'toward' a particular person, the correlative right being a right 'against' the person with the obligation.[43] This way of putting things is even thinner than the pared-down version of Hart's account I have proposed so far. It seems to me that by thinning things down this far we have lost something important. For one must at some point ask: what is it to have an 'obligation to' another person? What is it to have a right 'against' a person? These phrases become open to a variety of interpretations (which they have, indeed, received). Things are pinned down very little by the phrases themselves. I shall therefore not strip any more from Hart's characterization of obligations. I shall maintain within it the notion of 'owing'. In this way it retains some substance.

In the literature, obligations simply characterized as obligations 'to' another person, correlative with rights of that person against the person with the obligation, have become known as 'directed' or 'relational' obligations. Hoping not to confuse anyone, I shall in what follows use the phrase 'directed obligation', and related phrases such as 'obligation to', to refer to obligations directed in the more substantial sense I have specified. That is, I shall understand someone to have a *directed obligation* when and only when he owes another person an act of his own. His obligation is then an obligation to, or towards, that person, who has a correlative right against him to the act that is owed.

One should not think all that can be said about directed obligations has now been said. The notion of a directed obligation may at this point rightly seem puzzling. What is it for someone to owe an action to another person? On what basis can one be properly said to be in this position?

Assuming this idea can be made good, it is reasonable to suppose that directed obligations are obligations according to the partial characterization presented in this chapter. That is, it is reasonable to suppose that one who can plausibly be said to *owe* another an action will have an obligation according to that characterization. He will have sufficient reason for performing that action, sufficient reason that is independent of his own inclinations or narrow self-interest and that cannot be eradicated by his own fiat.

It seems that—failing special circumstances—the fact that one owes someone an action must trump one's contrary inclinations and considerations of self-interest from the point of view of what rationality requires one to do. If I owe you this action, how can I appropriately argue that my own inclinations or considerations of self-interest, as such, permit me not to give it

---

[43] Perhaps the most famous of these discussions is that of Hohfeld (1914).

to you? As noted earlier, it is often assumed to be true of genuine obligations in general that they trump inclinations and considerations of self-interest. It seems, then, that directed obligations fit well with a variety of common understandings about obligation.

2.4 Imputed Obligations

I now turn to a species of so-called obligations that are not of the general kind I have characterized in this chapter. When an imperator issues a directive to the effect that certain people are to act a certain way, this is sometimes described as a matter of imputing an *obligation* to those people, an obligation to act as directed. I shall call a so-called obligation of this type an 'imputed obligation'.[44] Often when people speak of one's 'legal obligations' they are speaking of a particular set of imputed obligations. More precisely, they are speaking of *what a particular system of laws directs one to do*.[45] To state that one has a particular legal obligation, in this sense, is not to state that one has a particular obligation of the kind I have characterized. To see this, suppose that Pamela is passing through territory T. She knows that the legislature of political society S has passed a certain law, L: all those who pass through T are to pay a certain tax. Thus L imputes to Pamela, qua person passing through T, an obligation to pay the tax. Given all this, Pamela may still go on intelligibly to ask whether she has an obligation to pay the tax, that is, an *obligation of the general kind characterized earlier in this chapter*. That L, in effect, says she is to do so or, in other terms, imputes this obligation to her, is not in and of itself a positive answer.[46] The same goes for obligations imputed by social rules and conventions.

To distinguish my quarry from imputed obligations is not to deny that such obligations are of primary importance for the membership problem. A central

---

[44] Several authors use other terms to mark roughly the same category of so-called obligations. Stocker (1970) writes of 'institutional obligations'. Simmons (1979) refers to 'positional duties'. It does not appear that all imputed obligations need be positional in Simmons's sense. In principle an edict might address me not as the holder of some position, such as professor, or US citizen, but as myself, this particular person. The same distinction would need to be drawn between the obligations *imputed* to me by this edict, and my genuine obligations.

[45] See e.g. Singer (1973: 2–3); Simmons (1979: 16 ff.); Kramer (1999: 382). The phrase 'legal obligation' may also be used in a more complex sense to mean something like 'genuine obligation one has by virtue of the content of certain laws and some factor linking one to these laws in an appropriate way'. In other words, this phrase, along with related phrases like 'institutional obligation', is importantly ambiguous.

[46] Simmons (1979: 148–51) discusses an example suggesting the same basic point.

aspect of this problem could indeed be put—if somewhat confusingly—as follows. It is the problem of whether membership in a political society obligates one to fulfil the-obligations-imputed-to-one-by-the-political-institutions-of-that-society. This, after all, is just a broader version of the question: am I obligated to conform to the laws of my society?

3

In Pursuit of a Theory
of Political Obligation

For present purposes a theory of political obligation is a reasoned affirmative solution to the membership problem. In this chapter I propose that a satisfactory theory of political obligation will satisfy a number of specified criteria. I then detail a number of less than promising notions of membership in order to clear the ground before proceeding.

3.1 Desiderata for a Theory of Political Obligation

A theory of political obligation, as that is understood here, is a theory that purports to provide a reasoned affirmative answer to a particular question: is it the case that, in plausible senses of the terms, obligations inhere in membership in a political society—a society with political institutions—the obligations being to uphold the institutions in question? More briefly, are there political obligations? In the course of the following chapters I pay attention to a number of competing theories of political obligation. These include the classic theory I label *actual contract theory*, and the theory I shall myself defend, which I label *plural subject theory*. It will be helpful to develop, at the outset, some tests or criteria by reference to which these theories can be assessed and, indeed, compared with one another. I first summarize these criteria and give each one a label. Later I discuss those that require further clarification or justification.

The first criterion stands somewhat apart. I label it the criterion of *affirmativeness*. According to this criterion, a maximally satisfactory theory will allow that there are political obligations. I say more about this criterion in the next section. The rest of the criteria assume this one and can be roughly divided into two related groups. I refer to these as *analytic* criteria, on the one hand, and *interpretative* criteria, on the other.

As to the analytic criteria, first on the list is the *explanatoriness* criterion: to some degree or other, the theory will explain how membership in a political society is such that members have political obligations. Lack of satisfaction of this criterion can lead to a relatively casual dismissal of general analytic membership arguments or, in other terms, theories of political obligation. Ideally, the explanation given by the theory will not be overly rough or sketchy. It will involve a careful explication of the relevant concepts of a political society, membership in such a society, and obligatoriness. This is the criterion of *explicativeness*. As to the concepts in question, they should be plausible or intuitive in ways I discuss below. This I shall call the *intuitiveness* criterion. Crucially, the theory will show precisely how, given these carefully explicated intuitive concepts, membership in a political society is such that by virtue of one's membership one is obligated to uphold that society's political institutions. This is the *intelligible grounding* criterion: what is desired is that one show precisely how the relevant obligations are grounded in one's membership in a political society.

Evidently, theories may meet each of these four criteria to a greater or lesser extent. The more complete the explanation, the more thorough the explication of each of the relevant concepts, the more intuitive each of these concepts, the more carefully the intelligible grounding is made out, the more satisfactory the theory.

The next two criteria have to do with the obligations that the theory posits. The first of these is what I shall call the *puzzle-solving* criterion. With respect to the obligations in question, a maximally satisfactory theory will respond in a coherent manner to the immediate concerns about analytic membership arguments noted in the first chapter. These relate, in effect, to certain puzzles about the very idea that there are political obligations. They are, first, the puzzle: how can membership in a political society—which seems to be something natural—be conceptually tied to obligation—which does not? Second, there is the puzzle about morally unacceptable laws: how are political obligations compatible with morally unacceptable political institutions? Third, there is the puzzle about the nature of the obligation at issue.

One pertinent concern that was mooted earlier in this connection may now seem less pressing. That is the worry that it may sometimes be best, all things considered, to break a particular law. Given that one with an obligation has sufficient reason for action but not necessarily an absolutely conclusive reason, this worry disappears. What, though of cases where the supposedly obligatory act itself is of negligible consequence—such as stopping at a stop sign in a desert? Can one really be obligated to stop? If so, is the same kind of obligation at issue when people say such things as 'if it leads you out to war, to be wounded or killed, you must comply'?

Before proceeding with the second criterion relating to obligation, I should note that the five analytic criteria listed so far—the explanatoriness, explicativeness, intuitiveness, intelligible grounding, and puzzle-solving criteria—are those I take to be fundamental with respect to the *adequacy* of an affirmative solution to the membership problem. These core tests have to do with the nature of and relationship between certain key ideas—political society, membership in a political society, and obligation. If a theory does well on these tests, it is an adequate theory.

There are other tests I take to be important also. A theory will be better if it satisfies them. I take it that a *maximally adequate* theory of political obligation will satisfy the further criteria I specify below. The first two criteria are, once again, analytic criteria.

With respect to the conception of obligation at issue, it is notable that in the literature we find reference not only to political obligations but also (as if the same thing were at issue) political 'bonds'.[1] There is also much talk of 'binding' and 'being bound'. Though a theory of political obligation might be considered adequate without doing so, a maximally satisfactory theory would, I suggest, explain the tendency to speak of bonds and the like here. If it fails to do so, this tendency will remain something of a mystery, since it is not immediately obvious why it should seem so apposite. As a mnemonic, I shall refer to this as the criterion of *political bonds*.

In relation to this criterion, a theory of political obligation that invokes directed obligations would appear to have an advantage. If I owe you an action of mine, to which you have a correlative right, this could produce in me a sense of being bound *to you*. Similarly, if I owe a certain action to all of my fellow members in a given political society, this could produce in me a sense of being bound *to all of them*. If we are all in this position, then all would appropriately have a sense of being bound to all the rest. In short, if political obligation is directed obligation, it is apt to give rise to a sense of political bonds. A maximally adequate theory of political obligation would make it clear who, if anyone, was bound up with whom.

A further criterion relates to a question that, in the eyes of many, is closely linked to what they see as the problem of political obligation. This might be called the problem of political authority.[2] It can be couched as follows:

---

[1] Simmons (1979) frequently uses this language in relation to what he also refers to as political obligations (though the term 'bonds' is not in the index to his book); see, e.g. pp. viii ('political bonds', twice); 3 ('moral bonds', three times); 51 ('firm bonds'); 55 (political bonds'); 115 ('political bonds'). See also e.g. Horton (1992: 13) 'moral or ethical bonds'.

[2] Though the title of his book refers only to political obligation, the kind of obligation Beran is interested in is 'the correlative of political authority' (1987: 54).

how is political authority possible? At its most general: how does one person gain the standing to command another to do something? In recent times political philosophers have not tended to regard this as a major problem in the field.[3] Witness the fact that the 'problem of political obligation' is a standard phrase, whereas 'the problem of political authority' is not. Though some have seen these problems as essentially the same, there are whole books on political obligation, let alone articles, that make little mention of the problem of political authority.[4]

One can see why these problems appear to be closely connected. To have the standing to command is to have the right to be obeyed, where this right is correlated with an obligation of conformity, or, more fully, an obligation to obey. So political authority, construed as the right or standing to command, involves obligations on the part of those who are commanded. At the same time, one could be obligated to conform to the edicts of a certain person or body by reason of something other than its standing to command one to do things. I suggest, then, that a theorist who offers an affirmative solution to the membership problem should at a minimum answer the question: is there a conceptual link between political obligations—as the theory understands these—and political authority or not? Whatever the answer, it should be explained. Call this the *authority* criterion.

The next three criteria are interpretative.[5] A theory of political obligation, as so far characterized, may be expected to help one to understand what at least some of those who take themselves to be politically obligated have in mind, though they may not be able to articulate it. In other words, it may be expected to satisfy the *interpretation* criterion. Associated with this are the criteria of *reasonableness* with respect to the beliefs of these who take themselves to be politically obligated, and *accuracy*. I discuss these criteria in a separate section below.

To sum up the discussion so far: I have specified eleven tests that a maximally adequate theory of political obligation will pass with flying colours. There is first the criterion of affirmativeness, about which I say more shortly. Satisfaction of this test engages five core analytic tests. On these any adequate theory will do well. The affirmativeness criterion also engages two further analytic criteria—the political bonds and the authority criteria—and three

---

[3] Some do focus on political authority. See e.g. Anscombe (1978); Raz (1979, 1986); Hampton (1997); and R. P. Wolff (1970)—who argued (in brief) that there wasn't any.

[4] Simmons, for instance, leaves the issue of a government's right to command till the last section of his book on political obligations (1979: 195–200).

[5] In Gilbert (1999b), I focused on these interpretative criteria. That now seems to make the issue overly subjective.

interpretative criteria. Evidently, a given theory will be more or less adequate, depending on whether and to what extent it meets all of these tests.

It is possible that a given theory of political obligation has features in addition to those so far specified that make it attractive. It may have certain formal virtues, for instance, such as an appealing simplicity, or it may help to illuminate other topics. For now I shall take it that if a theory fully satisfies all of the specified criteria it is as good a theory as one can reasonably hope for—in that sense, then, it is a maximally satisfactory theory.[6]

Evidently there could be more than one such theory. Maximally adequate theories need not be in competition with each other. They might propose different, yet still intuitive, notions of membership in a political society and mount a different, yet still compelling, argument for the existence of political obligations, given that notion of membership. Thus to say that a theory is as good as one can reasonably hope for is not to say that it is the only such theory in the field.

There may also be theories that do not meet the affirmativeness criterion but show, rather, that on a particular intuitive conception of membership in a political society, such membership does not involve obligations, on any plausible conception of an obligation. Insofar as one accepts the affirmativeness criterion, such theories will not be adequate. They will nonetheless be significant since they will explain an important aspect of the situation of members of political societies in the sense with which they are concerned.[7]

Some of the criteria for a satisfactory theory of political obligation that I have outlined do not require much explanation or justification. I now say more about those I think will usefully be further clarified.

Affirmativeness: The Theory Allows that there are Political Obligations

If one offers a negative solution to the membership problem, one must reckon with the intuitive judgements of those whose instinct is to give a positive one. This includes those, like Robert Paul Wolff, for whom various assumptions lead them to reverse their initial, intuitive judgements.[8] It also includes those philosophers who propound general analytic membership arguments. Faced with such arguments, sincerely proposed, there is reason to think a positive solution can be found. That is, there is reason to think that there is a sense

---

[6] I shortly reject the idea of positing an additional 'generality' criterion.

[7] Though Simmons (1979) does not focus on a specific conception of membership in a political society, it might be possible to articulate his form of philosophical 'anarchism' in such a way that it falls into this class—primarily by clarifying the relevant notion of membership.

[8] See the quotation from R. P. Wolff (1970), in Ch. 1, above. I say more about Wolff's negative position in the text below.

of 'political society' or 'membership in a political society' such that the latter involves obligations.

These theorists argue that it is part of the meaning of the phrase 'political society' that the members of such a society have the relevant obligations. Though the theorists could be wrong, a connection of meaning is the kind of thing about which one is least likely to be in error. One need not be clear about the analysis of this meaning, or be able adequately to articulate the purported connection between membership and obligation, but one's intuitive judgement that there is a certain analytic connection should be taken seriously. Of course, the phrases 'political society', and so on, are open to different construals. Given these intuitive judgements, however, there is reason to suppose that there is at least one affirmative solution to the membership problem, in terms of one such construal.[9]

Another problem with a negative solution is that it leaves open the possibility that the search has simply not gone on long enough. To close off that possibility one would have to offer a convincing proof that no positive answer can be found. A. J. Simmons attempts an argument of this sort in relation to the problem he considers in *Moral Principles and Political Obligations*. He begins by expressing the belief that the moral principles he will investigate are the only ones relevant to the case. If, therefore, his negative argument takes them all into account and is valid, there is nothing more to investigate, and his negative conclusion stands.[10]

Someone might wonder whether Simmons's negative conclusion in relation to the problem he considers is enough to warrant such a conclusion in relation to the membership problem. Setting aside the matter of the validity of his complex argument, I think not. There are at least two reasons for this. First, though in places he sets out the problem he is concerned with in terms that suggest an interest in what it is to be the member of a political society, he sets it out in different terms in other places, and fails to make it his focus.[11] In other words, he is not specifically concerned with the membership problem. It is reasonable, indeed, to see him as concerned with what I have called the residence problem. A negative solution to that problem does not

---

[9] It could be that theorists who claim a connection of meaning are really talking about their sense of the *metaphysical essence* of a society (see Kripke 1972). Then their fallibility in the matter would be easier to argue, though one might think it worth pursuing the possibility of their correctness nonetheless.

[10] See Simmons (1979: 56).

[11] This statement in the preface, for instance, suggests an interest in the membership relation: 'It is natural in such contexts to wonder if our relationship to our government constrains us to obey...' (Simmons 1979: p. viii). This suggests that 'we' are members of a political society. Shortly after, one finds Simmons referring to 'citizens in normal political environments' (1979: p. ix), which does not so clearly carry this suggestion.

entail a negative solution to the membership problem. Second, Simmons limits himself to the consideration of obligations understood to be a matter of moral principles. This precludes the discovery of pertinent obligations of another kind. It seems fair to conclude that one cannot rule out an affirmative solution to the membership problem on the basis of Simmons's discussion.

The last point applies, with appropriate changes, to Robert Paul Wolff's argument in his book *In Defense of Anarchism*. He allows that one may conform to the laws of any country in which one finds oneself for reasons of prudence, for the sake of the value of order, and so on. He disputes, however, that one has a special obligation to conform to the laws of one's own country. He believes he has shown that any feeling to the contrary is 'purely sentimental and has no objective basis'.[12]

As he would describe it, Wolff's argument is a moral one.[13] At its core is the contention that there is a primary moral obligation to be autonomous, so that one can never be morally obligated to do something just because another person or body—such as the government of one's country—says one is to do it. As is well known, his argument is open to criticism on several fronts. In particular, his central contention that every human being has a primary moral obligation to be autonomous needs careful attention. *Is* there such an obligation? If so, precisely what does it rule out?

Even if there is an obligation of an important kind to be autonomous, and even if it rules out an obligation of a similar kind to do what one's government says one is to do, because it says so, that may not prevent one from incurring an obligation *of another kind* with this content. This is something that Wolff does not address. In sum, for more than one reason, it would be premature to give up on an affirmative solution to the membership problem in face of Wolff's argument.

Intuitiveness

A satisfying theory of political obligation will offer an intuitive account of a political society such that membership in such a society involves political obligations. By referring to the account of a political society as intuitive, I mean that it answers well to a central everyday concept.

I am assuming that a political society is a type of social group—in a central sense of the term—and that this assumption reflects a central everyday concept of a political society. The sense of 'social group' in question has so far been

---

[12] R. P. Wolff (1970: 19).   [13] Cf. R. P. Wolff (1970: 10 ff.).

specified only by reference to examples. It will be explored in depth in due course. A satisfying theory of political obligation that invokes this concept of a political society should ground the obligations in question in a feature common to all such societies, or at least to clear cases. Otherwise it is, in effect, invoking a different concept of a political society, which may not be an intuitive one.

Similarly, the theory should show that membership in a political society grounds *obligations* in an intuitive sense of the term. In Chapter 2, I gave a partial general characterization of the kind of so-called obligation I take to be at issue. This is what I refer to as genuine obligation, where one with a genuine obligation to do A has sufficient reason to do A. I added some further marks, such as independence of inclination and self-interest, that I take to characterize obligation in particular. I also introduced the category of directed obligation construed as a matter of owing. My discussion offered only a partial characterization of the terrain of obligation. A satisfactory theory will appeal to something that is a genuine obligation according to my characterization and has whatever other features it needs to (perhaps out of a certain range) in order to be, intuitively, an obligation.

The Interpretative Criteria

With respect to the interpretation criterion, I shall assume that a maximally adequate theory will reflect an assumption common among those who believe they have political obligations. I have in mind the assumption that political societies can be of considerable magnitude.

The proponents of analytic membership arguments in particular tend to assume that they themselves have political obligations with respect to what they see as a political society with many millions of members. In other words, the concept of a political society that is argued to be analytically tied to a concept of obligation is at the same time judged to apply to very large populations. Indeed, it is taken to apply to specific, existing large populations such as the citizens of the United States, or the citizens of the United Kingdom. Insofar as a theory of political obligation hopes to explain the pull of these arguments, then, it should appeal to a concept of political society that can at least in principle apply to such populations. I believe that one can indeed appeal to such a concept while remaining within the bounds of the central, relatively narrow concept of a social group on which I am focusing.

Suppose one has specified concepts of a political society and of membership in such a society that are interpretatively fruitful in the following way. One can argue that membership in the intuitive sense in question obligates the members to support the relevant political institutions, and that the society in question can be extremely populous. Should one require of a theory of political obligation, in addition, that the concept of a political society it invokes is such that by and large at least some of those who currently believe they are politically obligated would be *reasonable* to suppose they are members of such a society?

There is reason to require that, by and large, these people would not *clearly be wrong* to think that they were members of such a society. This is not a matter of charity pure and simple. It makes good sense as an interpretative maxim. It would be hard to understand their conviction that they are politically obligated were evidence to the contrary staring them in the face. It would be easier, indeed, if there were at least some evidence that they were right. Hence the interpretative criterion of reasonableness: the concept of a political society invoked by a maximally satisfactory theory would be such that those who take themselves to be politically obligated are at least somewhat reasonable to do so.

There is no need from an interpretative point of view to demand of a theory of political obligation that, according to the account given, those who take themselves to have political obligations be right. A maximally satisfactory theory would, however, explain what it would be for these people to be right, and give some pointers as to how that might be ascertained. I shall understand the interpretative criterion of accuracy—perhaps somewhat misleadingly labelled—accordingly.

'Generality'

Should one demand of a maximally adequate theory of political obligation that, if it is true, most (or at least many) actual people in the world today are bound to support and uphold a particular set of political institutions? A. John Simmons can be read as adopting such a 'generality' criterion of adequacy for an account of 'our political bonds'.[14] He does so because 'most of those who have advanced accounts of political obligation have regarded generality (or even "universality," . . .) as the primary criterion of success'.[15] He had previously rejected a universality criterion as overly demanding. As a proponent of such a criterion he cites John Ladd. Ladd, he says, 'insists that political obligation must be a single "universal moral requirement binding on everyone in the society" '.[16] Though Simmons appears to see his generality criterion as simply a

---

[14] Simmons (1979: 55–6). Cf. Klosko (1992: 3) who cites Simmons.

[15] Simmons (1979: 56).

[16] Simmons (1979: 34) citing Ladd (1970: 27). Simmons also argues that the demand for a *single* ground of political obligation is too strict. See the text below. In asking whether membership in an intuitive sense grounds political obligations I do not mean to imply that there could be no other bases of obligation to support the political institutions of one's own country. Nor do I deny that there could be different intuitive concepts of membership such that membership of the different kinds at issue obligate in the same or different ways. Suffice it to say that a single satisfying solution to the membership problem would be good to have.

loosening of such a universality criterion, it suggests a different, more empirical direction of inquiry.

Some guiding questions, including the membership problem, are at root conceptual. It is natural to posit some kind of universality test if one's project is of this kind. My own core criteria incorporate such a test: if it is shown that membership (in a central sense) involves obligations—as I require—then it will be shown that *all* those who are members *in that sense* will be obligated.

Other guiding questions are closer at root to this: do many people at the present time have special obligations to support a particular set of political institutions? This is an empirical, statistical concern rather than a conceptual one. In spite of the possibility of putting a more conceptual gloss on his project, this often seems to be Simmons's own guiding question, his answer being: 'no'.

Some might think a theory that failed to meet an empirical generality test would have insufficient practical relevance. People are very reasonably concerned with the question, 'In what ways am *I* bound?' Among other things they want to know whether they are obligated to support and comply with the political institutions of what they would refer to as their country. A theory that met a statistical generality criterion would give one reason to think one was so obligated oneself. It would not, of course, close the question for any particular individual.

In order to respond to the concerns just noted to the best of one's ability, however, one needs to know what the possibilities are. In what ways might I be bound? In what ways might those living in the territory of a given imperator be bound? Does membership in a political society, on some central intuitive construal, involve political bonds, and if so of what kind? What does such membership amount to? Then one can ask: 'Who, in the world today, has such membership? Do I?'

Of the first set of questions, a theory of political obligation that is maximally satisfactory according to the criteria I have already set out would answer the last two. It would therefore directly bear on the first two also. It would accordingly allow each person more clearly to judge what obligations he has. If he does not have obligations of the kind invoked by the theory, it would clarify the nature of some obligations that he might have had, but does not. If he thinks it would be good if he and those around him had such obligations, it will indicate how that might be brought about. Similarly, it will indicate how he might continue to avoid them. It seems unnecessary to demand of a theory of political obligation as that is understood here that it pass the essentially statistical generality test as opposed to the interpretative tests I have offered. Nonetheless, such a theory might well pass such a generality test. If it does, that will clearly be of great interest both from a practical point of view and for social science.

Whether or not most or, at least, many people in the world today are obligated *as members* of a political society in an intuitive sense, many questions will remain to be answered. In particular, there may be other sources of obligation in the political realm. A maximally satisfactory theory of political obligation in my sense need not reveal all such sources of obligation. It will reveal one, but only one, particular source: membership in a political society in one intuitive sense of that phrase. Several other such bases have been suggested in the literature—benefits received, for instance, and a natural duty of justice.[17] Many people may be obligated in some sense to support the political obligations of their countries on one or more such basis. I have already allowed that, given the criteria of adequacy proposed here, the membership problem itself may have more than one adequate solution. To offer but one such solution is the task of this book.

3.2 Some Less Than Promising Notions of Membership

This section looks briefly at two broad notions of membership in a political society that might initially appear to be of some interest in relation to the membership problem. It argues that they are far from promising in that respect.

Membership through Residence

According to the first notion, membership in a political society is equivalent to residence in the territory of an imperator. This is a very spare notion: it does not require habitual obedience or even a tendency to obedience on anyone's part, it does not rule out a variety of imperators covering the same territory, and it says nothing about the possession of any kind of coercive power by the imperator in question. Its very spareness allows one to bring out an aspect that could seem decisive but is not. Insofar as a more intuitively plausible notion builds on or incorporates this spare one, it is by virtue of new elements that it is indeed more plausible.

By definition, an imperator is one who addresses imperatives to the members of a certain territorially defined population. Consider a given population, P, and a given imperator, 'Imp'. Imp addresses imperatives to P. Can one infer from this that all members of P are obligated to do as Imp says? All members

---

[17] On arguments from gratitude and natural duty see Simmons (1979: chs. 6 and 7). I briefly discuss another argument, from 'fair play', in Ch. 11, below.

of P have a number of *imputed* obligations, obligations to do as Imp says. As noted earlier, however, to say that the members of P have imputed obligations is not to say that they are obligated in a sense appropriate to the membership problem. What of the particular facts concerning Imp and his (or its) intentional relationship to the members of P? It seems far-fetched to suggest that any member of P has an *obligation* to do what Imp says merely by virtue of the fact that Imp has addressed one or more imperatives to members of P, whether or not he thereby *has reason* to do so.

Membership as Imputed Membership

According to the second notion, membership in a political society is what may be called *imputed* membership. This notion may be introduced as follows. Using some natural pre-theoretical construal of the relevant terms, imagine that certain young people found a political society on a remote island. They draw up a list of rules for the society and ordain that each member of the society must work for one week per year on a parcel of common land on the island. They ordain, further, that among the members of the society are the parents of the founding members. Now suppose that Bill, who is not one of the founders, and does not live on the island, is the father of one of them. According to the rules of the society he is a member of the society. Further, he has to work for one week per year on a parcel of common land on the island. This being so, one must grant that Bill has an imputed obligation to work on the common land once a year. It is hard, however, to grant that he has any other kind of obligation to do so.

The example makes clear that imputed membership is not a good candidate for the kind of obligation-generating membership that a theory of political obligation is looking for. At the same time, it allows for the existence of such membership. This may be exemplified, indeed, by the young people in the story.

4

Actual Contract Theory: Attractions

In this and the next chapter, I discuss what may be the best-known theory of political society and political obligation. I call it *actual contract theory* for reasons I explain. As this chapter argues, it has significant attractions as a solution to the membership problem. These points set the theorist an interesting goal: retain the attractions of actual contract theory while avoiding what is problematic about it—I discuss a number of objections to it in the next chapter.

4.1 Actual Contract Theory

Actual contract theory invokes an agreement as opposed to a contract in law. It is commonly referred to as 'contract theory' or 'social contract theory'. I use the term 'contract' in deference to this practice. I use the qualifier 'actual' in order to emphasize that the theory I have in mind invokes an actual as opposed to what has come to be known as a 'hypothetical' agreement, that is, an agreement people would make in such-and-such circumstances, but did not actually make.[1]

The idea that an agreement may give rise to political obligations is mooted at least as early as Plato's *Crito*. There Socrates imagines the laws invoking 'undertakings by which you agreed to live as a member of our state' in support of their claim that he must comply with their commands.[2] Other writings

---

[1] The most famous contemporary invocation of a hypothetical contract in political philosophy (Rawls 1971) is part of a theory of justice as opposed to political obligation. Rawls argues that in a carefully specified (and highly unrealistic) hypothetical situation ('the original position') the people involved would agree on certain distributive principles. The general concept of an hypothetical agreement does not require that the situation in which the people in question would agree is itself unrealistic in the way of Rawls's original position. See Ch. 5, below.

[2] Plato (1978a: 37, 52d; see also e.g. 35, 50e). Socrates imagines the laws invoking other factors also. Woozley (1979) reviews the discussion.

associated with one or another version of this idea include, perhaps most famously, Thomas Hobbes's *Leviathan*, Jean-Jacques Rousseau's *On the Social Contract*, and John Locke's *Second Treatise on Government*.[3] Many commentaries on and interpretations of these classic texts are available. Even a summary of this historical and interpretative material is beyond the scope of this book. I shall, indeed, tend to eschew references to it, and to the work of authors with related views, given that my main aim is the exposition of my own theory.[4]

For present purposes it will suffice to start by considering the following standard version of actual contract theory. To be a member of a political society is to be party to an agreement—an agreement to accept a particular set of political institutions. By virtue of this agreement the parties constitute a political society with the institutions in question. Members of this society are obligated through the agreement to uphold the relevant set of political institutions. People are obligated, then, to uphold the political institutions of their own political society by virtue of their membership. Insofar as one can be a member of more than one political society by means of entering a relevant agreement, one can be obligated to uphold the political institutions of more than one such society by virtue of such an agreement. There are various further elaborations that could be made to this broadly specified theory. This broad specification suffices to show both why it has been found attractive and why certain standard objections have been raised to it.

The theory just specified may sometimes be referred to as 'consent theory' in the literature. At other times the quoted phrase is used to refer to something that does not necessarily involve an agreement, let alone an agreement of the type described.[5] Suffice it to say that my focus here is on actual contract theory as I have just characterized it.

In this chapter I focus on the attractions of the theory. It may be found attractive for a variety of reasons. These fall into two broad classes. The

---

[3] Locke (1980: ch. 8, sects. 119–22, pp. 63–4) distinguishes between 'perfect members' who enter an agreement, and another class of obligated persons.

[4] Contemporary theorists with what might loosely be termed actual contractarian views include Tussman (1960); Walzer (1970, 1977); and Beran (1987) (see n. 5, below).

[5] Beran (1987) advances what he refers to as a 'consent theory' of political obligation. He argues that the acts with which he is concerned are largely a matter of 'unilateral' rather than 'mutual' promises or (as he sees it) contracts (1987: 153–5). A unilateral promise by person A need not be accompanied by anyone else's promise. Beran also says that he is 'not committed to a contractarian account of society' (1987: 52). Simmons (1979) goes to some pains to distinguish consenting 'in the strict sense' from entering an agreement or making a (unilateral) promise: 'consent in the strict sense is always given to the actions of other persons' (1979: 76). In discussing what he refers to as 'consent theory' he focuses on consent in that sense. Simmons insists that consent cannot be given 'under the direct threat of serious physical violence' (1979: 77). In some contexts of its use the term 'consent' may be defined in this way. I argue in Ch. 10, below, that the everyday conception of an agreement is not.

first class has to do with the plausibility from an analytic point of view of linking political obligations to agreements. They stem from intuitive understandings as opposed to empirical observations or moral judgements. I refer to these as *analytic* attractions. The second class concerns the supposed moral desirability of linking political obligations to agreements. The moral considerations in question are not strictly relevant to my concerns in this book. Nonetheless, it is important to understand what they are. Just as they may motivate acceptance of the theory, they may motivate rejection of alternative theories unless their irrelevance is clear. I refer to these as *moral* attractions.

Several of the attractions mentioned depend on assumptions about what a society or an agreement is. My mentioning the relevant attraction here implies only that these assumptions either have been or might well be found plausible, and hence facilitate the acceptance of actual contract theory. Some will be discussed in detail later in this book. The list I give is not intended to be exhaustive or to detail what might have attracted people to the theory in a particular historical context.[6]

4.2 Analytic Attractions

Agreements are a Canonical Source of Obligation

One clear attraction of actual contract theory as a theory of political obligation is this. It stipulates as a basis for membership in a political society something that is an uncontroversial basis for obligations—an agreement. The precise nature of the obligations is, presumably, less clear, if only because this raises a further question.[7]

It is worth emphasizing that it is actual agreements as opposed to hypothetical ones that are a canonical source of obligations. It is hardly clear, and it is probably not true, that from the premiss that people *would have agreed* to something if asked, or given other more restrictive conditions, one can infer that they have obligations to do what they would have agreed to do.[8]

---

[6] This contrasts with Simmons's procedure in Simmons (1979).

[7] Simmons (1979: 70) writes: 'the model of promise lends clarity and credibility to a theory of political obligation; for promising is surely as close to being an indisputable ground of moral requirement as anything is. Basing a theory of political obligation on consent, then, lends it plausibility unequalled by rival theories.' For present purposes what a maximally adequate theory must invoke is something that is an indisputable ground of *obligation*. It may then not be necessary that it invoke an indisputable ground of *moral requirement*.

[8] Cf. Dworkin (1989a), discussing Rawls (1971).

Agreements are Tightly Tied to Obligations

It may seem that the connection between agreements and obligation is extremely tight. Thus the moral philosopher H. A. Prichard remarked: 'Once call some act a promise and all question of whether there is an obligation to do it seems to have vanished.'[9] There is something a little awkward about this quotation. I take Prichard to be saying, in effect, 'Once say that *I have promised to do something* and all question of whether *I have an obligation to do it* has vanished.' I assume he would have been equally happy to assert: 'Once say that I have entered an agreement and all question of whether I have an obligation to conform to it has vanished.'

Prichard suggests that the connection between entering an agreement and having an obligation to carry it out is knowable *a priori*. That is, knowing that one has entered an agreement is sufficient for knowing that one has an obligation to conform to it. He is not the only person to have said, or implied, something like this.[10] To give it a label, however, I shall refer to it as 'Prichard's point'.

Returning to actual contract theory, if Prichard's point is correct, and if political societies are, by definition, founded on relevant agreements, one can know a priori that there are political obligations. This accords well with the general analytic membership argument to the effect that—never mind precisely why—it is true as a matter of logic that membership in a political society involves obligations. Were that the case the obligating quality of membership in a political society would be knowable a priori. The quotation from Prichard refers to 'obligation', full stop. Obligation is not qualified as 'moral'. Quite likely Prichard would be happy to add such a qualification. The main point, for present purposes, is that his unqualified claim has some intuitive plausibility. More will be said on this matter in due course.

Agreements Provide Directed Obligations

Let us suppose that the members of the war cabinet have agreed to meet in the usual room at five the following day, and that each is thereby obligated to come to that room at the appointed time. It is surely part of our intuitive understanding of the case that each is obligated to each to come to the room then. That is, each owes each his appearance at the place in question.

---

[9]   Prichard (1968: 198).

[10]   Beran (1987: 6) says that if someone is coerced into saying 'I promise' 'the utterance does not count as a promise and no obligation is created'. The context makes it clear that, in Beran's view, *were* there a promise it *would* obligate the promisor—*by definition.*

That is not to say that it is easy to see how precisely the act of entering an agreement brings this about. Nor does actual contract theory as so far adumbrated tell us that, since it relies on an intuitive understanding of what an agreement is. It can, in any case, stoutly maintain that agreements give rise to directed obligations in the parties. They may indeed be the most salient source of such obligations, along with promises.[11] Actual contract theory is thus fitted to explain, among other things, why people are so inclined to talk of 'bonds' in connection with the obligations of membership.

Agreements Provide the Right Kind of Ground for Obligations of Membership

It may be that one is in some way obligated to support the political institutions of any country whatsoever, or of any country that is just or has some other political virtue or virtues not possessed by all countries as such. It is not intuitively plausible, however, to suppose that every such country is one's own or that a country becomes one's own simply because it possesses some particular political virtue or virtues.[12] A country's being *my* country has to do with some relationship I bear to that particular country irrespective of, or at least in addition to, its virtues. My participating in the agreement that constitutes the political society that is that country would provide such a relationship, and hence provide the right kind of ground for political obligations in the sense of this book.

Agreements Provide Special Obligations

One's participation in the agreement that constituted the political society that is one's own country would explain how one could have a special obligation to uphold the political institutions of one's own country in particular. Similarly, it would explain why one might feel that one's relationship to the political institutions of one's own country was different from one's relationship to the political institutions of other countries.

One may, it seems, have more than one country. One would then, if the membership problem has an affirmative answer, have special obligations to uphold the political institutions of whichever countries are one's own. Actual contract theory provides an explanation of how one can have more than one country and how one will have special obligations to each of one's countries: by virtue of one's participation in the constitutive agreements of each.

---

[11] Cf. Hart (1955: 183).

[12] Some rhetorical statements might suggest otherwise. Think of J. F. Kennedy's pronouncement 'Ich bin ein Berliner' (I am a Berliner) at the conclusion of a speech delivered in Berlin on 26 June 1963 in which he praised Berlin as a place of political freedom. In spite of the sentiment, he would probably have refused to pay Berlin city taxes, if there were such, on the grounds of *not* being 'ein Berliner'.

An Agreement is Sufficient to Found a Political Society

The analytic attractions of actual contract theory discussed so far relate to the tie between agreements and obligation. The remaining analytic attractions relate to the nature of social groups in general and political societies in particular. Here I refer to social groups in the relatively narrow sense indicated earlier, such that discussion groups and trade unions are among the paradigmatic examples.

It is clear that an agreement is sufficient to found social groups of many kinds, large and small. As to some cases, a number of people may get together and agree to form a social club, a discussion group, a trade union, a political party, and so on. Two people may agree to 'go steady' and become an established couple or, as it is sometimes said, 'an item'. The agreement both creates the group and constitutes the parties to the agreement as its members. It seems that relatively populous, territorially extended political societies can in principle be formed in this way. Given new technologies, there may be no limit in practice on the number of people who can be involved in making an agreement of an appropriate kind.

New Members can Perpetuate a Society by 'Signing On' to an Existing Agreement

Once a social group has formed by agreement, new members can, in effect, 'sign on' to the founding agreement. A social club, for instance, may offer membership to those who are not yet members, explaining its terms. A would-be member may then accept the offer. Or a would-be member may solicit membership, understanding its terms, in which case the club may accept the would-be member's offer. Perhaps there will be some stipulation as to something one must do before becoming a member, such as paying dues or renouncing membership in some other group or groups. Still, the matter of 'signing on' will be central.

Political societies may incorporate new members in similar ways. In contrast with what is sometimes supposed, therefore, actual contract theory does not have to say, implausibly, that all of those with political obligations are either original founders of the society in question or are somehow obligated by an agreement to which they are not party. Over time, all of the founders may have been replaced by others who signed on after the society was founded.

Agreements could be Necessary

Agreements may be sufficient to found and—through 'signing on'—perpetuate a political society, but are they necessary for this? Though I shall argue that they are not, it is worth considering why one might come to think they are.

Consider first mere aggregates of persons such as the worldwide population of blue-eyed people, or all those who enjoy the music of Bach, populations that may on occasion be referred to as groups or, for that matter, social groups. A salient aspect of membership in such groups, in the context of the present discussion, is that it requires no particular preamble. One has blue eyes or one doesn't, one enjoys Bach's music or one doesn't. Certainly one need enter no agreement to be a member in groups such as these. Conceiving of a political society as *more* than a mere aggregate of persons, one may find it hard to see how such an aggregate—those residing on a given tract of land, say—can be transformed into such a society *without* a founding agreement.

One may reach this position after considering various alternatives. One may doubt the sufficiency of mere residence in the territory of an imperator, for instance, whether or not the imperator is generally heeded, or accompanies its edicts with credible threats. With Rousseau, one might judge that general compliance with an edict under threat does not of itself create a genuine society, only disparate persons—still a mere aggregate—all complying with the edict for their own reasons.[13] Though a population of such residents may superficially appear more 'society-like' than the worldwide population of blue-eyed people, or of those who like Bach, it may still not seem intuitively to rise to the level of a social group or society in the sense at issue here.

One may go on to conjecture that nothing that can be fully described in terms of what the various individual members of a population personally believe, feel, want, decide, and do can be more than a mere aggregate of persons, however smoothly or happily they interact.[14] A human society, it may be argued, is a collective body if it is anything at all, albeit a collective body made up of individual human beings. Whatever it is precisely, a collective body is surely not simply a matter of members of a given population personally believing, feeling, wanting, deciding, and doing certain things. An agreement is evidently sufficient to create a collective body, since an agreement is sufficient, intuitively, to create a society.[15] There being no clear alternative candidate,

---

[13] Rousseau (1983: bk. I, ch. 5, p. 23). See also Kavka (1983).

[14] Compare the argument in Gilbert (1989: ch. 2), on the difficulty of constructing a social group out of social actions in the sense of Weber (1964): a social action is (roughly) an action oriented in its course by reference to one or more persons other than the agent.

[15] Thus Locke (1980). See also Tussman (1960). The point is intuitively clear.

one may conclude that an agreement is not only sufficient but also necessary for such creation.

One may be encouraged to rest with agreements as the necessary foundation of political societies on considering their relationship to three conditions that are plausibly judged necessary for membership in a paradigmatic social group. These are intentionality, unity, and consciousness of that unity.

i. Intentionality As to the first, it may seem that, intuitively, membership in a social group, or membership of the most basic or central type, is always intentional to some degree. This marks a distinction between social groups and mere aggregates. It also distinguishes social groups from mere 'groupings' of persons for which an internal, psychological criterion is less persuasive.

Making an agreement the foundation of a political society would clearly accommodate the judgement that membership in a social group is always intentional. Entering an agreement is an intentional, indeed a conscious, process. One makes or accepts a proposal, intentionally communicating what one is doing to another person. Not necessarily in so many words, one understands that the other's or one's own acceptance is the final stage in the creation of the agreement. Someone who apparently agrees, but later is shown not to have had the appropriate intentions, will be judged not to have agreed in spite of the appearances. To say that agreements must be entered intentionally is of course not to say that the necessary intentionality of membership is a matter of entry into an agreement. It is only to say that an account of membership that appeals to such entry will have no problem with this requirement.

ii. Unity The sense that a human society is something other than an aggregate may be expressed in terms of unity. Membership in any social group unifies the participants, it may be said, in a substantial way.[16]

Those who enter an agreement seem thereby to constitute a unit of a substantial kind. In Hobbes's terms, an agreement creates 'a reall Unitie' of the parties.[17] It is not surprising, indeed, that the legal term 'contract' comes from the Latin *con-trahere*—bring together. This observation supports the judgement that an agreement creates a collective body. It supplies a kind of unity that is arguably necessary for the transformation of an aggregate of persons into such a body and hence into a social group proper.

[16] See Gilbert (1989: ch. 4) for a discussion of the capacious general notion of a 'unit'.
[17] Hobbes (1982: 227).

iii. Consciousness of Unity   The sociologist Georg Simmel wrote that, in order for a society to exist, the members must be *conscious of* their unity.[18] Whether or not the consciousness of unity is sufficient for societal existence—and whatever precisely that would mean—it may seem to be at least necessary. That is, it may seem that members of a social group or society must both constitute a unit in a more than trivial sense and perceive themselves and their fellow members as together constituting such a unit. Precisely what degree of awareness is necessary, assuming that some is, is an important issue.[19] In any case, the following points may be made in favour of the actual contract model of society. Those who have entered an agreement are unified in a substantial way. In the paradigm case, at least, they will know they have agreed. Roughly speaking, they will know that each party has done his part in creating the agreement. Hence they will know, at some level, that they constitute a unit of a substantial kind.

Actual Contract Theory as a Solution to the Membership Problem: Interim Assessment

I have noted seven analytic attractions of actual contract theory. It may well have other such attractions. Suffice it to say, now, that there are obviously many such attractions, enough to make this a theory worthy of attention.

With respect to the desiderata listed in the previous chapter for a solution to the membership problem, actual contract theory is affirmative and to some extent explanatory. Given that a political society is understood along the lines it proposes, everyone has a special obligation to uphold the political institutions of his own country in particular. These are obligations of agreement. The theory thus provides an answer to the question raised by the bare claim that there is an analytical link between membership in a political society and obligations to uphold the political institutions of that society: what links membership in a political society to those obligations? Since the obligations actual contract theory invokes are directed, it does well on the criterion of political bonds. It meets the criterion of intuitiveness at least to the extent that agreements are sufficient to found political societies and those who have agreed satisfy three conditions plausibly thought to be necessary for paradigmatic membership. I return to its relationship to the desiderata at the end of the following chapter.

---

[18] Simmel ([1908] 1971). He in fact suggests, somewhat gnomically, that consciousness of unity is both necessary and sufficient societal existence. I take the claim of sufficiency to be more problematic. See Gilbert (1989: ch. 4). See also the text below on more recent appeals to 'identification'.

[19] Graham (2002: 72–5) argues for the possibility of 'unwitting collectives', citing the case of a clique as an example. Gilbert (2004b: 132) argues in response that the possibility of different degrees of awareness must be taken into account.

By then I shall have discussed the most common objections that have been levelled at the theory.

4.3 Moral Attractions

In addition to its analytic attractions, the idea that political obligations are founded on agreements may be judged to have a number of moral attractions. In other words, it may be judged that, on various grounds, it would be a good thing if political obligations were indeed founded on agreements as opposed to any other foundation. Attractions of this kind are quite numerous.

One Must Intend to be Bound

It may be judged a morally attractive feature of political obligations founded on agreements that one cannot incur them without intending to do so.[20] This morally attractive feature connects with one of the analytic attractions mentioned above: membership in a social group arguably requires some degree of intention, as does participation in an agreement.

It has been proposed that, relatedly, one virtue of actual contract theory is that it ensures individuals are 'protected from being automatically bound at birth, and from becoming bound unknowingly, to a tyrannical or unjust government'.[21] Presumably the protection at issue, if it exists, is quite general: one is protected from being automatically bound to *any* government.

This seems to imply that agreements are the only possible source of obligations to support political institutions, and it is sometimes assumed that the actual contract theorist is committed to the claim that *all obligations whatsoever* come through agreements. That is, a person cannot be obligated to do anything unless he has first agreed to do it. Proponents of some versions of actual contract theory may have made such a claim. And something like it may be true for a special kind of obligation. If, however, we are operating with the relatively broad usage of the term 'obligation' that is current, and assuming that the obligations are genuine, there is no reason for a proponent of actual contract theory to hold that agreements alone can give rise to obligations.

At least one type of actual contract theorist would verge on inconsistency should he try to maintain this. Thus consider the standard view that construes the obligations most closely associated with agreements as a matter of moral requirement, where the existence of moral requirements is not a matter of

---

[20] Simmons (1979: 70).   [21] Simmons (1979: 66).

the making of any actual agreement. The making of an agreement is simply the occasion on which such a requirement comes to apply to the person who makes the agreement. There seems to be no principled reason why an actual contract theorist who takes this view should deny the possibility of *other* moral requirements that come to apply to one for reasons other than one's participation in an agreement, including requirements to support one or another political institution.[22]

Whether or not the actual contract theorist takes the view that the obligations of agreement are a matter of moral requirement, it seems possible for him to allow that even where there is no relevant agreement, a person may have an obligation of one kind or another to support a particular set of political institutions. These will not, however, be obligations or requirements grounded in the fact that the person in question is a member of the political society in question, such membership being—according to the actual contract theorist—a matter of participating in an agreement.

Clarity

Another aspect of agreement-based political obligations that may be found attractive is their clarity. Given that the language of a given explicit agreement is understood in the same way by all of the parties—not a trivial assumption, of course—people will be particularly clear about at least some of their obligations through the agreement: those that are explicitly specified within the agreement itself.

Agreements Ensure Premeditation

A further feature of the invocation of agreements that may be found morally attractive is the kind of premeditation they involve. This, it may be argued, allows for a special form of self-determination or freedom of action. Agreements and personal decisions have such premeditation in common.

Consider first a case of personal decision. On a certain morning, Sharon may get out of bed at six o'clock. She may simply wake up and then start getting up. Alternatively, she may have decided the night before to get up at six the next day, and she may get up—reluctantly perhaps—in order to conform to her decision. Her getting out of bed in the latter case is premeditated: she thought about it, indeed resolved to do it, before she actually did it, and she did it because she had previously resolved to do it. In this case she had resolved

---

[22] Hume (1965) makes a related point, arguing against actual contract theory as positing an unnecessary shuffle in the story of (roughly speaking) political obligations.

to do it about twelve hours prior to doing it. In other cases the time lag could be shorter; in others, far greater.

What is attractive about premeditation? It may be argued to be a condition of actions that are free in an important sense.[23] When Sharon acts so as to conform to her personal decision, she may then be said to act freely in the sense of acting in light of her own self-addressed demand.

There is an analogy here with the case of interpersonal agreements. If Sharon acts so as to conform to an agreement she has made with Emma, one might say that *they* decided she would so act. Sharon then acts freely in the sense that she acts in light of a prior demand *they* have made, where she is one of them. They are, if you like, co-authors of the demand. If this picture is correct—as I believe it is—then acts of conformity to agreements to which one is a party are at least partially self-directed. If people enter societies by agreement, then, their subsequent actions in conformity to the agreement—their heeding particular laws, for instance—can be regarded as to some extent free.[24]

One is Bound Voluntarily

Some have argued that the only agreements that obligate are voluntary in the sense of not being coerced. They assume, therefore, that actual contract theory must appeal to voluntary agreements only, insofar as it is a theory of obligation. Some will say that this is no real restriction at all, claiming that a coerced agreement is not a genuine agreement.[25] I argue against this claim in the next chapter, and later look closely into the question whether only voluntary agreements obligate.

For now suffice it to say that many theorists have found attractive the idea that people are only subject to political obligations as the result of a choice that is voluntary, and have seen actual contract theory as according with this idea.[26] They have, accordingly, seen the theory as an essentially liberal doctrine—one that applies only to political societies allowing their members significant freedom of choice.[27]

Note that this moral attraction and the first one mentioned are distinct. Doing something intentionally is not the same as doing something voluntarily,

---

[23] Cf. Pink (1996).

[24] It seems, then, that one can be 'forced to be free' in the following sense. Having entered an agreement, one is in a position to act (to some extent) freely in the sense of the text. If one is then forced to act in light of that agreement, one is being forced to act (to some extent) freely. The idea that one might be 'forced to be free' is familiar to many from Rousseau (1983: 6k. I, ch. 7, p. 26). I shall not attempt to connect what I have said here with that discussion.

[25] Cf. Simmons (1979: 82) (on 'consent').

[26] Simmons (1979: 66, 70); Walzer (1970: pref.).   [27] Walzer (1970); Beran (1987).

in the sense at issue here. This distinction is not always clearly marked in discussions of the topic. To see the point, consider that one may well choose to get up from one's chair, say, as a result of another's threat to kill one if one fails to do so. Then one will have acted intentionally. At the same time one will not have acted voluntarily in the sense that precludes acting as one does as a result of another's coercion. Thus even if it turns out that one can, according to actual contract theory, accrue political obligations in coercive circumstances, one still cannot accrue them unintentionally. The attraction of premeditation, such as it is, will also be retained.

The Self-interest of the Parties is Respected

The idea that political societies are founded in voluntary agreements may be found attractive because it seems to respect the self-interest or at least the perceived self-interest of each of the parties. The rough idea is this. Since the parties only enter the agreement without coercive pressure from others, one can assume they take the outcome to be in their self-interest. Otherwise, why would they have agreed?

Of course, since a number of different people are involved, compromise may be necessary. Thus supposing a range of possible agreements, all of which Jane judges to be better than no agreement at all from the point of view of her own self-interest, she may decide to opt for one that is not the best from that point of view. All equal, she would have preferred a different agreement. While negotiating the agreement, however, she decides to accept a compromise.

It may seem, then, that if Jane voluntarily enters an agreement, the agreement must at least be better for her, or better in her estimation, than her entering no agreement would have been. It may not give her what is best in terms of her self-interest, or her judgement of what that is. It still accords with her self-interest, or her judgement of it, in being better in that respect to no agreement at all.

This idea may be questioned insofar as morality is distinct from self-interest and one may enter a given agreement for moral reasons. For instance, a mature, extremely self-sufficient person may agree to join a particular society deeming that his doing so will be best for the world as a whole, though not for himself personally. Compare the position of the rulers in Plato's ideal political society, who would personally rather philosophize than rule. Perhaps then the point is best understood in terms not of self-interest but something broader like overall desirability in the judgement of any given party.

The Theory Treats Appropriately the Case of Evil Governments

Many assume that agreements to do evil things do not obligate. This assumption will be explored in some detail in a later chapter. Taking it on board for now, it can be argued that one cannot then be obligated by an agreement to support an evil government, obey evil laws, and so on. Not only can one not be bound unintentionally to such governments. One cannot be bound at all. If this is so, actual contract theory may be found attractive from a moral point of view. For one might find it morally odious, if not actually unintelligible, to suppose that a person can be obligated to perform evil actions.

Contrary to what might be thought at this point, the assumption that agreements to do evil do not obligate does not work in favour of the actual contract theorist from the point of view of the membership problem. In the next chapter, I note an analytic *objection* to the theory that depends on this assumption.

Moral Attractions, Moral Problems, and the Question of Analysis

Actual contract theory clearly has a number of moral attractions. It is good to understand what these are. It is important to realize, however, that they and any other such attractions are not immediately relevant to the question of analysis. They are reflected in judgements of the form: 'It would be a good thing if political obligations were founded in agreements, because then the following would be true...'. There may or may not be flaws in some of the reasoning involved. Assuming for a moment that the reasoning is flawless, it is hard to see how these attractions bear on the questions of how a political society is constituted and whether such constitution grounds political obligations.

In the context of this book, the critical question for actual contract theory is: are political societies founded in agreements that ground political obligations? If so, then one or another happy consequence may follow. That some happy consequence does or does not follow is irrelevant to the evaluation of the theory for present purposes. One should have some understanding of the moral attractions of a theory, however, if one is not to be irrelevantly swayed towards it by such considerations.

Any objections to actual contract theory arising from its being morally *un*attractive will be similarly irrelevant to the question at hand. Once again, however, it will be worth understanding what moral concerns have tended to work against its acceptance.

As one central moral criticism has it, actual contract theory involves a repugnant conception of society as the product of something like a business contract, arrived at by a process in which self-interested, mutually disinterested people bargain with one another, each with the aim of doing as well as possible for himself. This conception may be characterized as tainted by a capitalistic ideology or by an overly masculine perspective, depending on the critic's point of view.

Whatever the historical origins of the classic forms of actual contract theory and, indeed, standard assumptions about the theory, this objection involves an unnecessary gloss on the bare bones theory as it has been characterized here. A business contract may be a kind of agreement, but agreements themselves are of many kinds. There can be fond, mutually beneficial agreements between friends and lovers, agreements neither party would have entered had they not been understood to be mutually beneficial. In signing on to an agreement one may not even consider the effect of doing so on oneself. For instance, one may sign on because one judges the enterprise that is set in motion to be admirable, and to deserve one's support. Or one may sign up on a whim.

A variety of situations may obtain with respect to the whys and wherefores of particular society-constituting agreements. In the version presented here, however, actual contract theory tells no particular story. I turn now to the primary analytic objections to actual contract theory.

5

Objections to Actual Contract Theory

In spite of its long history and evident appeal, actual contract theory has been attacked from many different quarters. It tends to be dismissed by reference to two standard objections.[1] These have presumably been judged to be the most telling of all the objections offered. I focus on them this chapter, referring to them as the *no-agreement objection* and the *no-obligation objection*. I explain why the no-agreement objection makes actual contract theory a less than optimal solution to the membership problem. I then suggest that it may be possible to counter the no-obligation objection. This is important in relation not only to the overall assessment of actual contract theory but to the theory I shall propose as well. After noting a number of other objections that have been made to actual contract theory, I briefly consider some alternative proposals that invoke subjective identification and relationships, arguing that as so far formulated they leave many questions open.

5.1 The No-agreement Objection

The no-agreement objection is probably the most popular objection to actual contract theory, and, when properly presented, it is the most telling objection to that theory as a solution to the membership problem. It will be good briefly to restate that problem. In its conceptual formulation it runs: can it be argued that, in specified senses, membership in a political society in and of itself involves obligations to uphold the relevant political institutions? I turn now to the no-agreement objection.

---

[1] See e.g. Gans (1992: 49–57). This is a relatively nuanced discussion; others may invoke one or both objections in a more cursory manner.

In its standard formulation the core of this objection is an empirical claim: most people have not agreed to uphold any political institutions.[2] I shall refer to this as *the no-agreement claim*. It is generally made in a cursory fashion without any attempt to back it up. Sometimes an author simply states that he, for one, has never entered any such agreement. Clearly more than that is needed for a full defence of the claim. There is little doubt, however, that appropriate supplementation is available.

Starting with the no-agreement claim, the no–agreement objection may be developed in different ways. One version runs as follows. Given that most people have not agreed to uphold any political institutions, only a few actual people will have political obligations according to actual contract theory. The actual contract theorist could reply that, if so, so be it. Perhaps, indeed, few actual people have political obligations. That would be an important fact, if it were a fact.[3] It does not rule actual contract theory out as an adequate solution to the membership problem.

In response, a second version of the objection may be offered. If indeed few people have agreed, then according to actual contract theory it is not only the case that few actual people have political obligations. It would follow, also, that insofar as there are political societies at all, these are much smaller in extent than is usually supposed. Thus suppose a certain island has ten thousand inhabitants, and one hundred of these have agreed among themselves to uphold a certain set of directives. These directives refer to all the inhabitants of the island. For instance, one directive states that all residents of the island are to live in fireproof dwellings, another states that no resident is to imbibe alcoholic beverages, and so on. Actual contract theory would have to say that only the hundred people who agreed to uphold the relevant set of directives constituted a political society such that those directives were *its* directives. The other islanders would not be members of this society since they were not parties to the agreement. Though the directives refer to them, they would not be obligated to follow them as members of the political society in question.[4]

---

[2] Thus, e.g. 'many persons have never so agreed' (Smith 1973, in Edmunson ed. 1999: 84); 'The paucity of express consentors is painfully apparent' (Simmons 1979: 79); 'relatively few individuals expressly consent to their governments' (Klosko 1992: 142).

[3] Beran (1987) argues for a 'reform' version of consent theory on these grounds. People can and should be given the opportunity to enter a relevant agreement, and so on. This would allow for widespread obligations to support particular political institutions.

[4] Cf. Hart (1961). He begins by imagining a certain authority-producing process taking place in a relatively large population. He later imagines this process taking place in a smaller sub-population of officials. I take him to think this more realistic. Yet his initial vision surely had something to it. The later one leaves open the question: by what right do the *officials* impose sanctions on the rest if they fail to conform to the laws?

This version of the no-agreement objection reminds us that *actual contract theory is, in effect, a theory of two things: political society, and political obligation.* A particular kind of agreement founds a political society and at the same time provides its members with obligations to uphold a given set of political institutions. The objection suggests that even if one does not find it problematic to accept that few people are politically obligated, one may find it harder to accept that few people are members of a political society. If actual contract theory has the consequence that this is so, that may then be regarded as an objection to the theory.

This too may not be an insuperable objection. Perhaps, in the present state of the world, few people are members of political societies in an important sense of the word that connects such societies with obligations.[5]

A third version of the no-agreement objection makes it clear that actual contract theory is a less than maximally adequate solution to the membership problem. Some people—such as Robert Wolff in his pre-theoretical phase—clearly take themselves to have political obligations. They take it, that is, that a certain country is indeed theirs in some sense that involves obligations. Suppose one accepts the no-agreement claim: few people have entered agreements of the type actual contract theory posits. Presumably, then, few of those who take themselves to have political obligations have entered such agreements. Consider those who have not. It is unlikely that *their* sense that they have political obligations comes from an understanding that they have made an agreement. They most likely *have* no such understanding. If we want a theory that is interpretatively adequate, then, actual contract theory does not look promising. In many cases, at least, *there is a concept of a political society in play such that membership not based on entry into an agreement obligates.*

This points to an even more serious, related problem with actual contract theory. Agreements evidently fulfil some important necessary conditions for political societies according to a central everyday notion, conditions such as intentionality, unity, and so on. They are in addition sufficient to constitute such societies. Yet in spite of the temptation to do so, it is hard to argue that they are required for such constitution. This suggests that *the concept of a political society on which the theory relies is an artificially limited version of a more intuitive concept.*

The actual contract theorist may attempt to shore up the theory in various ways. Thus it may be pointed out that one can enter an agreement without

---

[5] Cf. Locke's distinction between 'perfect members' of a political society (who have explicitly agreed) and other residents (including transients) in the relevant territory, who could presumably considerably outnumber the perfect members. He allows that the other residents are not obligated *in the same way* as are perfect members. See Locke (1980: 63–5).

saying 'I agree to that' or, indeed, saying anything at all. In other words, one may enter an agreement silently or, to use the standard term, *tacitly*. Though many people may be right in thinking that they never entered a relevant explicit agreement, this does not mean that they have not tacitly agreed. Hence their sense of obligation through membership may relate to a tacit agreement as opposed to an explicit one. In claiming that membership in a political society is a matter of entry into an agreement, actual contract theory can allow that the agreement in question may be entered tacitly.

When, though, can one be said tacitly to have entered an agreement? Insofar as a tacit agreement really is a type of agreement, the conditions for one's having tacitly agreed are surely quite restrictive.[6] For instance, one has been faced with a proposal, one clearly understands that one's silence will be taken as acceptance of the proposal, and so on. Such an understanding of tacit agreement—the understanding most appropriate to actual contract theory, which does, after all, appeal to *agreements*—prevents an appeal to such agreement from being much help to the theorist. It is reasonable to suppose that few of those who take themselves to have political obligations have entered, or think they have entered, an appropriate tacit agreement. Their sense of membership and political obligation surely has another basis. Once again, it seems that *a concept of membership in a political society broader than the one the actual contract theorist has adopted must be invoked from an interpretative point of view, and, relatedly, from the point of view of the intuitiveness of the concept involved.*

Sometimes an *implicit* agreement is appealed to when there is neither an explicit agreement nor a tacit agreement according to conditions such as those just mentioned. Indeed, an implicit agreement may be referred to in the absence of anything that would normally count as an agreement strictly speaking.[7] One problem, then, is that it is hard to know what an implicit agreement is supposed to be.

The phrase 'implicit agreement' and related phrases may be intended to allude to what people *would* agree to if asked. In other words, it may be intended to allude to a hypothetical rather than an actual agreement.[8] In that case, it is hard to be sure what normative consequences, if any, an implicit

---

[6] A point emphasized by Simmons (1979: 79–82) in discussion of tacit consent.

[7] Compare Simmons (1979: 88 ff.) on the distinction between acts that are signs of consent, and acts that imply consent. I echo this to some extent in the text here. (I have some criticisms of the details of Simmons's discussion.)

[8] The 'hypothetical' contract here is less hypothetical, in a sense, than the Rawlsian one, where both the situation of the contractors, and the agreement itself, are hypothetical: were people in the original position, and were a certain agreement proposed to them, they would enter that agreement. The idea here is rather that people *are actually* in a certain situation and *were a certain agreement proposed to them*, they would enter that agreement.

agreement has. It is in any case not intuitive to claim that the fact that people would agree to something is itself constitutive of a society. In appealing solely to an agreement 'implicit' in this sense, then, the actual contract theorist seems no longer to have even a halfway plausible solution to the membership problem. In addition, of course, he has gone beyond actual contract theory, when he invokes hypothetical versus actual agreements.

In order to evaluate the idea that *something significantly like an agreement* grounds political obligations, we need to clarify a number of things. These include: What relevant phenomenon is significantly like an agreement? In what ways is it significantly like one? How does it differ from an agreement? What, indeed, does an agreement proper amount to? Later in this book I offer answers to these questions. For now, I rest with the obvious point that if so-called implicit agreements are either hypothetical agreements, or not agreements proper, appealing to them takes us beyond actual contract theory.

It is time to summarize what has emerged with respect to the no-agreement objection. However precisely it is developed, its core is the no-agreement claim: most people have not entered a relevant agreement. In face of the actual contract theorist's reasonable insistence that society-constituting agreements may be entered without any verbal assent, the objector can reasonably respond with a no-tacit-agreement claim. Should the theorist appeal to implicit agreements that are not supposed to be agreements proper, he has evidently gone beyond actual contract theory proper. For now, we need not follow him.

The no-agreement claim has empirical, interpretative, and conceptual implications. Assuming it is true, it shows that if actual contract theory is accepted, one must also accept that in the world as it is few people have political obligations. For few people will have entered into relevant agreements. It would be a corollary of this conclusion that most of those who take themselves to have political obligations are wrong. That is always possible of course. Assuming, however, as proponents of the no-agreement argument do, that the no-agreement claim is quite obviously true, one can infer that many of those who take themselves to have political obligations will be obviously wrong. That would be an unfortunate conclusion from an interpretative point of view: it violates a reasonable interpretative principle of charity.

That might not be enough to turn one from actual contract theory, but it points to a conceptual conclusion that is in any case quite compelling. As a conceptual matter, it is not plausible to suppose that political societies must—by their nature—be constituted by what are literally speaking agreements, explicit or tacit. This raises the question as to what might be a plausible, broader conception of a political society. *Is there, in particular, a form of membership that does not require an underlying agreement but has the characteristics of intentionality, unity, and perceived unity for which agreements account so well? And is it such that obligations, ideally directed obligations, accrue to all members?*

5.2 The No-obligation Objection

In addition to the no-agreement objection there is a class of objections to actual contract theory that would apply even if agreements of the relevant kind were, indeed, the necessary foundation of societies. According to these objections, either the circumstances or the content of many society-constituting agreements would prevent them from obligating all of the participants. Hence membership in a political society as conceived of by actual contract theory would not ineluctably be obligating. This would destroy the credibility of the theory as a solution to the membership problem. I refer to these as the *no-obligation objections* or, when considering them together, as the *no-obligation objection* (in the singular).[9]

There are several reasons for considering them in spite of the force of the no-agreement objection. One is to arrive at a relatively comprehensive assessment of actual contract theory. Setting aside the no-agreement objection, how does the theory fare? How many biting objections to it are there? Related to this, and most important for present purposes, is the following. Suppose that there is another theory that avoids the no-agreement objection while retaining core elements of actual contract theory. Perhaps the theory will carefully specify a ground of obligation that might loosely be referred to as an implicit agreement—though it was not an agreement, literally speaking. If actual contract theory is proof against the no-obligation objections, this will bode well for this other theory.

Those who put forward these objections sometimes put their point in terms of *moral* obligation or binding. They appear to believe, meanwhile, that when the conditions in question are satisfied an agreement will not *obligate* the parties at all. For now, therefore, I take the crux of these objections to be this: if a certain condition is fulfilled, you cannot have an agreement that *obligates* all of the parties.

The Objection Concerning Coercive Circumstances

The first no-obligation objection is the most common. It runs as follows. Suppose we accept the actual contract theorist's account of what it is to be the

---

[9] Gilbert (1999*b*) refers to them as the 'not morally binding' objections. The present label now seems best for reasons explained in the text below.

member of a political society. There are many possible circumstances in which one's entry into an agreement of the relevant kind would be insufficiently voluntary for the agreement to bind one. Even if one's circumstances do not involve coercion strictly speaking, it would be as if one had been coerced into entering it.[10] Therefore, the argument concludes, membership in a political society, as such, does not suffice to obligate one to support its political institutions.

I intend to focus on the claim that coerced agreements do not bind the coerced person.[11] Clearly, the objection depends on it. Before addressing that claim, I say something about the circumstances theorists have argued to be tantamount to coercion or, in short, *coercive*.[12]

One argument focuses on those who have lived from birth in the territory of a given imperator—probably the most common circumstance that might be envisaged—and runs roughly as follows. Suppose that when he is sufficiently mature someone in this situation is presented with the option of entering an agreement of the type in question. Suppose, further, that the cost of refusing to agree is deportation. This would be extraordinarily unattractive to many if not most people. Deportation could mean the loss of emotionally important connections to family, friends, and to a local culture and place as well. One's ability to earn a living could be threatened. For many people, then, the circumstances envisaged would be coercive.[13]

It is not clear that the alternative to entering the agreement in question would have to be anything like as drastic as deportation. Beran envisages a special 'dissenters' territory' to avoid this problem.[14] Proponents of the objection concerning coercive circumstances, however, can reasonably focus on the case in which refusal would involve deportation. It is clearly a possible case, and others may be developed along similar lines.

The situation of some immigrants is also cited. For those fleeing oppression, or worse, residence in a given territory may be their only chance of a secure existence. If one's entering an agreement is a condition of entry into that territory, that agreement, it may be argued, is coercive.[15]

---

[10] Thus Woozley (1979: 104–8) argues that duress or coercion lies at the end of a spectrum of cases for which it is not clear that a relevant distinction exists.

[11] Philosophers generally take this to be so. See, among others, Becker (1981: 100); Beran (1977: 267); Kavka (1986: 396) (not 'morally binding'); Raz (1999: 172); Simmons (1979: 82) (on 'consent'); Walzer (1970: pp. xii–xiv); Woozley (1979: 104).

[12] As Horton emphasizes (1992: 31) there may be considerable dispute as to which circumstances are indeed coercive.

[13] See e.g. Woozley (1979: 106–8); Sartorius (1999: 150) who cites the discussion in Hume (1965). See also Simmons (1984: 809–17; 1979: 77–8), and elsewhere (on 'consent').

[14] Beran (1987: 125).   [15] See e.g. Sartorius (1999: 150).

For the sake of the argument here, there is no need to question the contention that the circumstances mentioned, or others that might be involved, are tantamount to coercion. For I shall question the claim that coercion itself prevents an agreement from binding the coerced person. There are two cases worth distinguishing here. In one, party A coerces party B to enter an agreement with party C. One might think of a 'shot-gun marriage' as a case in point. In the other case, party A coerces party B to enter an agreement with A, his coercer. I shall be talking about the second type of case unless I say something to the contrary. Some of the things that may be argued in relation to the non-bindingness of coerced agreements are most plausible for this case.

How is it, or might it be argued that coerced agreements do not bind? It should be emphasized that this is not a question of contracts in law. The rules regarding such contracts in the various legal systems in human societies have developed in light of practical and moral considerations as well as conceptual ones, not to speak of the impact of history and politics.[16] In short, the law's purposes and the various influences upon it may lead to stipulations about contracts in law that do not reflect the everyday concept of an informal agreement. The contours of everyday concepts are also subject to various pressures, of course. That said, I focus on what I take to be the everyday concept of an agreement.

To begin, it will be useful to address the following question with some care: are so-called coerced agreements really agreements? Some theorists have suggested that they are not.[17] If that is so, the question of their bindingness clearly becomes moot.

The issue could be clouded by the assumption that entering an agreement is a form of consent, *where 'consent' is explicitly or implicitly defined as un-coerced.* One may or may not define 'consent' this way. It seems to be false, meanwhile, that everyday agreements, as normally understood, are forms of consent in this particular voluntarist sense.

Consider what everyday thought and talk about agreements suggests.[18] As they go about their lives, people seem to suppose that it is logically possible to be coerced into making an agreement. Those who set out to force others to enter agreements presumably find their project feasible. They may not assume it will succeed, but they do not see success as ruled out from the start. Again, those who complain in such terms as 'She forced me to agree' presumably think they have agreed. Otherwise it seems, they would rather say, with relief: 'She forced me, so I *didn't* agree!' Finally, those who *refuse* to agree presumably

---

[16] Cf. Ibbetson (2000: 248–9).

[17] Cf. Beran (1987: 6).

[18] Compare Simmons (1979: 82) who suggests that it is neutral on 'consent'.

see themselves as choosing one of two available options. Such a person might well say, 'He tried to force me to agree, but I refused' implying that his pressure might have effected an agreement, though it did not. Why refuse, indeed, unless this is so? In short, the 'verdict' of everyday discourse appears to be that one *can* be coerced into making an agreement. This is of course not to approve of forcing people to do things. It is just to say that the idea of a coerced agreement—a genuine agreement such that one or more of the parties was forced to enter it—is not a contradiction in terms.

The sense that a coerced agreement is impossible could develop from an idea about the origin of the practice of agreement making in the life of human beings. It is clear that, in a situation where there is lack of force or pressure imposed by either side, agreements can work for the benefit of all. For instance, they facilitate voluntary, self-interested exchanges as in the dialogue: 'I'll give you my cow for your horse, okay?' 'Fine'. Suppose one surmises this is the purpose agreements originally served—their original function. Observing that coercion prevents an agreement from performing this function, one might suppose that a coerced agreement is impossible. It seems, however, that once a practice of making agreements has become established—once people know how to enter agreements—they will be able to make them whenever they choose. Then agreements may be made in situations in which one party is, indeed, pressuring the other to enter the agreement. For instance, one person threatens another with an abhorrent consequence, saying nothing about any agreement. The threatened person then says something like 'No, don't do it. I'll agree to anything you want . . . if you'll just not do that'. This person begs to enter an agreement in order to avoid an abhorrent consequence imposed by the other party.

An ambiguity in such terms as 'voluntary' and 'acting in accordance with one's will' may also give the idea that coerced agreements are impossible a spurious plausibility. Suppose Phyllis has decided not to sign her name to a certain written agreement. Someone nonetheless gets her to sign her name at the bottom of this agreement without realizing what she is doing. Perhaps he covers the writing up in such a way that she thinks she is simply giving him her autograph. She then signs the agreement 'against her will' or at least 'without willing to' in what might be called the *intention* sense: she never intended to sign it. In contrast, if someone puts a gun to Phyllis's head indicating that he will fire unless she signs the agreement, she may well decide in favour of signing it. Then, though her signing the agreement may be against her will, or not be voluntary, in an important sense, it will not be against her will in the intention sense.

Consider now the claim that one's entry into an agreement—where there need be no question of *signing* anything—must be voluntary. Suppose one allows, plausibly, that this is true if 'voluntary' is interpreted in the intention sense: the claim that one agreed can be defeated if one can show that one did whatever is alleged to have constituted one's entry into the agreement without any intention to agree. One must be careful not to slide from this plausible claim to the quite different point that one's entry into an agreement must be voluntary in the sense of un-coerced.[19] I have already argued that this is not the case from the point of view of everyday understandings.

Someone may object that in reality coercion, at least in its most forceful forms, is liable to render a person incapable of making a decision—it is liable to render them witless. Thus, it may be alleged, the idea of a coerced agreement, entered into with the proper understanding, is not a realistic one. This is surely not so. Compare the matter of a simple personal action such as getting up from one's chair. If someone convincingly threatens to kill you unless you get up from your chair, and you are physically capable of doing so, you may indeed become paralysed with fear, or become so hysterical that you are incapable of action at all. But surely neither of these things need happen. If you make an advance decision at all, you may decide to get up from your chair—in order to stay alive. Having decided or not, you may intentionally and with full comprehension of what you are doing and why, get up from your chair. Once this is accepted it is hard to deny that in similar circumstances you may enter an agreement with full comprehension of what you are doing and why, whether by signing papers or by verbal or other less formal means. It may indeed be perfectly rational to do more than *feign* entry into an agreement, given that such feigning is possible. One may know that the other party has a nose for deceptions. Or one may not wish to use this occasion to find out.

In short, it is not plausible to suppose that people must become so frightened in face of coercion that they are rendered witless. Though in some circumstances a person may be this frightened, which would indeed render the existence of an agreement doubtful, there is neither a conceptual nor an empirical connection between coercion and witlessness.[20]

---

[19] A related slide is from saying that in order genuinely to agree one must *be able to choose not to*, to saying that one must not be coerced. Cf. Medina (1990: 3). In the case where she is threatened with a gun, Phyllis is clearly being coerced into signing; there is meanwhile, a standard sense in which she could have chosen otherwise. Her hand is not being 'physically forced to sign a document' (Ibbetson 2000: 236 n. 108).

[20] Compare Lord Scarman: 'The classic case of duress is ... *not the lack of will to submit* but the victim's intentional submission arising from the realization that there is no other practical choice open to him' (my emphasis), quoted in Guest ed. (1984: 242). Some earlier judgements, condemned by Guest (Anson) as 'fallacious', argued that: 'in a successful plea of duress ... the party affected must show that the compulsion was such as to vitiate his consent, to deprive him of any *animus contrahendi*' (ibid.). Thus, there has been discussion in legal circles as to whether *duress* is to be understood in terms of an inability to agree or (as Scarman argues) in terms of the context of one's entry into an agreement.

My discussion has proceeded in terms of undoubted cases of coercion such as threats to one's life. If one can argue that coerced agreements are possible, one can argue that agreements are possible in the kinds of circumstances that theorists of political obligation have judged to be coercive.

Many agreements, indeed, are made in circumstances that leave one little choice as to whether or not to enter them. One may even say that one was 'forced' to enter them. For instance, Jack may agree to work for a particular company because there is no other employer with work available in his vicinity. Presumably his relative lack of options does not mean that he did not really agree to work for the company. I have argued, in effect, that the same goes for clear cases of coercion. To repeat, that is not to endorse its use in any way. Nor is it to say anything about what follows from it.

Assuming now that a coerced agreement is possible, do such agreements obligate? According to the first no-obligation objection, they do not. How plausible is this?

It may seem very plausible at first. The argument for it will run roughly as follows. Suppose one or more people have coerced me into entering a certain agreement with them. Surely it is morally permissible for me not to do what I agreed to do, given that I was coerced into agreeing. In other terms, I am not morally required or in that sense morally obligated to do it. Again, I surely do not owe my compliance to the others, morally speaking. After all, they coerced me to agree. Assuming that they had no business doing so, they would not be morally justified in demanding compliance.

The clause at the beginning of the last sentence is worth attention. In the foregoing discussion I have written of 'coercing' someone and of 'forcing' them to do things, without distinguishing between the two. Sometimes people think of coercion as a special case of forcing: one *coerces* someone if one forces them to do something *when one is not entitled so to force them*. The plausibility of the moral judgements just adumbrated may depend on understanding coercion in this relatively narrow way. For the purposes of the discussion that follows, then, I shall so construe it.

The moral judgements in question may well be plausible given a standard interpretation of their terms. One may yet wonder if it can be right to conclude from them that coerced agreements do not obligate in any way at all.

Recall Prichard's point: once one has called something an agreement, all question of whether the parties have an obligation to conform to it has vanished. This would seem to imply that once we allow that a particular person *has* entered an agreement, we are committed to the view that he is obligated to conform to it whether or not he was coerced into entering it. According to the judgements now being considered, he is not morally obligated to do so, nor does he owe the other parties his conformity, morally speaking. Acceptance of these judgements, along with Prichard's point, may sometimes lie behind the claim that so-called coerced agreements are not agreements at all. For otherwise there is the following problem: if a coerced agreement obligates, *what kind of obligation is this?*

It is not only a sense that all agreements, as such, obligate, that raises this question. Setting aside the question of agreements generally, one may have a sense that obligations accrue from coerced agreements in particular. Thus, even if A had no business forcing B into entering the agreement, one may sense that once it is made, it can be appealed to by A in ways that imply an action is thereby owed. 'Look,' A may say, 'you did agree to do it.' B may respond by citing the coercion: 'Why should you profit from your wrongdoing?' Both, it may seem, have a point. Could both be right?

If one accepts that there can be a coerced agreement, as seems to be the case, and has at least some inclination to believe that coerced agreements obligate, this question is pressing. As is the further question: *how?*

Though it may not immediately come to mind, there could be a plausible affirmative answer. Recall the intuitive, partial characterization of obligations in general presented earlier in this book. It is not essential to an obligation as such that one ought to comply with it, all things considered. In particular, there may be opposing considerations that mandate or at least permit one's not complying with it. Intuitive judgements on the obligations of agreements and promises, indeed, prompted this particular characterization of obligations in general.

It could be, then, that there is a sense in which one is obligated to comply with an agreement one was coerced into making, and owes the other parties compliance, in spite of the acceptability of the moral judgements just noted. In other words, one could be obligated in one sense, but not obligated in another sense, a sense standardly connoted by the qualifier 'moral'. If this is the way things are, then the actual contract theorist can maintain the position that membership, entered into by agreement, is obligating. That is, he can continue to assert that there is an inextricable link between membership in a political society and obligation, in spite of the possibility that one is coerced into entering a society-constituting agreement, or that one enters it in circumstances tantamount to coercion. Someone might say, in response, 'If it isn't moral obligation, why care about it?' A full response to this question would best wait on greater clarity about the type of obligation at issue. If all agreements genuinely obligate, however, we should surely want to understand how that is.

In order to go further with this line of defence of actual contract theory one needs to understand the obligations of agreement. For now I propose, simply, that the no-obligation objection from coercive circumstances is not conclusive.

The Objection Concerning Morally Suspect Political Institutions

The second no-obligation objection runs roughly as follows. Many of the laws and edicts of political societies are likely to be unjust or otherwise seriously flawed, morally speaking. Even in relatively good political societies some morally problematic political institutions are possible. Agreements to uphold such institutions, the objection runs, would not be binding. Any sense of obligation based on them would be illusory. So even if, as actual contract theory has it, a political society is constituted by an agreement to uphold a given set of political institutions, membership in such a society will not necessarily *obligate* one to uphold all of these institutions.[21] Membership in egregiously bad political societies will obligate one to uphold relatively few of their political institutions, and even in good political societies there may well be some institutions one is not obligated to uphold, whether or not one has agreed to do so.

This objection is not as prominent in the literature as the objection from coercive circumstances. It is implicit, however, in much of what is said on the topic of agreements and promises in general. Thus A. John Simmons writes of an imaginary 'unscrupulous villain': 'A promise to aid him in his villainy, of course, would not bind us.' And, summarizing a long discussion, James Altham maintains: 'Consideration of a blatantly wicked promise provided reason to believe that some promises put the promisor under no obligation to do what he promised.'[22] Presumably such philosophers would say similar things in relation to the political sphere, such as, 'If I agreed to support the political institutions of a certain political society, and it initiates a cruel and inhumane policy of some kind, I am not obligated to support this policy.'[23]

Simmons and other authors who discuss this topic allow that the promises and agreements in question are genuine promises and agreements. Thus Simmons: 'I make two promises to a friend—one to help him commit murder most foul...It is usually maintained, and it is certainly my belief, that...both promises are real promises...' (my emphasis).[24]

---

[21] See e.g. Horton (1992: 43–4). He comments, 'An oath of allegiance requiring one unconditionally to obey the government, no matter how voluntarily entered into, cannot reasonably be thought to issue in an obligation to obey the government whatever in fact it does' (1992: 43).

[22] The quotations are from Simmons (1979: 78) and Altham (1985: 20). See also Simmons (1979: 15): 'While the fact that an act is morally impermissible may make it impossible for that act to be obligatory (consider the case of a promise to commit murder)...'.

[23] Cf. Dagger (2000).

[24] Simmons (1979: 86).

The claim that promises of the kind envisaged—immoral promises, for short—do not create an obligation for the promisor may appear irrefutable. Surely I cannot be morally required to kill someone, for instance, just because I promised to do so? Morally speaking, surely I cannot owe the promisee this horrible act by virtue of my promise? Surely it is morally permissible for me not to do as I promised in this case? How, then, can I have an obligation to do it? These rhetorical questions are surely in order, given a standard interpretation of their terms.

Once again, however, it could be that there is a sense in which one *is* obligated to perform even an immoral promise (or agreement) though *at the same time* there is a standard sense in which one is not obligated to do so—the sense that people tend to have in mind when they speak of moral obligation. If this position can be sustained, then the actual contract theorist can continue to argue that membership, entered into by agreement, is always obligating. For now I leave the matter there.

Conclusion on the Standard Objections

The two standard objections to actual contract theory attack the theory on two fronts. One denies the existence of an appropriate agreement in the situation of many members of political societies. The other argues that either the circumstances or the content of many such agreements would result in their not obligating all of the parties. The membership problem is not always at issue when these matters are discussed. Be that as it may, if these objections held, they would militate against the theory from the point of view of the membership problem.

I hold no antecedent brief for the actual contract theory of political obligation. I believe, however, that more can be said in its favour than is generally thought. In particular, the no-obligation objection can be countered. In chapter 10 I argue this in light of an account of agreements and their obligation that I shall then be in a position to deliver. The no-agreement objection has more bite. Nonetheless it remains possible that something closely related to actual contract theory can constitute a successful theory of political obligation.

5.3 Other Objections

Some further analytical objections to actual contract theory are fairly common. I have in mind two groups of objections, one group relating to membership in society, the other to the character of agreements.

Membership Precedes Agreement-making Capacity

In the first version of what I shall call the *born into membership* objection, it is argued that one's membership in a political society typically occurs at birth, preceding one's ability to enter agreements.[25] In short, one is 'born into' such membership. It cannot be the case, then, that the only way to become the member of a political society is by entering an agreement. Like the no-agreement objection, this denies the actual contract theorist's claim about the constitution of political society. It does this in terms of a particular consideration: people are typically born into membership of such a society. If valid, this objection would hold against any solution to the membership problem in terms of capacities unavailable to a newborn infant. The actual contract theorist can plausibly argue, however, that what one is born into is imputed membership. This cannot plausibly be claimed to be the central type of membership.

There is a different objection to actual contract theory that is sometimes put in terms of one's being 'born into' membership. It runs as follows. Perhaps people are not fully-fledged members of a political society at birth. Suppose, indeed, that one does not truly become a member until one enters an appropriate agreement, as the actual contract theorist asserts. Since people are usually born to parents who are members of a particular political society, they will generally have little choice as to whether to sign on to the agreement that is constitutive of that society when they are capable of doing so. Hence, they cannot obligate themselves through any such agreement. This is a version of the no-obligation objection concerning coercive circumstances. It will, in effect, be addressed when I reconsider the no-obligation objections in Chapter 10.

The original born-into-membership objection may be conjoined with the further claim that people are commonly born into political obligations when they are born into membership. This suggests that there is a viable alternative theory of political obligation. If this is all that is said, however, the proponent of the membership-precedes-agreement-making objection fails to explain the supposed connection between being born into membership in a political society and being born into obligations. The claim that being born into membership one is born into genuine—as opposed to imputed—obligations is open to serious doubt. An analogue of the second no-obligation objection to actual contract theory may be posed in relation to this claim. One may be born into a society that is far from just. Is one supposed to be obligated at birth to support and comply with its political institutions?

---

[25] In a different context, Althoff (2000: 2): 'In the middle ages, a child became a member of a number of communities and groups the moment he was born.'

Perhaps an argument can be found to the effect that people can in some standard sense be obligated to comply with unjust laws. That is what I have suggested in relation to actual contract theory. An explanation of how this can be, however, is sorely needed. In the case of actual contract theory what is needed is some further insight into agreements and the way they obligate. It is not clear how one might salvage the 'born into obligations' idea in relation to this matter.

To be sure, there are important observations that suggest that one is born into obligations of membership: at birth most human beings are confronted by a pre-existing social order. Social rules may immediately impute to them both membership in a political society and a set of associated obligations—obligations that, to be sure, they are incapable of fulfilling for a while. In such a context a parent may intone to an infant 'It is your duty as a citizen to care for me in my old age'. The actual contract theorist can respond to observations such as these by noting that they only show that people may have political obligations imputed to them at birth. A theory of political obligation is concerned with genuine, not imputed obligation. These points, in sum, are very well taken, but it is at best unclear how they undercut actual contract theory or any other theory such that genuinely obligating membership in a political society involves greater mental competence than that of a newborn infant.

Agreements too Trivial

Another type of objection appeals to the triviality of agreements or of the obligations that flow from them. Thus it may be argued that typical agreements are trivial things. They are based on people's 'arbitrary wills, their opinion, and their capriciously given consent'.[26] One's becoming a member of a political society would not seem to be well represented by such a trivial process. Hence a crucial premiss of actual contract theory's solution to the membership problem must be rejected.

The actual contract theorist can reply that there are agreements and agreements. Some may be a matter of caprice, as when two friends agree to go to the beach for the day. There may have been no onus on either of the friends to enter this agreement. Others may be quite different. One may agree to raise another's child, for instance, when one is the only suitable person to do so, or to become the leader of a just political society when one is the only appropriate candidate. In so doing one is responding, it may be said, to a moral imperative.

---

[26] The quotation is from Hegel (1977: 157), who refers to contracts. I do not mean to probe his complex position.

It would in any case be wrong to say that entry into these agreements is a matter of caprice. There is nothing arbitrary about it.

It may then be objected that the obligations of agreement are too lightweight to be invoked in a solution to the membership problem. Our political obligations are surely very weighty, it may be argued. The obligations of agreement are surely not in the same class.

The actual contract theorist can respond as follows. One has shown something significant if one has shown that one is genuinely *obligated* to uphold the political institutions of one's political society by virtue of one's membership in that society. To show that one is indeed so obligated is all that is required for an adequate solution to the membership problem, as that has been articulated here. In addition, it is not clear how much can be said, intuitively, about the 'weight' of our political obligations, if such there be, in advance of a theory of such obligations. Nor is it clear how weighty or otherwise the obligations of agreement are.

We need a better handle on agreements. Actual contract theory alludes to obligations, indeed, directed obligations, but as so far presented does not include an explanation of how agreements support such obligations. In advance of such explanation, it can allow that some people, of course, do not take their agreements seriously.[27] That does not show that they are right not to do so. And it is clear that even an agreement that is entered frivolously may have great significance once made. Think of someone who agrees to marry, on a whim, and then has either to face the chagrin of his fiancée or keep to the engagement. Why should the fiancée be chagrined if an agreement is such an insubstantial thing?

5.4 Actual Contract Theory Assessed

It is time now to draw together the main threads of the preceding discussion of actual contract theory. Suppose that the no-obligation objections can be countered. Actual contract theory will then have a lot going for it as a solution to the membership problem. It is an affirmative, explanatory theory. It provides a tertium quid—a 'third thing'—that explains the connection between political societies and obligations. The obligations it invokes are directed. That is not a trivial achievement. Even if the no-obligation objections are rebutted, however, the theory falls down over the artificial narrowness of the conception

---

[27] This phenomenon has been positively associated with training in economics, where agreements and promises, as such, are generally regarded as 'cheap talk'.

of a political society that it appeals to, and hence does not meet the intuitiveness criterion. It similarly fails with respect to the interpretative criteria. Finally, unless and until actual contract theory is presented in more detail than has been given here, it does not meet the explicativeness criterion. Light needs to be shed on what agreements are and how they obligate. Indeed, without a satisfactory account of these things it is hard to assess the no-obligation objections. For present purposes I set aside consideration of the question of authority in connection with actual contract theory. The theory can do quite well with this, as will be eventually become clear in what follows.[28]

5.5 Some Proposed Alternatives to Actual Contract Theory

Recently a number of philosophers have put forward what are in effect special (as opposed to general) analytic membership arguments that purport to be preferable to actual contract theory. The proponents of these arguments may be more or less sympathetic to actual contract theory. They all see a need to look elsewhere to explain how membership in a political society obligates. I have in mind arguments from subjective identification and belonging, on the one hand, and arguments from the existence of relationships, on the other.

These arguments make important observations but tend to be sketchily presented and leave important questions open. For instance, what is the connection between obligation and the phenomenon on which they focus, whether subjective identification and belonging or relationships? What is the nature of the obligation? What happens to it in the case of unjust political institutions? Without clear answers to these questions the sceptic about political obligations in the sense of this book may not be inclined to move from his position.[29]

Arguments from Subjective Identification and Belonging

An increasingly popular approach to political obligation alludes to a particular perspective one may have on his or her relationship to a given political society. In the approach I have in mind this perspective is often referred to as 'identification' with a particular political society. Alternatively, there

---

[28] The relevant discussions are in Chs. 9 and 11, below.

[29] The reader could skip this section without losing the main thread of the argument. I briefly compare my own theory with those mentioned here in Ch. 11, below.

is a reference to a sense of 'belonging'.[30] It is argued, roughly, that such identification gives rise to obligations of the relevant type. The way in which this supposedly happens, however, tends to be left obscure.

Thus legal theorist and philosopher Joseph Raz writes of a 'kind of obligation to obey which arises out of a sense of identifying with or belonging to a community'. He also speaks of a 'feeling that one belongs'. He goes on to say, 'this feeling is nothing other than a complex attitude comprising emotional, cognitive, and normative elements'.[31]

If we are to understand how obligations arise in this context, it is crucial to know precisely what the elements of the relevant complex attitude are. Raz says that it is 'an entirely natural indication of a member's sense of belonging' that that person believes him or herself to be 'under an obligation to obey because the law is one's law, and the law of one's country. Obeying it . . . expresses one's identification with the community.'

If his claim is that the core cognitive element in a feeling of belonging is a belief that one has relevant obligations, then one must ask how obligations arise out of a belief that one has them. Perhaps Raz does not mean to claim this. In either case the way in which actual obligations come into being in the context he describes is not made clear.

Another appeal to identification is found in an extended discussion by political theorist John Horton, who sees himself as presenting a type of analytic membership argument for political obligation.[32] Horton sees the core of the relevant membership relation as involving a 'sense of identification'.[33] He connects this with one's sense of authorship of the actions of the relevant political society. Thus 'there is an important, though limited, sense in which we understand ourselves as the authors of such actions, even when we oppose them: they are the actions of *our* polity . . . '.[34] He connects this understanding, further, with a range of emotions that people may feel in relation to the actions of the relevant society, in particular shame, guilt, and pride. Thus, he proposes, people feel a sense of responsibility for the actions of the polity in question. He concludes, 'This sense of identity and the corresponding responsibility is part of what it means to be a member of a polity and to recognize one's political obligations.'

Horton continues by suggesting that characteristically the sense of identity he is talking about will be shared by other members of the relevant

---

[30] Relevant discussions are found in Raz (1999); Horton (1992: Ch. 6); Tamir (1993). Simmons (1996) critiques such views. See Ch. 11, below, for some discussion of Simmons's article.

[31] All of the quotations from Raz in this section are from Raz (1999: 173).

[32] Horton (1992: 147–8).

[33] Horton (1992: 153).

[34] Ibid. (my emphasis, corresponding to an earlier emphasis of Horton's).

society who, along with its government, will 'expect some recognition of this shared identity and the acknowledgement of some allegiance to the community'.[35] Thus characteristically the sense of identity is 'not *merely* a subjective feeling'.[36]

What is unclear in Horton's discussion, as in Raz's, is how identification as he characterizes it—whether shared or not—provides anyone with obligations. In other words, one may have a 'sense' of identity, responsibility, and, indeed, obligation, but how does it follow from this that one does in fact possess the obligations in question?

Horton may think it is not necessary to argue this because he urges that there is no need to appeal to any 'external moral principle' in arguing for obligations within a political society. We need not appeal to moral principles that concern how one is to behave towards a benefactor, for instance, or that concern what gratitude demands. One can accept this, yet still want to see the connection between identification—or shared identification—and obligations explained. At one point Horton seems to recognize this.[37]

Can a connection between obligations and identification be made out? It is tempting to conjecture that there is a missing link here. That is, those who identify with or feel that they belong to a certain political society may in many cases do so *on an appropriate basis,* a basis which both naturally grounds a feeling of belonging and is a foundation for obligations. What, though, might be this third thing mediating between and grounding both subjective identification and obligation?

Both Horton and Raz explicitly reject the idea that an agreement or act of consent is the third thing in question.[38] Raz suggests, however, that obligations of the kind he is talking about are, like those arising from agreements, voluntary or semi-voluntary. In this case they arise from 'developing relations between people', where the relationship itself is not 'obligatory'.[39] His subjective identification approach, then, both acknowledges some affinity to actual contract theory, and shades into another type of argument, one whose details are not developed.

Relationship Theories

An appeal to relations between people can take various forms. The argument for obligations of relationship on which I briefly focus here does not depend on the existence of a sense of identification. Nor does it appeal to such matters

---

[35] Horton (1992: 154).   [36] Ibid.   [37] See Horton (1992: 149–50 f.).
[38] Raz (1999: 173); Horton (1992: 146–7, 155).   [39] Raz (1999: 173).

external to the relationship as local conventions regarding relationships of the kind in question.[40]

Nancy Hirschmann has argued that non-voluntary, non-contractual relationships of an obligating nature are fundamental for understanding political obligation and, indeed, obligation in general. She suggests that the point that such relationships are capable of obligating someone may be easier for women to grasp than for men, because of the different ways they relate to their mothers from infancy onwards.

One example she proposes of a relationship that obligates is that of a woman and the foetus she is carrying as a result of a rape. The point Hirschmann wishes to make is that this woman can be said to have obligations in relation to the foetus in spite of her wholly unwilling participation in its conception within her. The same goes for a woman who intentionally had sexual intercourse while taking precautions against pregnancy. She hardly intended the pregnancy, but if she becomes pregnant she can be said to have similar obligations. Hirschmann does not claim that either woman must carry the foetus to term, all things considered. Her claim is that whether or not this is so, obligations of a kind are involved even in these examples of 'connection, relationship, bondedness'.[41] In sum, in order to understand the full range of obligations we must focus on human connection as well as human choice. Hirschmann rests her case on the persuasiveness of examples in which, she argues, there is connection and obligation but no prior decision in favour of either.

There are radically different types of connection, relationship, or bondedness that can exist between human beings. As they differ in their nature, the ways in which they involve obligation may differ and so, indeed, may the types of obligation in question. There is room for further exploration of this broad territory.

My own argument will not speak to such cases as that of a woman pregnant without intent, at any level, to incur an obligating connection. I do aim, however, carefully to articulate the way in which an important *type* of obligation is bound together with a central *type* of connection, relationship, or bondedness between persons, whose specifics I make clear. This relationship does not require any 'opening agreement', voluntary or otherwise.

---

[40] Cf. Simmons's characterization (1996: 253) of 'associational' obligations whose 'content is determined by what local practice specifies as required' for those in a certain position.

[41] Hirschmann (1989: 260; see also 1992: 236).

PART II

Societies, Membership, and Obligation

This part elaborates the account of social groups that lies behind my affirmative solution to the membership problem. The account is developed by reference to the case of a small-scale, unstructured group that is relatively transient. I later show that it allows for large, structured, enduring groups as well.

According to this account, in terms that are explained, a social group is founded on one or more *joint commitments* of the parties. That gives a social group a substantial kind of unity, a unity perceived by its members, without whose appropriate understandings it cannot be. This particular species of perceived unity provides a basis for a range of phenomena that have been associated with an individual's identification with a group including a sense of pride, and a sense of guilt, over the group's actions. It thus accords with much that has been thought about social groups both informally and by social theorists and political philosophers. In my technical phrase the parties to a given joint commitment constitute a *plural subject*.

I argue that those who are jointly committed have obligations towards one another. Thus membership in a social group in the plural subject sense carries obligations with it. Plural subject phenomena include collective goals, beliefs, and values, and social rules or norms. Attempts to characterize societies in general and political societies in particular often appeal to one or another of these. As argued here, they have a common core: joint commitment.

6

Social Groups: Starting Small

The problem of political obligation at issue in this book compels one to consider the nature of membership in a political society. In this chapter I begin working towards an articulated conception of a political society, with an initial focus on *society* and, indeed, the more general idea of a social group. In order to consolidate the discussion here I will at some early points repeat observations made earlier in the book.

6.1 Societies as Social Groups

Social Groups

People use the terms 'society' and 'social group' of both human populations and populations of a variety of non-human creatures. There are doubtless points of contact between the human and the other cases. I focus on the human case in what follows here. I take this to be the least opaque to our understanding.[1]

The conception of a political society that I develop is that of a certain kind of social group. Social groups, as I understand these, include families, clubs, protest groups, trade unions, and army units. The above list expresses a relatively rich concept of a social group.[2] It is clear that the phrase 'social group' as well as the unqualified term 'group' is sometimes used to express a less rich notion. In some uses it would include in its scope populations of people whose most salient connection is that they possess similar personal traits. I focus, then, on social groups for which the examples given are among the canonical ones.

Evidently, such groups differ in significant ways among themselves. Consider the list just given: families, clubs, protest groups, trade unions, army units. Each of the items on this list is a type of social group. Yet there are salient differences

---

[1] Gilbert (1989: 442–4) adopted a similar approach.

[2] For another list all of whose members are social groups in this sense see Bacharach (2005: p. xxi). He lists these as 'teams', on which see Gilbert (2005c: 22–3).

among them and still others that might be listed. Clubs, trade unions, and army units are likely to have a set of explicit rules of procedure and explicit goals. Families are less likely to have such rules and goals. Protest groups will have at least one explicit goal—to make the protest in question—but may or may not have a set of explicit rules of procedure. And so on. In setting out to give a general characterization of social groups one is evidently setting out to find something common, a common structure perhaps, among these in many ways different phenomena.

Since families, for instance, often figure in lists of social groups, it is reasonable to infer that paradigmatic families, at least, are paradigmatic social groups. In other words, at least clear examples of a family are clear examples of a social group.[3] Meanwhile, it is possible that some so-called families are neither paradigmatic families nor paradigmatic social groups. A case in point might be a single adult with an infant child. While the child is very small, it may be insufficiently developed to enter into the paradigmatic member relationship. The same goes for a single adult who is caring for a severely mentally disabled child, sibling, or parent. With respect to the membership relationship, the condition of autism in a child may be especially pertinent. Such families may be sufficiently like paradigmatic families that they have come to be referred to by the same label. Yet they may be neither paradigmatic families nor paradigmatic social groups.

The same goes, of course, for some so-called social groups as well. Here I do not mean types of social group, such as the type 'family'. Rather, I mean individual populations of no such identified type. Some of these may be referred to as social groups because of similarities or other salient relations to the paradigm cases, though they are far from prototypical or paradigmatic themselves. These populations may be such that their members are liable to form paradigmatic social groups, or would do well to form such groups, for instance.

As a result of such considerations, someone who is trying to give a general account of what it is to be a social group is liable to produce something that does not fit every so-called family, or, indeed, every so-called social group. This should not be considered a serious drawback. If an account can be given of the clearest cases, we have a basis for envisaging what might fall within the predictably ill-defined penumbra of less clear cases.

The same goes for membership in a social group: we can expect to discover that some so-called members of a given social group do not stand in the

---

[3] To be more cautious here, one might infer only that paradigmatic families are perceived by the list-makers as paradigmatic social groups. I suggest that one's initial inference should be the less cautious one. See the text below.

paradigmatic membership relation to the group in question. In order to decide what that relationship is, we need to look at a clear case of a social group and of the membership relationship within it.

A salient difference among social groups is that of size. It may be that the clearest cases of social groups tend to be relatively small. That does not mean that there cannot be very large populations with the structure that confers on small populations their status as paradigmatic groups.

Societies

Social groups of many different sizes may be called 'societies'—secret societies, for instance, may be quite small. At the same time, those using the unqualified phrase 'a society' tend to have in mind a relatively large social group, one that may include many smaller ones, such as families, political parties, religious and cultural organizations, and so on.

What is it for a society to *include* other, smaller social groups? There are at least two possibilities. First, a society may be an association of social groups. Its members are social groups rather than individual people. The type of society in question is not a mere aggregate of small social groups. It resembles certain international bodies whose members are individual nations—bodies such as the League of Nations, the United Nations, and NATO. A member of a given 'inclusive' society of this type can also be a member of other such societies with a different membership—just as the members of NATO are also members of the United Nations.

A second way a society may include smaller social groups allows for the society's members to be individual people. A society so conceived can be understood as including smaller social groups in the following sense. Some or all of its individual human members are also members of other, smaller groups such that all of the members of those groups are members of the larger—or as is said 'wider'—society as well. It is generally assumed that a given person can be a member of many different social groups at once. For example, one and the same person may be a family member, the member of a church, the member of a professional association, and a member of staff at a school. Consistently with this, one and the same person can be the member of a variety of smaller social groups and, at the same time, a member of a larger political society.

My focus in this book is on the relationship between individual human beings and the political societies of which they are members. I can, of course, allow that a political society is generally inclusive in the second way. That is, its members may at the same time belong to one or more of the other social groups within it. Its members may, at the same time, be members of other social groups whose membership is not wholly contained within it. Thus, the members of a given political society may include some members of an extended family whose other members belong to a different political society. Perhaps some members of the family left the first political society in search of a better life in another. They remain members of the original family.

How Large?

Supposing that membership in a social group involves the exercise of various capacities, one might wonder if there are limits on the size of a social group of human beings. Their cognitive and other capacities are, after all, limited. Membership in a social group could pose challenges that they cannot meet on a very large scale.

One might allude here to the context in which human beings developed. Thus social psychologist George Homans: 'For hundreds of thousands of years, the largest human societies were probably bands of hunters and gatherers, each band numbering no more than a few dozen members. Our genetic characteristics themselves may have been acquired in groups like these.' He had previously remarked, 'The small group is the unit in which mankind learned social behavior.'[4] Such considerations could give one pause as to the capacity of human beings to form social groups with vastly more than a few dozen members. They also suggest, as they were intended to, the importance of understanding the small group case if we are to understand human social behaviour.

It is common to proceed as if there is no limitation on the size of human social groups. Nations are sometimes included in the lists of such groups made up by sociologists and others. The populations referred to as nations can be huge, with a membership in the hundreds of millions. This could, of course, involve a mistake. The character of the vast populations referred to as nations could have been misperceived, misunderstood.

Though there could be a mistake here, it is best not to assume that there is one at the outset of inquiry. I propose that until we have a better idea of what intuitive principle lies behind these lists, we do better to accept all of the listed items as social groups. If and when an otherwise plausible systematizing principle forces us to move some originally listed item from the list, that would be a better time to do so.

Earlier in this book, I referred to three characteristics that have been held to be necessary to any social group of the kind in question here: intentionality of membership, unity, and consciousness of unity. These do not clearly preclude

---

[4] Homans (1974: 96, 3).

the existence of very large social groups. Before one has a better handle on the topic it seems best to leave the matter open. At the same time, it is reasonable to propose that one does not treat populations of the great size just referred to as the *clearest* cases of social groups. That such populations *can* be social groups, apt to be put on a list whose members include families, trade unions, armies, and the like, is best shown rather than assumed.

Starting Small

If one assumes that the crucial details of the membership relation are the same for all social groups, large and small, one can in principle find what is crucial to the membership relationship in either type of case. I shall favour the option of starting small.

It may be observed that in doing so, I take the opposite road from that favoured by Plato in his investigation of justice in the *Republic*. He argued that it was best to understand the nature of justice in a political society before trying to understand the nature of justice in a human being since one would find justice 'writ large' in the former case.[5]

In the present instance, a good reason for starting small is that it allows one to look closely at a situation that is relatively simple. If the crucial details of the membership relationship do indeed lie there one can expect most easily to discover it by this means. There is also the point that the relatively small group has a special place in both the history of the human race and in the life of most human individuals.

I shall focus on a group that is both small and relatively transient. That this is a viable procedure is suggested by the following observation from Georg Simmel:

Sociation [roughly, the process of forming a social group] ranges all the way from the momentary getting together for a walk to founding a family . . . from the temporary aggregation of hotel guests to the intimate bonds of a medieval guild.[6]

Simmel is not alone among social theorists in including not only small but also transient populations in a list of social groups. His reference to 'getting together for a walk' suggests that we can explore the nature of social groups in general by investigating such small-scale temporary phenomena as those of

---

[5] Plato (1974: 368d–369).

[6] Simmel, in Levine ed. (1980: 24). 'Sociation' is a translation of the German *Vergesellschaftung*. 'The process of forming a social group' is a more cumbersome, but more familiar-sounding rendition. Simmel prefers to talk of 'sociation', a continuous process, as opposed to 'society' or 'social group', which have less dynamic connotations.

two people going for a walk together, dancing together, working on a project together, and so on.

Some may find this idea unattractive because they judge such transient phenomena to be relatively trivial. Such phenomena are indeed likely to be less consequential in a number of ways than are long-lasting ones. Enduring groups presumably tend to have a greater impact on the lives and character of their members. Growing up in a given family, for instance, is likely to mark one—well or badly—for life. It is likely to help endow one with a particular set of values, aspirations, and beliefs. A protracted stint of army life, for instance, can have a similar effect. This is far less likely to happen as the result of a walk with a new acquaintance—though it might. Again, important emotions often stressed in connection with group membership—a sense of belonging, emotional identification, and so on—are less likely to occur the more transient the group, insofar as such feelings take time to emerge. In contrast, they are often associated with such enduring groups as families, religious orders, schools, and nations. In addition, the more enduring groups are likely to have a greater impact upon the wider society and, indeed, the world at large. Medieval guilds and modern trade unions, for instance, had and have the capacity to influence the decisions of politicians and industrialists to an extent that is generally beyond the power of an individual craftsman or labourer. Long-lived terrorist groups that spend considerable time training their members, investigating their targets, and amassing weapons are likely to do more damage than are transient groups. Supposing that the longer-lasting groups tend to be more consequential, social theory itself is likely to seem particularly important if it focuses on such groups, and can help us to explain and perhaps control them. None of this means that the more and the less enduring groups do not share a common core. It certainly should not blind one to this possibility or lead one to reject at the outset an inquiry that takes it seriously.

It may be questioned whether it really makes sense to think of small groups as having a common core with much larger ones. For, it may be argued, societies and other large groups such as religious organizations tend to have a number of consequential features lacked by small groups. In particular, in senses I explain, they tend to be hierarchical, impersonal, and anonymous.

As to hierarchy, large groups tend to be divided into leaders and followers, particularly when the group has existed for a relatively long period of time. A single individual may lead the group, perhaps as 'supreme commander' where his or her command includes other higher level individuals or groups. Perhaps the society is led by one or more of the smaller groups within it. In any case one can differentiate different levels in the society with respect to authority and, to that extent, to power. The leader or leaders give orders to the members-at-large. As to impersonality, no one member is likely to know every other member personally, in the sense of having had any relatively substantial personal interaction with them. They may never have talked together, walked together, made and kept appointments, and so on. In other words, many members will be strangers to one another. Even if they have set eyes on one another, and marked one another as individuals, they may just be 'faces in the crowd'. As to anonymity, many members will not even *know* of every other member as an individual. They may have only a vague idea of how many members there are, and never have set eyes on many of their fellow members.[7]

Clearly, any model of a society introduced by reference to small-scale cases involving people who know each other personally will have to deal with these points. One will need to know how membership survives the existence of hierarchy, impersonality, and anonymity, assuming that it does. Meanwhile one should bear in mind that even the smallest groups can be hierarchical. One of two friends, for instance, may clearly be 'in charge'—the dominant partner. Again, it is easy to think of relatively small, transient groups that have a high degree of impersonality and anonymity. Consider a meeting of disaffected citizens in a crowded town square. No member of this assembly need know every other member personally or know of every other member as an individual. In the example of acting together on which I focus there is no hierarchy, the people involved certainly know of one another and are in the midst of a relatively substantial personal interaction. I move later to the question of groups that differ from this in the respects noted.

How Small?

How small can a social group be? Perhaps in some circumstances there can be a social group with a single member. For instance, one person may be considered the single member of a certain group if the other members of a previously larger group have died or left the group. Thus one might hear statements like 'She is all that's left of the peace movement', or 'He is the Echapa tribe', meaning, not that he is the leader or otherwise most important member of the tribe, but that he is the sole remaining member. Such a group may still have some life in it, and the prospect of a future. 'I'm the only club member left,' someone might say, 'but I keep the club going. I make up the schedule, attend all the meetings, give all the speeches, take the minutes . . . I'm hoping we'll get some new members soon.' There is also the case of one who

---

[7] A point emphasized in Anderson (1983).

has just founded a club, which is open to members other than him. These one-person groups are special: they are not paradigmatic cases of social groups. The single member in question might, in the first type of case, be labelled a 'residual' member. Perhaps one could speak of a 'residual group' here as well. This 'group' had more members, and it may do so again. If a so-called group neither was larger nor has the potential for expansion, calling it a group can be little more than a *jeu d'esprit*.[8] In other words, the paradigmatic group has more than one member. In what follows I should be taken to refer to such a group when referring to social groups in general.

Philosophers and others sometimes conceive of individual human beings as themselves societies or, at least, society-like. Plato is perhaps the best known of these, with his supposition of a tripartite soul, ideally ruled by reason. What these philosophers are conceiving is precisely that the minds of individual human beings have two or more 'parts' or 'elements', or 'members' whose relations give rise to the behaviour of the individual in question.

If a paradigmatic social group contains *at least* two members, it may have *only* two members. The previous quotation from Simmel suggests that he was of this opinion, as are others. Simmel and others have made a point of emphasizing that a social group with two members—a 'dyad' in sociological parlance—has a number of special characteristics. One such characteristic is this. In a dyad each member's presence in the group has the greatest possible significance for its survival as a group. Thus if one member of a couple leaves the relationship there is no group left. In contrast, if one member leaves a discussion group comprising fifteen people, say, there is no question that he leaves behind a discussion group, albeit a slightly smaller one. In other words, the group that is left behind is as much of a group as any other. The same goes, a fortiori, for a large country. The larger the group, the less vulnerable it is, in its very being, to the loss of a given member.

While recognizing that a dyad has special characteristics, I proceed on the assumption that two people can constitute a paradigmatic social group and that two people who are doing something together fall into that category. I argue that exploration of an example of two people doing something together discovers a structure that is constitutive of social groups in general, and political societies in particular. This structure will be carefully characterized.

I choose the example of people doing something together to some extent arbitrarily. As I argue in due course, it is just one among several phenomena

---

[8] Such a 'group' is envisaged in this variant of a famous remark of Groucho Marx: 'The only club I'd want to join is one whose membership was restricted to me.' The supposedly self-deprecating Marx was averse to clubs that would *accept* him as a member.

the examination of which may discover the structure in question. At the same time, rightly or wrongly, a political society is often seen as, or as involving, a particular kind of common enterprise or cooperative venture.[9] An explanation of what it is for people to do something together, then, should illuminate a relatively standard conception of a political society.

6.2 Acting Together: Observations

What is it to do something with another person or with other persons? What, in other terms, is it to act together? One possible response to the question just posed should be forestalled at the outset. Those who do something 'together' in the central sense I have in mind may, but need not, be in close physical proximity. They need not be 'together' in *that* sense. For instance, some of those planning a revolution together may be in one country, some in another, their communications slow and arduous. The same goes for 'with' in the phrase 'doing something with another'.

The phrases 'joint action', 'shared action', and 'collective action' do not invite an interpretation in terms of spatial connectedness. I shall feel free to use these phrases, also, as ways of referring to acting together. All are potentially ambiguous, which is why I emphasize the way in which I shall be using them here.[10] It may be that even when so interpreted, the qualifiers 'joint', 'shared', and 'collective' are most appropriate to different types of cases. I shall not distinguish between them here.

Further examples of acting together include: conversing (with one another), hunting for food together, preparing dinner together, holidaying together, investigating the murder together, living together, building a bridge together, organizing a strike together, advancing towards an enemy outpost together, working out the details of a treaty together, founding a nation together. Clearly, cases range from the relatively trivial to the highly consequential, from the context of domesticity and play to the context of politics.

Without doubt cases of acting together are of importantly different kinds. For instance, sometimes (conversing, living) the 'point' of the activity is engagement in a particular more or less open-ended process; at other times (building a bridge, organizing a strike) it is procurement of a specific result

---

[9] See e.g. Hart (1955); Rawls (1971).

[10] In some discussions 'Sharing an action' may mean little more than 'doing the same thing'. In the language of rational choice theory 'collective action' refers to a combination of individual agents' actions, where these actions are not necessarily 'the same'.

or end-state. In asking what it is for people to act together, one necessarily abstracts from this diversity.[11]

My discussion of acting together begins with a number of observations on a particular hypothetical case. This leads to a consideration of the contexts in which people start doing things together. Enough questions will then have emerged to demand a theory of acting together that goes beyond such 'low-level' observations. I focus on the case of two people who are out on a walk together.[12] For brevity's sake, I sometimes refer to them as, simply, *walking together*. My use of this terminology requires a caution. In common parlance, two people may be walking together, in the joint activity sense, without being *out on a walk* together. They may be acquaintances, who have run into one another and, since they were individually headed in the same direction, have fallen into walking together—as it would be said—for a while. These people may also be said to be *walking along* together or walking *with* one another. There will be few cases of acting together more familiar to people in general. Almost everyone has had the experience of walking with another person, and has had such an experience from an early age. Going for a walk, with or without another person, is a somewhat more specialized phenomenon. For obvious reasons, it tends to be engaged in by people with more leisure at their disposal. Some will regularly 'go for a walk', others will never do so.

Going for a walk with another person is, nonetheless, a perfectly humdrum joint activity. As we shall see, informal observations on the way people think, feel, and react in this context raise difficult questions.

What is it to go for a walk, singly or with another person? I take two fixed points to be the following. In order to take a canonical walk, the person or persons in question must cover a certain amount of space on foot in the time allotted. 'A walk' might well take about an hour, though it might take half of that or even less, and it could also be considerably longer. In short, the time to be taken is flexible but it is not negligible.

I shall assume that the people in my example take their walking along side by side to be the conventional behavioural form of their joint activity—their walking together. To be sure, if they come to a fragile bridge they may have to go over it in single file, keeping some distance between them. Their physical

---

[11] My first discussion of this topic was in Gilbert (1989: ch. 4). Gilbert (1990a) is a briefer version. See also Gilbert (1997b). Though there is some overlap with these and other discussions here—my basic position has not changed—the exposition in this and the following chapter is clearer and more precise in important ways. Gilbert (2003: 53–5) explains some changes of formulation that have occurred since the initial discussion in Gilbert (1989).

[12] Examples other authors have focused on include painting a house together (Bratman 1993a, and elsewhere); making music together (Dworkin 1989b; see also Schutz 1970); preparing a picnic together (Kutz 2000); executing a pass play, making a sauce together (Searle 1990).

environment will impose this behaviour upon them. As soon as they are able, however, convention requires them to revert to double file. In some cultures, or among some people, different forms may occur. For instance, a woman may be required to walk several paces behind her husband. Nonetheless, I take the behavioural form I am assuming to be common.

Now, two people can walk alongside each other as a matter of coincidence. In my experience it is common for people to attempt to disrupt such a pattern once it becomes salient. Perhaps each desires to avoid any semblance of partnership. Nonetheless, people can continue to walk alongside each other for some while without being engaged in any joint activity: one may not have noticed the other; one may be trying to draw ahead, the other successfully trying to keep up, and so on.[13]

How is one to discover where the difference lies? How is one to give an account of walking together and, more generally, acting together? I propose that one takes seriously two aspects of the situation when two people are, by hypothesis, out on a walk together.

My initial discussion of the following case will assume that there are no special background understandings—agreements, conventions, and the like—that obtain, beyond the parties' understanding that they are out on a walk, which has the conventional behavioural form noted. Later I shall discuss in some detail the kinds of background understandings that may alter the parties' situation in a given case.

A Special Standing to Rebuke and Make Demands

Suppose that James and Paula are out on a walk in New York. They are heading up Fifth Avenue from Grand Central Station on their way to Central Park. This is how each understands what is going on, and each knows that each understands this.[14] James is a naturally fast walker and begins to draw ahead of Paula. One can imagine Paula calling after him, demanding that he slow down, rebuking him for going too fast, or both at once: 'James! Slow down! You're going too fast!'

She may not do either of these things. She may prefer to use a more gentle means of getting James's attention. She may decide to wait till he realizes what is happening and takes action without any prompting from her. She may struggle to keep up, hoping to deal with the situation that way. Though all this

---

[13] See Gilbert (1996: 178–9) for a variety of cases in which there is such parallel walking without any joint activity.

[14] Better, it is 'common knowledge' between them that they are out on a walk together. Roughly, it is out in the open between the two, and each is aware of this. For a somewhat fuller account see the text below.

is so, James and Paula will both understand that she has the *standing* to demand that he act in a manner appropriate to their joint activity, and to rebuke him should he act in a manner inappropriate to it. They will understand, moreover, that she has this standing by virtue of her participation with James in the joint activity of walking together. Of course, the same goes for James: should Paula draw ahead he has the standing to make demands and utter rebukes by virtue of his participation with her in the joint activity. For simplicity's sake I shall occasionally focus on the situation of one of the parties. It should be understood that the other's situation is the same.

That the parties have the standing to make demands of one another, and so on, does not mean that in a given case they ought, all things considered, to do so. Paula may be right not to rebuke James for letting himself get ahead of her, however conscious he was of what was happening. He may better be approached in a gentler manner. To say one has the standing to do something does not even mean that one has some justification for doing it. Rather, it means that one is in a position to do it. Anyone can speak 'demandingly' to another or speak harshly to them. Actually to demand or rebuke another requires the standing to do so.[15]

The standing of the parties that has just been referred to is special in two ways. It is special in the sense of being a standing that is not shared by people generally. Suppose Dan, a stranger, happens to see James drawing away from Paula and calls out to him: 'Slow down! You are walking too fast for her!' James might well question Dan's standing to address him in this way. In vernacular terms he may say 'What business is it of yours?' He need not do any such thing. He may find Dan's intervention helpful and focus on doing what he needs to do to enable Paula to keep up with him. Without special background conditions, however, if James and Paula are walking together it is hard to imagine him questioning *her* standing in the matter.

Other people could in principle have such standing. Paula's brother Abe would have the standing to rebuke James for moving ahead if James had promised him not to get ahead of Paula on their walk. Such promises to third parties sometimes occur in the context of joint action. Obviously, however, there need be no such promise.

The standing of the participants is a function of their joint activity. Thus it is special not only in the sense of not being shared by people generally, but also in having a specific source, namely, the joint activity.[16]

---

[15] See the discussion in Ch. 1, above, of 'authority presupposing' terms. I take 'rebuke', 'demand', and 'insist', among others, to be such terms.

[16] The first sense of 'special' is that in which 'special' is opposed to 'general'; the second means something like *distinctive*.

The Presence of Obligations

Paula would have a standing that is special in the two ways noted if, through her participation, she had some kind of right against James to action appropriate to the joint activity. James would then have correlative obligations towards Paula. His obligations would include walking alongside her when this is feasible and taking corrective action should he find himself drawing ahead. Thus he might slow his pace, stop and wait for Paula to catch up, or turn back towards her. He might turn and ask her if she is getting tired, or apologize for outpacing her. These are the kinds of things people do when they realize they have drawn ahead while they are out on a walk together.

There is reason, then, to think that those who are out on a walk together have rights of some kind against each other and correlative obligations towards each other. This is evidenced precisely by the kinds of interventions and actions I have described. I take those not to be limited to the case of two people walking together but to other numbers walking and to joint activity generally.

For several reasons, one may find puzzling the idea that obligations and rights are part and parcel of joint activity as such. In particular, I have in mind the following problem. That people are doing something together may seem to be a natural phenomenon, a matter of 'brute fact'. Rights and obligations may belong to a different order of things. Moreover (this is a second concern), it may seem doubtful that all of the joint activity humans are involved in could involve rights and obligations. What of joint projects such as carrying out a murder together? Can they involve obligations to perform murderous actions?

These are both very reasonable concerns. As to the second, it is possible that some joint activities have special features such that they do not involve the rights and obligations that others do. That this is so is not clear from what one observes, however. Those engaged in morally unacceptable joint activity may respond to each other in much the same way that James and Paula do in relation to their joint walk. Thus one of those carrying out a burglary may say to his partner, who is clearly having second thoughts, 'Okay, we shouldn't be doing this but we are . . . so get a move on!'

The two concerns together make it clear that it will be a challenge to explain the observations on joint activity that have been outlined so far. That does not mean the challenge cannot be met. Indeed, it would seem that an adequate account of joint action must meet it. What is at issue here is, in particular, the joint action of mature human beings.

I therefore propose the following criterion of adequacy for an account of joint action. Such an account should explain how it is that, at least failing special background understandings, each participant has obligations towards the other participants to behave in a way appropriate to the activity in question—walking together, planning a revolution together, or whatever it may be. More precisely, it should explain how such obligations and the correlative rights are *grounded in the joint activity itself.*

This will be referred to as *the obligation criterion.* It rules out a number of accounts of acting together that have been or might be proposed.[17] The proposal I shall develop in this and the following chapter meets the obligation criterion.

The Need for Concurrence

Though some of the components of a walk for two are fixed in advance, there is likely to be much leeway as to how a particular walk is to be conducted. Obvious details of importance are: where will the walk be taken, and how long will it last? How are such things to be settled? A typical case might go like this. James asks Paula, 'Shall we turn round now?' He entreats Paula's acceptance of his proposal. She might give this with a simple 'Yes', 'Fine', or 'Let's'. She might also suggest something different, and James may concur. Such interchanges need not be a matter of words. James, puffing hard, may pause for a moment. Paula may express her acceptance of a pause in their walk by pausing herself without demur.

Generalizing to the case of joint activity in general, this suggests that, absent pertinent background understandings, the following *concurrence condition* holds: no one party is in a position unilaterally to decide on the details of a joint action. The concurrence of the other parties is needed in order that such details are settled. The parties must make it clear to one another either verbally or by means of other behaviour that each is ready to endorse the detail in question.

Pertinent background understandings can be quite various. For example, the parties could make an appropriate agreement in advance. Recurring to the case of two people on a walk, they may agree that one of them will 'take the reins' of the walk, making all pertinent decisions as they come up. Or perhaps one will make decisions about where to go, other issues being left for the two of them to decide. The point is that if nothing like this has happened, and one party acts as if it is indeed up to him, something is amiss. Thus suppose James has not previously been given charge of his walk with Paula. He suddenly says, 'We'll cross the road here', implying that he will brook no demur. Paula could reasonably object 'But we're doing this together—don't I have a say?'

There could be circumstances in which one party had better take the reins, and realizes this. For instance, James spots Michael, someone Paula is trying

---

[17] As discussed in Gilbert ([1990a] 1996): 178–84; and (1998a); also Bratman (1999: 130–41).

to avoid, walking towards them. Attempting to protect Paula, and needing to act fast, James speaks as above, in peremptory fashion. Once the coast is clear, one can imagine James offering an apologetic explanation for his peremptory speech.

To suppose that there is a concurrence condition on joint action is not to deny that there may be circumstances in which a given party's failure to concur is strongly criticizable. For instance, if James proposes that they take a rest stop when he is puffing hard, it may be unreasonable for Paula not to concur. There are versions of this case where it would be positively immoral of her not to concur. According to the concurrence condition, her concurrence is needed in order for things to be wholly on track—failing pertinent background understandings.

To suppose there is a concurrence condition on joint action is not to deny that there are circumstances in which James would be well advised to take a rest even *without* Paula's concurrence. He may, indeed, be morally required to do so. Though in doing so he may then have the moral high ground, the concurrence condition implies that there will be something amiss from the point of view of their joint walk should he stop without her concurrence—in the absence of pertinent background understandings. I say more about the range of possible background understandings shortly.

Among other things, I take the concurrence condition to relate to the matter of a given party's *breaking off from the joint activity*. In a two-person case, one person's doing this will effectively put an end to the joint activity, as such, for the other party. This need not be so in cases where there are more than two people. That said, I continue my focus on the case of James and Paula in discussion of the case of breaking away. Once again, I suppose that in this case there are no special background understandings in play.

Suppose that Paula and James are some way short of their target, Central Park, which lies to the north. Paula suddenly turns away from James and, without a word, walks down West 50th Street. She has apparently broken away from their walk.

One can imagine that James will be surprised. He may not be disappointed. He may even be pleased. Their conversation may have annoyed him in some way and he may be relieved that it has ceased. At the same time, he may well judge that Paula has acted 'out of line'. Given that they were out on a walk to Central Park, she has done something that is open to criticism. James may not do anything about this, for a number of reasons, but he will understand it nonetheless.

Paula's leaving would have been less problematic in slightly altered circumstances. Suppose she had first clapped her hand to her brow and said to James

'Good grief... I was supposed to be at the doctor's office ten minutes ago!' And suppose he had then replied 'Goodness... you'd better go!' She would then have squared things with him before leaving, and the problem in the original story would not have arisen.

Would it have been enough if, just before turning away, Paula had turned to James and announced: 'I forgot... I was supposed to be at the doctor's office ten minutes ago! I'm on my way!' In other words, would it have been enough for her to make her intention to break away known to Jim before she carried it out? I suggest that for her merely to make this announcement would not be enough to remove a sense of mistake.

Consider this. Were she to make such an announcement, a likely response would not be a simple acknowledgement from James that he has heard her message, as in 'I hear you, Paula' or—without irony—'Thanks for letting me know what's happening'. Rather he would say something implying that he endorsed the decision that she should go, as in 'Fine... get going then!' or, simply, 'Fine!'

It seems, then, that in this case Paula needs to take her leave of James, and in order for her to take her leave, he must give it to her. In other words, he must concur in her quitting the joint activity. Without this, things are not properly on course.

That does not mean that, all things considered, Paula may not be justified in leaving the walk with James should he refuse to concur in her doing so. If she is late for a doctor's appointment he could presumably be criticized for refusing. That it is incumbent on James to concur, all things considered, does not mean that his concurrence is not needed for things to be wholly on track.

Whether or not the onus is on one party to concur in the other's quitting the joint walk will depend on the case. Sometimes it will be reasonable to demur, at least initially, perhaps offering reasons why that person's quitting is far from desirable in the circumstances. Sometimes it will not be reasonable to do even this.

I take it that, knowing they are out on a walk, both Paula and James will grasp the concurrence condition. Moreover, they will understand that it is a function of what it is for them to be out on a walk together. Thus if Paula, having moved off, gives as her reason 'I feel like a swim...' James might well demur 'But we're out on a walk!' citing the fact of their joint activity against the propriety of her making any such unilateral decision.

She can of course just move away. She has the physical power to do that, as does James. James may say, 'Please don't go!' in the manner of a suppliant, at the point where she seems bent on ignoring his standing in the matter of her disengagement.

On first considering it some may be inclined to deny that Paula needs James's concurrence in order to leave their walk without some type of fault on her part. More generally, people may resist the idea that there is a *concurrence condition on exit* from a joint activity that holds in the absence of special background circumstances.[18] As I now argue, there are plausible ways to explain such a reaction without endorsing it.

First, those who are initially inclined to reject the condition may not like the thought that those with whom they do things have the kind of power over them it implies.[19] Given a relatively strong desire that something not be true, one's judgement on the point is liable to be affected, at least as far as one's initial reaction is concerned.

Second, those who resist the concurrence condition on exit may have been affected by observations and experiences that, taken out of context, appear to refute it. Once their context is revealed, however, it becomes clear that they do not do so.

The first kind of context I have in mind involves some form of advance concurrence of the parties with respect to one or another's quitting the joint activity should they so wish. There are at least three possible situations here.

One type of case involves a prior agreement made with respect to a particular instance of joint activity. For instance, James asks Paula if she'd like to walk to Central Park with him. She says she isn't sure she wants to go for much of a walk today. He responds, 'Look, if you want to stop at any point, that's fine. I'll be happy to continue on my own.' She replies, 'Let's go, then.' Later, feeling tired, Paula wants to leave their walk. She says to James: 'I'll stop here.' He does not find her bald assertion problematic. He says 'Bye, then' as a way of acknowledging what she has said. He does not see himself as offering his concurrence with her decision. Taken out of context, James's comfort with Paula's assertion might seem to refute the concurrence condition. Taken in its context, however, it clearly does not refute it. James has, in effect, concurred in advance with any proposal Paula might make to leave their walk if and when she wants to. That he sees fit to do so suggests that his concurrence is required in order for Paula's leaving to be unexceptionable.[20]

---

[18] Bittner (2002) resists the idea that there is such a concurrence condition; so have some discussants. Those inclined to accept it could skip to the summary of this section on p. 114 without losing the main thread of the discussion.

[19] Ibid. explicitly avows this attitude.

[20] Cf. the example in Bratman (1993a): each party to a duet 'reserves the right' to call off the joint enterprise at any time. That 'reservation of right' may amount to an agreement to treat the situation *as if* each party had the right unilaterally to call off the joint enterprise (Gilbert 2000: 35 n. 36). The case in the text could be viewed as involving an agreement to behave *as if* one party does not require

An example of another type of case is this. Suppose that James and Paula know each other well and enjoy walking together. Both know, however, that she finds it deeply uncomfortable to have to await anyone's concurrence on anything. They may therefore have developed an understanding or convention such that, whenever they are out on a walk together it is up to her how long she continues to participate in the joint activity. Here, too, James has, in effect, concurred in advance with Paula's ceasing to participate in a given walk of theirs if and when she chooses to do so, though he has not done so explicitly. My understanding of what it is for there to be a convention in a population allows for this interpretation of the case.[21] This may be referred to as a case of *private convention*.

In yet another type of case, James and Paula may be parties to the convention of a broader population to the effect that when one goes for a walk with another person, one may withdraw from the walk if and when one chooses to do so. Once again, James has, in effect, concurred in advance to Paula's ceasing to participate in their walk if and when she so chooses. Conscious of the convention, when Paula says, 'I'm going to stop here', James may offer what is no more than an acknowledgement of her definitive decision: 'Right then. I'm sorry we can't go on a bit longer.... Shall I call you tomorrow?' This may be referred to as a case of *societal convention*.

A societal convention like the one just envisaged with respect to exit from a joint walk is probably more common in relation to other forms of joint activity such as joint sexual activity. Meanwhile, one would expect the specific conventions that obtain in a given society to depend on its character. For instance, the more emphasis a given society places on personal freedom and autonomy, the more likely—one would think—are conventions allowing people generally to break away from one or another form of joint activity. I consider how far such conventions might go shortly. Again, in a strongly patriarchal society one would expect there to be conventions allowing a man to break away from joint activity without the concurrence of his female partner, but not vice versa.

The distinction between private and societal conventions is not intended to be overly sharp. In the examples given the cases differ at least in the following way. With the private convention, the parties know each other personally and their convention develops in the course of their personal relationship. With

the other's concurrence on his withdrawal from the joint activity. That would amount, *in effect*, to concurring in advance.

[21] My position on the nature of conventions differs from the influential account in Lewis (1969). See Gilbert (1989: ch. 6), and the text below.

the societal convention, a given party to the convention may well not know every other member personally or even know of every other member. It may be or become apparent, however, that another person is a fellow member of the society in question.

It is possible, then, that in particular cases the relevant concurrence has been given in advance, as a result of an ad hoc agreement or prevailing conventions. Observations of apparently acceptable withdrawals without contemporaneous requests for concurrence do not, of course, show that there is no concurrence condition if they are made in the context of such agreements and conventions.

Evidently such background agreements and conventions are not always present. When engaged in what are understood to be joint activities such as going for a walk together, people often speak and act as if they are requesting another's concurrence and respond in concurring ways, however subtle. Perhaps one person says, 'I'm getting tired,' and the other responds 'Well, why don't you go back, then? I'll go on by myself.' 'Okay,' says the first. In contrast, if one party says, 'I think I'll stop here!' without any suggestion that the other's concurrence is needed, this is likely explicitly or implicitly to be registered as some kind of mistake.

To sense mistake is not necessarily to express this sense or otherwise to act on it. James may keep quiet and barely raise an eyebrow, all the while judging Paula to have been at fault in leaving their walk 'without so much as a by-your-leave'.

One should not deny the concurrence condition because of cases like the following. Someone is so used to others making the mistake in question in relation to him that he is no longer disposed to notice it. The problem for this person is precisely that he no longer perceives, or consciously perceives, something he would have perceived were it not for the particular course of his experience. His partners in joint action may have regularly treated him with a lack of respect. Or his partners may constantly face urgent crises that brook no delay. He now stands ready for them to break away from joint activity without notice, not expecting any request for his concurrence.

As noted earlier, in some cases, taking the time to wait for concurrence, or to communicate in any way with one's partners in joint action would be inappropriate, all things considered. Awareness of this fact may tend to mask any sense of mistake in the other parties.

Does the concurrence condition depend on facts about the genesis of, say, a joint walk? In particular, does it assume that the walk was initiated with an agreement? It seems not, since one who remonstrates with another who presumes unilaterally to decide to stop walking is likely to say 'but we were going to Central Park', for instance, rather than saying anything about an agreement. The crucial thought here is that they were doing something together. If their joint action was indeed prefaced by an agreement, that may well have dropped out of the picture.[22] As I argue shortly, an agreement is not generally necessary as a preface to joint action.

I have explained how background understandings may be such that the concurrence of a given party has, in effect, been given in advance to another party's quitting a joint activity 'at will'. Another possibility concerns a different type of background understanding that is of considerable importance. This is to the effect that there is a specific condition other than the will of one of the parties such that the joint activity in question is at an end if this condition fails to be satisfied—perhaps with the proviso that the joint activity may continue if and only if all parties agree to its continuance. Thus, suppose that two people are living together 'as man and wife'. I shall refer to them as partners. If one partner is discovered to have engaged in sexual activity with a third party, the offended partner may aver, 'We're through!' and the other may not question the point. The same thing may happen if one party engages in physical violence against the other. Such language suggests the existence of an established condition of the kind in question.

Clearly, it may be extremely important to establish conditions such that everyone knows they must be fulfilled if a given joint activity is to continue. Where there is any doubt, it may be necessary to clarify these conditions in conversation. Explicit agreements may need to be made, and sanctions, perhaps, established for straying from the defined path when engaged in the joint activity.

Clearly, too, the conditions that are established may vary from group to group, and individual to individual. In an 'open relationship', for instance, one partner's sexual activity with someone outside the relationship will not be regarded as concluding the partnership. Here it has been explicitly agreed that each partner is at liberty to engage in sexual encounters outside the relationship.

The nature of particular agreements and both private and societal conventions may reflect differences in coercive power among different classes of persons or different individuals. They may reflect diversity in moral codes, and so on. That is not to say that some conditions may not be universal or close to universal across cultures and persons.

One might think that incapacity would always be taken to determine one's exit from a joint activity, without the need for anyone else's concurrence. That this is so is not entirely clear. One's avowal that he 'can't go on' may be met with something that looks like a concurring response, rather than a simple

---

[22] Compare Lewis (1969), on the genesis of convention.

acknowledgement that the joint activity is, evidently, at an end. However that may be, there is no question that if one party genuinely cannot continue to participate the other would be more than unreasonable not to concur on his quitting the joint activity. People who demur in such contexts most likely suspect the person they are dealing with of exaggerating the problem.

It is surely significant that the language of incapacity so frequently precedes the ending of joint action, or one party's exit from it. Often, people who say they 'have to' stop, and so on, do not really *have to*. They may want to stop, for whatever reason, but they could go on if they chose. Whatever their reasons, they will not be as persuasive an argument for another's concurring with their stopping as their having to stop. So they say that they have to stop. The other parties may seek to discover precisely what degree of incapacity, if any, is present, or they may leave it there.

When people are engaged in joint action, they may understand that one or more of them—perhaps all of them—are participating in the joint activity under a certain description rather than simply as themselves. Thus suppose Paula 'signed on' for her walk with James with the words 'I need to be in Central Park at noon to meet Kit, so I'll come with you'. If Kit calls her on her mobile phone to say that he cannot come to Central Park, she may not then need James's concurrence to quit their walk. It may be enough to reveal that the description under which she was engaged in the joint activity—as a person in need of reaching Central Park by noon—no longer applies to her, and he will understand this. Thus she might say 'Oh, James, I no longer need to be in the Park at noon . . . I think I'll stop here.' He may then have no sense of offence.

One might wonder whether people always enter joint actions not so much as *themselves* but rather as persons *wanting* to participate in that joint activity. Were this the case, and the previous point correct, then all one would ever have to do would be to reveal one's dissatisfaction with the activity and the other party would understand that one did not need his concurrence with one's exit. The evidence suggests that this is not so. At the same time there clearly can be—and are—background understandings according to which one person's no longer wanting to participate in a given joint activity is enough to conclude the activity, or to entail that person is no longer party to it.

Could there be a society with the convention that one's merely wanting to break away from *any* joint activity always suffices to free one of the constraints of that activity? This looks like a consistent description, and a society that put an exceptionally high premium on personal autonomy might develop something approximating this convention. Whether such a convention would be sustainable over time is another matter. Whether the very idea of joint activity—and hence a convention with this content—could long endure in such a society is a moot point. The existence of such a convention would not refute the claim that there is a concurrence condition on exit from joint activity *absent* special background understandings, the point presently at issue.

I have said little here about what background understandings—agreements, conventions, and so on—themselves amount to, relying on the reader's pre-theoretical understanding. Later in this book I focus at some length on agreements and social rules, of which I take social conventions to be a species. I indicate, also, how to construe background understandings that are more aptly thought of as collective beliefs than rules.

Let me pull together the threads of my discussion of the concurrence condition so far. I have proposed that according to the conception of joint action implicit in everyday thought and behaviour, there is the following condition on such action. Absent pertinent background understandings, no one party is in a position to determine its as yet undetermined details. Rather, all parties must concur on them, including the matter who may cease to participate in the action. In support of this proposal I argued as follows. In the context of joint action, people often speak and act in concurring and concurrence-requesting ways when specification of the terms of the joint activity or withdrawal from it are at issue. Importantly, they found objections to the lack of such actions on the fact that the activity in question is indeed joint. There are reasons for viewing a theorist's doubts about the existence of the condition with caution. He may not want it to be true, or without realizing it, he may focus on observations and experiences that fail to refute it though they might initially be thought to do so. There is ample room for background understandings and conventions of various kinds to explain them. Though more can be said in defence of this condition, I shall not go further in defence of it here.[23]

The concurrence condition can be put in terms of rights and obligations that the parties have in relation to one another. Absent special background understandings, any given party, A, has an obligation to any other party, B, to obtain B's concurrence in any new determination of the details of the joint activity.[24] This includes A's exit from the joint activity. Alternatively, B has a

---

[23] There is further discussion of the concurrence condition (there referred to as the permission point) in Gilbert (2003: 45–6): might the concurrence condition itself be based on understandings or conventions that have come naturally to accompany joint activity, rather than somehow being inherent in such activity? I argue that two aspects of acting together that might be thought to give rise to the concurrence condition—the *rudeness* of one who breaks off without permission, and the unfulfilled *expectations* of those who are left—are more apt to be *explained by* the concurrence condition, or what underlies it, than to satisfactorily explain it.

[24] By 'new determination' I mean a determination that has not been settled at the outset of the joint activity either explicitly or by virtue of background understandings.

right against A that A obtains B's concurrence in any new determination of their joint activity.

I now propose the *concurrence criterion* of adequacy for an account of joint action. Such an account should explain how joint activity grounds the concurrence condition. Doing so may seem to be a significant challenge. Once again, the apparently natural, 'brute fact' nature of acting together may be invoked: how can acting together, and that alone, ground the concurrence condition?

Questions Arising

I have proposed two conditions of adequacy for an account of acting together. Focusing on an example I took to be paradigmatic, and assuming the absence of special background understandings, I observed, first, that those who are doing something together understand each other to have a special standing in relation to one another. This includes the standing to make demands and utter rebukes to one another with respect to their conduct as participants in the joint activity. This suggests that those engaged in a joint activity have rights against one another to action appropriate to the joint activity and correlative obligations towards one another, rights and obligations that are somehow grounded in the joint activity. Hence I proposed the obligation criterion for an adequate account of acting together. I also proposed the concurrence criterion. As noted, this can also be put in terms of rights and obligations of the parties in relation to each other. Here, too, there are related entitlements to demand relevant action, such as an appeal for concurrence, and to rebuke another party should it not occur.[25] These rights, obligations, and entitlements are held by virtue of the fact that the parties are indeed acting together. They are, somehow, an integral part of acting together.

Though there is reason to suppose these things, they might be thought almost incredible. How can something that seems natural, relatively primitive, a matter of 'brute fact' intrinsically involve something that seems to be of a different order: rights against persons and obligations towards them? Rather than assuming that what appears to be the case cannot be, I shall for now assume that it is, and ask: How are the rights intrinsic to acting together possible? If a satisfactory answer can be given, as I shall argue, that will help to confirm the assumption.

---

[25] I might have said (as I have elsewhere) that the parties have a *right* to rebuke and make demands of each other instead of speaking of an *entitlement* to rebuke and so on. Speaking of an entitlement in this context is a way of marking a distinction. One's right to another's continued participation is a right to another's action—something verbally marked in speaking of a right 'against' another; the standing or entitlement or right to rebuke pertains to one's own action; it is not a right against another.

6.3   How Joint Action Comes About

Prior Agreements

How does joint activity get started? Once this is understood it may be easier to discover what it involves. How, then, might Paula and James, for instance, have ended up walking together? Perhaps Paula said, 'Shall we go for a walk?' thus proposing a walk to James, and he accepted her proposal by saying 'Yes, let's'. In short, they agreed to go for a walk together. Having thus agreed, they set off on their walk. Such an agreement is, clearly, a standard way of initiating joint action.

Now, just as agreements are, intuitively, a source of obligations, they are a source of rights also. Certainly, in the specialist literature, agreements and promises are generally regarded as paradigmatic contexts for rights.[26] For example, if you and I agree that I will cook dinner and you will wash the dishes, I acquire a right to your washing the dishes and you acquire a right to my cooking dinner.

All this may suggest *the agreement hypothesis*: those who act together in a certain way must first enter an agreement to do so.[27] A significant attraction of this hypothesis is that it provides a ground for the rights of those engaged in such action, at least in the absence of special factors relating to content or context. If we have agreed to go for a walk together, then, failing special background understandings, we would for that reason have a right to each other's participation in this joint act until such time as it were completed or, alternatively, we agreed to bring it to a close.

The problem with the agreement hypothesis is that a prior agreement does not appear to be a necessary condition for joint action. This can be argued by reference to examples that themselves differ in significant ways.

First, suppose Paula runs into James by chance and asks him what he is up to. He says, in the most friendly manner, that he is on his way to take a walk in Central Park. He says no more, but looks at her expectantly. She exclaims 'Oh, what a nice idea! Can you wait a second while I make a phone call?' James says 'Sure!' Her phone call completed, Paula turns to James and says 'I'm ready!' Such an interchange could provide the foundation for a case of walking together. Whatever precisely transpired between them, however, it

---

[26] See e.g. Sumner (1987); Thomson (1990). This is not to say that theorists agree as to how agreements give rise to rights.

[27] Tuomela (1995) makes such a suggestion, though his examples suggest that he has something other than an agreement in mind. Gilbert (1989) and Bratman (1993a) explicitly reject the agreement hypothesis. Both naturally allow that joint activity *may* be preceded by an agreement. On Tuomela, see Gilbert (1998b).

seems wrong to say that Paula and James agreed to walk together. That is, whatever background understandings were taken into account and whatever was implied by what was said, there was no agreement between them.

In this case there is, indeed, an interchange between the parties that occurs prior to their walking together, an interchange that is apt to provide a foundation for their joint walk. To that extent it resembles an agreement and serves at least one of the primary purposes an agreement would have served, had the parties made one.

It may be tempting to say that in this case Paula and James 'implicitly agreed' to walk together. If one succumbs to this temptation, however, one must admit that there was no agreement strictly speaking. In other words, examples such as this still present a problem for the agreement hypothesis.

In addition, there are cases of acting together that involve no such preliminary interchange. Take quarrelling, for instance. I take this to be a case of acting together, though in some ways a special one. Certainly people say things like 'We quarrelled all day', using a standard linguistic marker for joint action. Again, one might think of a quarrel as a certain (heated) type of conversation.

People often begin to quarrel without preamble. This is probably the most common way for quarrels to occur. They tend to erupt spontaneously, on the basis of feelings of anger. For example, Rose angrily bursts out 'You never should have invited your sister to dinner!' Fred offers a sarcastic retort, and more angry back and forth ensues. The premeditative quality of an agreement sets it at odds with this aspect of most quarrels. Joint actions precipitated by forceful emotions are not the only ones that occur without a prior agreement or other anticipatory preamble, but these are particularly suited for such an unheralded beginning.

A friend of the agreement hypothesis might point out that there is an agreement-like structure in the situation described. One could say that, in effect, by bursting out as she does Rose proposes a quarrel, and by 'taking the bait' and returning hostilities Fred accepts her proposal. This may be so, but it does not save the agreement hypothesis. In common parlance, as the story goes, Rose and Fred did not agree to quarrel. They simply started quarrelling.

It might be questioned whether the example of quarrelling is sufficiently like walking together to qualify as an example of the type of acting together at issue here. One might wonder, in particular, if quarrels involve rights and entitlements analogous to those that appear to be present when people walk together. If they do not, that would make quarrelling significantly different from walking together. Rights and entitlements analogous to those involved in walking together *do* seem to be involved when people quarrel. Once Fred and Rose understand themselves to be quarrelling, Fred is likely to have a sense of mistake if Rose suddenly tunes out, for instance. Rose might have avoided this by saying something like 'Let's stop this!' inviting a permission-granting response such as 'Okay'. One party may of course, concede defeat, and have this concession accepted as in the following interchange. Rose: 'I guess you are right. It was time to invite her.' Fred: 'I'm glad you understand where I was coming from.'

As long as an analogous package of rights and entitlements is present, and without further reason to doubt its status, it seems reasonable to allow that both walking together and quarrelling are examples of the kind of acting together at issue here. Someone might wonder if the antagonistic aspect of quarrels disqualified them as joint actions. It is not clear why this should be so. It may be pointed out that we tend to speak of people quarrelling 'with' each other rather than as quarrelling 'together'. It is not clear what, if anything, is marked by this fact about usage. 'With' certainly does not of itself imply antagonistic feelings, since people can converse with one another, for instance, in perfect amity. The implication may be that, roughly, it takes two or more to do what one person does *with* someone else, whereas what people do *together* (walking, lunching, and so on) one *can* do alone.

As far as the agreement hypothesis goes, it is easy enough to provide non-antagonistic examples of 'unheralded' joint actions, that is, joint actions beginning without a prior agreement or any analogous preamble created by means of the activity of the parties. Thus people may quite spontaneously begin a friendly conversation, or kiss. Either of these joint actions might more easily begin with an agreement than a quarrel would ('Shall we talk?' 'Let's kiss and make up!'). Neither need do so, however, nor need there be any related anticipatory preamble.[28]

Here is another argument against the agreement hypothesis. It is plausible to suppose that making an agreement with another person is itself a case of acting together. Certainly it is a special type of acting together. It is, precisely, a type that frequently precedes other types in the role of explicit preamble. Nonetheless, it is a case of acting together. After all, one makes an agreement with another person. Suppose we accept this. Suppose we also accept the agreement hypothesis. Recall that this is the hypothesis that those who act together in a certain way must first enter an agreement to do so. Then we shall have to allow that any agreement itself requires a prior agreement. This would lead to an infinite regress of agreements going backwards in time,

---

[28] Why might the idea of agreeing to *quarrel* seem slightly absurd? For one thing, those who are quarrelling have, pretty much by definition, 'lost their cool'. One doesn't quarrel calmly, though one may argue calmly. Agreeing to quarrel is thus analogous to deciding to get angry. Conformity is not under the direct control of either party or of the parties in combination.

which would, depending on your assumptions about infinity, make agreements impossible. If we allow that agreements are (possible) joint actions, then, we must reject the agreement hypothesis. People can, of course, agree to agree, as they can agree to kiss. A relatively common type of agreement to agree is an agreement to enter another agreement with the intent, in entering the second agreement, to create 'legal relations'. In other terms, it is an agreement to create a legal contract. An example of this is an informal proposal of marriage. 'Will you marry me?' is, among other things, an invitation to agree to enter a legal contract of marriage at some future date, possibly years in the future.

Most agreements, however, are not preceded by prior agreements to agree at some future time. Nor are they preceded by any analogous preamble created by the activity of the parties. Insofar as these unheralded agreements are themselves joint acts they are on a par with other unheralded joint acts. One person makes a proposal and the other accepts it, just as, without prior agreement, James bends his head down so his lips meet Paula's, and she tips her head up so her lips meet his.

One might object to this that agreements typically ensue from some form of joint deliberation, and are hardly something one just falls into. In response to this one must certainly allow that many agreements are the result of joint deliberation. For instance, one party asks 'What shall we do?' A discussion ensues, and a course of action is agreed upon. Nothing like this need happen, however. Some agreements, like the one in the following scene, have the character of spontaneity at both the individual level and the level of joint deliberation. On a whim, Sally says to Don, 'Shall we go to the beach?' Without pausing to reflect, Don replies, 'Yes.'

Of course, to 'fall into' a joint act, in the sense at issue here, is not necessarily to participate in something that has not been deliberated upon or reflectively endorsed *by the individual parties*. It is rather that it has not been preceded by discussion among the parties or joint deliberation.

Unless for some reason we are forced to accept the agreement hypothesis, there is no need to insist that there are agreements in situations where common parlance would deny this. Is there anything that forces us to accept it?

One might think that the agreement hypothesis is the best we can come up with because one believes that, in contrast to the rights associated with joint action, philosophers generally understand well the rights associated with agreements. There is reason, however, to reject this latter belief.

Surprisingly, perhaps, agreements as opposed to promises have not been thoroughly considered by philosophers. The prevailing view has been that they are promise-exchanges. If promises are understood in the usual way, however, it is not clear that this view can stand.[29] As to the rights associated with promises, these are generally ignored in favour of the obligations of the promisor—the one who promises. There is a large literature of conflicting views as to the foundation of these obligations. Though one of these views may of course be correct, it cannot be said that philosophers generally understand this matter well.

In sum, it is premature to claim that philosophers well understand the rights associated with agreements. One cannot assume, then, that they would immediately understand the rights associated with a joint action if they stemmed from a prior agreement.

A General Condition

It seems best to set the agreement hypothesis aside. We need to go somewhere else to understand in general terms how joint action comes about.

One might try to discern what is common to the cases so far considered. These cases all involve joint activity on a small scale. That this is the provenance of any general condition that emerges will have to be borne in mind. Things could change when we move to a larger scale. For now I continue to focus on the cases that have been discussed.

These are cases where there is a prior agreement to engage in the joint action in question, cases where it is tempting to refer to an 'implicit' agreement to do so, and cases where reference even to an initial implicit agreement seems wrong. Here people simply fall into the joint activity, as two people might start to quarrel or to kiss or to enter an agreement without preamble. In order to give a general account of the genesis of joint activity, then, how might one attempt generally to characterize this range of cases?

One can say at least that each party to the joint action does something expressive of readiness to participate in that action. Further, each party makes this readiness manifest to the others. Something each party does or says makes their personal readiness clear, as it is intended to.

That is not to deny that more may be happening than this. In the case of an agreement proper, the parties, precisely, agree in advance to perform the action in question. In the case where there is only an 'implicit' agreement, something is nonetheless established in advance of the joint activity by dint of some exchange between the parties. In the 'falling into it' type of case one expresses readiness for a kiss, say, by beginning to play one's own part of that process, and the other does likewise.

---

[29] In Ch. 10, below, I sketch a positive account of agreements and the associated rights and obligations.

In spite of these differences, the mutual expression of readiness to engage in the joint activity seems to be common to all of the cases. We may then reasonably refer to it in generalizing over the three ways of producing joint action that have been noted. As far as the examples considered so far go, it seems appropriate, also, to add a reference to what has become known in the philosophical literature as 'common knowledge'. That is, it seems appropriate to require that the mutual expressions of readiness to engage in the joint activity are common knowledge between the parties. What is common knowledge? Roughly and briefly, if some fact is *common knowledge* between A and B (or between members of population P, described by reference to some common attribute), then that fact is entirely out in the open between them—and, at some level, all are aware that this is so. Among other things, it would not make sense for any one of these persons to attempt to hide the fact from another of their number.[30]

6.4 The Need for a Theory

So far I take myself not to have gone far beyond everyday observation and experience, including self-observation. I have noted some intriguing aspects of the way people act and speak when walking together. I have focused, in particular, on their sense of their standing in relation to one another. This cries out for explanation. I then considered the ways in which people come to be acting together, to see if this could provide further enlightenment. I argued that we could not rest with an appeal to a prior agreement and its production of rights, even though joint action is often preceded by an agreement. On the one hand, a joint action need not be preceded by an agreement. On the other hand, the way in which agreements produce rights and standing is not well understood. On the basis of consideration of a number of small-scale cases what seems to be necessary are mutual expressions of readiness for participation in joint action. To say this, however, leaves much to be explained.

What precisely is communicated from one party to another? What precisely is the outcome once these communications have occurred? How do entitlements to make demands and utter rebukes come into the picture? Insofar as an explicit

---

[30] 'Common knowledge' has been much discussed in philosophy and economics; several different, often quite technical, accounts have been proposed. The original discussions are in Lewis (1969) and Schiffer (1972); also Aumann (1976). See also Heal (1978). In Gilbert (1989: 188–95, etc.) develop the account on which the rough proposal in the text is based. I shall not attempt to go beyond that here. I emphasize an important distinction among types of common knowledge in Ch. 8, below.

agreement is not a necessary precursor of joint action, what does it add to the picture when it is part of it?

It is unlikely that either informal observation or more rigorously conducted experimental observation can provide an answer to these questions. If they cannot, then some form of theoretical construct must be developed in order to illuminate the observable data. The aim of such a construct will be to represent in a perspicuous way what is in some sense in the minds of the participating persons. It need not represent something of which these persons have explicit awareness. Most people may not, indeed, be capable of articulating their understanding, insofar as such articulation requires philosophical skills they lack. Nonetheless, something needs explaining, and it is something about the understanding of these very persons. What does it amount to? What, if we were to build a model of them, in the domain of artificial intelligence for example, would we have to put into that model to get the output we have observed: the demands, rebukes, and sense of entitlement (on both sides)?

Towards a Theory of Acting Together

Suppose that Paula, alone now, is walking to her doctor's office. What are the key elements in this process? The standard philosophical answer runs along the following lines. Paula has the goal of walking to her doctor's office, she is behaving in a way appropriate to the achievement of this goal, and she is doing so in light of the fact that it is her goal.[31] Instead of referring to Paula's goal, I might have referred to her intention. The term 'goal' may tend to suggest that we are talking about the ultimate point of what is going on, from the agent's perspective. To speak of her 'intention' may tend not to suggest this. I take the differences to be subtle ones and will stick with 'goal' for now. I think that nothing I say in this section will hang on this.[32]

Suppose, then, that an individual human being who is engaged in an action of his own espouses a specific goal in light of which he behaves in appropriate ways. How is it with those who do something together? A natural answer is that they *collectively espouse* a given goal. This obviously raises the question: what is it collectively to espouse a goal?

---

[31] To give an account of *walking to one's doctor's office* in terms of the goal of *walking to one's doctor's office* may seem to involve a troublesome circularity. As is common in discussions of this topic, I shall assume the propriety, in a rough description, of characterizing Paula's goal as above, and the same for other standard vernacular act descriptions such as 'painting the house', 'running for cover', and so on.

[32] Gilbert (1989, 1990a) discusses these matters in terms of goals; Gilbert (1997b) focuses on intentions, in part so as to align the discussion with those parts of the literature that are couched in terms of intentions, personal or collective.

Another possible answer is that each of them *personally espouses* a goal of a special 'collective' kind.[33] There is reason to doubt that the latter answer is the one to pursue. One pertinent reason is this. Suppose you come across two people you know and ask one of them what they are doing. 'We are going for a walk,' she says. You continue, 'I see. So your personal goal is to go for a walk with Sam?' She might well reply, 'I didn't say that. I didn't say anything about my personal goals. I said we are going for a walk. That's what *we're* doing. *Our* goal is to take a walk.'

This returns us to the previous answer, and the question it raises. What is it for two or more people collectively to espouse a goal—to make it *their* goal? That is not an easy question to answer. A number of proposals that might immediately suggest themselves can be argued to be inadequate. I shall not attempt here to review those that have been made, but will focus on the development of my own proposal about the collective espousal of a goal and the further components of acting together.[34]

The plausibility of the dialogue just presented strongly suggests that our collectively espousing a given goal is not a function of each one's personal goals, whatever their character. It seems, indeed, that one who is doing something with another, in the context of a goal he regards as 'ours', may at the same time not be prepared to ascribe any related goal to himself personally. This sets a task for any account of what it is for *us* to have a goal as this is understood in everyday life. For us to have a goal is for something to be the case that does not require each of us to have a concordant personal goal. Nor is it clear that either of us must *lack* a *dis*cordant personal goal.

This suggests, putting it without much content as yet, that *collective goals*—on the sense of goals collectively espoused—exist at a different 'level' from personal goals. In other terms, that *we* have a certain goal or aim *does not speak to* the issue of what goals *you* and *I* have, and vice versa. These are two separate realms in terms of goal possession. At the same time, what occurs at the collective level is enough to motivate the individuals who make up the collective. That is, 'our' goal is sufficient to motivate each of one of us.

How can a number of people bring it about that (in their eyes) *we* espouse a goal—where this does not involve each one's having that goal as a personal

---

[33] This is the approach of Miller (2001 and elsewhere); also Kutz (2000).

[34] Gilbert (1989: chs. 4 and 7; and 1990a) argues against various accounts of acting together with a 'shared personal goal' at their core. I argue that, among other things, these fail to account for the observations on acting together detailed in this chapter. See also Gilbert (1997b). Gilbert (1998a) summarizes a range of accounts of acting together and related phenomena including those of Tuomela (1984); Searle (1990); and Bratman (1993a, 1993b) and critically compares them with my own. Further critical discussions are cited on p. 164 n. 53.

goal—and that (consequently) our individual forces are directed to the goal by virtue of that espousal?[35] This is likely to seem like just another puzzle, and indeed it is. It is not easy to make sense of it, let alone to do so while at the same time explaining the other phenomena associated with acting together on which I have focused.

Here, in technical terms I shall carefully explain, is my own proposal as to how you and I can make a goal ours: we jointly commit to espousing that goal as a body. This suggestion—which will rightly appear opaque at first—introduces the notion that is central and crucial to my account of acting together: joint commitment. As I shall argue in what follows, if we accept this suggestion we find ourselves with an account of acting together that satisfies both the obligation and the concurrence conditions. At the same time, there is no appeal to personal as opposed to collective goals, which can be seen to exist at a different 'level' of goal possession.

---

[35] I consciously echo Rousseau (1983: ch. 6, p. 23). I do not say that my answer is the same as Rousseau's, but I suspect the question is the same. The passage in question is variously translated by different translators, perhaps because of the conceptual challenge it presents.

7

Joint Commitment
and Obligation

Pursuit of an acceptable account of acting together has led to the invocation of joint commitment. This will play a key role in the theory of political obligation I propose. This chapter gives an account of joint commitment, beginning with discussion of the kind of *commitment* at issue. It then argues that the parties to any *joint* commitment have obligations towards each other. These are directed obligations. They are perhaps the original or prototype of such obligations. In the final section of the chapter I complete the presentation of my account of acting together.

7.1 Commitment

I use the phrase 'joint commitment' as a technical phrase of my own.[1] I take the *concept* of a joint commitment to be a fundamental everyday concept. That is, I take it to be a basic part of the conceptual equipment of human beings functioning in social contexts. This is in part because it can be argued that the best accounts of many central everyday social concepts including acting together involve the concept of joint commitment.[2]

That the concept of joint commitment is fundamental to our everyday conceptual scheme has by no means been generally accepted by philosophers or other theorists writing today. Many contemporary theorists tend to prefer singularist accounts of phenomena such as acting together. A *singularist* account is, by my definition, one that ultimately draws only on the concepts of an

---

[1] Others have used this phrase, sometimes without an account of it, sometimes clearly in a sense other than mine. I stipulate a particular meaning for it in the context of my own discussions.

[2] This was the argument of my book *On Social Facts*, which introduced but only scratched the surface of the concept of a joint commitment (Gilbert 1989: 198 and elsewhere). I continue to refine both my understanding of joint commitment and my expressions of this understanding.

individual human person's beliefs, desires, goals, commitments, and so on.[3] The concept of a joint commitment stands outside this singularist conceptual scheme. The preference for singularist accounts may, of course, stem from lack of knowledge or understanding of existing alternatives. I concentrate here on the careful elaboration of the core of my own proposals, the concept of a joint commitment.

A joint commitment is a commitment of two or more people. It is, more expansively, a single commitment of two or more people. Before going further with respect to the jointness of the commitment, I discuss the commitment side of things. I take a particular kind of commitment to be in question. Not all so-called commitments are of this kind. Indeed, the commitments referred to in contemporary discourse are a motley crew.

Commitment in Contemporary Discourse

The term 'commitment' appears in many contemporary theoretical discussions—in action theory, in ethics, and in economic theory, to name a few. Thus, in a famous paper, economist Amartya Sen argues for the importance of commitments in the explanation of human behaviour, and recommends that economists develop their theories accordingly.[4] People also talk about commitment in a variety of contexts in everyday life and popular literature. Thus a recent book in popular psychology is entitled *Why Men Won't Commit*. I take it that Sen's concerns include those of that recent book. Others use the term 'commitment' in ways that go beyond his concerns. Thus, according to economist Robert Frank, a person who has not eaten for several days is 'committed' to eat. He adds, 'commitments of this sort are . . . merely incentives to behave in a particular way'.[5] If we use the phrase intuitively, it is clear that the kind or kinds of commitment with which Sen is concerned are not a matter of 'merely having an incentive'.

Consider also the popular psychology book. One might represent the core issue in such discussions thus: why do some men avoid entering an agreement with a woman to the effect that (roughly) they will love and cherish one another as long as they both live? In other words, the 'commitment' here crucially involves entry into an agreement. The agreement in question is, of course, an agreement with a particular content, just specified, and, when it is

---

[3] I introduced the term 'singularist' in Gilbert (1989). The term 'individualist', which might have been used, is well worn and undoubtedly ambiguous.

[4] Sen (1977).

[5] Frank (1988: 6). The first occurrence of the term 'commitment' in his text is in quotation marks. In the quoted passage he distinguishes between commitments that are merely incentives and those that are 'strictly binding' or 'irrevocable'.

formalized in marriage, it has a legal aspect.[6] It is surely those aspects of this agreement that may be found particularly intimidating.

Doubtless, the simple fact that one has entered an agreement is an incentive, in some intuitive sense, to conform to the agreement. Yet this is clearly an incentive with a difference. If nothing else, it is something that one *intended* to bring about. One's not having eaten for several days may by no means have been intended: one might be wandering lost in a desert; one might have been thrown into a jail cell and offered no food.

I shall not attempt to provide an account of commitment in general that encompasses all of the uses of the term 'commitment' that one finds in contemporary discourse. Rather, I focus on the kind I take to be involved in joint commitment.

Commitments of the Will

Consider, first, a decision to do something made by a particular human being. Joe, say, decides one morning to go swimming that afternoon. One who makes a *personal decision* of this kind is, I take it, thereby committed in some intuitive sense to do that thing.

To say only this much is to make it clear that a commitment—in the sense in question—does not necessarily involve more than one person, at least in a salient fashion. It also makes clear that it is not a condition of being committed to a certain course of action that one be morally required to perform that action in light of its nature or expected consequences. It may, presumably, be morally indifferent whether or not Joe goes swimming that afternoon. Nor need Joe think otherwise. One may, indeed, be committed to a certain course of action without there being good reasons of any kind for one's preferring that action to all alternatives. Nor need one think there are such reasons in the offing.

In saying this I assume something I take to be intuitive: one's decision need not be the result of any deliberative process, of any weighing of reasons for and against. Of course, Joe may have decided to go swimming because, for instance, he thinks this is the best way for his body to get the exercise it needs. He may explain this decision to his wife in these terms. Equally well, he may say that he decided to go swimming 'for no particular reason'. It seems reasonable to take him at his word. Perhaps the idea just 'popped into his head' and he thought, 'I'll do that!' thereby deciding to do so.

How might one characterize the kind of commitment at issue here? In discussing this I shall refer to Joe as the *subject* of the commitment insofar as

---

[6] I deliberately avoided mentioning *marriage* in representing the core issue since I take that issue not to be a matter of creating a *legal* relation.

he is the one who has it or is subject to it. Joe's commitment appears to be a simple function of his deciding. Can something more general be said about it? I take it that there is an intuitive sense in which a person's making a decision is an exercise of his *will*. The commitment that comes through his decision, then, is the result of such an exercise. It can be done away with in a similar way. Thus one who has decided to do something can, as we say, 'change his mind', and the commitment he accrued through his decision is at an end.

While a personal decision may be characterized as an *act* of will, a personal *intention* may be characterized rather as a *state* of will, or, to use a common philosophical phrase, a conative state.[7] Seeing his friend Maria standing on the corner, Joe might start walking towards her with the intention of getting close enough to talk. He may not at any point have decided to do so, as in the case where he thinks, 'Oh, there's Maria. I'll go and talk to her'. He simply sets off, intending to talk. His intention *forms*, one might say, he does not *form* it. In spite of this distinction between decisions and intentions, the thought that there is a sense in which merely intending to do something commits one to doing it has some plausibility.

With these points in mind, I shall use the technical phrase 'commitment of the will' to refer to a commitment *resulting solely from an act or state of a will or wills*. In creating a *commitment*, I take it that the productive will or wills in question in some sense *bind* the subject of the commitment.

Commitments of the will, as just defined, come in a variety of types. Among other things, there are different levels or grades of commitment, corresponding to different ways in which those who have such a commitment may be said to be bound.

Personal decisions can be argued to be binding in two ways, as I now explain. First, given such a decision, its subject has sufficient reason to act in accordance with it. As I understand this, it means that if one has made a certain decision, and not changed one's mind, and there are no countervailing factors, then rationality requires one to act conformably with one's decision. I argued for it earlier, by reference to an example.[8] In further support of this idea, consider that one might well ask someone why he did not do such-and-such, saying 'I thought you'd decided to do it', the implication being that he had

---

[7] The voluminous philosophical literature on intention often fails to distinguish between intentions and decisions. Exceptions here include Raz (1975); Robins (1984). Here I intend only to set out some points I take to be intuitive. On Robins see Gilbert (1991).

[8] Sect. 2.2, above, where I introduced this sense of 'having sufficient reason' and related phrases. Broome (2001) argues that intentions (which he conceives of much as I conceive of decisions) are not *reasons* but 'normatively require' conforming action. This may allow that they give their possessor sufficient reason, *in my sense*, to conform.

strayed from an apparently requisite course. Some may be inclined to argue that it is not the decision but the reasons assumed to lie behind it that would drive this judgement. On the face of it, however, the decision is what drives it. Indeed, the person speaking may know that 'you' decided on a whim, or made an arbitrary choice among equally justifiable alternatives.

I should emphasize that to say that a personal decision to do A gives one sufficient reason to do A is not to say that doing A, in itself, has anything to be said in its favour absent the decision. Nor does it mean that, given the decision, doing A is somehow transformed to that there is something to be said in its favour given its nature or expected consequences. In sum, to say that one's decision to do A gives one sufficient reason to act in accordance with it is not to say anything about the desirability of action A as such.

One might be said to be *bound*, up to a point, to do something one has sufficient reason to do. All else being equal, this is what rationality *requires* one to do.

What if one decides to do something that, considered apart from one's decision, is a wicked thing to do? There is no clear reason to deny that one's decision, as such, gives one sufficient reason to do the thing in question. To say this is, after all, consistent with the assumption that the action's wickedness counts as a countervailing circumstance. Indeed, if a countervailing circumstance is one that need have no more than an 'equal but opposite' normative force, one might think the circumstance in *this* case will be more than countervailing.[9] To use a standard term, it will at the same time be *overriding*. It is not just that one need not conform to one's decision, all things considered. Rather, one ought not to conform to it, all things considered. For then the action's wickedness has been factored in.

Thus one can allow that Jane's decision to do something wicked gives her sufficient reason to do the thing in question insofar as it is indeed a decision. At the same time one can accept, that, all things considered, she should change her mind or—if that is somehow impossible—simply act against her decision, in order to conform to the dictates of rationality.[10]

The second way in which a decision binds the one who makes it is illustrated by the following example. Suppose Tanya decides at noon that she will phone

[9] In speaking of a factor's 'normative force' here and in what follows I mean to allude to the role of that factor in determining what reason requires one to do. If factor A and factor B are the only relevant factors in a situation, and have an equal but opposite positive normative force, reason will not require one to do A, nor will it require one to do B.

[10] Could one be incapable of *changing one's mind* while at the same time capable of *acting contrary to one's decision*? This seems to be possible as a matter of logic; and many strange things seem to be possible in fact, as in the case of people with specific brain lesions.

Maureen at six o'clock that day. At this point, she has sufficient reason to phone Maureen at six (and hence to plan accordingly). But there is more. Unless at some prior point she rescinds her decision to phone Maureen at six, she still has reason, at six, to phone Maureen then.[11] Likewise, she had reason to phone Maureen at six at all times during the period in between. In the vernacular, she has reason to phone Maureen unless and until she *changes her mind*.

Decisions, then, have a kind of *trans-temporal* reach. They continue to give their subjects reason to conform to them up to the moment of conformity—*provided they are not rescinded at some prior point*. A decision that has been rescinded by its subject no longer has any normative force. Its existence has, if you will, been erased from the record.[12]

In sum, decisions give their subjects sufficient reason to conform to them. In addition, they have what I have referred to as trans-temporal reach. Once established, they stand as guides to action until they are wilfully undone. Thus they may be said to 'bind' their subjects in at least two ways.

What of intentions? One can argue that they bind only in the first sense.[13] The point applies not only to intentions but also, for instance, to cases of trying to do something where one cannot be said precisely to intend to do the thing in question. I take a particular state of the relevant person's will to be an integral part of both trying and intending.

I take it that if I intend to do something I have sufficient reason to do it. In other words, intentions are on a par with decisions in this respect. I do not, however, have to repudiate my intention in order that it cease to give me sufficient reason for action. I may *simply stop* intending to do the thing in question. In contrast, once I have decided to do something I cannot just 'stop deciding'. I have to repudiate my decision or I continue to have sufficient reason to conform to it. In short, a decision calls for repudiation, an intention or striving does not.

In the case of a given intention, my attention may be caught by something else. My intention may switch accordingly. The normative force of the prior intention ends at the time of the switch. In contrast, if I have decided to do something, and not wilfully changed my mind, the fact that I start intending to

---

[11] I take rescission to be a *deliberate* matter, though it need not be preceded by any *deliberation*. One *rescinds* one's decision by (in a more vernacular phrase) changing one's mind. I sometimes use the term 'repudiate' in the same sense.

[12] One might wonder what happens if, some time before six, calling Maureen at six becomes impossible. Does Tanya cease to have sufficient reason to phone Maureen at this point? It is not clear that she does. For to have sufficient reason to do something is for it to be the case that one is required by reason to do that thing, absent countervailing circumstances. Presumably, the impossibility of doing that thing is just such a circumstance.

[13] See Gilbert (2005b).

do something else or attempting to do so does not erase the normative force of the decision. On the contrary, I can be judged to be at fault insofar as I intend to do something that is incompatible with my conformity to a standing decision of mine.

One could stipulate that one has a commitment of the will proper only if one is bound in both of the ways a decision binds, or, indeed, in more ways than this.[14] Rather than making this stipulation, I am allowing that one has a commitment of the will if, simply by virtue of an act or state of one's will, one is bound in the way that is common to decisions, intentions, and efforts: one has sufficient reason to act in a certain way.

This permits me to acknowledge, indeed to emphasize, that there are different grades of commitment of the will. At the same time, it makes clear the connection between a number of things that are close cousins. Note that I have not said *how* it is that decisions, intentions, and efforts bind in the ways they do. Nor, indeed, have I tried to say what decisions and so on amount to. These are important questions, which may be set aside for present purposes. An adequate theory of decisions and so on will somehow accommodate the intuitive points made here.

How do commitments of the will, generally speaking, relate to other considerations in terms of what rationality requires of one who has such a commitment? In particular I have in mind personal inclinations—urges, impulses, and the like—and self-interest. I shall not attempt to reach a firm conclusion on this question, but the following considerations may be noted.

Clearly, commitments of the will can conflict with inclinations. After his conversation with a recruiting officer, Eric may decide not to join the army. He may subsequently find himself strongly tempted to join it. He may then change his mind. As long as he does not change his mind, however, there is at least one thing to stop him from joining the army: his decision not to do so.

Does rationality require one to conform to a standing commitment of the will in face of a contrary inclination? An inclination, urge, and so on, prompts a person to do a thing, at least in the sense of disposing him to do it. This does not yet mean that it gives him sufficient reason to do it. It could give him reason, but not yet sufficient reason. In any case, whatever precisely the status of inclinations, there is some plausibility to the claim that given only a countervailing inclination, as such, rationality requires one to act in accordance with a standing commitment of the will. This is suggested by the way such situations tend to be approached. Suppose Jan has decided to join the peace vigil tonight. Later, however, she finds herself shrinking from doing so: it is

---

[14] On the last possibility, see more later.

so cold outside. Mindful of her decision, she may steel herself to go to the vigil, contrary to her inclination. She may say to herself, 'Well, I did decide to go.' Otherwise, things are likely to go in some such way as this. Jan says, 'I can't bear the thought of going outside—I guess I'll give up the idea of going to the peace vigil.' Here her 'I'll give up the idea' amounts to the rescission of her previous decision. This may be necessary to make right her acting on her inclination.

It may be possible to argue, of specific inclinations, that it would be incumbent upon one, morally speaking, to satisfy them, in spite of a contrary commitment of the will. Perhaps the inclinations are so strong, their object unimpeachable, the personal and social consequences of denying them so grave, that in the circumstances one would be morally required to follow them—and, all things considered, ought to. Then a contrary decision would have more than an inclination, as such, to contend with, in terms of what one had reason to do.

What of self-interest? If one has a standing commitment of the will to the effect that one is not to do something, though it is in one's interest to do it, does reason require that one fulfil one's commitment? Often there is little distinction between the case of inclination and that of self-interest, insofar as one's personal comfort depends on the satisfaction of one's inclinations. At other times there may be a distinction, as when one understands intellectually that it would be useful to have more money, but has no inclination to seek it. Meanwhile it seems that someone might have occasion to say something like this: 'It would be good for me to have more money, but I've decided not to work any more.' This suggests that his decision is, in a word, *decisive*. Once again, it may be possible sometimes to argue that one is morally required to act in one's self-interest in a given case, in spite of a commitment of the will to the contrary. Then more will be at stake against the commitment than self-interest alone.

Focusing on personal decisions as examples, then, there is some plausibility to the view that, to echo Joseph Raz, reason requires one to treat one's standing commitment of the will as *excluding* from consideration one's contrary inclinations or the contrary pull of self-interest as such.[15] Assuming there is no other type of consideration in play, it requires one to act on one's commitment. This may not seem to be of great practical importance in the context of personal decisions and the like because one is in a position to rescind them if one wishes. Nonetheless, if it is true, it means that commitments of the will as such have considerable practical import while they stand.

---

[15] Raz (1975: 35–6 f.) distinguishes a special class of 'exclusionary' reasons.

In discussing commitments in what follows I shall generally have in mind some kind of commitment of the will. I should therefore now be understood to be referring to these when I use the term 'commitment' without qualification.

A personal decision, intention, and so on, gives rise to what may be called a *personal* commitment. By definition, I unilaterally create my personal commitments. I decide, intend, or try to do something, thereby *committing myself*.[16] Further, insofar as it calls for rescission, I can rescind my personal commitment on my own. All I need to do is change my mind.[17] A personal decision 'calls for' rescission: without it, the decision continues to have normative force up till and including the time to carry it out. A personal intention or effort may cease without any act of rescission.[18]

I have focused on the case of a personal decision, in particular, as a way of introducing the general notion of a commitment of the will. It is both a familiar and a relatively simple case and hence apt for the purpose. I should emphasize, however, that I do not mean to imply that a personal decision is the central or paradigm source of a commitment of the will. I am inclined to think that it is not. The type of commitment involved, though stronger than that for an intention or effort, is relatively weak. It remains to be seen what would make it stronger: an answer to that question will emerge when joint commitment is discussed. First, it will be useful to note some intriguing features of the situation in which one fails to conform to a standing personal commitment.

Suppose that, on Election Day, Alice decides to go to the polling station before noon, and does not change her mind about this. She finds, however, that she has put herself in a position where she will not be able to get to the polling station by noon. Having realized what is going on, how might she react? She may well say to herself 'How could you have let it get so late?' at one and the same time chiding herself for, and demanding an explanation of, her tardiness. That she demands an explanation indicates that she understands herself to be *answerable* to herself for any failures in relation to her decision. Failing special background circumstances, she is answerable *only* to herself in relation to such a lapse. Further, Alice may feel she *owed it to herself* to go to the polling station by noon. Her chiding herself may relate to this feeling.

Whether or not she chides herself or demands an explanation for her failure, Alice may feel a sense of self-*betrayal*—a betrayal of self-*trust*. 'Betrayal' may

[16] For some further discussion of what it is unilaterally to create a commitment, see Gilbert (2003: 48).

[17] The phrase 'personal commitment' has been used without this explicit stipulation, as in Farley (1990: *passim*).

[18] *Can* an intention or an effort be rescinded? I shall take it that by deciding against it, one will have rescinded it.

seem too 'big' a word for what has happened in this case. I take it, though, that there can be small betrayals. Phenomenologically they may barely register, yet they may register, nonetheless. If Alice much wanted to carry out this particular decision, the experience of self-betrayal might be quite strong, precipitating other unpleasant feelings such as self-directed anger, even self-hatred. She may then chide herself more harshly than she would have otherwise. She may not, of course. Much will depend on her general character and outlook. For now that is all I shall say about these aspects of the failure to conform to a personal commitment. The points will help to introduce important aspects of those commitments I refer to as *joint*.

7.2 Joint Commitment

The Basic Idea

It is worth repeating that I take the concept of a joint commitment that I shall discuss to be a fundamental *everyday* concept. I am reasonably confident of the broad outlines of the account that follows. At the same time, the topic is a rich one and my understanding of it to date is undoubtedly open to further refinements.[19] Though a number of important aspects of joint commitment will be noted, a very fine-grained discussion is not necessary here. Occasionally, therefore, references to a more extended discussion are given in the footnotes. I start with the basic idea, and focus on the case where a new joint commitment is created for the first time. Similar things can be said, with appropriate changes, of a case where one or more people sign on to a joint commitment originally created by others.[20]

A joint commitment is a kind of commitment of the will. In this case, the wills of two or more people create it, and two or more people are committed by it.

Recall that when I speak of the *subject* of a commitment I mean to refer to the one whose commitment it is, the one who has it. Use of this term is not intended to imply that its referent is or has a single centre of consciousness, or that it has a distinctive form of 'subjectivity'. Nor need the 'one' in question be a single human individual. In the case of a joint commitment, one can properly

---

[19] Most likely much can be learnt from a close study of the law relating to international treaties and domestic contracts in so far as these are at some level perceived as matters of joint commitment. Meanwhile, the law quite properly imports into its judgements moral and other considerations that could move a theory of joint commitment in the wrong direction. Thus informal understandings of non-legal contexts are a crucial resource.

[20] Cf. Gilbert (1989: 219–21).

say that its subject comprises two or more people. The joint commitment is the commitment *of* these people. The joint commitment of James and Paula, for instance, is the commitment *of* these two.

One can also say that these two comprise the *creator* of the commitment, insofar as each plays an essential role in creating it. I later explain how this is done. One way in which it is *not* done is by the creation, on each one's part, of a personal commitment in the sense introduced in the last section. It seems that one can generalize and say that a commitment of the will—a commitment that results solely from an act or state of a will or wills—is such that its creator is its subject. In the case of joint commitment, in particular, those who comprise its creator also comprise its subject.

In what follows, when I refer to the 'parties' to a joint commitment I mean not to differentiate between the (active) role of creator and the (passive) role of subject. Since the creator of a joint commitment is also its subject, it is useful to have such a generic term at one's disposal. The parties to a joint commitment, then, are those who comprise both its creator and its subject.[21]

As will become clear, two importantly different kinds of case meet the condition that all of the parties must be involved in the creation of a joint commitment.[22] All of the parties must also be involved in its rescission. This allows for a situation in which one party explicitly concedes the rescission of their joint commitment to another, either at the time of its creation or at some later point. In effect, the conceding party offers his own participation in its rescission in advance. It also allows for a case like the following. Peter and Johan are jointly committed in some way; Johan acts contrary to the commitment in a manner that leaves no doubt that he is not interested in sustaining it. One might want to say that this leaves it open to Peter to rescind the commitment. Here it could be argued that Johan has already done his part in its rescission, though it is still in force. If there are more than two people involved, the contrary action of one, however wilful, will not allow any of the others *unilaterally* to rescind their joint commitment. They will need to rescind it together.

Does a joint commitment always call for rescission or can it be ended prior to its fulfilment without it? That is a good question and the answer is, I suggest, twofold. Depending on their mode of creation, some joint commitments require rescission (as do personal decisions), others do not but are open to it (as with personal intentions). I take the point that joint commitments cannot be

---

[21] Cf. Rousseau's distinction in the political realm between the body politic (neutral), the sovereign (active), and the state (passive). See Rousseau (1983: bk. I, ch. 6, pp. 24–5).

[22] See the distinction between basic and non-basic cases in the text below.

unilaterally rescinded to stand for both types. As to which joint commitments require rescinding, it will be best to consider these after something has been said on the way in which such commitments can be created. How do joint commitments bind? Are there differences of type here too? It is plausible to suggest that there are. Discussion of this point is also best left till after more has been said on other matters.

Associated Individual Commitments

Though no one of them independently constitutes the subject of their joint commitment each of the committed persons is committed through it. Each is bound at least in the way in which a personal intention binds its subject: each has sufficient reason to act in a certain way. Bearing this in mind, one might speak of the parties' derived or associated 'individual commitments'.

As to the content of these associated commitments, each is committed to promoting the object of the joint commitment, in conjunction with the other parties, to the best of his or her ability. In order to fulfil his associated commitment it may be necessary for each to attempt to find out what the others are doing or, where that is possible, to discuss and perhaps negotiate with them who is to do what. I discuss the object of a joint commitment—what it is a commitment to do—shortly.

The associated individual commitments referred to here are not *personal* commitments as I have defined these. In particular, they are not the unilateral creation of the respective persons and they cannot be unilaterally rescinded. One party can, of course, deliberately act contrary to a standing joint commitment. What is done in that case amounts precisely to a violation of both the joint commitment and the associated individual one, as each party will understand.

Individual commitments of the kind associated with a joint commitment, are *interdependent*: there cannot be a single such commitment, deriving from a given joint commitment, in the absence of any other such commitments. The derived commitments of those creating a joint commitment *de novo* come into being simultaneously—at the time of the creation of the joint commitment. In a two-person case, simultaneity logically follows from interdependence, though not conversely.

The General Form of a Joint Commitment

Joint commitments all have the same general form. People may jointly commit to accepting, as a body, a certain goal. They may jointly commit to intending, as a body, to do such-and-such. They may jointly commit to believing, or accepting, as a body, that such-and-such. And so on. The general form of a joint commitment, then, is this: the parties jointly commit to X *as a body*. Different joint commitments involve different substitutions for 'X'.

What is the force of the qualifier 'as a body' in the above statement of the general form of a joint commitment? It is best to start with an example. Take the case, then, of a joint commitment to believe as a body that democracy is the best form of government. This can be parsed as follows: the parties are jointly committed *together to constitute, as far as is possible, a single body* that believes democracy is the best form of government. This constitution of a single body with the belief in question will be achieved by a suitable concordance of the several actions and expressions of the individual parties. Suppose there is a community in which the members are jointly committed in this way. When they encounter one another, they will conform to their commitment by saying things that imply that democracy is the best form of government and avoiding saying things that imply the opposite. They will not bluntly agree with anyone, from the group or from outside it, who speaks ill of democracy. To all intents and purposes, they will function as would the several 'mouths' of a single body with the belief in question. Evidently, they may on occasion say nothing that bears on democracy at all.

The idea of a 'single body' invoked above is not itself the idea of a *body of persons*, that is, of something with a plurality of members. An individual human being is a clear instance of a 'single body', or, as might have been said, a single person. A joint commitment to believe something as a body, then, is a commitment to constitute as far as possible a single body that believes that thing, where the concept of a 'single body' is negative with respect to the question whether the body at issue is in some sense composed of individual human beings.

It is worth emphasizing that a joint commitment to believe that such-and-such as a body does not—as I understand it—require the parties to the commitment personally to believe anything. The commitment is, after all, together to constitute, as far as is possible, a single body that believes that such-and-such. None of the individuals in question is that body. It is reasonable, then, to deny that their personal beliefs are in question.[23]

Though this is so, those conforming to such a commitment will often appear themselves to have the belief at issue. That one did not would come out clearly if he said something like 'In my personal opinion, democracy is not the best form of government'. Though someone who says such a thing may be viewed with some suspicion, the use of this preamble would enable him to avoid falling foul of the joint commitment itself.

---

[23] For more on this see Gilbert (1987, 1989, and, more recently, 2002d and elsewhere).

A joint commitment to accept as a body a certain goal will have the very same logic as that just described. It does not require the participants to have any particular personal goal. Each is required, rather, to act as the member of a single body with the goal in question. That may involve, to a large extent, acting as if one personally wanted the goal to be achieved by virtue of the activity of each of the members. One's personal goals, however, are not at issue. One must simply do what one can, in conjunction with the others, to achieve the goal.

The goal we are jointly committed to accept may be specified in 'neutral' terms, in the sense that it can in principle be achieved by one person acting alone or by a body of persons, or it may be specified in 'non-neutral' terms, in the sense that it can only be achieved by two or more persons. A neutral specification is 'going for a walk'. If we are jointly committed to accept as a body the goal of going for a walk, we understand that this goal will be achieved by our constituting as far as is possible a single body that goes for a walk. A non-neutral specification is 'playing a duet' or, indeed, 'sharing a walk'. If we are jointly committed to accept as a body the goal of playing a duet, or sharing a walk, we understand that the satisfaction of this goal involves each of us acting in such a way as to constitute a single instance of duet-playing or the sharing of a walk.

It is cumbersome at all times to write of people being jointly committed to *espouse as a body the goal of going for a walk*, and so on. I shall not be concerned always to spell things out in this long-winded way. Rather, I may write simply of a joint commitment *to go for a walk*, and so on.

How Joint Commitments are Formed

So far I have noted only that all of the parties must be involved in the creation of a joint commitment. I have not yet addressed the means by which such a commitment is created. Two central, very general points are as follows.

First, such creation involves a kind of expressive behaviour on the part of the would-be parties. In each case, each one's expressive behaviour is an expression of readiness *for joint commitment*: each understands what a joint commitment is, and expresses all that is needed on his or her part to bring such a commitment into being, namely, readiness to be jointly committed in the way in question.[24]

Second, the existence of the relevant expressive behaviour must be common knowledge among the parties. To repeat the rough and informal account of common knowledge presented earlier: if some fact is common knowledge

---

[24] For an extended discussion of what is *not* involved, contrary to the assumptions of some authors on the basis of earlier ways in which I expressed the point, see Gilbert (2003: 51–5).

between A and B (or among members of population P, described by reference to some common attribute), that fact is entirely out in the open between (or among) them, and, at some level, all are aware that this is so.

Should James have his deaf ear turned to Paula when she expresses her readiness to go for a walk with him, she will have expressed her readiness, but not in conditions of common knowledge, for James will not have heard her and so will not know she has done so. Such an expression of readiness cannot play the appropriate role in joint commitment formation. That is not to say that each party to a joint commitment must have been *directly aware* of each party's expression of readiness. Though this may happen and, I take it, often does, it is not essential. I leave further discussion on this point till later.

Though one must know what a joint commitment is in order to enter such a commitment, this does not mean, of course, that the phrase 'joint commitment' is part of one's vocabulary. According to my proposal about walking together, one knows what a joint commitment is if one knows what it is to go for a walk with another person, since one goes for a walk with another person only if he and that other person are party to a particular joint commitment. One need not be able to spell things out. The same is true, I take it, of many other common bits of knowledge.

Expressions of readiness for joint commitment may take various forms. When a joint commitment to endorse a certain goal as a body is at issue, these correspond to those contexts in which people come to be doing something together, some of which were adumbrated in the last chapter. They include but are not limited to what would count as everyday agreements, as when Bill says to Claire, 'Shall we work on our taxes tonight?' and Claire responds 'Yes'. For one who enters an agreement with another person to engage in some joint action is plausibly construed as expressing his readiness jointly to commit to performing that action as a body.

From the case of agreements there will be a spectrum of cases, some more agreement-like than others, in which expressions of readiness to be jointly committed in some way are made. They will include cases of expressing one's readiness for joint commitment by manifesting it in action. For instance, three people are running towards the scene of an accident, apparently jointly committed to espousing as a body the goal of helping the victims. Lee, a bystander, works out what is happening, moves towards them, and begins running with them, joining in the conversation as to 'I wonder how bad it is' and 'it's a shame none of us is a doctor'. Lee thus expresses his readiness to jointly commit with the others to helping the victims. They may reciprocate by treating his references to the four of them as 'us' without demur, and, indeed, by including him in the scope of their own references to 'us', as when one of the runners exclaims, turning to him, 'We need to hurry—can you run a bit faster?' At no time did the original three make an agreement with the former bystander. I say more about uses of the first-person plural pronoun shortly.

The original three in the above example could have agreed to try to help the accident victims. They might not have, however. Hearing a loud crash, one could have said 'I'm going over there!' and the others could have followed, keeping up with him and talking in much the way that the bystander does later.

That readiness for a given joint commitment is being expressed may emerge gradually, over time, and the joint commitment itself may relate not to a single episode, like doing something on a particular night or helping some accident victims. Thus two like-minded factory workers might find themselves chatting about the state of the nation for a few moments outside the factory one evening. After this has happened a few times, one might conclude their chat by saying 'Talk to you tomorrow', and the other may concur. If that happens a few times, it may become unnecessary to say anything. A joint commitment to endorse as a body the practice of chatting about politics after work may have been established. These people have, if you like, fallen into this practice. They have not set the *practice* up by agreement, even if they made one or two agreements on specific meetings along the way.

Basic and Non-basic Cases

It is important to distinguish what I shall call basic and non-basic cases of joint commitment. In the *basic* case, a joint commitment of the parties to the effect that they are to do a certain thing as a body is formed by virtue of the parties' expressions of readiness to be jointly committed *to do that thing* as a body. For instance, in conditions of common knowledge, Joan expresses to Rico and Paul her readiness to be jointly committed with them to espouse as a body the goal of forming a Green party, and they do likewise. One might think that all cases must be of this kind, but that is not so.

It is possible for people to be jointly committed to espouse a certain goal as a body, for instance, without having mutually expressed their readiness to uphold *that particular goal* as a body. That this is so is particularly important for the argument of this book.

An example of the kind of case I have in mind—a case of *non-basic* or derived joint commitment—is the following. Pam and Penny have mutually expressed their readiness jointly to commit to accepting as a body that Penny may decide what they will do on weekends without any consultation with Pam. That this is their situation may come out in such conversations as the following. Gunnar asks Pam what she and Penny are doing the following weekend. Pam turns to Penny and asks her, 'What are we doing next weekend?' She takes it that this has already have been determined, though she does not herself know how it has been determined. She may not yet have contemplated the goal in question. She believes, however, that she and Penny are jointly committed to espouse it as a body, their joint commitment deriving from a prior joint commitment of the basic kind.

Note that what is essentially at issue here is this. Each of the parties has expressed her personal readiness to be jointly committed to espousing whatever goal is specified by the operations of a specified mechanism. In this case, that mechanism is Penny's say-so. Here, then, one party to the basic joint commitment, determines the content of certain non-basic commitments and is, indeed, aware of that content. Neither of these things need be so, however. Thus, for example, the members of a certain population—who have perhaps a basic joint commitment to uphold the goal of winning a certain war—may also have a basic joint commitment to espouse as a body whatever war plan will be indicated, according to certain rules, by the occurrence or non-occurrence of some natural phenomenon involving none of them. In this way they may come to be jointly committed to a plan of which none of them are yet aware, since the phenomenon in question has occurred though they have not yet discovered this.[25]

How to be Freed from a Joint Commitment

How can one be freed from a joint commitment? Consider first basic joint commitments whose genesis is an agreement. It is plausible to suppose that these require to be rescinded if they are to come to an end prior to their fulfilment. Otherwise their normative force will survive. Rescission is a deliberate, explicit cancellation of the joint commitment. The obvious way to do this is by means of an agreement. For example, Geoff says to Kate: 'Let's not do this anymore!' and Kate says 'That's fine by me!'

This case is clearly analogous to that of a personal decision whose associated personal commitment is only removable in advance of its satisfaction by an act of the will of its subject designed for the purpose, as is expressed by 'No, I shan't do that after all!' There may be joint commitments initiated by something sufficiently close to an agreement that their conclusion also requires something that amounts to rescission.

Be that as it may, it is plausible to suppose that there is also an analogue of personal intention in the realm of joint commitment. Recall how it is

---

[25] The case where one party hands over to another (or others) a specific range of decisions as to what the parties are to do—providing for a multiplicity of non-basic joint commitments—should be distinguished from the case discussed earlier where one party hands the other (or others) the decision when to end a given joint commitment.

with a personal intention, which, like a decision, involves a form of personal commitment. A personal intention can be repudiated but need not be. Prior to its satisfaction, it can simply stop, or change. For an example of how a joint commitment comes to an end without a deliberate joint act of rescinding, we can go back to the case of the factory workers who developed the practice of discussing politics for a while when their workday had ended. One day Tom, one of the factory workers, comes to their usual meeting place and tells Fay, the other, that he can't stop to chat that day. She says 'That's okay.' The next day he says the same, and so does she. The following day, she shows up, but he doesn't. The day after that, she shows up again, and once again, he's not there. She considers that he is sending her a message—voting with his feet. The following day they run into each other as they are coming out of the factory building. She gives him a curt but not unfriendly nod, which he acknowledges. It would be stretching things for either of them to say, at this point, 'We agreed not to go on meeting after work'. Yet each could confidently aver that their practice of meeting after work was at an end. This case provides an analogue of the personal intention that comes to an end without being repudiated. Evidently there can be similar cases involving larger numbers of people and a more extended process of disintegration.

One joint commitment may be replaced by another as the result of distraction by an external stimulus, as a personal intention may. Consider the following case. A band of hunters from an ancient tribe has been ambling along in the forest. The members of the band are jointly committed to killing a deer for food. A small deer crosses their path in the distance and goes off to the left. Massing together, the hunters immediately run to the left in pursuit of the deer. By entering this formation each indicates to all his readiness jointly to commit with them to kill this particular deer. They are now jointly so committed. Suddenly another deer, a large one, appears. It is running in the opposite direction to the first. The hunters immediately change course. They are now jointly committed to espousing the goal of killing a different deer, the large one. Did they rescind their prior commitment? It seems not. There may have been nothing approaching an agreement to change course. When the large deer hove into view they changed course, as one, and a new joint commitment was thereby established. This new commitment came into being just as the previous one did, without agreement or other preamble. At one and the same time the previous one was extinguished, without any explicit rescission.

So far I have touched on three ways in which one may be freed of a given joint commitment of the basic kind. To give them labels, there is, first, *satisfaction*: the commitment may be fully satisfied, so no one has anything more to do as far as it is concerned. Then there is *rescission*, which cannot be unilateral.

The parties together rescind the commitment. Third, there is what one might call, for want of a better term, *fade-out*: Here rescission is not necessary for the commitment to come to an end before fulfilment. Nonetheless, in the paradigm case, all the parties are involved. Whether by a gradual process or all at once, whether through verbal exchanges or not, the demise of the commitment is the work of them all, as is common knowledge. To use a word intended to cover both rescission and fade-out, a joint commitment must be *terminated jointly*.

What of violation or, in other terms, failure to conform to a joint commitment to which one is a party? Precisely what results from it depends on the details of the case. Generally speaking, however, it will not cancel the commitment. Violation may be inadvertent, or it may be wilful. In the latter case it may sometimes be reasonable for the other parties to take it as an expression of readiness for joint termination of the commitment. Then it will be up to them to decide whether or not to terminate the commitment. They may have little option in the matter if one's default renders their own conformity either pointless or impossible. Thus, if Isaac is the only one who knows where Jackie lives, and he walks out on us, our plan of walking to Jackie's house may have to be put on hold. Violation in some two-person cases is somewhat special, not so much in terms of where it leaves the violator, but in terms of where it leaves the other party. I set aside this aspect of the matter for now.[26]

There are at least two ways of being freed from a joint commitment that do not have to involve the conclusion of the commitment—or of oneself. These correspond to the ways of exiting a joint activity without the concurrence of the other parties that were noted in the previous chapter.

One may be party to a joint commitment as this or that particular person (Joe, Jane, or whoever), or as someone with a particular feature (residing along the coast between the estuary and the mountain, and so on). One who is committed in this latter way will be freed of the commitment if and when he ceases to have the feature in question. Thus I may be jointly committed with the others in the auditorium, as such, to keep the room quiet enough for the speaker to be heard. There is nothing in this commitment that requires me to stay in the auditorium, however. If I slip out quietly at some point I free myself from the commitment without violating it. I am free simply by virtue of my loss of the feature in terms of which I was committed.

The feature in question need not be so obvious as one's physical location. Suppose that at the end of a long day some weary colleagues jointly commit to go to a town meeting. It has not been important to anyone, as is understood,

---

[26] As discussed in Ch. 10, below, it is highly germane to our understanding of agreements.

that any given colleague be part of this group. Each has put himself forward as having some degree of interest in attending the meeting. The somewhat ragged assembly starts moving towards the town hall. Nancy, who is at the tail end, suddenly loses interest in the venture. It seems that she might quite legitimately slip away from the others. She might attempt to tell someone what has happened, as a matter of politeness, but it is not clear that is called for. Nancy is unlikely to be seen as violating the joint commitment or, more complexly, attempting by her violation to express her readiness to participate in its rescinding. What she is doing is more likely to be seen as manifesting her loss of those properties that, so to speak, anchored the joint commitment in her person. She is, in other words, manifesting her freedom from the joint commitment. If someone notices she has gone, they may say, curiously, 'What happened to Nancy?', but it is unlikely that anyone will feel any sense of offence, or that a sense of offence would be appropriate.

Precisely what the situation is in an actual case may be a matter of subtle contextual clues and applicable private or societal conventions. Suffice it to say, here, that if one enters a joint commitment not simply as oneself, but rather as someone with some relevant feature or features, then, all else being equal, one's loss of those features will free one from the commitment.

Even those committed 'as themselves' may be freed without the demise of the commitment to which they are subject. They may fail to satisfy a presupposition or condition for their own subjection to the commitment. Sometimes such conditions may be explicitly specified. Thus at the foot of a steep incline an experienced climber might say to an anxious novice, 'You don't need to go any further than your comfort allows'. If the novice starts getting nervous, he is freed from their joint commitment to scale the incline. His 'I'm getting nervous now' will make it plain that he has been so freed. Such presuppositions or conditions may be a matter of background conventions with respect to particular forms of joint commitment. They may also be introduced ad hoc, most likely explicitly.

In what follows, when I write of the situation of the participants in or parties to a joint commitment, I should generally be understood to refer to those for whom all presuppositions and conditions are fulfilled and who are not in a position to manifest their freedom because they are not free of any features by virtue of which they are involved in the commitment.

Plural Subjects

It is useful to have a label for those who are jointly committed with one another in some way. I have elsewhere used the label 'plural subject' for the purpose and shall use it that way here. To put it somewhat formally: A and

B (and . . .) (or those with feature F) constitute a *plural subject* (by definition) if and only if they are jointly committed to doing something as a body—in a broad sense of 'do'.

I argued at length in *On Social Facts* that a standard use of the English first-person plural pronoun is to refer to a plural subject of some kind. Of course, this pronoun is often used not to refer to a plural subject but rather to refer to certain individuals—who may (at the same time) be conceived of as members of a plural subject. This usage is often appropriately marked as in the use of the phrases 'We all . . .', 'Both of us . . .', and so on. Thus an executive may say to an inspirational speaker who has visited his boardroom 'We were all inspired by your talk'. Or one member of a couple may say to a dear friend, 'We are both so concerned about you'. In many contexts, however, 'We' are said to think, feel, or do something without there being any implicit 'all' or 'both'. If Claire says of herself and her husband, Bill, 'We intend to work on our taxes tonight', she may deny that this is shorthand for 'We both personally intend to work on our taxes tonight' or, indeed, that it is shorthand for any statement of the form 'We both personally intend . . .'.

I argued, in effect, that there is good reason to think that what Claire says is best understood as a reference to what Claire and Bill are jointly committed to intend as a body. That, quite generally, is how to construe references to what *we* intend or, to use a more technical term, what we *collectively* intend. More generally still, sentences of the form 'We . . .' where the blank is filled with any broadly speaking psychological predicate, and where the insertion of 'all' or 'both' after 'we' is not accepted, are best interpreted as referring to a plural subject—'us'. In other words, there is good reason to think that the ascription of psychological attributes to populations of more than one person in everyday speech is commonly interpreted in plural subject terms. Further examples include 'We believe that . . .', 'We value . . .', 'We feel remorse over . . .', 'We accept this rule'.[27]

This would help to explain a number of observations in relation to the use of the words 'we', 'us', and so on. Well known to some is the unexpected, disassociating response Tonto gives the Lone Ranger, who considers Tonto his associate: ' "*We*", white man?' Transition to—or from—the use of 'we', is often noticed as an important move in relationships both public and private.

---

[27] See Gilbert (1989: ch. 5 and elsewhere) on 'We believe'; Gilbert (2005a) on 'We value', and Gilbert (2000: ch. 7) on 'We feel remorse over'. On, in effect, 'We accept this rule', see Ch. 10, below. This case merits an extended discussion here in view of its special relevance to political societies.

Someone may urge her partner to speak in terms of 'we' rather than 'I', hoping thereby to consolidate his sense of partnership.[28] Politicians may make sure to refer to those they address, inclusively, as 'we'. The use of this little word has been cherished and abhorred, derided and embraced, in the context of both personal and political relationships. A plural subject interpretation goes a long way to explain these kinds of reactions.[29] In the next chapter I argue for a conception of social groups as plural subjects. First, I return to the case I have been focusing on: two people out on a walk together.

7.3 Acting Together

What is it for a goal to be ours? At the end of the last chapter, I proposed that for two or more people to have a collective goal or, in other terms, for them collectively to espouse a goal, is for them to be jointly committed to espouse a goal as a body. Now that I have explained the key technical terms of this proposal, it should be a good deal clearer. Evidently, when people have a collective goal, on this account, the underlying joint commitment gives each sufficient reason to direct his forces in a particular way. More precisely, each has sufficient reason to coordinate his behaviour with that of the others in pursuit of the goal in question.[30]

A general account of acting together can now be proposed. This puts a collective goal at the centre of the account, which runs as follows: Two or more people are acting together (doing something together) if and only if: (1) they are jointly committed to espousing as a body the appropriate goal; (2) they are fulfilling the behavioural conditions associated with the achievement of that goal; (3) their satisfaction of these conditions is motivated in each case by the existence of the joint commitment. I have focused on an account of walking together as an example of acting together. The plural subject account of walking together will conform to the above schema, with appropriate substitutions.

Going back now to the discussion of how people come to be acting together, I proposed as a preliminary answer that each party must *express something* to the others, something that is expressive of readiness to participate in the joint action. The proposed account of acting together suggests that what must be expressed is, in effect, *a readiness to enter a joint commitment to espouse a certain goal as a body.* As discussed earlier, this subsumes a wide variety of

---

[28] Cf. the restaurant case in Gilbert (1989: 175–7).
[29] See also Gilbert (1996: ch. 8) ('Fusion: sketch of a "contractual" model').
[30] Cf. Gilbert (1997*b*).

contexts in which joint action gets going, from agreements and other contexts involving some kind of anticipatory preamble, to cases where people fall into the joint activity.

A crucial question for the assessment of this account remains to be addressed. Recall the range of phenomena intimately associated with walking together that were noted at the outset of this discussion: the standing to make demands of and utter rebukes to the other parties. Recall, too, the fact that were each to have a right against each to his performance of appropriate actions, the existence of this standing would be well explained, as would the phenomena that come under the heading of the concurrence condition. Can the proposed account of acting together account for all of these observations? I argue in the next section that it can. The implications of this argument are considerable.

7.4 Joint Commitment and Obligation

The Explanatory Power of Joint Commitment

If a phenomenon has a joint commitment at its core, that is immensely consequential. Importantly, the consequences I have in mind would not be provided by a suitable conjunction of personal commitments. With respect to a joint commitment, as I shall show, it is possible to argue as follows. By virtue of the existence of the commitment, and that alone, the parties have rights against each other to actions that conform to the commitment. As a result, they have the standing to demand such actions of each other and to rebuke each other for not so acting.

To repeat a point made before, that is not to say that their making such demands or issuing such rebukes is always *justified*, all things considered. Indeed, it is not to say that it is ever justified, under any circumstances.[31] To say that someone has the standing to do something means simply that he is in a position to do it. If someone lacks the standing to do it, the question whether he is justified in doing it does not arise. For he *cannot* do it. One who lacks the standing to make a certain demand or issue a certain rebuke can, of course, utter a purported rebuke or make a purported demand. He can speak in a rebuking or demanding tone. His target, meanwhile, may have little interest in this if it is possible to question his standing actually to rebuke or demand. His target may well respond in some such words as these: 'It's none of your business, so . . . forget it!' Thus, *standing matters* if only in terms of one's efficacy in securing the desired outcome.

---

[31] Those who are jointly committed, however, may be argued to have a case for rebuking those who violate the commitment. See the text below.

If one of the parties wishes to act contrary to the joint commitment, he can do so without fault only if the other parties have, in effect, waived their rights to conforming action, or, in other words, concurred with his decision not to conform. These rights are relatively stable. Absent special background understandings, no one can unilaterally get rid of the joint commitment itself, thus getting rid of the rights against himself that it brings with it.

In short, if there is a joint commitment at the core of any instance of acting together, the observations made in the previous chapter would all be accounted for. In particular, the phenomena that would be explained by various rights of the parties are explained, and this is done, indeed, by reference to rights of each against each that are grounded in the joint commitment.

Observations on joint action include more pleasant concomitants than those on which I have focused. I have in mind such things as attempts to help the other parties to keep up, offers to slow down, gentle enquiries as to whether anything is wrong, and the like. These are commonly observed in the context of joint action and, indeed, the parties may rebuke one another for their absence, or scoff at one who omits them behind his back. Such helpful behaviour can also be explained by reference to an underlying joint commitment. Helpful behaviour may be more likely when the parties have some degree of care and concern for one another. Insofar as it is the best means to keep the joint action on track, however, it is not necessary to posit such feelings in explanation of it, given an underlying joint commitment to espouse a certain goal as a body.

The last point also relates to the presence of those less pleasant concomitants of joint action, the rebukes and demands that actually occur. Though I have focused on the beliefs of the parties as to their standing in relation to one another, actual rebukes and demands are also observed in the context of joint action. The presence of an appropriate joint commitment, would both provide the parties with the *standing* to rebuke, and so on, and help to explain the *occurrence* of such rebukes as well as the kinder, gentler reactions just mentioned.

To see this, recall the general form of a joint commitment: one is party to a joint commitment to constitute with others as far as is possible a body of some kind. In order to act accordingly one may need to do more than act in a certain way oneself. That will depend on whether or not others will fall by the wayside unless one does something to spur them on to do their parts as well. One needs, in short, to see to it, as best one can, that the other parties fall into line. As long as there are no countervailing reasons that mandate or allow that one may act otherwise, and assuming that a rebuke is the best means of spurring another on to better conformity with the commitment, one has sufficient reason to issue such a rebuke. This will presumably often explain why people issue rebukes and engage in the other kinds of behaviour noted, given their knowledge that they have the standing to do so.

What, then, of that standing? I turn now to the association of joint commitment with rights to conformity. It may strike one as obvious that if James and Paula, say, are jointly committed in some way, then they have rights against each other—and corresponding obligations towards each other. In particular, James has a right to Paula's conforming action, and Paula is under a corresponding obligation to James, an obligation to conform to the joint commitment. It may seem obvious, too, that it is the jointness of the commitment that brings this about. These points may be made without reference to any articulated understanding of the nature of rights and obligations. This was my own original reaction to the idea of a joint commitment.[32]

For others, specific understandings of the nature of rights and obligations may get in the way of granting this point. I am not saying that these understandings are wrong, which would be to deny that there are rights and obligations in the senses in question. Rather, I am saying that these particular understandings are not at issue here. To have those understandings at the forefront of one's mind, then, is to make oneself less receptive to the points to be made. It is better to approach them by setting aside one's assumptions about the nature of rights and obligations, and, in particular, obligations other than directed obligations.

The Jointness of Joint Commitment is Key

It is not hard to argue that, by virtue of his involvement in a joint commitment with Paula, and that alone, James gains a *special standing* with respect to Paula's actions, and vice versa. The emphasis here is on the *jointness* of the commitment rather than the fact that each party is committed through it. I shall note four significant aspects of this standing, all of which can be brought out by reference to a comparison with the situation where one has made a personal decision. The fourth will bring us specifically to rights and obligations.

i. Betrayal   Consider first the idea, mooted in my discussion of a personal decision and the personal commitment it produces, that one who acts contrary to a standing personal decision may experience a sense of self-betrayal. I noted that 'betrayal' may seem to be too big a word in some cases, but argued that a sense of betrayal may be quite mild, though it is likely to be at least somewhat unpleasant.

---

[32] In Gilbert (1989), I took the connection to be obvious and did not make a serious attempt to explain it. I focus on it in Gilbert (1999a, also 1993a). The present discussion both builds on and extends that material.

Now one may think, reasonably enough, that the primary or central case of betrayal involves more than one person. That is, one person betrays another, or several others. This is not to decry as illusory or unintelligible a sense of self-betrayal through one's failure to act as one decided. It is, rather, to suggest that the intrapersonal case is, for whatever reason, not the paradigm.

I suggest that a joint commitment is the clearest possible context for interpersonal betrayal. If Deb fails to conform to a joint commitment she is party to with George she has—to some extent—betrayed him. She would betray many people at once should she fail to conform to a joint commitment she is party to with many others. In contrast, failing special circumstances, no one else need be implicated if Deb fails to carry out a personal decision of her own. In particular, she need not have betrayed any other person.[33]

The details of a joint commitment may be expected to affect whether or not a sense of betrayal becomes psychologically salient. I have in mind, in particular, an informal analogue of the legal idea of 'fundamental breach'. [34] Suppose Nan and Felicity are jointly committed to love and cherish each other till death parts them. They may have made an explicit agreement to that effect. Conformity to their commitment will, evidently, involve countless acts and omissions throughout the lives of the parties. Precisely what 'loving and cherishing' amounts to is open to interpretation. Suppose, though, that Nan and Felicity are of one mind on that, and this is common knowledge between them. Suppose now that Nan, feeling irritated, speaks a little roughly to Felicity one morning. Were they to consider the matter the parties might judge that Nan has violated their commitment, but not in a fundamental way. Felicity's reaction may be so muted it barely registers in her conscious mind. Suppose that after this Nan commences verbally to abuse Felicity and finally hits her hard across the face. Here they may well judge that there has been a fundamental violation of their joint commitment—and here, presumably, Felicity is most likely to experience a full-blooded sense of betrayal.[35]

Note that in the context described Nan may feel that she has betrayed not only Felicity but also *herself* in hitting Felicity across the face. She may not feel

---

[33] One's having promised someone else that one would not make that decision would be a 'special circumstance'. I argue that promises are joint commitment phenomena later in this book.

[34] For a fine-grained legal essay on fundamental breach whose conception of 'dependent promises' approaches the conception of informal agreements as joint commitment phenomena advanced in Ch. 10, below, see Dawson (1975).

[35] As will emerge, this point can be brought to bear on the distinction in political societies between behaviour that is judged to be treasonable and other behaviour that is not supportive of the political institutions in question.

this while 'in the act' but, once her fury has waned, she may wonder at herself like one betrayed: 'How could I have done that to Felicity?'[36] There could be many reasons for her thinking a thought so expressible, but a sufficient reason would be her violation of their joint commitment.

In the context of a joint commitment one betrays whomever one betrays in their capacity as participants with oneself in the joint commitment in question. This is another way of saying that the commitment is the ground of the betrayal. It is not that *I* did this to *you* that is the issue—though one could express oneself in such terms—it is that I did this to you *in face of our joint commitment*, which required that I not do it. One can assume that Felicity would have reason to *judge Nan adversely* for hitting her across the face even if this did not violate a joint commitment of theirs. The joint commitment gives her reason to feel *betrayed*—in her capacity as a party to that commitment.

This means that what one does may be felt—and count—as a betrayal irrespective of the various parties' personal desires in the matter. Thus suppose that Jacob and his sister Jill (a computer whizz) are jointly committed to meet on Tuesday evenings to help Jacob improve his computing skills. Jacob is quite uncomfortable with computers and is not looking forward to this evening's meeting. Suppose now that Jill arrives full of talk about the upcoming elections. She ends up failing to spend any time helping Jacob with the computer before she has to leave, in spite of his prompting. At one level Jacob may be quite relieved. Yet he could experience a sense of betrayal as well. After all, the joint commitment he and Jill were party to has been violated, and egregiously at that. He could express his concern, while there is still time to do so, in a relatively impersonal fashion such as: 'What about our computing project?' Similarly Nan, in the previous example, could say, 'Is this what we planned? Is this loving and cherishing . . . ?'[37]

Reactions of the project-focused or more generally *impersonal* type are predictable in the case of a large-scale joint commitment among persons with a specific common feature, where many of the parties are not even known to each other personally. I argue for the possibility of such large-scale commitments in the next chapter. The points made in this chapter apply to joint commitments generally.

---

[36] Here I echo Wordsworth (1982: Act III, scene 1): 'Action is transitory—a step, a blow, | the motion of a muscle, this way or that.—| 'Tis done, and in the after-vacancy, | we wonder at ourselves like men betrayed'. Wordsworth's use of 'like' here suggests that paradigmatic betrayal, in his eyes, involves more than one person.

[37] The last two paragraphs respond to a query (and example) from John Horton (personal communication, 2004).

The example of Nan and Felicity suggests an important question about joint commitments generally. Does any joint commitment, irrespective of its content, require a certain level of care from the parties towards each other? I shall not attempt to probe this question here.[38] In general terms at least the following would seem to be true: those with a joint aim, for instance, are required to behave in a caring manner towards each other to the extent that this is necessary to promote their joint aim. One must bear in mind, however, that people may make (distasteful) joint commitments that either enjoin or allow one person's suffering at the hands of another party or parties.[39]

The form of the examples in this section should not obscure the fact that betrayal in the context of a joint commitment may involve behaviour towards parties other than the betrayed. Marital infidelity, one paradigm of betrayal, may fit in here. Treason, another such paradigm, may do so as well. By this, I mean that an underlying joint commitment may be involved in both of these cases. Betrayal in the context of a joint commitment may also involve a solitary act, such as taking an alcoholic drink in private when the parties are jointly committed to achieving each party's long term sobriety.

The central point for present purposes is this. Given that a sense of betrayal is appropriate in the context of a joint commitment, such a commitment clearly gives the parties a special standing in relation to one another's actions. There are certain actions that one party can only perform at the cost of betraying the other party.

ii. Trust Corresponding to the previous point is one about trust. There is a central type of trust such that it makes no sense to say that you trust someone unless certain background conditions obtain. One who says that they 'trust so-and-so' to do something when those conditions do not obtain is speaking in 'as if' mode, and this may be understood.

If anyone is *in a position* to trust another person to do something, one who is party to a joint commitment is in that position in relation to the other parties' conformity to the commitment. Evidently, that is not to say that they are necessarily justified in trusting the others, all things considered. That will depend on what they know or can reasonably assume about the character, temperament, and, in short, trustworthiness of each.

One reason for saying this is the following. If I am not in a position to trust you to do something, you cannot betray me when you fail to do it. You can surprise me, disappoint me, wound me, but you cannot betray me. Whatever lays me open to betrayal legitimates my trust (as opposed to justifying it).

---

[38] It recurs, in another guise, in Ch. 11, below.   [39] Cf. Gilbert (1996: 220).

Betrayal, one might say, is the dark side of trust. Nothing has been said yet about *why* a sense of betrayal is intuitively in place in the case of a personal decision, on the one hand, and joint commitment on the other. I turn to that issue shortly.

iii. Answerability Failing special background circumstances, one who makes a standing personal decision is answerable only to himself for failing to act against the decision. One might justify this claim by observing that it is, after all, *his* commitment he fails to live up to—his, and no one else's. By parity of reasoning, if one acts contrary to a joint commitment one is answerable to all the parties, as such, including oneself. Each can say 'You have acted contrary to our commitment—the one we made together!' Each is surely in a position to demand an explanation of the violation. Most clearly this is 'his business'.

One's answerability to the others for acting contrary to the commitment may not clearly imply that so acting will be some kind of offence against them. That one has betrayed them, in however 'small' a way, does imply this. So what precisely is the offence? What was the basis for legitimate trust?

iv. Owing Recall once again how it is with a personal decision. Given that she has not rescinded her decision, Alice may feel she owes it to herself to carry it out. As with betrayal, however, it would appear that the primary case of *owing* involves a relationship to someone or something other than oneself, so that the self-directed case is secondary. In any case, if Alice is liable to feel she owes herself conformity to her personal decision, the parties to a joint commitment are surely liable to feel that they owe *each other* conformity to the commitment.

If we allow that they would be right to feel this—that they do owe each other conformity—then we have gone a long way. Indeed, we have gone the necessary distance. For, according to the construal of directed obligation adopted earlier, I am obligated *to* someone to perform a particular action if and only if I owe him that action. He has a correlative right against me to the action that is owed. In short, directed obligation is a matter of owing.[40]

I have been assuming, as is standard, that once the owing relation is present, the standing to demand what one is owed follows. If I owe you an action of mine, you have the standing to demand it of me. I take a rebuke to be the correlate of a demand. It may be seen as an after-the-fact demand—a demand that acknowledges its own frustration. Thus I have been assuming

---

[40] See Ch. 2, above.

that, if someone owes you an action you have the standing to demand it from that person or to rebuke him for not supplying it. That is not yet to say what precisely grounds that standing.

It may seem obvious, intuitively, that the parties to a joint commitment owe each other conformity to that commitment. If it does then the main point of the section has been conceded. At the same time, a more articulated understanding of the matter may be sought. This should help us further to understand the owing relationship itself. In particular, it should help to lay bare the structure of a situation in which one person owes another an action of his own, where such owing grounds a special standing to demand that action and so on. There is more than one way of approaching this question. For present purposes I propose the following.

For each party to enter a joint commitment is for him to allow his will to be bound at least in the way in which a personal intention would bind it: he has sufficient reason for acting conformably to the commitment. Importantly, it is for him to allow his will to be bound *by the creator of the commitment*.

Does an individual party to a joint commitment owe conformity to the creator of the commitment? Here is one way of arguing that he does.

In the situation envisaged, the creator of the joint commitment can say of the conforming actions of each one that in an important sense it *owns* these actions—now that the joint commitment has been established. Such ownership can exist, evidently, without the thing owned being in one's possession. In the case in question, the creator of the commitment will presumably count as *possessing* the actions that are its own if and when those actions have been performed. Until they are possessed, they are *owed* to the one who owns them. Their owner, if anyone, has the standing to demand them. For their owner is in a position to say of each conforming action 'Give me that, *it's mine!*' If that is now impossible, its owner has the standing to rebuke whoever would have performed it. This argument links the ideas of owing an action and its being owned in a way I take to be intuitive. I shall now assume that owing and owning are linked in this way.

Suppose, then, that I have helped to create a joint commitment whose subject I and the relevant others now comprise. Given that I owe conforming actions of mine to the creator of the commitment, as such, what about those other individuals who, along with me, comprise it?[41] It is plausible to suppose that any one of these individuals is in a position to demand conforming actions from me in the name of this creator, by virtue of his constitutive relationship to it. Thus he does not demand it in his own name, or as this particular person,

---

[41] Cf. Shockley (2004).

but as co-creator of the joint commitment and co-owner of the actions in question. He is thus in a position to say, 'That action is *ours*! Perform it!'

Can the same story, with relevant variation, be told of a personal decision? In this case, insofar as anything is owed to anyone, the decision-maker must owe it to himself alone. It seems, then, that if this story is to be told in the case of a personal decision, the decision-maker must be seen in two guises. In deciding to do something he must be seen as, in effect, coming to own his future action, in the relevant sense of "own". Then, as its owner, he is in a position to claim the action from himself as prospective performer of the action. Insofar as the idea of owing an action to oneself makes sense, this elaboration of it has some appeal. It also supports the idea that the single-person case is secondary.

In the case where one is jointly committed with others, his owing conforming action to himself is a matter, more precisely, of his owing it to himself as its co-owner, rather than as its sole owner. So, as one would expect, the situation here is different from that where a person owes himself something through a personal decision of his own.

Given the above considerations, one can see that (and how) *those who are jointly committed with one another owe each other conforming actions.* I believe this point to be intuitive. The fact that it can be explained as above goes some way to support this belief. There are other ways of supporting it, but I shall not pursue these here.[42] From now on I shall consider it firm. To put it as it can equally well be put: the parties to a joint commitment have *obligations.* These are obligations of the directed kind—*obligations towards each other.*

In arguing for this conclusion no appeal has been made to the necessity of joint termination that is an integral aspect of joint commitment. Though this aspect was not appealed to as part of the argument, it is of great practical importance in relation to the obligating character of joint commitment.

To see how important the joint termination condition is in practical terms, suppose that it did not exist. That is, generally speaking, without special background understandings, anyone could unilaterally terminate a given joint commitment he was party to by personally deciding to do so. Were that the case, then one party, Tess, say, could ruminate as follows: 'It's true that given our joint commitment I have an obligation to go to London, and Sergio has a right to my doing so. But that's of no consequence! I'll just unilaterally terminate the joint commitment!' Setting aside the question of how she might do this, imagine that, believing that she has done so, she fails to go to London. Were Sergio to complain later about her not going to London, she could reply, 'I terminated our commitment, so you have nothing to complain about.'

---

[42] Gilbert (1999a) suggests some other approaches.

'How was I to know you would terminate the commitment?' Sergio might ask. 'How were you to know that I *wouldn't*?' Tess could reply, 'You knew that I was perfectly entitled to do so . . . as were you'.

Given the necessity of joint termination, the situation is quite different. All else being equal, if Sergio has not concurred in the rescission or fade-out of their commitment, it remains in force. Tess then violates an obligation towards Sergio if she does not go to London, and he has a basis for complaint.

What if a joint commitment could be unilaterally terminated, but only after the other party had been informed of one's intention to terminate it? Were this the situation of Tess and Sergio, he would be able to rely on the existence of the commitment until he had received word from her of her intention to rescind it. He would still know, however, that he could be faced with the imminent termination of the commitment at any time, purely at Tess's pleasure.

Though it does not appear to be essential to an argument for the obligating character of joint commitment, therefore, one can see why an everyday concept of joint commitment would include a defeasible condition of joint termination. The obligations of joint commitment are of far more practical import given such a condition. This is particularly so when contrary inclinations or a conflict with self-interest are likely to arise after the joint commitment has been formed, or, indeed, if it was formed in the face of such inclinations or self interest. I say more about this shortly.

There are other reasons for supposing that there is an everyday concept of joint commitment with this feature. If all of its parties must be involved in the creation of a joint commitment, the supposition that all must similarly be involved in its termination has an intuitively appealing symmetry. At the same time the explanatory adequacy of the concept of a joint commitment in the context of an account of acting together and other common phenomena is enhanced if one makes this supposition.

The Obligations of Joint Commitment

For the purposes of this book, the central conclusion of the previous section is this. The parties to a joint commitment owe each other conformity to the commitment. Thus, they have obligations towards each other. To emphasize the source of these obligations I shall sometimes refer to them as *obligations of joint commitment*.[43] The argument appealed only to the structure of a joint commitment. It may be more perspicuous to say it appeals only to the *lack* of structure of a joint commitment. From this, of course, many things follow.

---

[43] This is not to imply that *all* directed obligations have this source—nor is it to rule out this possibility.

Are there really *obligations* here? This question may stem from a continued focus on another type of so-called obligation, which may also be referred to as a moral requirement. I say more about this shortly. The question may also call for discussion of how those who are jointly committed stand in relation to the general characterization of obligation offered in Chapter 2.

Following common understandings in relation to a central class of cases—the class I referred to as *genuine* obligations—I said that one who has an obligation to perform some action will have sufficient reason for performing it, sufficient reason that is independent of his own inclinations or self-interest and that cannot be eradicated by his own fiat. This was presented only as a partial characterization of obligation, bringing into focus some of obligation's central features. Does one who is jointly committed with others have something—call it what you will—that has the features in question? The answer is surely: yes.

If one has an obligation of joint commitment, one is jointly committed and hence the subject of a commitment of the will. One therefore has sufficient reason for performing actions that conform to the commitment, sufficient reason that is independent of one's inclinations and self-interest. In the case of a personal decision, intention, and so on, the normative force of this commitment can be eradicated by one's own fiat. Failing special background understandings, that is not so in this case. Since one cannot unilaterally terminate the joint commitment, one's personal fiat cannot destroy its normative force. Such destruction is, indeed, to some extent dependent on one's will, but it is not dependent on one's own will alone.

Now, the obligations of joint commitment have to do with a particular relationship between people. This is something that my partial, general characterization of obligation does not mention. It is, however, an aspect of a central concept of obligation—the concept of a directed obligation—as that has been interpreted here, along the lines of Hart. To have such an obligation is to owe someone an action. As I have just argued, any joint commitment sets up a relationship of owing: each party owes the others his conforming action.

At the end of my discussion of directed obligation in Chapter 2, I suggested that one who owes another an action thereby has sufficient reason to perform that action, sufficient reason that conforms to the partial general characterization of obligation given. I suggested, further, that one's owing another an action trumps considerations relating to one's own inclinations and personal self-interest—as such—from the point of view of what rationality requires. Failing special background circumstances, it seems insufficient to argue against giving someone what is his that one is not inclined to do so, or that it is not in one's self-interest to do so. One may of course fail to give someone what is his for these reasons, but that is another matter. Assuming, as I shall, that this point about 'trumping' is right, one who has an obligation of joint commitment has something—call it what you will—with yet another feature commonly associated with obligation. This could, indeed, be the source of the idea that obligations generally have this trumping feature. There is no need to pursue that speculation here. It makes it clear, however, that if joint commitments are to be countered, or overridden, it will be with something special, something itself independent of what one is inclined to do or what lies in one's self-interest. This is how morality is often viewed. The development of such a concept of morality may have been stimulated at least in part by a need to find reasons that could trump joint commitments themselves.

In sum, the obligations of joint commitment are powerful inputs to reasoning about what to do. They trump inclinations and self-interest as such, and they are recalcitrant to a person's own fiat. They could be feared, if one worries about having to act in ways that go against one's current inclinations and one's self-interest. They could also be welcomed. One reason for this is as follows. One is never the only person to be obligated by a joint commitment. The price of having to act against one's own current inclinations in certain respects may be well worth paying if one receives, in return, another's having so to act as well. Thus a joint commitment to espouse as a body the decision that each will be sexually faithful to the other, say, may appeal to Tammy if she prefers Tom's fidelity to the freedom she might otherwise enjoy. Tom may not *conform* to their joint commitment, but at least it will limit what he can do from the point of view of the constraints of rationality.

One can argue that joint commitment has a further important power in the context of practical reasoning. Suppose Tom is a party with Tammy to the joint commitment just envisaged. Alone at a club, he spots Billie whom he finds very attractive. He decides to forget the joint commitment and approach Billie. From the point of view of what rationality requires, one can say that there is already something amiss insofar as he has made a decision that demands action contrary to a standing joint commitment he is party to. In any case, his decision, now, is a fait accompli.

What does rationality require of him, taking only the fact that *there is a conflict between a personal decision he has made and a joint commitment to which he is party*? Here I mean to remove everything else from consideration, including the content of the joint commitment, on the one hand, and the personal decision, on the other. This is a question of some general interest.

One might point out that though Tom cannot unilaterally rescind the joint commitment, he can unilaterally rescind his decision. So, one might say, he should rescind it, in order to remove the conflict. There is another argument in favour of his rescinding his decision also.

His personal decision gives him sufficient reason to conform to that decision, as his joint commitment gives him sufficient reason to conform to that commitment. It is possible that in both cases contrary inclinations and considerations of self-interest are trumped. I left open that possibility in relation to decisions, and I shall not pursue it here. Even if joint commitment and personal decision are on a par in this respect, however, there is a consideration inherent in the joint commitment that is not inherent in the personal decision: Tom owes Tammy his conformity to their commitment. This is in itself enough, one might argue, to give such conformity the edge over his conformity to his decision, as such.

It might be said that, given his decision, he owes *himself* conformity to it. But now he has a choice. Rescind his decision and remove the conflict with the joint commitment, or go with the decision, and fail to give Tammy what was owed her. All else being equal, then, it seems that Tom should rescind his decision. Only then can he act without fault.

One can argue, therefore, that a joint commitment, as such, trumps a personal commitment, as such, from the point of view of what reason requires. That this is so is obviously of great practical importance.

I conclude this general discussion of the obligations of joint commitment with some remarks on two ways in which such obligations are to be distinguished from another class of obligations. Those in this other class are often referred to as *moral* obligations.

i. On Context-sensitivity—and its Lack Someone might propose that the obligations of joint commitment are not worthy of the name 'obligation' because they lack a feature I shall refer to as *context-sensitivity*. Consider the following example. At 4.30 p.m. Jane is out on a leisurely walk through the neighbourhood when she sees a small child a few yards in front of her trip and badly hurt its arm. The child starts screaming. There is no one else in sight. One may well judge that in these circumstances Jane has a *moral obligation* immediately to help the child. Now suppose that at 4.31 p.m., before Jane has had time to reach the child, she spots an elderly woman who has just left her house collapse with an apparent heart attack in a nearby driveway. One may well judge that Jane now has an obligation immediately to help the elderly woman, who may otherwise soon die, and that she no longer has an obligation immediately to help the child. That is not to say that she can now forget the child. She may well have an obligation to help the child immediately after she has done what she can for the woman, if no one else has taken care of it by then. What she no longer has is a moral obligation *immediately* to help the child. For now a more urgent matter has arisen. Her moral obligation is immediately to attend to that.[44]

Whatever precisely its nature, then, obligation of the type invoked in these judgements on Jane's developing situation is context-sensitive in the following way. Even when an obligation of this type is present in one context, it may in principle disappear if the context is enlarged. Then an obligation of the same type but with a different content may stand in its stead.[45]

In contrast, the obligations of joint commitment are not context-sensitive in the way in question. As long as a given joint commitment is in place, these obligations remain, for they are a function of the existence of the joint commitment, and that alone. If it is there, so are they.

Why might one try to insist that anything worthy of the name 'obligation' would have the type of context-sensitivity in question? If I really have an *obligation* to do something, one might think, reason cannot permit me not to do it, let alone require me to do something else! Obligations are more powerful, more pre-eminent than that, from the point of view of what reason requires.

This may indeed be true of obligations such as Jane's obligation to save the heart attack victim once she appears. It may be of a kind reason cannot permit Jane not to fulfil. To assume this is true of all obligations, however, is to take one type of so-called obligation as canonical, and to refuse to allow that any other type is properly so called. There is nothing to prevent someone from making this stipulation, but it would not be true to ordinary usage, and it is therefore likely to be difficult to stick to it.

As to its not being true to ordinary usage, one can cite the case of agreements and promises. As discussed in Chapter 2, common judgements suggest that promissory obligation is not context-sensitive. It can be argued, then, that obligations of joint commitment fit into an already established category of so-called obligations that lack the feature of context-sensitivity. It is therefore not plausible to refuse to call them 'obligations' because they lack this feature.

As I have argued, there are in any case good reasons to speak of obligations in the context of a joint commitment. We have here as good a case of one person's owing another an action as one can imagine, and hence as good a case of a directed obligation as one can imagine. Many consider such obligations paradigmatic, and it has even been argued that they are the only obligations strictly speaking.

---

[44] Evidently, the judgements on Jane's situation that I have envisaged invoke a type of obligation akin to Ross's 'duties proper'. See Ross (1965: 18 ff.).

[45] There is concordant discussion in Davidson (1969:108–9).

At the end of the day, one does not want to argue about how a word is or should be used. What we are talking about here are *inputs to practical reasoning of importantly different kinds*. It will be good, then, to mark the distinction I have elaborated with some appropriate terminology.

In order to avoid ambiguity, in what follows I shall generally refer to so-called *moral obligations* of the context-sensitive type as *moral requirements*. I take it that those who speak of 'moral obligations'—as in the case of Jane—often have such context-sensitive obligations in mind. Because of their context-sensitivity, it will be a feature of moral requirements, as I understand the term, that if I am presently morally required to do A now, I am not presently morally required to do anything that would prevent me from doing A. It follows that moral requirements cannot directly conflict.

Unless it is clear that a so-called obligation is a moral requirement in the sense just noted, I shall refer to it simply as an obligation. The context should make clear when I am talking specifically of obligations of joint commitment. I am at all times concerned with so-called obligations that conform to the partial description of obligations given in Chapter 2. In particular, they are genuine obligations in the sense there defined.

Joint Commitment and Owing

By virtue of being party to a joint commitment I owe my conformity to the other parties in their capacity as parties.[46] In this capacity, therefore, they all have a special standing in relation to my conformity: they have *a right against me* to it, and they will rightly take themselves to have *the standing to demand it* from me *and to rebuke* me if it is not forthcoming. In addition, they will be in a position to *trust* me to conform. Correspondingly, they will appropriately feel *betrayed* if I fail to conform. Further, they will rightly take me to be *answerable* to them for nonconformity. No one will deny that these are important interpersonal connections. The existence of each of these connections, when present, may always be a function of the existence of a particular joint commitment. The aspects of joint commitment noted will then not only be distinctive of joint commitment but unique to it.

In this book my primary aim is to develop a single adequate theory of political obligation according to the criteria stated in Chapter 3. The possibility that there is no *other* source that generates this package of interpersonal connections is, therefore, not a pressing issue. It is, however, a matter of great theoretical

---

[46] More strictly, as co-creator of the commitment. I shall not always trouble with such strictness since any party is a constituent of the creator, or, more broadly (in the case of those who 'sign on' later) the sustainer of the commitment.

and practical importance. It raises, among other things, the question whether an account of directed obligations in terms of moral requirements is sustainable.

Though I shall not attempt to argue this in any detail here, I believe it is not. Some reasons for thinking this follow.[47] To say that John owes Mary a certain action is to imply that this action is already in an important sense *owned* by Mary. It is hers. That is why he can be said to owe it to her. It explains, indeed, her standing to demand it and to rebuke John for not producing it. This conception of 'owing' is nicely instantiated by the parties to a joint commitment. Where, if anywhere, might a case of one human being owing another an action be instantiated in the realm of moral requirements?

It is hard to argue that this conception is instantiated in every case that one person is *morally required* to do something. In particular, it is hard to argue, as someone may contend, that every human being owes every other human being his conformity to moral requirements as such. It seems rather that no human being owes any human being his conformity with moral requirements as such. Recall Pothier's reference to obligations—those he refers to as 'imperfect'—'for which we are accountable to God alone'. One who wishes to avoid theistic assumptions might say that moral requirements do not carry with them any kind of accountability at all. Or perhaps he might say that one is accountable to oneself alone for their fulfilment.

In support of such judgements, one can point out that it is by no means clear that every human being has the standing to demand of every human being that he conform to moral requirements as such, or to rebuke every human being for the violation of such requirements.[48] Yet this would be the case if human beings owed each other conformity in the sense of 'owing' in question here.

One sometimes comes across appeals to 'the moral community' in this connection. These may take the point on board to the extent that they imply that something other than bare humanity—some form of community—is at issue. Then one must of course ask whether what is in question here is a community in a sense appropriate to the generation of mutual directed obligations.[49]

What of cases where one person is morally required to do something *for the benefit of another*? An example here would be a moral requirement to rescue a stranger if one can do so without endangering oneself. There seems to be no basis for going further and saying that the required action is already in an important sense owned by the other party. One could of course stipulate that, by definition, someone who is morally required to act in a certain way

---

[47] There is sustained discussion in Gilbert (forthcoming; see also 2004a).

[48] See Gilbert (2005a) for discussion.

[49] For concordant remarks see Kamm (2002), discussing Scanlon (1998).

for another's benefit 'owes' that person the morally required act. This would, however, be a different sense of the term 'owing' to the one at issue here, one that lacked important implications.[50]

What of the case where it is another's *prior benefits to me* that are the ground of the moral requirement that I do something to benefit them? This is the situation in which I may be said to have a duty of gratitude to another. It is a situation in which people do speak, in the vernacular, of 'owing' as in the statement 'I owe him a favour'. It has long been thought and argued, however, that duties or so-called debts of gratitude are not correlative with rights in the prior benefactor.[51]

Intuitively, one does not have the standing to demand the return of a favour. One may be disappointed that it is not returned, and even express one's disappointment in no uncertain terms. Speaking of what people 'owe' in such contexts, however, is best considered an extended or secondary usage, given that the one I am concentrating on is primary. For now, I leave there the matter of the relation of moral requirements to owing in this sense.[52]

I say more about the practical relevance of joint commitment and its obligations later in this book. Among other things, I consider whether the circumstances of its creation or its content affect the obligating character of a joint commitment. In particular, what of coercive circumstances, or immoral content? This important topic will be taken up in the context of a joint commitment account of agreements and an ensuing reconsideration of actual contract theory. The fundamental point can be mentioned at once. A joint commitment obligates by virtue of its structure, that is, by virtue of its jointness. If such a commitment can be made in the circumstances, or with the content, at issue, then the obligations will be there as long as the commitment is.

Acting Together and More

It is now possible to see how my account of acting together takes account of all of the associated phenomena I have noted. In particular, the joint commitment that is at the heart of acting together, on this account, gives the participants rights against each other to conformity to the commitment, and corresponding obligations towards each other. The obligation criterion is thus satisfied.

---

[50] I have in mind those theories of rights known as benefit or interest theories, of which the version in Raz (1984) is an influential example. For more on this see Gilbert (2004a: 100–1).

[51] See e.g. Pothier (1802), quoted earlier. Also Card (1988: 120). Simmons (1979: 14 n. c) allows that one is not dealing with a clear case of (directed) obligation here: 'The moral bond in question has interesting features that make it look both like a duty and like an obligation.'

[52] For some related material see Ch. 10, below, when I discuss moral requirement accounts of the directed obligations of promises.

In addition—as usual, absent special background understandings—no one is in a position unilaterally to terminate the joint activity, since no one can unilaterally terminate the joint commitment that is the core of that activity. Nor is there any room for a given party unilaterally to dictate the details of the joint activity—it is for the parties together, not one party alone, to organize. A given party can, of course, decide not to act in conformity with the joint commitment. He has that power, whether or not it is rationally permissible for him so to act. However, if he chooses without the others' concurrence to act in a way that is not conformable to their joint commitment, they are in a position to rebuke him and to demand that he desist. In short the concurrence criterion is satisfied.

Though this account was developed in terms of two people out on a walk together, there is reason to see it as generally applicable to cases of different joint activities involving more and more people. In the following chapter it will be seen that there is no barrier in principle or, indeed, in practice to the existence of common enterprises on large scale.

I have focused on the presentation of my own account and have not attempted to argue its superiority to others that have been put forward. I have discussed a number of these other views elsewhere.[53] Suffice it to say, here, that I believe this to be the most adequate theory of the phenomena.

I have introduced the idea of joint commitment and its obligations in the course of an investigation of acting together. As has emerged quite clearly, this key idea can illuminate far more than this particular phenomenon.

Acting together was chosen for examination in large part as an example of a situation in which people are said to constitute social groups. People can do things together for a brief time in twos, or over a far longer stretch and in far greater numbers (tracking down the murderer, devising a new constitution, seeking justice for a prisoner, storming the Bastille, routing the enemy army, carrying out a revolution, installing a new leader). In so doing they count as having formed a social group of sorts, whether a small temporary one or a large and enduring one. Acting together is sufficient to constitute a social group. It may not be necessary, however. Indeed, there is reason to think it is not. It is now time to proceed to a general account of social groups.

[53] These discussions include Gilbert (1998*a*), also (1997*b*), on Bratman (1993*a* and *b*); (1998*b*) on Tuomela (1984 and 1995); (1998*c*) on Baier (1997); (2001*a*) on Searle (1990 and 1995); and (2002*c*) on Kutz (2000).

8

Societies as Plural Subjects

Drawing on the ideas elaborated in the last two chapters, this chapter argues briefly in favour of an account of social groups as plural subjects. The particular type of social group at issue in this book is a society, understood as at least a relatively large social group that may include within it a number of other social groups on a smaller scale. I argue here that a plural subject conception of such a society is both viable and important. My discussion involves several distinct lines of argument. All of these go to show that understanding social groups as plural subjects fits well with common ideas about social groups in general and large, inclusive societies in particular.

8.1 The Range of Plural Subjects

In a nutshell, the proposal to be discussed is this: a social group is a plural subject. As before, I am concerned with social groups in the relatively narrow everyday sense pinpointed earlier. In support of this proposal, I have so far observed that it is common to take those who act together as constituting a social group, and have argued that such people constitute a plural subject in my sense. I now argue, in effect, that it is *because* they constitute a plural subject that they constitute a social group.[1] I first attempt to defuse some concerns one might raise about this proposal.

Someone might wonder if an account of social groups as plural subjects was too narrow. This worry might occur for various reasons. I address two of these here.

One might think this account too narrow if one assumed that all plural subjects involved a joint commitment *to espouse as a body a certain goal or aim.* For, one might reasonably aver, it is not the case that every social group must have an overarching goal or aim. Consider, for instance, the case of a

---

[1] See also Gilbert (1989: esp. Ch. 4).

family. Families may tend to formulate plans and projects and carry them out. However, it is by no means clear that families as such must be characterized by some overarching goal. That is not to say that a particular family could not be characterized by such a goal. There is a variety of possibilities that might serve as such a goal: maximizing the welfare of individual family members; serving God as best they can as a body; running the family farm; keeping alive the tradition of political service of earlier generations of family members. Be that as it may, it seems forced to insist that every paradigmatic family has its overarching goal. The same may be said of groups of friends, and other kinds of social groups as well.

A plural subject account of social groups can easily deal with this concern. The definition of a plural subject allows for plural subjects with a variety of attributes. The general idea of a plural subject, then, goes beyond the idea of a plural subject of goal acceptance or, derivatively, of acting together.

This accords with the proposal that the ascription of psychological attributes to populations of more than one person in everyday speech is commonly interpreted in plural subject terms. This can most easily be argued in relation to first-person plural ascriptions such as 'We believe that . . .', We value . . .', 'We feel remorse over . . .', 'We accept that . . .'. When these cannot plausibly be parsed as relating to 'all of us' (the distributive reading) a plural subject reading recommends itself. Evidently, 'we' are capable of more than the espousal of a goal. Such statements are, of course, commonly made by group members with respect to the population in question. Family members, for instance, may well refer to 'our' beliefs, values, and so on.

Concern that a plural subject account of social groups may be too narrow may also relate to certain types of population that have often been the focus of social scientific interest, and which may be found in social scientific and other lists of social groups. An example here is that of an economic class. Another example is that of a population defined by reference to its members' presumed 'racial' distinctness. Such populations may well not be plural subjects. Is that a problem for a plural subject account of social groups? I think not.

A given list of social groups may be a somewhat rough and ready thing. For instance, it may include cases that are not, intuitively, paradigmatic. An account that captures in a principled way a large number of cases that are commonly listed—including the intuitively paradigmatic cases—is most likely the best one can do if one wants to home in on a relatively homogenous kind of thing. My proposal that social groups are plural subjects can best be understood on this light.

Determining that a particular population is not a social group in a given sense is (of course) in no way to argue that it is not of great importance from a number of points of view. It is likely often to be helpful, meanwhile, to distinguish plural subjects from other populations, insofar as different things can be said about these different kinds of populations and their members. Insofar as economic classes, say, are not plural subjects, it is important to recognize that fact.[2]

One might wonder if the plural account subject of social groups is too *broad* in certain respects. It seems, for instance, that people can constitute a plural subject by virtue of having a single joint commitment—hence, a single collective goal, belief, value, or whatever. Aren't most actual social groups more richly endowed?

In response one can agree that a proliferation of collective beliefs, goals, and so on, characterize many social groups, and may, indeed, tend to arise in the course of any given plural subject's career, the longer that lasts. At the same time it is not uncommon for a social group to be conceived of as having one primary goal, and so on. For instance, people may come together precisely to form a group of 'students against the war'. Think also of the 'pro-choice lobby', the 'pro-life lobby', the National Rifle Association, the Flat Earth Society, and so on.

One might also wonder if the plural subject account is not too broad in countenancing very transient plural subjects, such as two people whose brief conversation produces a collective belief or two, but then they are off on their separate ways. Did they really constitute a social group?

These people constitute, indeed, a very small, very transient plural subject and hence they will constitute a social group of the same kind, if they do. Agreed, such encounters constitute something close to the thin end of a long wedge.[3] If the nature of this wedge is otherwise well captured by the concept of a plural subject, however, it seems arbitrary to insist on a particular cut-off point.

8.2 Plural Subjects and Common Ideas about Social Groups

Many common ideas about social groups fit well with the idea that social groups are plural subjects. Here I bring several ideas that have already been mooted in this book and discuss their fit with the plural subject proposal.

---

[2] Recall Marx's famous distinction between *Klasse an Sich* and *Klasse für Sich* (classes in themselves and classes for themselves), the latter alone involving some form of self-awareness. See e.g. Marx and Engels (1977: 214).

[3] I say 'close' to the thin end, thinking of the mutual recognition discussed in Gilbert (1989, 2003).

There can be Small-scale Ephemeral Groups

At this point the most salient, perhaps, will be the judgement, not unique to Simmel, that social groups can indeed be small and ephemeral, and that an example of a small and relatively ephemeral social group is a party of two persons out on a walk together. If walking together is a matter of plural subject formation, as I have argued at length, this not only suggests that small and relatively ephemeral social groups generally are plural subjects. It suggests, also, that larger and less ephemeral social groups—insofar as they are indeed social groups in the same sense—are similarly constituted.

Intentional Entry, Unity, Perceived Unity

There are also qualities commonly ascribed to groups in general, and to their members, that mesh well with a plural subject account of social groups. Some of these were mentioned earlier in connection with the attractions of actual contract theory. I have in mind the following three points that were mentioned there. The core type of group membership is at some level intentional—it is not acquired unwittingly, such as by inheritance simply; social groups involve a substantial kind of unity; core group members will perceive that such unity exists.

If social groups are plural subjects these things will hold true. As to unity, a joint commitment unifies the parties to it in a salient way. Each is both co-creator of and subject to one and the same 'commitment of the whole'. A related point made about social groups is that the collective 'we' is a standard way of referring to one's group: we are doing this, we think this, we have these rules, standards, principles, and so on. As noted, one can argue that the intended referent of such statements is understood to be a plural subject of the relevant kind, a set of persons unified in a particular way.

To enter a joint commitment, the parties must express their readiness to be jointly committed with certain others. I take this to imply that entry into a joint commitment is at some level intentional. That is not to say that it must be a matter of deliberation or forethought, and, though its implications must be understood, they need not be consciously noted or dwelt on at the time. Nonetheless, there is a big difference between a supposed acquisition of membership by inheritance, say, and its acquisition as a result of an expression of one's readiness to be a member in the relevant sense.

The parties' concordant expressions must be made in conditions of common knowledge; and the joint commitment exists when there is common knowledge of the existence of these expressions. I take it that generally speaking, at least, when something is common knowledge, this is at some level known to and in that sense perceived by the parties.[4] Thus when there is a joint commitment the parties will at some level know that there is. Again, there need be no explicit reference to that fact or any conscious dwelling upon it.

Agreements Sufficient but not Necessary

A point about the genesis of social groups made in discussion of actual contract theory was that they may be created by means of what is properly speaking an agreement. It is plausible on the face of it to argue that a plural subject account of groups accords with this point. As noted earlier, to agree to engage in some action is plausibly construed as expressing one's readiness jointly to commit to doing it as a body. This appears to be true of agreements to 'do' something together in a broader sense. Thus suppose, for example, that the inhabitants of a small island have agreed to set up certain rules to govern their interactions. Intuitively, this would be to constitute a social group characterized by the rules in question. At the same time, it would create a plural subject. Whatever precisely an agreement is, it is intuitively clear that by agreeing on certain rules of procedure the parties have manifested their readiness to be jointly committed to endorsing those rules as a body.

In discussion of actual contract theory it was also noted that, though a social group may be founded by agreement, it need not be. This point, too, is consonant with a plural subject account of social groups. As we have seen, a plural subject can be created by expressions of readiness to be jointly committed which do not, at the same time, constitute an agreement. In sum, as with social groups, so with plural subjects: an agreement may create one, but an agreement is not a necessary part of its production.

The cases of plural subject formation not involving agreement that have been noted earlier involved several possibilities. Perhaps most important for present purposes is the possibility of a process that may be considerably extended in time. During such a process it gradually becomes clear to all that everyone is ready jointly to commit in a certain way. For instance, by dint of observation of one another's speech and behaviour over an extended period of time, people come to understand that they are jointly committed to upholding as a body a certain social practice. As discussed earlier, it is possible for the joint termination of a joint commitment to take a similar form. There may be no easily identifiable moment when things 'come apart', though there may be some salient steps along the way. Thus there may be a significant though not at all obvious trigger for general dissatisfaction with a given process.

---

[4] Cf. Gilbert (1989: 187–95).

Identification

As noted earlier, group membership has often been seen as a matter of 'identification' with a particular social group, whether large or small. A 'sense of belonging' has also been referred to in this context.[5] Such feelings as pride or guilt over what a given group has done have been taken as an index of identification. So has linking the members of a given group together with oneself under the rubric of 'us'.[6]

As noted, it can be argued that standard references to what 'we' are doing, and so on, refer to plural subjects. The feeling of guilt over what one's group has done is of considerable interest in this connection. It has puzzled philosophers and others, particularly when it is experienced by those who did not even take part in the relevant group action. Thus a suddenly reflective gang member who was home sick on the night of the gang's rampage through a peaceful village may feel guilt over the gang's action: 'That was a dreadful thing for us to have done!' The philosopher-psychiatrist Karl Jaspers, at the end of a careful and nuanced discussion of several other kinds of guilt one might have and experience, said that such feelings, though he himself experienced them, went 'beyond conception'.[7] He could not see how to make them intelligible.

As I have argued elsewhere, the understanding that one was party to a joint commitment that linked one to the group's action would make intelligible feelings of guilt over the action of the group as such. Suppose, for instance, that the gang in the example is a plural subject founded in a joint commitment of the members to find things to do when they are gathered together of an evening. That night, urged on by some outsiders, the gang went on its violent rampage. The reflective gang-member was not present and did not, therefore, take part in the rampage. Perhaps, had he been there, he would have been repelled by what was being done and refused to join in. Perhaps he would have spoken against the urgings of the outsiders, and somehow turned things around. Be that as it may, he understands that he is a party to the joint commitment that lay at the foundation of the whole thing. He therefore has a basis for saying 'We did it' (and thus identifying with the gang) and, given that he is himself one of 'us', for feeling guilt over what *we* did. That is *not* to feel guilt over what *he personally* did, or even, necessarily, over his participation in the joint commitment. Nonetheless, that participation links him in a clear way

---

[5] Max Weber (1964: 136), writing of 'communal relationships', defines these in terms of a sense of belonging. Contemporary writers not yet cited include Hardin (1995) and Mason (2000).

[6] For both of these see Horton (1992).

[7] Jaspers (1947). He famously distinguished legal, political, moral, and 'metaphysical' kinds of guilt.

to what was done. Far more can be said on this topic, but for present purposes I leave it there.[8]

Bonds of Association

Another idea about societies and social groups in general with which a plural subject account sits well is the idea that the association of people in groups involves some kind of binding or bonds.[9] This thought may go beyond the idea that social groups involve a substantial kind of unity of persons. For instance, the type of bond in question may be seen as a type of 'bondage'—involving restrictions on the behaviour of the people in question.[10]

It has been suggested by distinguished authors that in order for there to be bonds of the type in question there must be 'shared values', 'common thought', and so on.[11] Clearly, if we understand such phrases as referring to a situation in which people are jointly committed to believe or to value certain things as a body, we can say that they do indeed involve a special kind of unity. That is the special kind of unity that any joint commitment provides. Such an understanding of these phrases can be argued to be a central everyday construal, though some theorists approach the issue in different terms.[12]

As to 'bondage', this kind of unity does indeed involve restrictions on the behaviour of the people in question. Not only are they subject to one and the same unifying commitment which itself mandates a particular kind of action, all else being equal. Unless and until he is in a position to withdraw from it or to bring about the concurrence of the others in its termination, each is continuously subject to it at the pleasure of the rest. Moreover, each owes each action that conforms to the commitment. Hence, he will understand that he ought to prefer that action to any recommended only by his current personal inclinations or self-interest. Should he nonetheless act contrary to the joint commitment, the others have the standing to rebuke him for doing so; and each has the standing to demand compliance when contrary action is threatened. Insofar as this constellation of circumstances involves a kind

---

[8] For longer discussions of the plural subject perspective on this particular issue see e.g. Gilbert (1996: ch. 16; 1997a).

[9] This is distinct from the point that *political obligations* are often characterized as 'bonds'. I return to that point having developed the plural subject theory of political obligation.

[10] Devlin (1965) uses the word 'bondage', referring also to 'bonds'.

[11] Rawls (1971); Devlin (1965). Rawls refers to 'public agreement on questions of political and social justice'; this, he says, 'secures the bonds of association' (1971: 540). Devlin refers to the 'bonds of common thought' (1965: 10).

[12] A different construal is implicit in Kymlicka (1995: 188). For an extended discussion of the import of different construals of what it is to 'share values' see Gilbert (2005a).

of 'bondage' in relation to those others the plural subject account of groups accords well with the line of thinking noted.

It accords particularly well with the suggestion from Lord Devlin that people gain the standing to 'intervene' in one another's actions when there is a 'collective moral judgement' in the offing.[13] He contrasts collective moral judgements with resembling individual moral judgements spread throughout a society: the latter do not give the standing in question. Devlin suggests that the collective moral judgement, rather than the generalized individual ones, make one person's action 'the business' of the others. That is, an action that is not in the spirit of the collective judgement is open to public comment, an action that is not in the spirit of purely private judgements is not. Devlin clearly accepts these points himself. At the same time he takes them to be common, pre-theoretical assumptions.

I take it that by 'intervening' Devlin intends to include demanding certain actions of others and rebuking them for actions already performed. Unless someone else's action is 'one's business' one does not have the standing to do these things. One should therefore, to use a standard phrase, mind one's own business and refrain from presuming that one has this standing.

Evidently, a plural subject interpretation of the idea of a collective moral judgement would bear out what Devlin says about such judgements. Given that the plural subject concepts are standard everyday concepts, as I have argued they are, the point that he is reflecting common opinion would seem to be a fair one. By virtue of the underlying joint commitment people gain a special standing in relation to others' actions. Each can properly see the question of whether or not the other conforms to the commitment as 'his business'. After all, by virtue of the jointness of the commitment each party can argue that every other party owes him conformity. Rather than it being appropriate for him to mind his own business, he has the standing to demand compliance or issue rebukes for non-compliance.

It can also be argued, concordantly with Devlin's claims and his representation of common opinion, that mere sameness of individual judgement, moral judgement or not, fails to effect what a joint commitment to endorse as a body certain beliefs does. It does not, in and of itself, change the standing of the parties in relation to one another. In particular, it does not make the parties' conforming actions the business of the other parties, nor in any other way give them a special standing to make demands or issue rebukes.[14]

----

[13] Devlin (1965: 8).   [14] Gilbert (2005a).

8.3 Large Populations as Plural Subjects

I now turn to the capacity of the plural subject account of social groups to cover societies understood as large-scale groups that commonly have certain special features. This is particularly important in relation to the potential of this account to provide a solution to the membership problem. The features I have in mind are what I have called inclusiveness, impersonality, anonymity, and hierarchy. I start with some comments on inclusiveness.

Inclusiveness

A given plural subject will be inclusive if there are smaller plural subjects constituted by subsets of its members. All but the smallest and most fleeting of plural subjects are likely to be inclusive to some degree.

This can be argued in terms of the following consideration. Suppose there is a plural subject with more than two members. If two of its members exchange a few private words they temporarily constitute a plural subject themselves—the plural subject of a brief episode of communication. Such encounters are by no means insignificant for the life of the larger plural subject. This is one way that information about what is going on in that larger group may reach individual members.

Many included plural subjects will endure for a long time and be of great significance in the lives of their members. A small-scale example in which both the including and the included plural subjects are relatively long-lasting is suggested by a common observation on families cited earlier: within a given family there may be a variety of coalitions involving less than the full complement of members.

Thus suppose the four members of a family—mother, father, son, daughter—are jointly committed to uphold as a body a variety of goals, to accept as a body a variety of beliefs, and so on. Perhaps a primary goal is to pull together to survive their harsh environment, and they have various beliefs and values that relate to this goal, such as the importance of hard work and thriftiness. The members of the family constitute, then, a richly textured plural subject. At the same time father, son, and daughter may be party to joint commitments in which mother does not share. For instance, they may be jointly committed to the belief that mother is too sensitive to be exposed to certain kinds of information. In this connection they may refer to themselves in plural subject terms—'We mustn't tell this to mother'—not including mother in the plural subject on these occasions. Thus father, son, and daughter constitute a plural subject that is included within the plural subject that the whole family constitutes. Evidently the family could include more than one such plural subject: mother and daughter may have one or more joint commitments of their own, and similarly for father and son, son and mother, daughter and father, and so on.

This example makes plain the capacity of a given, relatively enduring plural subject to include smaller plural subjects of a similar kind within it. If this is possible in the small compass of a family it is clearly possible on a larger scale.

Impersonality and Anonymity

A social group involves a degree of *impersonality* if a given member fails to know a given other member personally. That is, at least one member has had no relatively substantial personal interaction such as a face-to-face conversation with at least one other member. An obvious contrast case is a family of two parents and two children who live together under one roof and regularly eat together, talk to one another, and so on. Evidently there are many degrees of impersonality. In a very large society, a vast majority of members may not be known personally to a vast majority of members. One may know one's family, friends, co-workers, various service people, and so on, and these may be just a tiny fraction of the general population.

It is likely that such a society will involve a high degree of *anonymity* also. A society has a degree of anonymity when a given member does not even *know of* another given member as an individual: the first member has no idea that this other, particular person exists. A case of impersonality that is not also a case of anonymity is that of the devoted fan of a particular movie or sports star. Jane may know all too well who the star is, and so on, but she has never had any personal contact with her.

The first question to deal with is whether a large population in which there is a high degree of anonymity can be a plural subject. The question can be answered in the affirmative if one can describe at least one process by means of which there can be common knowledge in the population that the members of the population have expressed their readiness to be jointly committed in some way. This common knowledge will be of a kind I have elsewhere referred to as population common knowledge.[15] I say more about this shortly.

I see no barrier to the existence of such a process in principle. Nor are there any obvious practical barriers that must obtain in large human populations. Here I assume that we are talking of those members of the population who have the mental capacity to meet the condition. These will be, roughly, 'normal' human beings of a sufficiently advanced age.

---

[15] Gilbert (1989: 212–13).

Breaking it into two conditions, what is necessary is this. First, all members of the population must have expressed their readiness to participate in the relevant joint commitment with all other members of the population. Second, this must be population common knowledge.

It may be clear enough that the first condition contains nothing problematic. Nonetheless, it is worth isolating certain parts of it in turn to consider them separately. That way any incipient doubts on the matter may be forestalled.

Fulfilment of this condition requires, first, that all members of the population share a conception of the population. Simple examples of such a conception are 'people living on this island', 'fishermen of the north shore', 'those who farm in the river delta', 'mushroom pickers', 'people of small stature who live in the forest', 'those who acknowledge their descent from the great warrior Obi'. These are simple in the sense that they make no reference to complexes of social rules or institutions—they make no reference, in particular, to already constituted countries. Thus they contrast with such conceptions as 'Americans', 'British', 'citizens of Europe', and the like, which are also conceptions of a particular population of persons. There is no obvious objection in principle or practice to the idea that a very large number of people can share either kind of conception of a population.

Next, all of these people must be ready to enter a particular joint commitment with all of the others. This too is unproblematic. Finally, these people must express their readiness jointly to commit with one another under the description in question. About this, the following concern may arise.

It is plausible to think of the requisite expressions of readiness to enter a joint commitment with certain others as being in some sense *directed towards* those others. One might wonder if this way of understanding what is involved in a relevant expression of readiness can apply to a situation of high anonymity. Consider in this connection a case involving face-to-face interaction. Phyllis is alone in a room with Ramon. She looks directly at him and speaks directly to him. When she says 'Let's go now' it is clear that she is expressing *to Ramon* her readiness jointly to commit with him to espousing the goal of 'going'. The details of this situation may suggest that expressions of readiness jointly to commit must always be directed towards others who are known of as individuals.

It is not necessary to insist that the directionality of expressions of readiness is of this kind. That it is not can be made plausible by considering a case involving a fair degree of anonymity, in which whatever kind of directionality is necessary appears to be present. Suppose that a large starving crowd has gathered. One of their number, Dee, urges that they storm Longbow, the residence of a local corn-dealer. After a while she cries 'So, shall we storm Longbow?' Everyone in the assembly howls out an affirmative answer. Each can be understood as expressing his readiness jointly to commit with the others present to espousing as a body the goal of storming Longbow. How, if at all, were these expressions *directed towards* the others? One might suggest that they are not directed towards the others generally, but rather towards the speaker. Yet her call was in the name of them all. It is more plausible to say that the expressions are in some sense directed to the members of the crowd, including the one who has just spoken in their name. In what sense, though, are the expressions directed to the members of the crowd?

A preliminary point to be made is this. We can reasonably suppose that each knows that many are present, but no one knows of each one as a particular person. It is in any case natural to suggest that the expressions of readiness relate to those who are in the crowd—*whoever exactly they are*. In other words, each is ready to commit with those who fit a certain description—*being part of this crowd*.

This is a good place to say more about what population common knowledge is. As was implicit in what I said when I introduced it earlier in this book, common knowledge is of two kinds. I refer to these as 'individual' and 'population' common knowledge. Roughly, *individual* common knowledge is common knowledge between particular people considered as such by those involved. For instance: it is common knowledge between Liz and Joanna that such-and-such; it is common knowledge between you and I that so-and-so. In contrast, *population* common knowledge is common knowledge between people considered by those involved as members of a population individuated by means of a certain general description. Descriptions such as 'Those gathered in the town square tonight', or 'Those who live east of the mountain' are examples. Thus it may be entirely out in the open among those who live east of the mountain that *everyone who lives east of the mountain speaks Spanish* and everyone who lives east of the mountain may be aware of this. Then—by definition—the existence of this situation is population common knowledge between those who live east of the mountain.[16]

In the case at hand, there could be population common knowledge of the kind needed to 'clinch' the existence of a joint commitment of the members of the crowd to storm Longbow. In particular, it could be entirely out in the open among the members of the crowd both that every member of the crowd has expressed his readiness jointly to commit with the other members

---

[16] It is possible that, in a given population individuated by reference to a general description, there is less than universal participation in some situation of common knowledge. See note 18 below.

of the crowd, and that *this expression has been directed in the appropriate fashion towards these other members, under the relevant description.*

I shall not attempt to give a general account of the conditions under which an expression of readiness has the necessary kind of directionality. In light of the foregoing, however, one can argue that they are not very stringent.

One key factor, I take it, is this. There should be no attempt on the part of those who express their readiness for joint commitment with certain others to conceal this expression from the others in question. An example of such concealment would be a case like the following. Hana says to her confidant Paul 'I am ready to join the army—but for now that's between you and me. I'll go and sign on later.' This expression of readiness is not directed to the relevant military personnel. Indeed, it is explicitly not directed at them. Similarly, those who express their readiness should not clearly be assuming that the expression in question is private in the sense that it will not be relayed to all of the relevant parties. They should clearly be comfortable with the idea that their expression is open to all of these people.

I conclude that appropriately 'directed' expressions of readiness for joint commitment are possible in situations where there is a high degree of anonymity among the members of a given population. The presence of such directedness as is necessary is no barrier to the possibility of a joint commitment in such a context.

The example of the anonymous crowd suffices to forestall another possible concern.[17] How can anyone be sure under what description people are conceiving of the population with whose other members they are ready jointly to commit themselves? Here, at least, is a case in which scepticism seems to be unwarranted. Doubtless there are other such cases. That is not to deny that this concern represents a consideration it is important to bear in mind—both as participant and observer—in assessing what is going on in a given situation. It suggests, indeed, that in many cases the relevant common knowledge may take some time to emerge, as interpretations of what precisely is going on are tested in various ways.

A further concern in relation to cases where people may be 'lost' in a given population, whether a crowd or a vast territory, is as follows. What if, in a given crowd, say, a few people, dotted here and there, remained silent? Perhaps they even shouted 'No!' when the others were roaring approval. That such people did what they did may well not be perceived by many, if any, of the others. More generally, it may only be open to members of the population that *almost everyone* expressed his readiness jointly to commit in the relevant way.

---

[17] Balzer (2002) raises this and the following concern.

The larger the crowd, the more likely this would seem to be. What if the Longbow case had been like this?

I propose the following. If you were one of those roaring approval, you rightly understand yourself to be party to a joint commitment created in part by your roaring. If you come across someone else who says he was in the square, you are entitled to assume, as a matter of probability and evidence, that he is a party to the joint commitment also. But you could be wrong. In certain circumstances you may do well to be circumspect on the matter, in order to find out where this person stands. Nonetheless, as was clear to you, the vast majority of those in the crowd expressed their readiness jointly to commit with all or (at least) almost all of those in the crowd. And this was population common knowledge in the crowd. Those who expressed their readiness under these conditions, whoever precisely they are, are jointly committed one with the other. At the same time, the precise boundaries of the plural subject so created are unknown.[18] There is, nonetheless, such a subject; and each member of it knows whether or not he himself is a member of it.

Evidently, not all plural subjects are of this kind. Even in very large populations there are ways of knowing that every member has expressed his readiness for a given joint commitment. Perhaps, for instance, everyone eligible to vote in a referendum voted a certain way, and there is no reason to doubt that they so intended, given the nature of the referendum. That is not a problem, since there is no reason to expect all plural subjects to be the same in all significant respects.

A crowd around a speaker is an assembly whose boundaries, one may assume, are not that far flung. This is not to say that such a crowd may not be huge; such assemblies can number in the hundreds of thousands, if not more. All that is needed for a very large-scale version of the Longbow case is a large enough area for the gathering to take place, and the possibility that everyone hears and responds to the one speaker and, indeed, that the response of pretty much the whole crowd is somehow open to all.

It would be good, however, to move to a different kind of scenario, approximating more closely the situation of those in a large, inclusive society whose members are not necessarily gathered together in any kind of crowd.

---

[18] A related question about boundaries can arise for population common knowledge, given certain broad descriptions of the population. Some members of the population can be assumed to be excluded at the outset, in particular those who lack the necessary cognitive capacities such as infants and those with various mental disabilities. There may still be an issue as to whether everyone who is left is party to the common knowledge (Balzer 2002). Once again, it is not clear that some vagueness as to its boundaries should be a major concern. In order not to complicate matters I am assuming in discussion that there is no such vagueness.

Consider, then, the following example. A long broad valley that certain people have farmed for years is about be invaded by a neighbouring group that intends to enslave them all. This news has been carried by messengers from hamlet to hamlet. Each time, one of the several messengers learns from those able-bodied men and women who live in a given hamlet that they are ready jointly to commit with other farmers of the valley to defend their freedom in a particular manner. As the farmers knew they would, the messengers pool their information. They then spread the word to all the valley farmers that all of them have expressed their readiness jointly to commit to defend the valley in a certain way. They make it clear that this word is being spread throughout the population, and that this process will be complete within a week. It seems fair to say that by that week's end the relevant joint commitment will be in place, all else being equal.

I conclude that, in terms explicated above, the following is possible. In a large population, P, with a high degree of anonymity, whose members reside in a territory of great extent, there is population common knowledge—involving all members of P—that all of the members of P have expressed to one another, as members of P, their readiness to participate in a certain joint commitment among the members of P. When these conditions are fulfilled, the members of P are jointly committed in the way in question. This is what I envisaged in the case of the valley farmers above. There is also the following possibility, which may be particularly pertinent to large populations. This involves an approximation to what may be referred to as the *perfect case* just described. It is true and common knowledge in population P that *most members of* P have expressed to members of P as such their readiness to participate in a certain joint commitment among the members of P or among a large majority of such members. Here it is those members of P who have expressed their readiness who are jointly committed with one another in the way in question. For practical purposes the jointly committed persons may continue to think of the plural subject in question as comprising the members of P. They will in any case be unable precisely to specify the boundaries of the collective they now constitute. The issue of how it may be proper to treat members of P who are not subject to the joint commitment for whatever reason is essentially a moral one. There is some discussion of this topic in Chapter 12.

Hierarchy

There is little problem allowing for large-scale plural subjects with a hierarchical structure. Given that one can have a joint commitment on a large scale, a large population can participate in a joint commitment to the effect that one or more person or body within it has some form of rule over the population as a whole.

Clearly, situations with this abstractly described structure can vary enormously. There may be many different persons or bodies (or both) with partial non-overlapping domains in which their word is law. There may be a single individual or body that is the sole and thus, in that sense, supreme ruler. And so on. I do not mean to argue a historical or sociological case here. The point is that any form of rule can in principle be backed up by an underlying joint commitment.

This would not necessarily render all of these forms morally attractive or even morally attractive relative to resembling situations where no joint commitment is present. That would depend on the case. Thus if the edicts of two imperators, in my technical sense, are equally cruel, and there is a joint commitment supporting the rule of one, the situation in which it obtains is arguably worse. For there the populace will be more motivated than in the other to comply with the cruel imperator's edicts. Perhaps one could argue, by parity of reasoning, that given two really good imperators, the situation in which there is an underlying joint commitment supporting one's rule is the better. The question of rule or governance in general is the topic of the next chapter, so I shall not attempt further to develop the plural subject approach to it here.

Societies as Plural Subjects

Societies as opposed to social groups in general are often conceived of as large-scale inclusive social groups involving a high degree of impersonality and, indeed, anonymity, often with a hierarchical structure. In this section, I have argued that a plural subject account of societies allows for them to have all of these features. Large-scale inclusive plural subjects are possible. They can involve much impersonality and anonymity, and they can be hierarchical.

The plural subject account of a society provides an articulated model in relation to which the realities of the world can be assessed. The perfect case is, if you like, an *ideal type* in the sense of Max Weber. It is not necessarily a good thing—it is not ideal in that sense. Rather, it is the clearest possible case of its kind.

Precisely when and where there are large-scale plural subjects is an empirical matter. Given the consequential nature of plural subjecthood it is highly desirable to know the answer to this question. Even when there is only a relatively imperfect approximation 'on the ground', many members of the population in question will, think, act, and feel accordingly, and it will be important to understand what the relevant conception amounts to. Whether or not the world today contains large-scale plural subjects, it is important for practical purposes to understand that they are a real possibility. Given that the plural subject concepts are as central to human thinking as I have argued they are, building a large-scale society on the plural subject model is a feasible task.

Before concluding, I briefly address a concern that some have raised about the plural subject model of a large scale society in general. This has to do with the plausibility of a concurrence condition on one's exit from such a society. Surely, it may be asked, people should be able to leave their society whenever they choose? Now this, I take it, is a moral concern, expressing a positive evaluation of the freedom to give up one's membership in a given society at will. Such an evaluation is not of immediate relevance to analysis. Nonetheless, it is worth emphasizing the following general points about the plural subject account in this connection.

A joint commitment may be made by particular individuals as such, or by individuals insofar as they have certain features. In a large scale society whose members are jointly committed qua those who live in a certain geographical area, say, one need only move from that area to 'exit' the commitment—one will simply no longer be subject to it in that case. Otherwise, a given society may develop rules stipulating that, say, one's statement that one is exiting the fundamental joint commitment clinches the matter. One may then in effect renounce one's membership at will.

The plural subject account allows, then, for particular societies in which one can renounce one's membership at will. It implies, however, that this possibility needs to be founded on understandings that either limit membership in the first place to those with certain features that a person can discard, or—explicitly or implicitly—establish this option in relation to the particular society in question.

That is not to say, of course, that a given individual or body of persons is never justified, all things considered, in breaking away from a given society *without* the concurrence of the other parties. What individuals or social groups are justified in doing in a given case, all things considered, is a matter that goes beyond the confines of the plural subject account of society to the realm of morality and case-by-case argumentation.

It is reasonable to suppose that most if not all societies of the large-scale kind will have political institutions and will, therefore, be political societies in the sense of this book. To these I now turn.

PART III

A Solution to the Membership Problem

The central materials for a solution to the membership problem have now been assembled. In this part I develop and defend this solution. I start by filling out the account of political societies adumbrated in Part I. I focus attention on three very general forms of political society. Though all are constituted by one or more social rules of a specific type, they encompass a vast range of possibilities. I argue that a plural subject account of social rules in general is preferable to the influential account of H. L. A. Hart. A positive solution to the membership problem emerges. The members of a political society as that is characterized here are obligated to uphold that society's political institutions. Their obligations are obligations of joint commitment.

It remains to evaluate this plural subject theory of political obligation, both as it stands in itself and in comparison with some closely related theories, including actual contract theory. Before this particular comparison can be done well, a theory of agreements is needed. I argue that standard philosophical approaches to agreements are seriously lacking. A plural subject account of agreements is to be preferred. If one accepts such an account, one sees that actual contract theory is a special case of plural subject theory.

One can then defend an actual contract account of political societies against one of the standard objections to it, the 'no-obligation' objection. The no-agreement objection remains. The broader plural subject theory is not subject to this objection. As far as the two standard objections go, then, actual contract theory is better than has been thought, but plural subject theory does still better. Importantly, it offers a more intuitive account of a political society and a broader stage for political obligation.

The plural subject solution to the membership problem does well when tested against the full set of desiderata for an answer proposed in Part I. It does better than several other proposals that bear interesting relations to it. A number of possible objections to a plural subject theory of political obligation are noted and replies are made. Some matters arising in the context of the theory are noted. Key aspects of the plural subject theory of political obligation are then reviewed and some avenues for further research proposed.

9

Political Societies

I have argued for a plural subject account of social groups in general and societies in particular. I have previously characterized a *political* society as one with political institutions or, in other terms, institutions of governance. These institutions are 'its' institutions. Pre-theoretically, this characterization might be continued as follows: the members understand these institutions to be *theirs*. Given the ideas developed in the previous chapters, it is clear that one way of amplifying this is in terms of joint commitment: the members are jointly committed to uphold these institutions. It is clear, too, that if this amplification is made, the members of political societies are obligated to uphold the institutions in question, their obligations being obligations of joint commitment. I now put more flesh on this skeletal idea.

I consider three very general forms of political society. Each form is constituted by social rules of a particular type. These three general forms cover a wide spectrum of more specific cases. They constitute a natural hierarchy, in the sense that understanding the simplest form enables one to understand the next, and so on for the third and most complex form. I do not discuss in detail how these forms of political society might arise. Sometimes an agreement may start things off. Sometimes there may be no initial agreement. That said, no particular originating process need be posited in characterizing the social rules at issue here. As will later become clear, the underlying structure of both agreement-based and non-agreement based forms is the same: it is the structure of joint commitment.

9.1 Social Rules: Hart's Account

I take it that a political society may be constituted by one or more social rules without there being a special governing person or body distinct from the population as a whole. Its institutions of governance are social rules with a particular content. I shall refer to these as *governing rules*.[1] I shall not try to differentiate rules of the right type from others with any clear-cut criterion, but some pointers follow.[2]

Some social rules are not best thought of as governing rules. Those that are naturally referred to as rules of etiquette are a case in point—the rule, for instance, that one is to wipe one's nose with a handkerchief.[3] Another example is the rule that men are to wear trousers but not skirts and women may wear either skirts or trousers. Such rules may certainly be related to broadly speaking political matters. But in themselves they are not good examples of governing rules.

Here is a case with the right kind of character. The valley farmers have the rule that if a dispute over farm boundaries breaks out between any two of them, the dispute is to be settled by consulting the entrails of a goat according to certain established procedures. If one asks what makes it plausible to characterize this as a governing rule, a rough answer is that it settles a matter that demands settling for the sake of the peaceful progress of life in the valley. More specifically, it relates to the maintenance of social order among the valley farmers.

Some other examples with the right kind of character are as follows. The valley farmers occasionally have to deal with gangs who come from across the sea to plunder and pillage the valley. The farmers have the following associated rules: anyone who sights a plunderer is to send messengers throughout the valley. After the messenger arrives, all able-bodied farmers are to assemble at the meeting point a particular spot to organize and prepare the defence of the valley. These particular rules relate to the way in which external attacks on the valley farmers are to be repelled or, in other terms, to the 'defence of the realm'.

There may also be rules about how those who violate the various governing rules are to be dealt with. For instance, there may be a rule to the effect that if

---

[1] Later I refer to rules of *governance*, a distinct type of rule. Hampton (1997) speaks of a 'governing convention'. She has in mind something close to my rules of governance: 'a convention defining not only governmental offices and office-holders but also the nature of the authority held by those in office' (1997: 78). Hampton says (1997: 116 n. 25) that she might have used Hart's term 'rule of recognition'. She herself speaks of conventions rather than rules. Her understanding of convention is different from mine, insofar as it does not require an underlying joint commitment. It seems close to that in Lewis (1969) to which she refers. Though there are significant differences, there are important commonalities between Hampton's discussion and my own and I have benefited from it.

[2] I do not think the famous distinction between 'primary' and 'secondary' rules in Hart (1961: 89–96) can be used insofar as, first, it is not clear that all social rules that are primary in Hart's sense will intuitively be governing rules and, second, governing rules may include both primary and secondary rules (roughly, rules relating to (other) rules) without bringing in people or bodies who are rulers in any intuitive sense. See the text below.

[3] On the development of such rules in European culture see Elias (1978).

a given farmer is found not to have joined the defenders of the valley after a messenger has reached him, his neighbours are to mark the delict by refusing to help him harvest his crops when the next occasion arises.

In sum, among the set of social rules found in a given population some may settle matters that need to be settled for the peaceful progress of the lives of its members. These may appropriately be thought of as institutions of governance and hence, as I understand these, political institutions.[4] The central question raised by this observation is that of the nature of social rules in general.

I understand a social rule to be the rule of a given population.[5] Social theorists, it should be noted, often use the phrase 'social norm' as an alternative to 'social rule'. Such norms are considered to be fundamental features of human societies.[6] An important distinction is made between, roughly, *statistical* norms or regularities in behaviour and *prescriptive* (also permissive and proscriptive) norms. The latter can be described in terms of what members of the population in question 'are to do' or 'may' or 'must not' do.[7] Social rules in the sense in question here are of the latter kind. Thus the examples of governing rules given earlier were all described in sentences about what people 'are to' or 'may' do. Related phenomena include (social) conventions, customs, and traditions. As conceived of in everyday life, these can be argued to be subsumed under the general category of social rules.[8] What, then, is it for a given rule to be the rule of a particular population?

Perhaps the most famous and influential account of social rules to date is that proposed by H. L. A. Hart in his classic jurisprudential text *The Concept of Law*. It has been said, indeed, that the 'central and distinctive element in Hart's contribution to descriptive jurisprudence' is his 'elucidation of the idea of a social rule and the methodology he applies in that elucidation'.[9] Hart's

---

[4] Should someone argue that rules of the type just described are not *political* institutions strictly speaking, because they do not relate to a ruler or governing body other than the whole population, I would think it best not to spend time arguing that they are. As will emerge, the plural subject theory of political obligation does not depend on it.

[5] Cf. Raz (1975: 52): 'A social rule is a rule of a certain society or community.' It is plausible to argue that, intuitively, any population that has a social rule *thereby* constitutes a social group. The account of social rules I shall espouse supports this judgement. see the text below.

[6] Durkheim (1951) famously argued that 'anomie' or the paucity of social norms, contributed to higher suicide rates in human societies. On the ambiguity of the phrase 'social norm' in social science see Gibbs (1965).

[7] See Gilbert (1998c).

[8] See Gilbert (1989: 403–7) for some discussion of custom and tradition; Gilbert (1989: ch. 6) contains an extended discussion of social convention. The relevant terms may sometimes be used to express broader notions, as is often the case.

[9] MacCormick (1981: 43). The extensive literature on Hart's philosophy of law includes monographs by Bayles (1992); MacCormick (1981); and Martin (1987).

account is a rich one, incorporating a variety of features. It can usefully serve as a starting point for any consideration of the topic. I shall not attempt a review of the extensive critical literature on Hart's discussion of social rules.[10] I first review his account of such rules, then move directly to my own concerns.[11] After explaining one central problem for Hart's account, I argue that a plural subject account of social rules is superior to that of Hart on several grounds. Among other things, important observations incorporated into Hart's account strongly support a plural subject alternative.[12]

Hart on Social Rules

Hart asks: 'What is the difference between saying of a group that they have the habit, e.g. of going to the cinema on Saturday nights, and saying that it is the rule with them that the male head is to be bared on entering a church?'[13] He goes on to describe a number of features that he suggests must be present when a social rule is present. He can be understood as proposing at least a partial analysis of the statement that a group has a certain rule in common parlance.[14] I shall critique his account from this perspective.

In his discussion of the nature of social rules in general, Hart focuses on rules of a particular and central type. I shall do so as well. First, such rules are prescriptive: they can be formulated in terms of what is 'to be done'. Second, they are basic or primary at least in the sense that they do not exist by virtue of the operation of any special rule-generating rules such as 'We are to do whatever Regina tells us to do'.

Hart's discussion is relatively informal. I shall set out his account of social rules somewhat more formally than he does himself, characterizing it in terms of four central features the details of some of which will be amplified later. For purposes of easy reference, I give each feature a label of my own. The account refers to a perfect case and is intended to allow that some approximations to this case involve social rules by virtue of their closeness to it. It runs as follows.

There is a *social rule* in a group G to the effect that action A is to be done in circumstances C if and only if every member of G: (1) regularly does A in C (this behaviour need not be invariable) (the *regularity* feature); (2) regards

---

[10] See e.g. Raz (1975); Dworkin (1977); MacCormick (1978, 1981); Sartorius (1987); and Bayles (1992). See also Hart's 'Postscript' (1994) to *The Concept of Law*.

[11] For a fuller discussion see Gilbert (1999a) on which the present discussion draws.

[12] The reader could move to Sect. 9.2 without losing the main thread of the argument.

[13] Hart (1961: 54).

[14] See Hart (1961: 9), for instance, where he writes of 'what is meant' when one says that a rule exists.

doing A in C as a 'standard of criticism' for the behaviour of members of G (the *standard of criticism* feature); (3) regularly criticizes any member of G who does not do A in C and puts pressure to conform on members of G who threaten not to do A in C (the *criticism and pressure* feature); (4) believes that such criticism and pressure is legitimate or justified in the following sense: non-performance of A in C by any member of G provides any member of G (either the defector or any other member) with a good reason to express criticism and exert pressure (the *criticism and pressure thought justified* feature).

One further aspect of Hart's account may be mentioned at this point. He is at pains to avoid the idea that the significant internal or psychological aspect of social rules is 'a mere matter of "feelings" '. He does allow, however, that when there is a social rule the members of the relevant group typically feel that they are in some sense 'bound' to behave according to the rule. Though he does not make much of this, and it should not be placed at the core of his account, we might add to the above list the following feature. Every member of G:

(5)   feels in some sense 'bound' to conform to the pattern: doing A in circumstances C (the *felt bindingness* feature).

Whatever else might be said about these five features, as so described, each one is commonly present in those contexts where people deem there to be a (prescriptive) social rule in a given population. It is therefore worth considering them carefully. Are some more fundamental than others? Is the list incomplete in some important way?

Note that feature (3)—criticism and pressure—involves certain actions and utterances, whereas feature (4)—criticism and pressure thought justified—involves the belief that these actions and utterances are justified. One can argue that feature (4) is the crucial feature here. For one thing, it seems to be primary from an explanatory point of view: once it is present, it will help to motivate the actions and utterances in question. More important, it is unclear how much actual criticism and pressure is required even for a perfect or paradigmatic case of a social rule. There is likely to be some, in reality, though extraneous factors such as the timidity or kindness of an observer may complicate the picture of what actually happens. In a population of punctilious rule-followers, however, actual criticism and pressure will rarely, if ever, be called for.

Precisely what kind of criticism is at issue? I take it that group members believe they are justified in doing more than simply *judging* deviants adversely. Indeed, they believe that they are justified in doing more than merely *communicating* a judgement of error. The criticism in question is a matter of *reproofs, rebukes*, and the like, directed at those who deviate from the pattern of behaviour at issue.

It is clear from a passage early in his book that Hart conceived of 'informal reproofs administered for the breach of non-legal rules' as the equivalent, in a non-legal context, of legal punishment.[15] I take this to be correct. Indeed, it is possible that punishment is best understood as reproof.[16] In order to keep the kind of criticism at issue clearly in mind, I shall refer to it as *punitive criticism*. It contrasts with what one might call *descriptive criticism*, which merely notes or points out an error, either privately or in a communication to the person described.

Hart emphasizes that where there is a social rule people will take themselves to be justified in pressuring would-be deviants to conform. He speaks of 'demands for compliance' in this context. Presumably, any such demands will be 'backed by threats' at least to the extent that—as Hart assumes—punitive criticism can be expected should the deviant act be performed. To characterize feature (4) succinctly, I shall say it invokes the belief that it is justifiable to meet deviance with *punitive pressure*. This is to be understood to include both punitive criticism (reproofs and the like) and demands for conformity backed by threats of punitive criticism.

Suppose we assume, with Hart, that an adequate account of our everyday concept of a social rule will either include or imply the existence of feature (4). It is natural to wonder *why* people would think it justifiable to meet deviance with punitive pressure. What would justify punitive pressure in the context of deviance or threatened deviance from a social rule? Prior to the question of justification, however, is the question of *standing*. Those with a social rule surely take themselves to have the standing to reprove one another in the strong central sense that requires such standing. Similarly, they themselves make authoritative demands. They do not simply speak 'demandingly'. So the prior question is: why would they think they had the standing to impose punitive pressure (so understood)?

Consider the following dialogue between a valley farmer and two of her fellows. She knows they have been in conflict over the boundaries of their farms, and she finds them locked in armed conflict.

Farmer 1 (reprovingly): 'Men, you're fighting! Over the boundaries of your land!'

Farmer 2: 'Are you telling us off?'

---

[15] Hart (1961: 10–11).   [16] See Ch. 11, below.

Farmer 1: 'Indeed I am. We've a rule about such disputes! We are supposed to follow the appropriate procedure!' or 'Why not? You're breaking one of our rules!'

The point to be made is that Farmer 1's response to Farmer 2 appears to be perfectly in order from a conceptual point of view. That this is so suggests the following important point about what it is for a group to have a rule: if a particular group has a given rule, this entitles group members to impose a form of punitive pressure on members who deviate from it.

Can one be more precise about the presumed basis for this entitlement? Consider a slightly different dialogue with the same background:

Farmer 1 (speaking as if the other farmers had somehow offended against her): 'You're fighting over boundaries!'

Farmer 2: 'What's that to you?'

Farmer 1: 'It's against our rule!'

Once again, I take it that there is nothing untoward in Farmer 1's responses, including her offended surprise.[17] This suggests the following: a group's having a rule grounds a right of each member against every member to his or her conformity to the rule. This right would be correlated with a directed obligation of every member, an obligation to each member to conform to the rule. Here Farmer 1 regards herself as having been offended against by the other two farmers' nonconformity to the rule, citing their rule as the ground for her implied right against them.

One can now add the following feature to Hart's list, assuming the preamble 'There is a social rule in group G that action A is to be done in circumstances C if and only if every member of G:'

(4′)   believes that every member of G has a right against every other member to the performance of A in C, and a consequent title to exert punitive pressure on any other group member in favour of doing A in C.

In describing feature (4′) I have written that every member of G *believes* certain things. Why should a theorist be so agnostic? When party to a social rule oneself, one is confident in this matter. One takes oneself not only to believe but also to *know* that these rules, in and of themselves, ground rights and entitlements of the sort in question. Rather than altering feature (4′) I shall, accordingly, simply add the following assumption to Hart's list of features of social rules:

---

[17] Compare the discussion of 'offended rebukes' in Gilbert (1996: ch. 14).

(A):   The existence of a social rule in a group G, in and of itself, gives members of G the standing to exert punitive pressure on one another for conformity to the relevant pattern, when deviance occurs or is threatened. It does this by virtue of grounding a right of each member against every other member to conformity.

Assumption (A) might be said to describe a 'structural feature' of social rules. We understand that it is because of its truth that feature (4′) is present when there is a social rule in some group. Members believe that they have a right against one another, and so on, because they do have a right. More precisely, members know, rather than believe, these things. Analogous points can be made for feature (4).

A Problem for Hart's Account

I now set aside features (4) and (4′) as features invariably correlated with social rules, features we can expect to be explained by the existence of such a rule. Once we do this, the key features remaining on Hart's original list are the regularity feature and the standard of criticism feature (features (1) and (2) respectively).

Here is a question with respect to each of these features (and, eventually, with respect to their conjunction). Is it the case that, by virtue of the presence of the feature in question, and that alone, members of the relevant group have a right against other members for conformity to the pattern in question, and a consequent title to exert punitive pressure for conformity in the appropriate circumstances?

I am supposing that, according to our everyday understanding, it is our having a given rule, and that alone, that grounds the right at issue. The pertinent question, therefore, whether there is what I shall call a *direct* argument from one of the features in question, or their conjunction, to the claim, no new information should be introduced. If there is no such direct argument, one can conclude that Hart's account is in need of amendment. To anticipate, I shall argue in what follows that this is indeed the case: the answer to the question just mooted is negative.[18]

i. *The Regularity Feature*   As to the regularity feature, surely the fact that the members of group G regularly do A in circumstances C is not enough to give members of G a claim on one another to the performance of A in C.[19]

---

[18] Those who feel that this is obvious for one or both of the features—or wish to take it on trust—may skip these sections without losing the thread of my discussion of Hart.

[19] I take it here and elsewhere that having a 'claim' on another to a certain action (or actions) is the same as having a right against them to their performance of that action.

Compare what Hart himself says at one point: 'habits [of obedience] are not "normative"; they cannot confer rights or authority on anyone'.[20]

It is worth briefly considering two arguments that introduce assumptions that do not go far beyond that of a regularity in behaviour. I refer to these as the *expectation* argument and the *moral* argument.

The expectation argument invokes an 'entitlement to expect' conformity. It may assume, rightly or wrongly, that given the regularity in question the crucial premiss follows.[21] Be that as it may, the argument runs thus. Suppose members of G have reason to believe that members of G will continue to do A in C in the future. It follows that members of G are entitled to expect future performance from one another. So each member of G has a claim on other members of G to the performance of A in C.

There is an intransigent problem with this argument. From the premiss that members of G have reason to believe that . . . , it follows that they are 'entitled to expect' performance only in the sense that they are entitled *to predict that performance will be forthcoming*. Such an entitlement, however, is not in itself sufficient to ground a claim on others to their performance.

The moral argument starts from the same premiss. A further premiss takes the form of a moral judgement. Various such judgements, with various grounds, might be appealed to in variations of the moral argument. The version on which I focus includes the judgement—call it M—that all persons have a moral right not to be put in a position where they may rely on a reasonable expectation to their own detriment. This argument, also, concludes that members of G have a claim on one another to the performance of A in C.

One problem here—apart from any doubts one might have about the precise meaning or acceptability of M—is that this is an indirect argument. One can argue for its indirectness in the following way. It seems one can grant that members of G fully understand what it is for there to be the relevant regularity or entitlement to predict conformity without themselves endorsing M. To invoke M, then, is to invoke something that could, for all we know, be quite foreign to members of G themselves. Either they disagree with it or they have never considered it. So an argument that invokes M is an indirect argument in relation to the regularity or expectation feature. The same can be said, evidently, of all arguments from either the regularity or the expectation feature which appeal to moral judgements.

For many, moral judgements like M, that invoke moral rights, can be rephrased without loss of content in terms of a moral requirement. In this case the requirement would look something like this: all persons are morally

----

[20] Hart (1961: 58).   [21] On this see Gilbert (1999c: 153 n. 38).

required not to put another person in a position where they may detrimentally rely on a reasonable expectation. If that, or something like it, is the gist of M, there is the following further problem with this argument. As argued in Chapter 7, there is reason to doubt that one can infer from anything like this that the members of G have rights against each other to the fulfilment of their expectations. This, however, is what needed to be shown.

ii. The Standard of Criticism Feature   What of the standard of criticism feature? I construe this as follows: group members regard a certain pattern of action as a standard in relation to which the behaviour of group members may be judged correct or incorrect. One should first ask what kind of standard is at issue. Are correctness or incorrectness, here, matters of moral rightness or wrongness? Here, as usual, I understand the qualifier 'moral' as invoking an intuitive notion of morality that is substantive rather than residual.

Hart's examples of social rules suggest that, in his view, moral rightness and wrongness are not what is at issue. The example rule 'Whatever actions Rex specifies (perhaps in certain formal ways) are to be done' does not look like a moral rule and surely need not be so viewed.[22] It is, rather, a stipulation or fiat, which could have been quite different without losing whatever authority it has. Another example 'the male head *is to be* bared on entering a church' (my emphasis) is similar.[23] It could apparently be understood without the application of any moral understanding, whether or not moral ideas of some kind led to its adoption. It is explicitly couched in the form of a simple fiat: such and such is to be done. No reasons are given, or obviously implied. Again suggesting a fiat Hart writes 'if a social rule is to exist some at least must look upon the behaviour in question as a general standard *to be followed* by the group as a whole' (my emphasis). The word 'standard' here could presumably be replaced by 'pattern' without loss of content to this sentence, since the implied normativity of the term 'a standard' is made explicit by the phrase 'to be followed'.

It seems, then, that we should construe regarding a pattern as a standard of criticism for one's group as regarding the pattern as, simply, a pattern that is to be conformed to, which implies that members are in error if they fail to conform to it, all else being equal. The nature of the error, and the provenance of the fiat are not specified. This accords with intuitive judgements. Intuitively, there can be a social rule that is not itself at the same time a moral rule. Something seen as a rule is, meanwhile, something seen as 'to be conformed to'.

---

[22] Hart (1961: 56).   [23] Hart (1961: 54).

Having specified its meaning, we can now ask if Hart's standard of criticism feature, in and of itself, grounds a set of rights to performance, rights that entitle the claimant to exert punitive pressure in favour of conformity. It seems not. Certainly the fact that I personally regard this pattern as a standard for all members of a certain group, including myself, does not seem to give me any special title to exert pressure in favour of performance. The same seems to go for the fact, if it is a fact, that I prefer that others conform. Recall that we are eschewing moral aspects of the situation. Thus even if it could be argued that it is morally required that one conform to existing preferences, all equal, this would be extraneous to the preference condition itself.

What of the presumed fact that *everyone* in our group regards this pattern as a standard? Does that directly ground rights of the type in question in each member of the group? It is hard to see how a direct argument from a standard 'shared' in this way can be found. Perhaps a standard 'shared' or 'common' in some other sense is at issue. I shall shortly argue for such a conclusion. Much more needs to be said, however, than is given in Hart's text.

I conclude that Hart's features (1) and (2) are not singly such as directly to ground the relevant type of mutual claims to performance or the corresponding entitlements to exert punitive pressure. Nor would they appear to be more powerful in conjunction. Hart's account of social rules, suggestive though it is, is therefore in need of amendment.

9.2 Three Issues for an Account of Social Rules

Discussion of Hart has brought this issue into focus: what is it about a social rule that immediately grounds rights to performance and the standing to exert punitive pressure—something that we believe our social rules to do? Call this *the grounding problem*. It is a problem any fully adequate account of social rules must solve.

At least two other important questions are raised by Hart's account. The first can be brought into focus by once again considering Hart's claim that when there is a social rule in a group the individual group members personally 'regard such-and-such as a standard that all should follow'. I have argued that this is best construed in terms of the endorsement of a certain fiat. Now in this context a fiat is plausibly regarded as a purported command. This construal raises the question whether individual members of the group are conceived of, and conceive of themselves as, in effect, issuing a command to the population as a whole. If so, it seems reasonable to ask: by what right or authority or title do they take themselves to do so?

Paradoxically enough, there is here a problem analogous to that Hart uses his appeal to social rules to solve. This is the case of his imaginary Rex, who specifies what is to be done by the members of a certain population, but lacks the authority to do so.[24]

Hart proposes that Rex's problem (lack of authority) would be solved if there were a social rule in the relevant population precisely granting him authority to 'introduce new standards of behaviour into the life of the group'.[25] 'In its simplest form this rule will be to the effect that whatever actions Rex specifies (perhaps in certain formal ways) are to be done.'[26] Intuitively speaking this proposal has some plausibility. Given Hart's account of social rules, however, it is problematic. For, as I now argue, Rex's problem recurs at the core of this account of social rules—with the consequence that the problem about rules must be solved if Hart's solution to Rex's problem can be sustained.

Suppose each member of a given population regards obeying Rex as a standard to be adhered to by the members of the population. What entitles any of them to issue commands—voiced or unvoiced—for the population as a whole, with respect to who may give them orders or anything else? The fact that each issues the same command does not seem to make a difference. There may be safety, but it is by no means clear that there is authority, in mere numbers.

Rex's problem was this: how can he be entitled to specify what is to be done for the group as a whole? Hart's solution—in terms of social rules as he characterizes them—reraises this problem at the level of social rules themselves.[27] Assuming that social rules involve, in effect, the issuing of a fiat by someone or something, we have what I shall call *the group standard problem*: who or what has the right to issue a fiat that applies to every member of the group?[28] In order to solve this problem, I believe we must abandon one general aspect of Hart's account of social rules, and of many related accounts. That is its singularism—a specific type of individualism.[29]

Finally, there is *the bindingness problem*. Though he downplays its importance, Hart himself observes that in the context of a social rule people 'say they "feel bound" to act in certain ways'.[30] The following question arises: Is there an appropriate basis for this feeling of being 'bound'? Or must this be written off as illusory or as reflecting something other than genuinely being bound?

---

[24] See esp. Hart (1961: 56–7).   [25] Hart (1961: 57).   [26] Hart (1961: 56).

[27] I believe this also applies to Hart's more recent discussion of the authority of a 'commander' in Hart (1982).

[28] Some would dispute the viability of any 'imperative theory of norms', in other words, they would question the assumption in the text above. See Raz (1975: 51). I believe, however, that a kind of imperative theory of norms can be defended. See the text below.

[29] 'Singularism': see the text above on pp. 125–6.   [30] Hart (1961: 56).

Where there are social rules are group members indeed bound to perform in some relevant sense?

Hart himself may be willing to side at least to some extent with those who take the 'feelings of being bound' to be illusory, insofar as he eventually singles out a proper subset of social rules as 'rules of obligation'.[31] Suffice it to say that an account of social rules that did not restrict being bound to a subclass of such rules would appear to be most satisfactory. When someone claims that a prevalent sense of things is in whole or in part 'illusory' this always leaves open the possibility that one has missed the correct explanation—unless one shows that there *must* be an illusion in this case.[32] The bindingness problem is the problem of finding a warrant for the felt bindingness of social rules—or demonstrating the impossibility of such a solution.

9.3 Social Rules: a Plural Subject Account

As it turns out, a plural subject account of social rules suffices to solve the three problems I have argued to face any account of social rules. Precisely how this account should run need not be debated here. The main thing is to say enough to show that if a foundational joint commitment is incorporated into an account of social rules, then the grounding problem, the group standard problem, and the bindingness problem can all be solved. Such an account of social rules in general can help us to understand not only 'ground-level' governing rules but other social rules that are constitutive of political societies as well.

Consider, then, the following plural subject account of social rules:

There is a social rule in a population P if and only if the members of P are jointly committed to accepting as a body a requirement (or fiat) of the following form: members of P are to perform action A in circumstances C. (That there is a particular reason for doing A in C may be specified as part of what is required, or it may not.)

---

[31] His inclination to draw a distinction between social rules that are 'rules of obligation' and others may stem from his connecting at one point the notion of 'bindingness' with the terms 'obligation' and 'duty'. These can have strong moral overtones. Then of course it will not just be odd but wrong to claim that, for example, one has an obligation to say 'You were' rather than 'You was'. Given the plural subject model of a group's language (see Gilbert (1989: ch. 3), there is a sense in which the speaker of such a language is indeed 'bound' to say, e.g. 'You were' rather than 'You was'. But this is not a matter of morality. This is true to the way things are perceived. One who is learning English may have a feeling of 'compulsion' with respect to saying 'You were'. He won't think of this as a moral requirement, nor as something he can't help doing, a compulsion in that sense. Rather, it may be something he finds difficult to do but knows that (as an English speaker) he is bound to do.

[32] In Gilbert (1989: 123) I argued, in a different context, that to criticize an intuitive doctrine as 'mysterious', is nothing like the presentation of a knock-down argument against it.

One can shorten this slightly by introducing first the notion of joint acceptance of a requirement, thus: Members of a population P *jointly accept a requirement R* if and only if they are jointly committed to accepting R as a body. Given that 'joint acceptance' is so understood, we can now write, alternatively (and equivalently):

> *There is a social rule in a population P* if and only if the members of P jointly accept a requirement of the following form: members of P are to perform action A in circumstances C. (That there is a particular reason for doing A in C may be specified as part of what is required, or it may not.)

In writing that members jointly accept a requirement of the form: members of P are to do A in C, I mean to capture the idea that such joint acceptance *amounts to the imposition of a requirement*.

As I understand it, participation in a joint commitment to accept as a body some requirement does not involve one's personal acceptance of that requirement. One's personal stance is not an issue. As I have argued in discussing the group standard problem, it is not clearly *intelligible*—without some special stage-setting—that a given individual personally requires that we are all to do A in C. That it does make sense that *we* require that we are all to do A in C is one way of arguing that *our* requiring this is not constituted by a set of personal requirements.

I have elsewhere proposed that a social *convention* as ordinarily understood was a species of social rule seen by those accepting it as 'to be done, full stop' as opposed to 'to be done, for some specifiable justifying reason'. This was not to say that a particular convention must be seen as having no justifying reason; rather, it was to say that to see something as a convention is to see it as 'to be followed, irrespective of any reasons for doing so'.[33] The notion of a social rule is, I take it, more general. That is, it allows for the understanding that there may be kinds of social rule that carry with them the understanding that they have a particular type of justification.

People may perceive a given rule as a *moral* rule independent of particular social rules and conventions. They could have a social rule that reflects this perception. They might refer to that rule somewhat as follows: 'We accept that we are to be kind to animals *because that is the right thing to do.*' 'We are', they might add, 'a moral people.' This does not, of course, entail that moral rules, as such, are a species of social rule. Nor does it entail that the supposed moral rule is not indeed a moral rule that is independent of particular social rules.

---

[33] Gilbert (1989: ch. 6). There I critique the account in Lewis (1969).

I have already shown how joint commitments can arise in populations of a variety of types and, in particular, sizes, so there is no need for a lengthy discussion here of the genesis of social rules, in particular, as these are characterized in the plural subject account. The following points are worth emphasizing, however.

Consider the expression 'our rule'. This may clearly be intended to refer to a social rule in (or of) the population P, and hence, according to the plural subject account, to a requirement we jointly accept. Suppose now that Josie has recently come to live on a small island and has entered various joint commitments with the established Island-dwellers. She observes that they regularly light fires on the beach at sundown and assume that in so doing they are complying with a established social rule. Running into a fellow islander one day she refers, accordingly, to 'our fire-lighting rule'. She thereby expresses her readiness to participate in a joint commitment to require as a body with the other island-dwellers that fires are lit according to the practice she has observed. Her tone may suggest that she takes herself already to participate in such a commitment with the others. Be that as it may, her fellow islander may accept her reference to 'our fire-lighting rule' without demur. Consequently, such references may spread until it is common knowledge among the islanders that everyone is ready to be party to the relevant joint commitment. The initial reference to 'our rule' may be tendentious, but once this way of talking is generally accepted in conditions of common knowledge, later references are no longer tendentious but well founded.[34]

These uses of language will not stand alone. Other things people say and do will confirm the plural subject interpretation of 'our rule'. In particular, precisely the kind of behaviour Hart alludes to—expressions of the assumption that islanders have the standing to exert punitive pressure on one another in favour of conformity to the fire-lighting practice—will help confirm this interpretation as will dialogues of the kind imagined earlier in this chapter.

How does the plural subject account of social rules compare with that of Hart? The main point of contrast is this. There is a holism in this account, which is absent from that of Hart.[35] By 'holism' here I mean to point a contrast with singularism: Hart's account is couched in terms of the personal beliefs of individual human beings. The plural subject account goes beyond singularism in that it invokes joint commitment.

---

[34] Gilbert (1989) discusses both tendentious and initiatory uses of 'we'.

[35] Cf. Cotterrell (1995: 226): 'if [in the work of Hart and others with the "imperium" conception of law] legal authority is no longer traced back to a sovereign it is still not traced back to a community—to the social group as an entity whose values provide law's foundation'. This citation is not intended to imply that the account of social rules I present here invokes a notion of a community's values specifically.

In spite of this important difference, I argue shortly that if something like the plural subject account of social rules is correct, one can expect Hart's listed features to be present when there is a social rule. The existence of some of these features is derivable from the plural subject account as a matter of logic. Others are such that, in standard circumstances, one can expect them to result from the existence of social rules in the plural subject sense.

I turn first to the relationship of the plural subject account to the three problems that stand as challenges to any account of social rules, challenges that appeared to be fatal to Hart's account. I start with the grounding problem. That is the problem of finding a ground, in the nature of a social rule itself, for mutual rights against one another of those whose rule it is.

As the discussion earlier in this book makes clear, by virtue of the joint commitment present when there is a social rule, each member of the population in question has a right against every other member for conformity to the rule. Each member has the standing to impose punitive pressure on those who threaten not to conform or in fact fail to conform. That is, they will have the standing to demand conformity and to rebuke one another for nonconformity. Members of the population will understand this, since all are party to the relevant joint commitment and understand the structure of such commitments. Thus the grounding problem finds a solution here.

I turn next to the group standard problem. On the plural subject account a social rule's existence is a matter of a joint commitment to accept as a body a certain fiat relating to all of the parties to that commitment. The group standard problem now seems to have disappeared. No one is issuing a fiat relating to some other person or persons in addition to himself. On this conception of social rules, it seems fair to say that *we* issue a fiat for *us*. The plural subject account of social rules constitutes, therefore, a version of the 'imperative theory of norms' in which these are regarded as 'imperatives issued by a society to itself'.[36] The account also accords with the idea that social rules have the authority of society behind them.[37]

The proposed account of social rules is couched in terms of a 'population' rather than a 'social group'. As I argued in Chapter 8, any population in which the members are linked through a joint commitment will count as a 'social group' on one standard understanding of that phrase.

I prefer to define a social rule in terms of a population as opposed to a social group, more specifically, for the following reason. A given population may in

---

[36] The quoted words are from Raz (1975: 51), who there assumes the falsity of the imperative theory.

[37] Woozley (1967).

principle constitute a social group by virtue of having a given rule, and within the consciousness of the people concerned the extent of the population may be determined by some description that does not obviously refer to an already constituted social group, a description such as 'the townswomen' or 'people living beside Lake Clearwater'. Thus they understand their rule to be the rule of the population so specified. A social group constituted by joint acceptance of a single rule may of course get a name of its own and accrue a variety of further joint commitments under that name.

I turn finally to the bindingness problem. That seems well taken care of by the plural subject account. As I argued earlier, a joint commitment can be said to 'bind' the participants to it in more than one way. One is bound to conform, in that one has sufficient reason to conform. One is so bound unless and until the other parties to the joint commitment are willing to accept one's freedom. One is also bound to the others, in that one owes them conforming action or, in other terms, is obligated to them to conform. A constitutive joint commitment, then, is well suited to explain a sense of being bound to conform to a social rule.

The sense of being bound that is grounded in a joint commitment is not, clearly, a matter simply of 'feelings of compulsion'.[38] Nor is it a matter of 'something external, some invisible part of the fabric of the universe guiding and controlling us in these activities'.[39] It is grounded, but it is not grounded in an invisible part of the fabric of the universe. It is of our own making. If there is a type of obligation that is not of our own making then, as I see it, the obligations associated with social rules are not of that type.

Critical consideration of Hart's account of social rules has led to another account, the plural subject account. Hart's account brings into focus the fact that, when there is a social rule, punitive pressure on deviants and would-be deviants is generally accepted as justified. From this starting point I argued in favour of the plural subject account. It seems that we regard our group's rules as themselves grounding rights in each against each to conformity, and corresponding entitlements to impose punitive pressure when appropriate. This argues against Hart's own account of social rules and in favour of the plural subject account, which accounts for these rights and entitlements.

As I now argue, if a social rule is a jointly accepted requirement, we can expect most of Hart's features to be present whenever a group has a rule. Thus, though I have rejected Hart's account of social rules in favour of an account distinct in every particular, the plural subject account remains quite close to

---

[38] Cf. Hart (1961: 11).

[39] Hart (1961: 11–12). Mackie (1977) makes a similar (sceptical) characterization of the everyday conception of the way morality is grounded, which he sees as an obvious error. How can anything that is 'intrinsically action-guiding' be part of the 'furniture of the world'?

Hart's observations on social rules. The existence of these points of contact with Hart's discussion helps to confirm the plural subject account.

Consider, then, Hart's regularity feature: every member of G regularly does action A in circumstances C. It does not follow from the fact that one is party to the relevant joint commitment that one will conform to it.[40] One may be swept away by blind passion, for instance, or act contrary to the commitment on account of weighty moral reasons one takes to forbid one from conforming. Nonetheless, one who acts according to the requirements of rationality can be expected to perform the relevant action A in many instances of C. There may of course be further considerations in favour of following a particular social rule—a point of considerable importance in the context of this book. This will be so in the case of governing rules, for instance, insofar as they settle matters that need to be settled for the sake of the peaceful progress of life in the population in question.

Again, some rules may come to be seen as typifying the population in question.[41] Members of P may come see themselves as 'the X-ers'—those who have the rule that our members are to X in circumstances C. An example of this type of rule is the rule that male infants are to be circumcised. Those who are not members of the group, if they are thought not to have this rule, may become known within the group simply as 'the uncircumcised'. Violation of such a rule by a group member is likely to incur particularly strong negative sanctions from the other parties. In short, in addition to the normative force of any joint commitment, there will often be further conditions in favour of conformity to a given social rule. Conformity then becomes even more likely.

Consider, now, Hart's feature (3). This posits a regularity in the imposition of rebukes and demands in connection with actual and threatened nonconformity to the pattern of behaviour in question. On the plural subject account a social rule provides a *basis* for such rebukes and demands. Among other things it justifies the belief that members have the standing to impose them.

As noted earlier, one should not require such punitive pressure to be rampant in order to judge that a social rule is present. The plural subject account helps to explain why this is so. The appropriate exercise of any one party's right to conformity to a joint commitment will always depend on considerations external to the existence of the relevant joint commitment. In

[40] Cf. Sartorius (1987: 51): 'contrary to what seems to be a virtually universal assumption among philosophers, it makes perfect sense to speak of a social rule as existing in a community' in which it is not generally conformed to. Finnis (1987: 66 n. 53) agrees. On this issue see also Ben-Menachem (1987: 76–80); Woozley (1967: 72). I argue, contra Lewis (1969), that a social convention can survive undiminished in the face of diminishing conformity in Gilbert (1989: ch. 6).

[41] Hardin (1995) emphasizes a related point. See Gilbert (1998d).

some circumstances it may not be appropriate to do anything. For instance, it may be clear to all that a nonconformist was not able to help himself and had no culpability in the matter. Or a nonconformist may be so sensitive that even a slight rebuke will cause him to collapse.

There may be a more permanent argument against the imposition of punitive pressure facing those in a given social context. Thus there may be a rule—if you like, a meta-rule—in the population in question to the effect that kinder, more conciliatory approaches are to be attempted in the first instance in every case of deviance or threatened deviance from a given rule. (This rule appears to be perfectly self-applicable.) Most people, after all, do not enjoy being rebuked.[42]

Irrespective of the existence of such a social meta-rule in a given population, the requirement of doing things as kindly as possible in the context in question may be a moral requirement. Be that as it may, those who *thought* it was a moral requirement would be likely not to issue rebukes when a more gentle approach was available.

Realistically, then, the plural subject account of social rules does not predict that parties to a social rule will exercise punitive pressure on every occasion of deviance or threatened deviance. Should one party wish to rebuke another for nonconformity, however, his standing in the matter will be perfectly clear. That he is, in the relevant sense, in a position to issue a rebuke will not be in question.

It may be clear, too, that he has reason to issue the rebuke. After all, he is party to a joint commitment to constitute *with the others* as far as is possible a *body* that upholds the requirement in question. In order to act as he is committed to act, then, his own behaviour is not his only concern. He needs to see to it, as best he can, that all conform to the requirement in question. He has sufficient reason, then, to demand what is owed to him qua party to the joint commitment. This is something that he can be presumed to know. This point accords with Hart's feature (4)—criticism and pressure thought justified. As long as there are no countervailing reasons that mandate or suggest that it would be better to proceed otherwise, and assuming that a rebuke will achieve the desired end, a given party to the rule has both standing and sufficient reason to issue a rebuke and may be expected to do so.

Clearly there is a great deal to be said about the role and impact of social rules in human societies. The main point of this section has been to develop a reasoned account of such rules.

---

[42] For a detailed scholarly survey of the nuanced approach of a particular religious tradition relating to the matter of how to approach those who have engaged in deviant behaviour see Cook (2001).

9.4 Three Forms of Political Institution

Governing Rules Again

I shall understand governing rules to be social rules according to the plural subject account. As I have shown, this account accords with Hart's well-taken observations on human behaviour and perceptions in the context of what are understood to be social rules. In arguing for the plural subject account I have not invoked a particular type of situation that evidently calls for such rules. I have in mind those situations or structures sometimes characterized by theorists as *problems of interdependent decision*. In such situations there is more than one person who must make a personal decision as to what to do. Each person ranks the various 'outcomes' in his own way. These outcomes are the different combinations of the different parties' possible actions. There is a problem for at least one of the parties if his ability to achieve the best outcome according to his ranking depends not only on his own contribution to that outcome but on the action of another party also. A variety of such problems have been studied by game theorists and others. Indeed, much of contemporary social and political science is dedicated to understanding the world in such terms.

I do not believe that the nature of social rules is best characterized in terms of such problems. This goes for the various species of social rule, including social convention.[43] That is, we need not appeal to such problems in order to understand what social rules and their species amount to. Nonetheless, once they are established, social rules can serve people well in problematic situations of this type. This may help to explain why there are such rules and why they tend to endure or to be replaced by an alternative rule once established.

How are we to understand the way a social rule works in the context of a problem of interdependent decision, given the plural subject account of social rules? This is not the place for a fine-grained discussion of this issue. It can quickly be made clear, however, that given a certain plausible conception of problems of interdependent decision, an appropriate joint commitment will fruitfully direct the actions of those participants who are rational in the broad sense at issue in this book.

Economists and others who attend to problems of interdependent decision tend to refer to a given structure of outcome rankings as a structure of

---

[43] In contrast, in the most influential discussion of social convention to date, Lewis (1969) makes a specific underlying structure of outcome rankings (namely, 'a coordination problem') part of the definition of a (social) convention. For arguments against doing this see e.g. Jamieson (1975); Gilbert (1983, 1989: ch. 6).

'preferences'. Often one's preferences are understood to represent one's judgements about which combinations of actions are the most choice-worthy, all things considered. In terms of the best understanding of human action and reasoning about action this is not necessarily the best way to go.

An alternative perspective invokes the parties' inclinations antecedent to considerations of the dictates of morality and antecedent to any commitments on the matter. This is a perfectly intuitive interpretation of 'preference' as far as ordinary language is concerned. It is the interpretation I shall adopt in what follows.

Taking it on board, one can see that any problem of interdependent decision can be effectively resolved once an appropriate joint commitment is added to the picture.[44] In brief, such a joint commitment gives each party sufficient reason to conform to it, while trumping inclinations as such from the point of view of what rationality requires.[45]

An ubiquitous and much-discussed class of problems of interdependent decision is the class of coordination problems or games. Here there is no radical conflict of preferences between different individuals but, nonetheless, it is not clear from the situation itself what each is to do. Roughly, there are two or more disjoint combinations of the relevant parties' actions such that all parties prefer—perhaps very strongly prefer—these combinations of actions to others. For instance, all prefer that all drive on the right, or that all drive on the left. It is no good if some drive one way, others the other. This is, indeed, a life or death matter. The question for each agent is: which combination of actions should I do my part in? For instance, should I drive on the right... or on the left?[46] Social rules on the plural subject account are able to give precisely the kind of direction needed.

Some prototypical governing rules will constitute responses to coordination problems. The problem of settling on a way to resolve disputes and the problem of settling on a procedure for defending the territory in which the parties reside are both likely to be coordination problems.

Governing rules that respond to such problems may do so in a way that is arbitrary in that an alternative rule would have accorded equally with the personal preferences of those who have it. Even such a rule may not be arbitrary in other ways. It may accord well with the other rules of the group,

---

[44] I don't say that it can be 'solved' in the sense in which a solution is a matter of what rationality requires given only the structure of the preferences involved.

[45] The same point can be made for a common interpretation of 'preference' in terms of self-interest.

[46] There may be some conflict. In the 'battle of the sexes' (when there are two action options for each player and two players) the two most preferred outcomes are differently ranked by the players. Thus there is a sense in which one can 'win' while the other 'loses'.

and with its beliefs, values, goals, and so on. It is then not arbitrary in relation to these things, which may have helped to produce it.

Not all social rules that give direction in coordination problems will be of great moment. Thus matters of etiquette, though considered important by some, are generally regarded as relatively insignificant. They have to do with 'manners' as opposed to actions necessary to fulfil vital ends. Insofar as they are linked to coordination problems at all, they may arise out of conformism: each prefers to do whatever most others are doing.[47]

Another much-discussed class of problems of interdependent decision for which a social rule in the plural subject sense can provide a solution are those with the well-known 'Prisoner's Dilemma' structure. An excellent example of this structure is to be found as far back as Plato's *Republic*.[48] This is particularly pertinent since it is represents, in effect, the need for a social rule or rules that prohibit people from harming one another. Insofar as such rules are crucial for the peaceful progress of life in any population it is plausible to think of them as another type of governing rule.

Here one of the characters in the *Republic*, Glaucon, is describing what most people see as the nature and origin of justice:

They say that to do wrong is naturally good, to be wronged is bad, but the suffering of injury so far exceeds in badness the good of inflicting it that when men have done wrong to each other and suffered it, and have had a taste of both, those who are unable to avoid the latter and practice the former decide that it is profitable to come to an agreement with each other neither to inflict injury nor to suffer it. As a result they begin to make laws and covenants, and the law's command they call lawful and just. This, they say, is the origin and essence of justice; it stands between the best and the worst, the best being to do wrong without paying the penalty and the worst to be wronged without the power of revenge. The just then is a mean between two extremes...

In a Prisoner's Dilemma, as Plato indicates, there is considerable conflict between the parties in terms of the ranking of the possible combinations of their actions. In the situation envisaged, if each were to follow the dictates only of his inclinations, they would be on the way to destroying one another. Nonetheless, if they have to compromise, there is an obvious choice. This is the choice that would be implemented by a social rule of mutual non-aggression. On the plural subject account, if people have such a rule, rationality will require that each conform regardless of his inclinations. If one deviates, overcome by persisting inclination, the others have the standing to rebuke him. Ultimately

---

[47] On conformism and coordination problems see Lewis (1969); Gilbert (1983).
[48] See Plato (1974: 358e–359a).

all benefit from the system of sanctions built into the joint commitment, in this case, insofar as all benefit from general conformity to the rule as opposed to the 'state of nature' without it.

Though governing rules in particular may answer to important needs, a given governing rule may be far from optimal. The situation in which it is the rule of a group could be worse than that in which there is no governing rule at all. It may sometimes be better for members of a given population to proceed in a haphazard, case-by-case way than to adopt a rule it is painful or degrading to follow. Some rules, though better than none, may still be far from the best possible, given the inclinations and self-interest of each member of the population. The activities of powerful pressure groups, for instance, may generate social rules that unfairly advantage a particular class of people within the population—the rich, perhaps, or those of a particular skin colour or creed. Not only governing rules but the two kinds of political institution I turn to next may be far from ideal.

Personal Rule

I first consider a political institution I shall refer to as *personal rule*. It crucially involves an imperator comprising a single person or body of persons fewer than those who comprise the society's members. Before doing so it will be useful to recall the account of a political society with which I am operating. Broadly speaking, this is the conception of a society with political institutions or, to use another phrase, institutions of governance.

In speaking of personal rule I do not mean to imply that a particular person or body is an institution. The institution is rather that person or body's *rule*, or that person or body *as ruler*, as opposed to the person or body itself.

In considering the topic I follow Hart and consider the case of a particular individual, in this case Regina. As will shortly become clear, the conception of personal rule I elaborate goes beyond that of an imperator introduced in Part I. It is clearly akin to the conception Hart develops with respect to his character, Rex. Thus, I take it that a plausible notion of personal rule can be explicated in terms of a social rule relating to the person or body in question. An important difference between us is our differing accounts of social rules quite generally.

In what follows I take it that, with respect to their content, the pertinent edicts of the imperator in question will relate to matters importantly germane to the peaceful progress of life in some population P. This is indeed a rough description but it will suffice for present purposes.

A simple social rule of the requisite kind would look something like the following, which I shall refer to as rule R:

(R)   If Regina says x is to be done in circumstances C by members of
population P (perhaps subject to certain conditions such as age, sex, and so
on), members of P are to regard her as instituting a social rule or collective
command of P to the effect that x is to be done by members of P (subject
to whatever conditions) in circumstances C.

In stating (R) I have not tried to represent the following points which may
now be noted. First, various qualifications on the circumstances of Regina's
utterance may be included. Thus the rule may stipulate that only her utterances
made when she is sitting under a certain oak tree are to be regarded as instituting
a rule or command of P. Second, various qualifications on the range of the
imperatives in question may also be understood. For instance, it may be
understood that if Regina attempts to interfere with the religious practices of
members of P her edicts are not to be regarded as instituting social rules or
collective commands of P. What rule R does, in effect, is give Regina—within
whatever limits on context and content—the standing to create new governing
rules and commands of P.

As I am using these terms, Regina will institute a social *rule* if her imperative
is of the form 'Members of P (subject to whatever conditions) are to perform
action A in circumstances C'. For instance, 'Male members of P are to have
two years of full-time military training once they reach the age of 18'. In
contrast, she will institute a collective *command* if her imperative is rather of the
form 'Members of P (subject to whatever conditions) are to do A now.' For
instance, 'All members of P who have completed their military training are to
report for combat duty at noon tomorrow'. In some contexts I shall also use a
broader notion of a collective command that includes what I am calling social
rules as commands with a special kind of content.

Various versions of rule R are possible. For instance, a variant rule R+
might add an 'exclusivity' clause to the effect that no individual or collective
body other than Regina may institute new governing rules of P. Another
variant, R+* might add a 'dominance' clause with regard to imperatives
issued by other individuals or collective bodies to the effect that members
of P are to disregard these if they conflict with any imperatives issued by
Regina. R+* allows for the existence of other 'rulers' in smaller populations included in the whole, while not allowing these rulers effectively to
countermand Regina's orders. The same goes for population P itself: it may
include itself in the dominance clause. Its situation is special, however, as I
explain below.

Such rules as R and its variants can be regarded as extending the ruling
capacity of the population as a whole to Regina or whichever person or body

is in question. In saying that the population as a whole has the capacity to rule I mean to refer to something noted earlier. The population as a whole, suitably united through a joint commitment, has the *standing* to issue commands to every member of the whole as such.[49] Regina's continuing capacity to rule rests on the continuing extension of its own capacity to rule by the population as a whole, through its maintenance of the social rule that grants her personal rule in the first place. Were that rule somehow to disappear, Regina's capacity to rule would collapse. It would be without foundation.

Note that there is no joint commitment, in this model, between Regina and the population as a whole. Were there such a commitment, Regina would need to be a party to its rescinding or otherwise concur in its demise. Nor need Regina be a member of population P herself. If she is a member, then she will need to concur in the demise of the joint commitment that is the foundation of her rule, but only as a member, not as an independent party. Her authority is ultimately vested in the people—the members of population P. Another way of putting this is as follows. Regina's capacity to rule is a matter of collective stipulation by the population P. That population's capacity to rule itself is not.

Two Contrast Cases

Here is a stark contrast with the case of Regina in the context of rule R. A given person or body issues imperatives to the members of a population, P, and backs them with threats. I shall call this person or body Imperatrix. Conforming behaviour on the part of the individual members of P follows as a result of fear of reprisal or, perhaps eventually, habit, *without any joint commitment coming into the picture.*[50] It is possible that the members of P constitute a social group or even a political society, at the point at which Imperatrix enters their lives. Nonetheless, no joint commitment arises in P with respect to her. Each member conforms to her imperatives for personal reasons and without respect to any presumed joint commitment.

In this case, clearly, population P as a whole does not extend its ruling capacity to Imperatrix. Thus it makes good sense not to speak of Imperatrix's *rule.* One might say, in other terms: she has political power but not political authority. Again, she has the capacity to compel compliance but she lacks the capacity to rule.

---

[49] It can probably be argued that without special background understandings, *only* the population as a whole has the standing to issue fiats that apply to every member of the whole. For now I bracket that question.

[50] Cf. Kavka (1983).

There is, doubtless, a thin sense of 'rule' in which Imperatrix does rule. This would be an instance of a familiar phenomenon: there is a relatively thick authority-presupposing sense of a term ('punish', 'obey', 'command', and so on) and also a thinner sense that picks upon some key elements—in this case, issuing imperatives and motivating compliance—without implying the existence of any special standing or authority. Be that as it may, the situation involving Imperatrix is not pertinent to the membership problem. I now explain why this is so.

Suppose that population P does constitute a political society. Imperatrix lets much of its life proceed as before. She dominates its members' lives in relation to some of the matters to which governing rules apply. One cannot say that Imperatrix's *rule* is a political institution of that society, since Imperatrix does not rule. Nor is there any other *political institution of P* that involves her. There is no such institution, that is, that members can properly say is *theirs* collectively. The situation involving Imperatrix, then, is not one that has direct relevance to the membership problem, since that concerns one's obligations to uphold the political institutions *of the political society* of which one is a member.

I now turn to another type of case. Here, as in the case of Imperatrix, a person or body issues imperatives to the members of population P. These imperatives may or may not be backed by threats. In this case, however, population P as a whole does have something to say about this person or body, whom I shall refer to as Imperatrix+. There is the following social rule in population P. Call this rule C (for 'conformity'):

(C)   Members of P are to do whatever Imperatrix+ says they are to do.

Rule C could be complicated in various ways. For instance, it might be qualified by such a condition as 'unless you can get away with it', or 'insofar as doing so is necessary to prevent our society from being totally destroyed'. The condition in question need not, in principle, suggest a negative attitude to Imperatrix+. Thus it seems that a version of rule C might be qualified 'insofar as the imperatives of Imperatrix+ continue to be wise and just'.

One might wonder if the situation of Imperatrix+ is much different from that of Regina. It is importantly if subtly different. Rule C says nothing about regarding Imperatrix+'s imperatives as instituting *social rules* or *collective commands* of P. It simply tells members of P to *comply* with these imperatives. Thus it does not of itself elevate Imperatrix+'s imperatives to the level of the population's self-addressed rules and commands.

Perhaps this will be questioned. Someone might invoke in this connection Robert Paul Wolff's dictum 'Obedience is not a matter of doing what someone tells you to do, it is a matter of doing what he tells you because he tells you to do it.'[51] It may be asked: in following rule C, will not members of P be doing what Imperatrix+ says they are to do because she says they are to do it? Will they not, therefore, be *obeying* Imperatrix+ and, in so doing, treating her imperatives as self-addressed rules and commands?

The answer to the last question is: no. As I argue, in effect, in Chapter 11, Wolff's dictum—if interpreted in terms of the issuing of imperatives, simply—reveals only part of the story of what it is to obey the command of another person. If that is right, then the following can be said of both Imperatrix and Imperatrix+. Either of these may be said to create *de facto* rules or commands for P, if this means that those to whom their imperatives are addressed can be expected to conform to those imperatives. At the same time, it can be argued that neither is in a position to issue *de jure*—genuine—commands.

One might put things this way: rule C allows members of P to retain a high degree of detachment from Imperatrix+. Rule R requires members of P, rather, to identify with Regina.

Does the joint acceptance of rule C by the members of population P create a political institution of P? The answer would seem to be: 'yes, but'. The case of Imperatrix+ is not a case of personal *rule*, since she has neither a natural ruling capacity in relation to P, such as P itself has, nor a ruling capacity by virtue of P's stipulation. It seems, though, that rule C can be regarded as constituting Imperatrix+ as a mechanism by virtue of which a class of governing rules is set up. In short, it sets her up as a *governing mechanism*. Members of P are not committed to regarding her as their ruler, but they are committed to doing what she says they are to do in an appropriate domain—subject to whatever conditions apply.

From this perspective, giving a particular person or body *rule* also sets up a governing mechanism, one that demands a special kind of attitude to a given person or body. In short, it constitutes them as one of the *rulers* of the population in question.

The type of political institutions a given political society has need not remain static. In particular, there can be movement between the different types of case considered in this section. Thus the case of Regina, as originally imagined, could gradually change. After she has made several disastrous decisions regarding the course that population P should take, the original joint commitment with respect to her could be replaced by joint acceptance of a version of rule C. She would now constitute not a ruler but a governing mechanism of P, like Imperatrix+. Regina's status could later come to correspond with that

[51]   R. P. Wolff (1970: 9).

of Imperatrix. Population P may have ceased to be a society. Its members, meanwhile, do what Regina says outside any framework of joint commitment.

Clearly, the reverse process is also possible. After complying with the imperatives of Imperatrix as a matter of personal decision, members of P might come jointly to accept a version of rule C with respect to her. There may not yet be any joint commitment to regarding her imperatives as those of population P itself. Her status is that of a governing mechanism. After she has helped the population to repel numerous invaders, however, and demonstrated much benevolence and largesse, such a joint commitment may come into being, finally establishing her as the ruler of P. Members of P are now happy to intone: 'God save our Queen!'

Rules of Governance

It is easy enough now to cover the case of what I am calling rules of governance. As Hart made clear, it is a short if significant step to go from a social rule granting the imperatives of a particular person or body the status of rules issued by the populace, to a social rule that refers not, or not only, to a particular individual or body but rather to individuals or bodies, whoever they may be, that satisfy certain conditions. The main point to be made here is that the conditions that may be invoked range across a vast spectrum of political forms including both hereditary kingship (Regina will be succeeded by her closest blood relative, where age breaks a tie, and so on, in perpetuity) and liberal democracy (with such rules as: whoever is elected to office by a particular process engaged in every four years will rule for the next four years).

There can clearly be transitions between, say, the existence of personal rule and a particular rule of governance, and between rules of governance and governing rules. An example of the first kind of case: Regina performs impeccably, and persuades the people to accept her heirs as their rulers in perpetuity. An example of the second kind: Members of a population P endorse a certain form of democratic process. A body that rules as a result of this process becomes so unpopular that its imperatives are regarded less as the commands of a ruler than as something members of the population are jointly committed to conform to, for the sake of avoiding the total breakdown of society. At the same time, the joint commitment to the democratic process has itself broken down.

Political Obligation

The stage has now been set for the presentation of a plural subject theory of political obligation. This is a theory of political obligation in the sense of this book. It constitutes a reasoned affirmative answer to the membership problem.

I have argued that certain consequential social rules may reasonably be regarded as *governing rules* and hence political institutions. This argument was followed by an account of social rules in general such that they are plural subject phenomena: those who are parties to a social rule are jointly committed to accept as a body the requirement in question. It follows—as argued in Chapter 7—that the parties are obligated to one another to act accordingly.

As argued in Chapter 8, people may constitute a social group by virtue of their possession of a social rule. For they then constitute a plural subject. Accordingly, they may constitute a society on the plural subject model. In particular, they may constitute an inclusive social group whose membership is quite large and which possesses a high degree of anonymity. A political society, in its turn, may be constituted by one or more governing rules. These will be its political institutions. By the previous argument, the members of any political society of this type are obligated to uphold these political institutions. As obligations of joint commitment, these are obligations to one another. The same goes for political societies of the other types envisaged here.

Personal rule is the rule of a given person or body as such. Given the way this is understood here, members of a political society whose central political institution is the personal rule of a given person or body are jointly committed and hence obligated to uphold the ruling status of that person or body.

Political societies constituted by governing rules or by personal rule may be quite 'primitive'. They are plausibly regarded as political societies nonetheless. The argument that applies to them applies equally well to a political society constituted by *rules of governance* (as opposed to governing rules). In order to avoid confusion with the names, and perhaps more perspicuously, I shall sometimes refer to these as *constitutional rules*—which is not to imply that they must be embodied in a written constitution. Such political societies can be extremely sophisticated and complex, and the corresponding political obligations multifarious.

Evidently, the conception of a political society as a plural subject with political institutions allows for a wide variety of types of political society, from the very simple to the very complex. These range from acephalous groups to populations ruled by a particular conqueror to hereditary monarchies to liberal democracies. One interesting aspect of this conception is that it helps to explain the sense one might have that the source of political authority in every case lies with 'the people'. Here a joint commitment of the whole population in question—the people—is taken to underlie whichever kind of rule is in place, whether governing rules, personal rule, or rules of governance.

The potential for all forms of rule to be backed up by an underlying joint commitment is something of which Plato appears to have been aware when he described the political society he took to be optimal in *The Republic*. He described his ideal political society, or, in his terms, city, as involving 'rule by the best'. The populace at large had no opportunity to vote in or out of office particular rulers. This was hardly a democracy, then, in any standard sense of the term. The ruling class of morally and intellectually superior individuals was to live apart from the rest in frugal communal circumstances and get on with the business of ruling, while the others made their own contributions to the society in terms of the production of goods and services, with the possibility of relatively luxurious living conditions.

In spite of this clearly anti-democratic tendency, Plato makes what could be regarded as a significant concession to democratic ideas, or, if you prefer, to the idea that in an important sense one lacks the authority to rule over a population if that population has not endorsed one's rule. This comes out in his claim that an ideal society will have the virtue of moderation. He conceives of this virtue of a city in a somewhat unexpected way. It is the function of an agreement among the members of the population in question to the effect that the morally and intellectually superior individuals should be the ones who rule over the others.

I doubt he would have insisted that there be a specific moment in which an explicit agreement was endorsed by all parties. Rather, he would allow that the relevant understanding could have developed by more subtle means. In other words, in my terms, he would allow that what was required was not so much an explicit agreement but the coming into being of a joint commitment among the members of the population to the effect, roughly, that the morally and intellectually superior members of the population were to rule in the city. This would make these 'aristocrats' rulers, whether or not they had been elected to office through the workings of a democratic voting process.

Evidently, a given set of political institutions may be wholly admirable or seriously lacking in terms of their moral qualities, or they may lie somewhere between these two extremes. This, I take it, answers well to intuitive understandings of what a political society is. Few would want to rule out a deeply flawed *political society* by definition. Many, however, are inclined to deny that members of a deeply flawed political society have a general *obligation* to uphold the institutions of that society. As a result, they are inclined to regard the membership problem as susceptible only of a negative answer. As may already be clear, that would be a mistake. I return to the point in the next chapter.

10

Reconsidering Actual
Contract Theory

In this chapter I return to the actual contract theory of political obligation. I argue, first, that actual contract theory is a special case of the plural subject theory I have just outlined. The core of this argument is a plural subject account of agreements. I briefly explain why such an account is preferable to those currently prevailing. I then argue that when agreements are understood in plural subject terms, the 'no-obligation' objection to actual contract theory as a solution to the membership problem can be resisted. This involves further consideration of coerced agreements, on the one hand, and immoral agreements, on the other. I do not propose that actual contract theory is an adequate solution to the membership problem. It is important to see, however, that it can be defended against the no-obligation objection. Apart from the intrinsic interest of the point, it implies that the more general plural subject theory can also be so defended.

10.1 What is an Agreement? The Joint Decision Proposal

Anyone who wants fully to probe the merits and demerits of actual contract theory needs a theory of everyday agreements. This chapter begins, therefore, by presenting such a theory. My understanding of agreements and the way they obligate the participants runs counter to standard philosophical opinions on the topic in various ways. I first say what my own view is. Then I explain why it is preferable to these other opinions.

As a way of exploring the nature of agreements, I use a simple example involving two people. Lynn and Oliver agree that she will go to the polling station this morning, and he will go tonight. Perhaps this is done by his saying 'Shall you go to the polling station this morning, and I tonight?' and her responding 'Sure'. I say that this is simple not just because it involves only two people, but because the agreement specifies a single future act for each of the parties. This is a familiar type of agreement. It corresponds to a form of what is known in law as a bilateral executory contract.[1]

I propose that the sample agreement is, in effect, a joint decision. I construe a joint decision in plural subject terms: those who have *jointly decided* on a course of action are jointly committed to uphold as a body the decision in question. In the example, they are jointly committed to uphold as a body the decision that Lynn will go to the polling station this morning and Oliver will go tonight.[2] Thus, given the agreement, she is obligated to go to the polling station this morning and he is obligated to go tonight. I shall call this proposal about the sample decision *the joint decision proposal*.

If agreements of this familiar type are joint commitment phenomena, this is a good reason to suppose that other types of agreement are also. These include: agreements with more than two parties, agreements that specify several acts for each party, agreements to the effect that just one of the parties will do a certain thing, agreements to the effect that each party will act in generally specified ways in the future, agreements to the effect that the parties will act together in some way, and so on. Closest to the concerns of this book are: agreements to accept as a body a certain governing rule or rule of governance as a rule of the group, agreements to regard the imperatives of a given imperator as commands, and agreements simply to comply with the imperatives of a given imperator.

One possible worry about the joint decision proposal is this. Doesn't the fact that we have a special term, 'agreement', suggest that an agreement is *not* a joint decision? One can talk about 'what we decided'. Mustn't talk of having our agreed be talk about something different? Not necessarily. One and the same thing can, after all, have more than one name. It is possible that, though the core phenomenon is the same in each case, talk of 'our decision' is more appropriate in one type of background circumstance, 'our agreement' in another. Whether or not this has to do with the semantics of the terms, or something else, need not be considered here.

It may be that when one speaks of 'our decision' one (in some sense) implies that before entering the decision-making process the parties already formed a plural subject of some kind. Perhaps they constituted a committee, a trade

---

[1] Bilateral: involving two people for each of whom some action or actions is specified in the contract; executory: the specified actions are to be performed at some time after the contract is made.

[2] Often when a personal decision is at issue, one speaks of a decision *to do something*. One can also say one has decided *that one will do such-and-such*. If one wanted a 'plural' version of the first form, one could speak, with respect to the example in the text, of the joint decision to constitute a body one of whose members (that is, me) votes in the morning, the other of whom (that is, you) votes in the evening.

union, or a less formal association such as a group of political activists. Thus one activist might say, 'We decided to hold a peaceful demonstration in the town square every Thursday.' This usage suggests that in arriving at the decision, the parties were not so much engaged as separate individuals, but rather as members of a social group with its own agenda. One may speak of an agreement, meanwhile, when one wishes to make no such suggestion. The parties to an agreement may constitute a plural subject of some kind prior to the making of the agreement. In speaking of their agreement, however, one is viewing them as separate individuals with possibly distinct personal agendas. In discussions of the international scene, accordingly, one might expect nations that were not initially allies to be said to 'agree', whereas allied nations might be said to 'decide'. In sum: collectives decide collectively; individuals agree. Should this be so, it could still be true that by entering what we refer to as an agreement the parties thereby achieve the same immediate result as those who collectively decide: they are jointly committed to uphold as a body a certain decision.

I shall not attempt fully to elaborate the joint decision proposal here. For present purposes its central feature is this: it implies that making an agreement is a way of producing a joint commitment. It implies, further, that the obligations to which agreements give rise are (at least) obligations of joint commitment. These points have further implications, in their turn. In particular, they have implications for the no-obligation objections to actual contract theory. I return to these after adumbrating my argument for the joint decision proposal.

This argument has two distinct parts, in each of which it goes against the prevailing philosophical grain. The first part argues that the structure of the sample agreement is different from what is commonly supposed.[3] Though I shall not attempt to examine other cases, this strongly suggests that what they, too, produce, is a joint commitment among the parties. The second part of the argument concerns the nature of the obligations involved in the sample agreement and others. This part of the argument, too, would appear to be generalizable to the other kinds of case I have noted.

Three Salient Features of a Sample Agreement

According to the prevailing philosophical account of agreements, an agreement is an exchange of promises. Thus Hampton, 'the parties . . . give promises to

---

[3] I put forward related points in Gilbert (1993a and, in far greater detail, 1993b). Bach (1995) finds my argument conclusive with respect to the spare notion of 'exchange' in terms of which I argue. He suggests, however, that the view I contest can be rescued if one uses a richer notion of exchange, a notion he does not articulate. I suspect that articulation of the richer notion of exchange may well uncover a problem about *exchanging* akin to the original one about agreements. Prichard (1949) suggests it will. See Gilbert (1993b).

one another. The action each agrees to undertake is therefore considered to be binding, unless the party to whom the promise is made in the agreement releases the other from his or her commitment.'[4] It would be assumed, then, that my sample agreement—the agreement between Lynn and Oliver that she will go to the polling station this morning and he will go tonight—is of this form. The core of my argument against this account is that no one promise-exchange can capture three salient features of this agreement. At the same time, a joint commitment to uphold as a body the relevant decision has all three features. Here is the argument.

We would normally understand that, given the sample agreement, and absent any countervailing factors, Oliver has an obligation to go to the polling station tonight and Lynn has an obligation to go this morning. This is not intended to imply that no other obligations are produced as well. These, however, are the *performance* obligations of the agreement—they are *the acts explicitly specified in the agreement as to be performed by one or another party*. Our understanding of each one's performance obligation is this: it is an obligation *to go to the polling station*, not an obligation *to go to the polling station, if the other person does*. To summarize the point, I shall say that—in this case—the performance obligations are *unconditional*.[5] Second, these performance obligations are arrived at *simultaneously*. They are arrived at when and only when the agreement is complete.

Now, it is possible for a promise-exchange involving at least one conditional promise to achieve a set of *unconditional* obligations arrived at *simultaneously*. Thus consider the following exchange. I say: 'On condition that you promise to go to the polling station tonight, I promise to go this morning.' So far, I have not promised anything. Rather, I have made what I shall call an *externally conditional* promise, whose condition has not yet been met. You reply: 'I promise to go tonight.' You thus fulfil the condition governing my promise. At this point—one and the same—both of us accrue unconditional obligations, I to go to the polling station this morning, you to go tonight.

What is impossible is for the obligations resulting from any promise-exchange to be all of the following at once: simultaneous, unconditional, and, in a sense

---

[4] Hampton (1980: 324). Hampton is discussing 'contractual agreements' and explicitly draws on the *American Restatement of the Law of Contracts* (1932). The relationship of the various (changing) legal conceptions of contract and the everyday concept of an agreement is a question of some delicacy. Whether influenced by legal texts or not, philosophers commonly assume that everyday agreements are made up of two promises. See e.g. Lewis (1969: 34, 45, 84); Atiyah (1981: 204–5); Raz (1984: 202–3); Robins (1984: 105).

[5] Conditional performance obligations are possible. For instance, we agree that I will work on our taxes tonight if you are too busy to do so. The point to be made is that, on the face of it, many performance obligations are not conditional in form.

I shall explain, *interdependent*. Yet it can be argued that if a promise-exchange is to mirror the structure of our sample agreement, the ensuing obligations need to have all three features.

Consider the sample agreement. Suppose Lynn fails to go to the polling station this morning though she and Oliver have agreed that she will do so. Her failure is completely wilful: she could go to the polling station, she has no good reason not to go, she is fully aware that she is breaking her promise, and fails to make any effort not to do so.[6] As far as her own (one) performance obligation is concerned, she has totally failed to conform to the agreement. That she has failed in this way is transmitted to Oliver, and this is common knowledge.[7] As far as their agreement goes it seems that at this point he is free not to go to the polling station tonight. That is not to say that the agreement has been rescinded. Since Oliver and Lynn were the only parties to it, however, its fate is now in his hands. Insofar as he is still obligated through it—as perhaps he is—his current obligation is an obligation with a difference. In effect, it is up to him whether to maintain it or not. Perhaps he will decide to stand by the agreement, conforming to it, for his part.[8] Whether *it* stands is now up to him. It is now, to use a legal term, voidable at his discretion.

As far as the sample agreement goes, then, the performance obligations of the parties are *interdependent* at least in the following sense: if one of these obligations is wilfully ignored, this affects the status of the other. It affects, indeed, the status of the agreement itself.

There are things that could be said about the relevance of particular aspects of the example to the point just made. In order to get at the underlying structure of the sample agreement, however, these may be set aside. What is crucial is that in this case, intuitively, *Lynn's* wilful violation directly affects the status of the agreement and hence of *Oliver's* obligation. His present freedom not to do what he agreed to do is not such that considerations of fairness or equity, for instance, need be brought in to establish it. It is a matter of *what an agreement is*.

So much for how things stand, intuitively, with the sample agreement. Now suppose you have made a simple unconditional promise to me and I have made a similar 'counter-promise' to you: I promised to vote in the morning and you promised to vote in the evening. If I break my promise, this does not affect the status of your promise as a robust promise. You

---

[6] I qualify the violation as wilful because this seems to be the clearest case in relation to the point to be made. For purposes of uncovering the structure of agreements it does not matter what might be the case for violations that are less starkly 'wilful'.

[7] This condition may not be necessary to arrive at the point to be made. I leave that matter open.

[8] Thanks to John Horton for emphasizing this point (personal communication, 2004).

could perhaps argue that your fulfilment of the promise is not required from the point of view of fairness or equity. That may be so. But it is not an argument to the effect that your promise is now voidable at your pleasure, so you can now remove its obligation. The point, rather, is that in spite of the fact you made a promise that is still robust, it is permissible, all things considered, to break that promise. The more complex exchange involving a conditional promise discussed earlier also fails to provide interdependent obligations. Indeed, it seems that no promise-exchange, however complex, is capable of simultaneously delivering unconditional, interdependent obligations to the parties.[9]

A joint commitment account of our sample agreement is better than an exchange-of-promises model in this respect. If the agreement involves a joint commitment to uphold the relevant decision as a body, then unconditional obligations accrue to both parties simultaneously, when and only when the joint commitment has been established. These obligations are a function of the joint commitment. This would help to explain the judgement that one party's wilful violation changes the status of the agreement.

It seems that Lynn's deliberately disregarding her performance obligation would reasonably be taken as an expression of readiness to rescind the joint commitment involved in the agreement, leaving it open to Oliver—the only other party—to clinch its rescission at will. At this point, though still obligated, Oliver has the power to remove that obligation by his own fiat. This is, then, an obligation with a difference, as was apparent in pre-theoretical discussion of the case.[10]

What of promises? It is true that here only one person, the 'promisor', has an obligation to perform an action the parties explicitly specify. Nonetheless a joint commitment account of promises, also, has some merit. I shall not try to do more than briefly explain this here. I should say, first, that I shall understand promising in a broad sense such that one can promise without saying 'I promise' or using some similar established formula. For instance, Helen says to Natalie, 'You'll be there, won't you?' obviously looking for something more than a prediction, or, indeed, an expression of intent. She is likely to take the response 'I will' as a promise in the broad sense in question. She may similarly rebuke Natalie with 'You said you'd be there!' if she does not show up. She may not say 'You promised' but the gist of her complaint

---

[9] For discussion of several other candidate promise-exchanges see Gilbert (1993b).

[10] If the gist of this discussion is correct, it seems that in some special, specifiable circumstances an *obligation* may not be recalcitrant to the obligated person's will. This will be so of obligations of joint commitment such that the other party or parties have, one way or another, left it to a single party to decide whether or not to rescind the commitment.

is much the same. Should Natalie attempt to defend herself by saying 'I did not say "I promise" ', this would reasonably be considered a pretty thin excuse.

Consider, then, that with typical—and arguably paradigmatic—promises, there is a promisee who must accept the promise in order that it come into effect. Such acceptance amounts to more than a simple acknowledgement that the promisor has promised. It helps to constitute the promise *as* a promise. Second, though only the promisor has a performance obligation—the promised act or acts are his to perform—it would be untoward, all else being equal, should the promisee act so as to thwart the promisor's performance. For instance, should Anne promise Ben that she would join the protest in the square at nine tomorrow, he would then fail her should he arrange for her to be distracted in such a way that she could not get to the square at nine. This suggests that both promisor and promisee take on obligations and accrue rights with respect to a given promise, something to whose creation both must contribute. These considerations, among others, support an account of promising as some kind of joint commitment phenomenon.

There is some plausibility, indeed, to the idea that a typical promise is a joint decision. Such a decision can, after all, assign an action or actions to one person only. Thus Jim and Julia—a married couple—may jointly decide that he will stand for public office. The members of a trade union, including Sylvia, may jointly decide that she will represent the union in talks with the management, and so on. The ensuing obligations of the other parties are then somewhat vague, but they presumably include not setting out to thwart the designated person from performing the act decided upon. There is some reason, therefore, to see a typical promise as a joint decision of the promisor and promisee to the effect that the promisor is to act in a certain way. According to the account of joint decisions just given, promises would then be joint commitments to uphold as a body the decision that one party (the so-called promisor) is to do a certain thing. Given my understanding of agreements, they would be a kind of agreement.

The literature on promising often suggests, if it does not state, that there is an important asymmetry between promisor and promisee in addition to the fact that only the promisor has a performance obligation through the promise. The suggestion is that the promisor's obligation is *under the control of the promisee*. In other words, if the promisee so desires he can cancel the promise without the agreement of the promisor, thus 'releasing' the promisor from the promise. The promisor, meanwhile, cannot release himself from the promise. Is this a problem for the joint decision model of promising? The following considerations suggest it is not.

First, it is not at all clear that the suggestion in the literature is correct. Certainly—absent special background understandings, at least—a *promisor* cannot say to his promisee 'I am taking back my promise'. That point, however, is taken care of by the joint decision model, since the promisor will need the promisee's concurrence in the cancellation of the promise.[11] At the same time it is not so clear that a promisee, as such, has the standing unilaterally to cancel a promise that has been made to him. Sometimes it will look as if he does, for the following reason. Promises are often made at the request of the promisee, in order that something he desires come about. The promisor may make the promise out of a desire to please the promisee, without having any independent desire to do the thing promised. He may, indeed, prefer not to do it, all else being equal. Suppose, then, that at her prompting, Wlodek promises Marianne that he will return her book tomorrow. Reflecting that she does not really need the book, Marianne may call Wlodek and say, 'Don't worry, you can keep the book for now'. This may look as if she is unilaterally cancelling the promise. However, she may speak in this way because she knows that Wlodek would be happy to keep the book and is taking his concurrence for granted. This assumption could be false, however. Wlodek might be someone who prides himself on keeping his promises. He might then respond, 'No, I promised to return the book tomorrow, and that's what I'll do.' That such a response is intelligible suggests the falsity of the suggestion that a promisee, as such, has the standing unilaterally to cancel the promise.[12]

The point just made to the effect that the promisor's concurrence may be necessary for cancellation of the promise does not deny, of course, that in some contexts a promisor's refusal to accept cancellation of the promise would be pig-headed or worse. As discussed shortly, there is plenty of room for moral (and other) argument around a promise. If a promisor's refusal would clearly be out of bounds for whatever reason, it may be that a promisee will reasonably treat the situation as one in which he is in a position to cancel.

One who was still convinced that the promisee is in a position unilaterally to cancel the promise—finding some way around the example of Wlodek and Marianne—could still accept a version of the joint decision account of promises. He could maintain that a promise was a joint decision to the effect that the promisor is to do something, subject to the pleasure of the promisee.

In informal discussion of the joint decision proposal for promises, people tend to bring up as purported counter-examples cases that are arguably not

---

[11] The promisor can of course say 'I know that I promised but I can't—or I won't—do it,' which is different.

[12] There is concurring discussion in Vitek (1993).

paradigmatic, where the nature of their divergence from the paradigm is fairly clear. If an account of promising works well for the clearest cases that may be the best one can hope for.

I shall not pause further to defend or elaborate upon the joint decision model of promising. For present purposes the main point to be made is this: there is something to be said for the idea that a plausible account of promising will put a joint commitment at its core.[13]

If the concepts of an agreement and of a promise are concepts of joint commitment phenomena one can see why some moral philosophers have thought, and indeed emphasized, that the fact that they obligate is knowable a priori. It is indeed knowable a priori. What precisely is knowable a priori is, of course, the existence of an obligation of joint commitment.[14]

In a late work, Kant makes a distinction between rights that stem from (or inhere in) contracts, and another kind of right—a moral right?—that, he says, has to do with 'the choice of all united *a priori*'.[15] Playing on this Kantian phrase, the rights and obligations of agreement (and rights and obligations of joint commitment generally)—which he would refer to as *contract rights*—could be referred to in contrast as stemming from 'the choice of *some* united *a posteriori*'. There is no need for present purposes to explore Kant's understanding of the other side of the contrast.

10.2 Agreements and Promises as a Source of Obligation

If one accepts that the obligations most closely associated with agreements are obligations of joint commitment, one will be adopting a view of these obligations that goes against the standard understanding of contemporary moral philosophers. Is that a problem? I think not, for several reasons.

Before going into them, I should emphasize two things. First, these philosophers tend to focus on promises rather than agreements. It is not clear why

[13] There is further discussion is Gilbert 2005d.

[14] This may be less satisfying to the philosophers in question. For, depending on one's understanding of the bounds of the moral realm, it may well not amount to knowledge of an a priori connection of a non-moral fact (that one has made an agreement or promise) with a moral fact. Whether or not knowledge that one has an obligation of joint commitment is best characterized as moral knowledge, it is surely going to be knowledge of something morally *significant*. This may or may not be of some comfort to these philosophers. See Gilbert (1996: 297).

[15] Kant (1991: pt. J, Ch. II, sect. II, subsect. 20, p. 93). I thank Christine Korsgaard for alerting me to Kant's discussion as having much in common with views I was expressing. It seems to me to do so. Other Kant scholars I have approached have varied on the issue.

that would be, except for the assumption that an agreement is an exchange of promises, which takes promise to be the more fundamental notion. I have argued against this assumption. Since moral philosophers have focused on promises, however, the remarks that follow relate to that literature. The points to be made apply, with appropriate changes, to the case of agreements as well.

In Chapter 5, I noted the possibility that there is a sense in which one is obligated to perform even an immoral promise while at the same time there is another sense in which one is not obligated to perform such a promise. The second preliminary point to be made relates to this. Contemporary moral philosophers do not generally allow that there are different senses in which a given promise may obligate the promisor. They take themselves to be discussing the one and only sense in which promises obligate the promisor—if and when they do.

My account of the relationship of promising to obligation diverges from the standard philosophical account in two ways. I take it that *a given promise may obligate in more than one sense*, including the sense at issue in the standard view; and I argue that *every promise obligates in a way the standard view does not contemplate*. As I see things, then, the common phrase 'promissory obligation' is importantly ambiguous. It could refer to any obligation a given promisor incurs as a result of his promise, or it could refer to that kind of obligation most closely associated with promising. In describing the standard understanding of promises in what follows there is no need to distinguish between these two possible construals, since on that understanding there is only one kind of obligation associated with promising.

The standard understanding I have in mind is as follows. Promissory obligation is a matter of what one is morally required to do. One is morally required to do something if one's situation falls under a prescriptive moral principle that is general in the sense that, logically speaking, it is not limited in scope to particular individuals or situations. Thus Thomas Scanlon: 'when promises give rise to clear obligations, these can be accounted for on the basis of general moral principles . . . '.[16]

Putative moral principles tend to be presented in a sentence of the form: 'In circumstances C, one must perform action A.' A pertinent example is Scanlon's highly nuanced Principle F (for fidelity). Scanlon has conjectured that the situation of a paradigmatic promisor falls under this principle and that it thus accounts for a promisor's obligation to act as promised. Principle F runs as follows:

[16] Scanlon (1998: 315).

If (1) A voluntarily and intentionally leads B to expect that A will do X (unless B consents to A's not doing so); (2) A knows that B wants to be assured of this; (3) A acts with the aim of providing this assurance, and has good reason to believe that he or she has done so; (4) B knows that A has the beliefs and intentions just described; (5) A intends for B to know this, and knows that B does know it; and (6) B knows that A has this knowledge and intent; then, in the absence of special justification, A must do X unless B consents to X's not being done.[17]

The way Scanlon's principle is written indicates the context-sensitivity that promissory obligations are presumed to have. The promisor is obligated to or 'must' carry out the promise only 'in the absence of special justification' for doing otherwise.

Moral principles as such are generally conceived of, indeed, as having 'a distinctive importance and authority' in relation to practical reasoning.[18] Their source or provenance is a matter of debate, but it is generally assumed that they are not necessarily embodied in any legal system or other such institution or in any actual agreement or kindred production. The existence of principles answering to the above description has been disputed. There is no need to enter that question here. The point is that moral philosophers tend to invoke principles supposed to be of this kind in the explanation of promissory obligation. The obligation, to repeat, is conceived of as consisting entirely in the fact that in his particular circumstances the promisor is required to act in a certain way, in accordance with a certain moral principle.

Now, I am arguing that one who promises immediately incurs an obligation of joint commitment. The jointness of the commitment creates an owing relationship, or directed obligation, of the promisor towards the promisee. There appears to be nothing like the standard appeals to moral principle in this picture.

How troubling is this radical divergence from standard opinion? There are several reasons not to be concerned by it. First, there is the question of what a promise is. Some philosophers do not seriously attempt to probe this question, relying on their intuitive understanding of the matter. Others operate with a more or less fine-grained account that may, of course, be mistaken. It should not be surprising if a new account of promising invokes a different source of promissory obligation.

Second, there is no consensus among moral philosophers as to *how* promises obligate, even given the consensus that their obligation is a matter of moral

---

[17] Scanlon (1998: 304). See also Scanlon (1990, 2001).
[18] The phrase is from Scanlon (1995: 345).

requirement. No one view is so compelling it has swept the field.[19] Each view has found its critics, even as ever more thoughtful and sensitive accounts, such as Scanlon's, are proposed.

Third, a problem for moral principle theories generally is that, reasonably enough, they allow that, 'all may not be equal'. That is, they allow that you may promise in circumstances such that you are not morally required to perform the promised act. What is not obvious is that in these circumstances you do not have an obligation of some kind through your promise. As previously discussed, it is common to judge that one's promissory obligation does not disappear when, according to the kinds of moral principles invoked by philosophers, one is not morally required to perform the promised act. It remains, and you fail to fulfil it if you fail to perform the promised act. This fits well with the idea that those who promise create a joint commitment—with attendant obligations—that remains in spite of the moral permissibility of not doing what you promised to do, in the circumstances.

A fourth point about theories that 'moralize' promissory obligation is this. They often take as their starting point Hume's well-known dictum to the effect that one cannot will an obligation into being. Hume himself was aware that this dictum went *against* everyday assumptions. He suggested that the contrary was 'entirely conformable to our common way of thinking and expressing ourselves'.[20] He argued, however, that from a philosophical point of view the truth of his dictum was clear.

Hume may well be right about moral obligation in the sense of moral requirement. He would be wrong, however, to deny that joint commitment—a kind of (joint) willing—is enough to bring an obligation into being. It can, after all, bring it about that one person owes another an action, and to owe someone an action is to have precisely the kind of obligation that promises intuitively bring about. Perhaps this is the gist of the 'common way of thinking and expressing ourselves' to which Hume alludes. Be that as it may, once one recognizes joint commitment as a source of obligation, a primary reason for attempting to explain promissory obligation by appeal to a moral principle is removed.

A fifth point about moralizing theories notes a significant problem for them. One can argue that they are unable to account for an important aspect of promissory obligation. When one makes a promise, the obligation one incurs is directed: one owes one's performance of the promise to the promisee, who

---

[19] It is not necessary for present purposes to present a typology of moral principle theories here. Scanlon (1998: 295) makes a point of contrasting his own theory with those which appeal to the existence of a valuable social practice of promising. See also Gilbert (2004a: 84–6).

[20] Hume (1978: 3.2.5.3).

has a correlative right against the promisor. This may be referred to, then, as *the problem of promisees' rights*. I discuss this in another place with a focus on Thomas Scanlon's account of promissory obligation.[21] I shall not go through the details of the argument here, but summarize its general conclusion. Quite generally, an account that makes promissory obligation a matter of subsumption under a moral principle such as Scanlon's principle of fidelity cannot adequately account for the special standing of the promisee to demand performance of the promise (or related actions). This special standing is a function of the promisee's right to performance, the right that is correlated with the promisor's directed obligation. In the case of Scanlon's principle, there is a special 'consent' clause to the effect that one must perform the promise, all equal, *unless the promisee says one need not*. Though in devising this clause Scanlon may have hoped it did, this clause does not suffice to give the promisee a special standing with respect to demands for performance and so on. It simply adds a condition to the applicability of the principle. These remarks on promissory obligation accord with those in Chapter 7 where I explained the difficulty of giving an account of directed obligations generally in terms of moral requirements.

Once promissory obligation is allowed to be the obligation of joint commitment, the problem of promisees' rights—and the correlative directed obligations of the promisor—is immediately solved. The same goes for the obligations incurred through an agreement, as well as those incurred through acting together, accepting a social rule, and so on. Invocation of a moral requirement, it can be argued, does not have the needed result.[22]

Reflection on these matters may be complicated by the possibility that the promisor incur more than one type of obligation through a given promise or agreement. This possibility can now be fleshed out in more concrete terms. Suppose things are as I am proposing: those who enter agreements or make promises immediately and inevitably incur obligations of joint commitment. It is then quite possible that one is morally required, all else being equal, to conform to the agreement.[23]

10.3 Moral Argument Around the Promise

Evidently, my account of promissory obligation does not rule out moral argument with respect to promising. The detailed morality of promising, entering

---

[21] See Gilbert (2004*a*).

[22] This, then, is a problem for Bratman (1993*b*) and others who invoke Scanlon's principle of fidelity to account for the obligations associated with acting together, either given an initial agreement or not.

[23] Gilbert (2004*a*) connects this point to Scanlon's Principle F.

agreements, and related matters is of great importance to our understanding of the moral rights and wrongs of human action. The broken promise or violated agreement may, indeed, be one of the basic spurs—if not the basic spur—to moral reflection. Certainly it is the topic of its fair share of plays and operas.

An example of moral—and legal—argument around an agreement is found in Shakespeare's play *The Merchant of Venice*. There are several facets to this argument. Among these is Portia's proposal, in a famous speech, that a promisee should bring considerations of mercy to bear on the question whether to insist on the performance of the promise. Contemporary legal judgements in contract law often reflect such considerations. Considerations of mercy are relevant in the context of all joint commitments, given the general concurrence needed to end the commitment and so on. The important general point is one I have by now often made: to have the standing to insist and, indeed, to have sufficient reason to do so, is not the same as being justified all things considered in insisting. In Shakespeare's play, Shylock focuses on his standing; Portia insists on the relevance of further considerations to what ought to be done, all things considered.

Philosophers have considered, in particular, two cases pertinent to the morality of promise keeping. The first case is that of coerced promises. The second is the case of what I have referred to as immoral promises. As we have seen, these cases—given their analogues involving agreements—are highly germane to the evaluation of actual contract theory.[24] Those who assume that promissory obligation is a matter of moral requirement often say that such promises do not obligate, full stop. I argue in what follows that they do obligate. This will not be surprising in light of my discussion so far. Since the issues are important both within and outside the territory of political obligation it is worth explaining my position on each of these cases in turn.

Coerced Promises

I argued earlier that someone could indeed be coerced into entering an agreement. The same points apply to promises. Let me summarize them briefly. Everyday thought and language suggests that it is indeed possible to be coerced into making a promise. It is indeed the case that, as a conceptual matter, one cannot promise without intending to do so. One must understand what one is doing. This point is not enough, however, to preclude one's being coerced into making a promise. For one can be in coercive circumstances without being rendered witless by fear.

---

[24] See the discussion of the no-obligation objections in Ch. 5, above.

Once one accepts that there can be a coerced promise, there is the question whether it obligates. It may help to have a concrete example in mind. Suppose that Carol is surprised by Jack in the act of robbing his house. She gets him to promise, at gunpoint, not to call the police after she has left the building.

Many would make the following moral judgements on this case: Jack is not morally required to keep this promise. If anything, he is morally required immediately to call the police to report that an armed robber who has already broken into his house is now at large in the neighbourhood. He certainly does not owe Carol his silence, morally speaking. After all, she has wronged him both by being in his apartment, and by putting a gun to his head in order to extort his promise. Carol would surely not be morally justified in now demanding that Jack keep the promise or rebuking him for going to the police.

These moral judgements may well be correct. But suppose it is inferred that no obligation of any kind accrues to Jack through his promise. This, it may be argued, is counter-intuitive. One might appeal to a general sense, such as Prichard's, that all promises, as such, obligate. One might also return to the example. Surely Carol is in a position to rebuke Jack for calling the police, citing his promise. In other words, not only did he promise, his having promised gives her the standing to rebuke him. She can, of course, have the standing to do this without being morally justified, all things considered, in going ahead and doing so.

Given that a coerced promise is possible, and that such a promise in some sense obligates the promisor, those who view promissory obligation as a matter of moral requirement, have what looks like an insoluble problem. This is so in spite of the plausibility of the moral judgements just described. Given a plural subject account of promising, one can argue as follows: coerced promises are promises and do bind, in the way every promise binds. One is not, however, morally required to keep every promise. A plural subject account thus supports plausible judgements on promises and the validity of conventional moral think-ing. I take its ability to bring order into this difficult terrain to count in support of a plural subject account of promising. It is not, of course, its only support.

The implications of all this for the actual contract theory of political obligation will be pursued later in this chapter. First, I consider immoral promises and agreements.

Immoral Promises and Obligation

Suppose Alice promises Belle that she will kill Cass. It would generally be agreed that, in the absence of further pertinent facts, Alice is not morally required to carry out her promise. It would generally be agreed, indeed, that she is morally required *not* to carry it out. Importantly, these judgements would be made on the basis of the description of the promise itself, in particular on the basis of its content.

Alice's promise in the example is a clear case of what I am calling an immoral promise. If a general account of such promises is desired I propose the following for present purposes: a promise is *immoral* if, given its content, and on the assumption that there are no further facts pertinent to this conclusion, the promisor is not morally required to do what he promised and, indeed, is morally required *not* to do what he promised.

Given this account, there could be further facts relevant to the evaluation of such a promise such that many would judge it to be morally permissible or even mandatory to carry it out. Thus consider a version of the example given. Suppose Cass has a terminal illness that will soon kill him and that he is in pain that no medical treatment can alleviate. In a phone conversation from his hospital bed he has begged his bedridden wife Belle to arrange for someone to kill him and end his misery sooner rather than later, something trained medical personnel have refused to do. Belle agrees that she will do this and gets her only friend Alice to promise to kill Cass. In circumstances such as these, many would take back the judgement that Alice is morally required not to kill Cass.[25] That said, I focus on the case of an immoral promise where, by hypothesis, no such further facts obtain.[26]

Does an immoral promise obligate the promisor? As noted earlier, several philosophers are prepared to give negative answers, with or without argument. This is completely consonant with the standard view of promissory obligation. What I would argue is that though an immoral promise may not *morally bind* or *require* the promisor to do what he promised, there is an important sense in which such a promise *obligates* the promisor.

This position is consistent with all of the following points. First, insofar as there is a general moral requirement that one keep one's promises, it is a moral requirement 'all else being equal'. It is not a moral requirement 'whatever else is true' or, in other terms, a conclusive moral requirement. Second, as Thomas Scanlon puts it, 'various factors . . . can make it [morally] permissible not to do the thing promised'.[27] Third, one such factor is the consideration that the promise in question is an immoral promise. In that case, indeed, not only is it morally permissible not to do the promised thing: it is morally required that one not do it.

---

[25] Here I respond to a comment from Dan Egonsson (2004).

[26] Cf. Altham (1985: 3), 'I take as my main example a promise to kill someone, and ask the reader to suppose that in the circumstances to carry out the promise would be murder.' I am assuming that absent special mitigating circumstances it would be morally wrong to carry out a promise to kill someone.

[27] Scanlon (2003: 284).

My position does not, therefore, stand in opposition to authors such as Simmons and Altham who say that in and of itself an immoral promise does *not* obligate the promisor, insofar as what they maintain amounts to or entails that those who make immoral promises are *not morally required* to do as they have promised, all else being equal. This much is trivially true, indeed, given my account of an immoral promise. The issue, as I have indicated, is whether there is *another* sense in which every promise, irrespective of its content, obligates the promisor. According to the letter of quotations made earlier in this book, these authors would say that there is no such sense.[28] They may have meant to do no more than assert that a promisor may not be morally required to do as promised. On this we are in agreement. What, though, of the other matter?

Irrespective of my preferred account of promising, is there anything to be said in favour of the view that there is a sense in which all promises, as such, obligate? Once again, one might cite the suggestion of Prichard and others that to find an act was promised is to establish that the promisor is obligated to perform it—there is simply no room for doubt here. If this is correct, and if, as is agreed, one who makes an immoral promise is not morally required to carry out his promise, promises must obligate in some *other* way.

One way to resist this suggestion would be to deny that immoral promises are genuine promises. Those who deny that immoral promises obligate do not accept this. Simmons sees his position as consonant with common opinion and does not provide any reasons for it. A reason is offered by James Altham, who puts the point in the following way.[29] (I have changed the names in his example so as to fit mine.) Suppose that, in the original version of this case, Alice has received money from Belle in exchange for her undertaking to kill Cass. If Alice does not kill Cass, Belle can invoke the promise in demanding that the money be returned.[30] If there was not really a promise, Belle would have nothing to invoke in demanding her money back.

It is worth looking more closely at this example. As Altham describes it, Alice received the money 'in exchange for her undertaking to' kill Cass. Perhaps the money was handed over after the promise was made, and in that sense one was 'exchanged' for the other. Still, one might argue, there is a puzzle here. The promise was made. How can Belle demand her money back if it was given in exchange for the promise itself?

Elizabeth Anscombe, in a passage that inspired Altham, wrote rather of receiving money 'for an evil deed that was not yet done'.[31] This suggests a

---

[28] See Ch. 5, above.   [29] Altham (1985: 9).

[30] As Carol can invoke Jack's coerced promise as a basis for rebuking him in a previous example.

[31] Anscombe (1981: 16).

number of points about promising that I take to be correct irrespective of how they may be explained. What Alice's promise to Belle achieved could be put this way: *Alice's future action was now Belle's own.* Not, of course, in the sense that Belle was to be the performer of the action, but in the sense that she could say it was 'her thing'. This she could do once the promise was made. At this point, however, the action was not yet in her possession. In order for that to happen, Alice had to perform the action. Until she did so, she would *owe* the action to Belle.

So what did Belle pay for? In light of the points just made it now seems plausible, after all, to say that she paid for Alice's promise, and that alone. For *in paying for the promise she was paying for Alice's future action*. This being *owed* her, as a result of the promise, Belle would be in a position to demand that it come into her possession—that is, be performed—within a reasonable time. Should it not be forthcoming, perhaps now being precluded, she would be in a position to demand, among other things, some form of compensation for her loss. The money she had paid for the action would be the obvious choice.

Quite similar things can be said for a case in which Belle did not give Alice money. Suppose Alice simply promised Belle to kill Cass, having been asked to do so. Belle would now be in a position to demand that Alice kill Cass within a reasonable time. Suppose that Alice does not do so and that it is now impossible for her to do so. Belle cannot demand her money back, since she gave Alice no money. She can, however, make other pertinent demands, including a demand for some form of compensation for her loss. There is a loss here, though no money has changed hands. For by virtue of Alice's promise, and that alone, Alice's future action of killing Cass became 'Belle's thing', something Alice owed her. In this case, if you like, it was a 'free gift'.

Belle can also invoke the promise in demanding an explanation for Alice's non-performance of the promise and in demanding some kind of compensation for any losses she has incurred on the basis of her reliance on it. She will presumably not be able to get the law to press her case and would be foolish to attempt to do so. Nonetheless the non-performance of Alice's promise seems to give Belle a case to be answered. She can, in short, 'invoke' the promise in the course of making various demands. This promise apparently both makes Alice's action Belle's 'thing' and entitles her to 'get' it. Until she gets it, Alice owes it to her.

The preceding account of what Alice's promise to Belle achieved suggests that (by virtue of being promises) immoral promises, like other promises, give the promisor a *directed* obligation, this being a matter of owing an action to another person. This accords with my proposal about promises generally: a promise is a joint commitment of the promisor and promisee. More precisely it is a joint commitment to uphold as a body a particular decision as to how the promisor will act. The promisor, then, owes the promisee performance of the promise.

What if a promise is immoral? If such a promise is indeed a promise, as I have suggested is intuitive and as the theorists cited agree, then on the above account it will obligate the promisor to fulfil the promise. This will be a directed obligation toward the promisee. That said, a promisor might, on occasion, reasonably say to himself: 'I am party to a joint commitment with this person (the promisee). I therefore owe him conformity. This consideration gives me sufficient reason to conform and "trumps" certain types of consideration that might in principle favour not doing so. However, what I am jointly committed to do is something that, absent special circumstances, is wicked. All aspects of this joint commitment considered, reason requires that I do not conform to it.' This allows that though the joint commitment continues to have its usual normative force, there is an overwhelming moral counterforce in play.

I am not here addressing the question of precisely when it is plausible to claim there is an overwhelming moral counterforce to an obligation of joint commitment. Suffice it to say that the joint commitment account of promising can allow that such a counterforce is *possible*. It can accordingly allow that the immoral promise as defined here is a case in point—all else being equal. Meanwhile it implies that such a counterforce *does not destroy the obligation*, which stands as long as the joint commitment does.

Does an immoral promise in any sense *morally* bind or obligate the promisor, on the joint commitment account? If one understands that someone is *morally bound* to do something if and only if he is morally required to do it, and this is an 'all things considered' matter, then one can consistently argue that wicked promises do not morally bind. One can, indeed, argue that one is morally bound not to perform such a promise because of its content. This judgement is consistent with the idea that promises as such endow the promisor with obligations of joint commitment. If one understands that someone is *morally bound* as long as he is genuinely obligated in *some* sense, then of course the joint commitment account will say that an immoral promise does morally bind the promisor, since it gives him an obligation of joint commitment.

From a practical point of view the main issue is the bearing, if any, of an immoral promise on what one has reason to do. The issue is not how the qualifier 'moral' should be used. These questions, however, are not unrelated. In order to give a reasoned answer to the latter question, we need to develop a plausible answer to the first.

What, then, is the practical relevance of an immoral promise? If, in this case, reason does not require the promisor to act as he promised, as is plausible, what difference can his promise make to him? If reason does not permit the promisee to demand performance of the promise, as may seem plausible too, what difference does the promise make to *him*? Some indication of this has already been given. In brief, the promise is there to be invoked. The promisee may badly want what was promised him, or have some other motive strong enough to lead him to ignore reason's dictates and demand performance or compensation. The promisor may respond by disparaging the promisee's action, but he cannot deny that he has the promisee's 'thing'. Something, it seems, may need to be done to rectify this. This is close to the structure of the crisis in *A Merchant of Venice*.

10.4 Implications for Actual Contract Theory

I have argued that both coerced and immoral promises obligate the promisor towards the promisee. This will be so if a promise creates an appropriate joint commitment, an idea that has some plausibility. Prior to that I gave an account of an everyday agreement as a joint commitment to uphold as a body a certain decision. Clearly, my conclusions on coerced and immoral promises apply, with relevant changes, to agreements so conceived. I now discuss the implications of these conclusions for actual contract theory, beginning with the question of agreements entered into in circumstances that are coercive in nature.

If actual contract theory construes an agreement as suggested, it can allow that coercive circumstances do not deprive an agreement of its obligating quality. In other words, it will be no part of the theory that political obligations *must* be voluntarily assumed. Rather, they must be assumed intentionally, at some possibly quite low level of awareness.

This, some may argue, is not actual contract theory as they know it. It was part and parcel of that theory that political obligations were voluntarily assumed; this was one of its great moral attractions.

In response one can point out, first, that there are doubtless different versions of actual contract theory. Insofar as the theory is characterized solely in terms of agreements as these are conceived of in everyday life, however, there is no automatic assumption of voluntariness. Everyday understandings allow for one to be coerced into entering an agreement. To argue that political societies are founded on agreements, then, and that membership requires entry into an agreement, is not to say that such entry must be voluntary. This is the version of actual contract theory under consideration here.

Second, as discussed earlier, its moral attractiveness or otherwise is irrelevant to an analytic theory of political obligations. What a solution to the membership problem requires is a satisfactory analytic theory, in particular a theory that shows that and how membership in a political society, being what it is, involves obligations. If one has a plausible account of such membership, such that it obligates, that is sufficient for a solution to the problem. That there is something unattractive, if there is, about a solution such that one may have political obligations one did not voluntarily assume is beside the point.

It is not beside all points, of course. If the possibility of being obligated through an act one had no real choice about is a real one, and is morally repellent, one can start thinking of ways to deal with, or ameliorate, the situations where it arises. Philosophers have discussed such matters, with suggestions, for instance, as to how to facilitate someone's withdrawal from a political society of which he no longer wishes to be a member.[32] The main thing for present purposes is to see if there is a theory of political obligation that satisfies at least the core criteria sketched in Chapter 3.

In conclusion, from the point of view of the membership problem, actual contract theory is proof against the first no-obligation objection, the objection in terms of coercive circumstances. Even one who is coerced into entering an agreement still has obligations under that agreement. One might wonder about the practical consequences of such obligations, assuming that one is not morally required to fulfil them. I have already made some suggestions along these lines, and return to this question.

First, I turn to the second no-obligation objection. This runs as follows: even granted a foundational agreement to do so, the members of political societies with unjust or morally unacceptable political institutions of any kind cannot be obligated to uphold these institutions.

In arguing against this, the actual contract theorist need not allow that anyone is morally required to uphold morally unacceptable institutions. In particular, he need not allow that members of a society with immoral political institutions are morally required to uphold those institutions. In the area of moral argument and judgement, his judgements may go one way or another without his changing the core of his theory of political obligation. Suppose he comes to argue that members of a political society are morally required to subvert rather than uphold its immoral institutions, insofar as that does not demand more of them than is reasonable. He does not then have to give up the idea that the members of any political society have obligations to support and uphold the political institutions of that society quite generally. For he can argue that they have obligations of joint commitment deriving from the agreement they have made, the agreement to found the society in question with its

---

[32] Cf. Beran (1987) on 'internal emigration'.

particular political institutions. Given that these institutions are immoral, there is reason enough (he can argue) *not* to fulfil them.

Richard Dagger has argued that theorists of any stripe who argue for a positive solution to the membership problem are wrong because of what he nicely calls 'the problem of group character': some groups are just too bad for there to be political obligations. What I have argued, in effect, is that a joint commitment version of actual contract theory avoids this problem. Its proponents can argue that membership in a political society—as a matter of participation in an agreement—is accompanied by obligations to uphold its political institutions, whatever the moral character of that society. In this way it can, after all, offer a positive solution to the membership problem.

I say more about the case of societies of considerable injustice in the next chapter.[33] At this point in the discussion of actual contract theory, however, it will be well to make some further comments on that topic now.

If the political obligations of actual contract theory are obligations of joint commitment, how will things play out on the ground, so to speak, given that one is in that way obligated to obey an evil law? Suppose that Emma is morally required to break a particular, evil law. Realizing this, she goes ahead and breaks it. I take it that a morally astute person would not call her on this violation, irrespective of his standing to do so. One might indeed say that the correlative rights of joint commitment are also overridden. That is, one might say that her compatriots have no *moral* right to her compliance. A morally astute compatriot would approve her action and, if his circumstances and courage are similar, do the same.

Not all of one's fellow members need be morally astute, however. Knowing that they have the standing to do so, they may invoke the agreement at any time. They may say, in effect, singly or in unison, 'You have not given us what was ours!' Alternatively they may stand behind their leaders as these act accordingly. Thus the existence of political obligations of joint commitment may have significant practical consequences even given that they are obligations to do extremely bad things. I take it that Emma may not be morally required to break an evil law if the consequences for her personally will be too grave. Some political leaders and regimes call for heroes, as opposed simply to morally upright people, as opponents.

Evidently, questions about how things will play out 'on the ground' are somewhat ambiguous. They may relate to an ideal world in which people act in accordance with the fullest understanding of their situation and impeccable practical reasoning. Allowing for the moment that some immoral political

---

[33] Sects. 11.1 and 11.4, below.

institutions have somehow become part of the landscape, it may be that political obligations with respect to them will have no effect on what is actually done in such a world. The other interpretation concerns an imperfect world like our own in which people act on partial or temporarily salient information and for a variety of bad reasons. In this world the political obligations of an immoral society will most likely be impediments to that society's good. They will tend to prevent people from acting morally: people may be diverted by salient joint commitment obligations, they may be afraid of others' making demands they have the standing to make and so on.

Clearly, the actual contract theorist need not assume that the political obligations he takes to exist in immoral societies are all, always forces for good. Many people have followed the orders of their political 'superiors' to the great shame of mankind. To say this is not to say anything untoward. It is generally understood that obligations are not always best fulfilled, all things considered. What can be obscure, given this understanding, is precisely how that can be. Things become clear once one understands that the obligations that inhere in joint commitments are neither (in and of themselves) moral requirements, nor context-sensitive.

My conclusion on actual contract theory to this point, then, is that it can be successfully defended against the no-obligation objection: coercive circumstances and immoral content do not rule out a society-constituting agreement that obligates all parties. To show this, I have argued for a joint commitment account of agreements and of the obligation most closely associated with agreements.

This does not mean that actual contract theory is a maximally adequate theory of political obligation. As was argued in Chapter 5, a theory that articulated a broader concept of political society would better fit the criteria of adequacy mooted earlier.

Such a theory has already been mooted: plural subject theory. This is proof against the plural subject version of the no-obligation objection. It too invokes obligations of joint commitment; if a relevant joint commitment is in place, so are they.

11

The Plural Subject Theory
of Political Obligation

This chapter returns to the plural subject theory of political obligation and evaluates it as a solution to the membership problem. The theory is brought up against the targets that were proposed for a solution in Chapter 3. It is then compared and contrasted with some theories of political obligation that are close to it in content or spirit, including a theory not yet discussed in this book, the theory that political obligations are obligations of fair play. A number of possible objections to plural subject theory are noted and responses to these objections are given. The importance of political obligations according to the theory is discussed, and some substantive moral questions relating to these obligations are noted.

11.1 The Theory Assessed

Review of the Theory

In the terms of this book a theory of political obligation is a theory that offers a reasoned positive solution to the membership problem. At the end of Chapter 9 I adumbrated a plural subject theory of political obligation. As is already clear, closely related theories are possible. Actual contract theory, as construed in Chapter 8, is a case in point. It is a special case of plural subject theory. That is, the class of political societies it contemplates is smaller than, and included within, the class contemplated by plural subject theory. Variants of the more general theory proposed here are also possible. That said, I shall in this chapter discuss the theory articulated in Chapter 9 and shall refer to it as *the* plural subject theory of political obligation.

It may be good briefly to focus attention on this theory before proceeding to its assessment. The theory argues that, according to a central everyday conception, a political society is constituted by an underlying joint commitment to accept certain rules, rules that count intuitively as political institutions. Those who are parties to the joint commitment are the members of the political society in question, or, if you prefer, they are its core members. They may stipulate that others, for instance, their children, are to be regarded as members for some or all practical purposes. These others then have imputed membership. They will not be core members or members proper unless they come to participate in the joint commitment that constitutes the political society in question.

I should emphasize that my purpose in proposing this theory is not—or not just—to meet the challenge of showing that the membership problem is susceptible of a positive solution. I believe, and have argued, that the concepts of a political society and of obligation invoked by the theory are central everyday conceptions and that their linkage, therefore, is of great importance for understanding much of the discourse, feeling, and action that takes place in the course of human life.

Assessing the Theory

I return now to the criteria of adequacy for a solution to the membership problem that were set out in Chapter 3. Given that the theory satisfied the affirmativeness criterion, one set of criteria were, I suggested, central. Any adequate theory of political obligation should meet them. A theory that did well according both to these and to the additional criteria would be about as good as any theory could be. The fact that one theory met all of the criteria would not mean that no other theory could do so: in principle, there would be another maximally adequate theory that appealed to a different notion of membership in a political society, a different notion of obligation, or both.

How does the plural subject theory of political obligation fare in light of the criteria? I have in mind, of course, the theory as it has been developed to this point in this book. Plural subject theory clearly meets the affirmativeness criterion: according the theory, there are political obligations. Given its proposed understanding of what a political society is, its members are obligated to uphold its political institutions. What, then, of the core criteria?

i. The Core Criteria Plural subject theory satisfies the explanatoriness criterion: the theory does not merely state that membership in a political society is such that members are obligated to uphold the political institutions of the society in question. It explains how this is. It argues, of course, that membership in a political society—or membership of the central, society-constituting type—is participation in a joint commitment to uphold as a body with the relevant others the political institutions of the society.

Plural subject theory meets the criterion of explicativeness, according to which the explanation given by the theory should be backed up with a careful explication of the relevant concepts of a political society, membership in such a society, and obligatoriness. In doing so, I would argue, it also meets the intuitiveness criterion. Its intuitiveness breaks down into several parts.

First, I take the society aspect of the plural subject account of a political society to meet the intuitiveness criterion. According to a standard conception of societies, these are social groups in a relatively narrow, intuitive sense. I have argued that the concept of a plural subject as articulated earlier approximates the relevant intuitive concept of a social group. As was explained, there can be small and transient plural subjects, but also large, enduring ones whose many members, anonymous in relation to one another, are spread over a territory of great extent. Such large plural subjects may include other, smaller plural subjects, and they may be hierarchical or non-hierarchical. That societies are often understood to be large, enduring, and so on, is thus no barrier to the intuitiveness of the plural subject account of societies.

Second, I take the way the plural subject account understands the 'political' aspect of a political society to be intuitive also: a political society is a society with political institutions. Intuitively, again, a society's political institutions, or institutions of governance, are *its* institutions. A plausible way of under-standing the relevant relation of ownership—of understanding what it is for an institution to be the institution *of* a particular society—is in plural subject terms. It is for the members of the society to be jointly committed to uphold, as a body, the institutions in question. They can then meaningfully claim that those institutions are collectively *theirs*.

I do not take either of these conceptions to be the only ones that might count as reasonably intuitive. The point is that if we want something precise enough to give us an adequate theory of political obligation, we must opt for a particular, specifiable conception. Given other reasonably intuitive conceptions there could be different, perhaps negative, results.

As to the conception of obligatoriness invoked by the theory, I have argued that an obligation of joint commitment is a fundamental type of obligation. Such obligations are constantly at issue in everyday thought, as people do things together, and live together in the context of a variety of social groups.

The type of obligation in question is directed: a given party to the joint commitment is obligated *to* the other parties to the commitment, as such, who have corresponding rights to conformity to the commitment. Such directionality is here understood along the lines of Hart and others at least to this extent: one party owes performance to another, who is, then, in a position to demand it of him.

Though theorists have attempted to explain how the owing relationship arises, it is unclear that the explanations that are generally given are adequate. It may be claimed, for instance, that the owing relationship exists when one person (the one who 'owes' the action) is morally required to do something and another's interests are the ground of the moral requirement (this person being the one to whom conformity to the requirement is 'owed').[1] But this does not accord with the intuitive character of the owing relationship at issue here. For that gives the one who is owed the action a special standing to make demands and the like, demands of the one who owes. If the whole thing is simply a matter of moral requirement, however grounded, then it is by no means clear that the one who is 'owed' has this special standing.

Plural subject theory shows how the owing relationship can arise. Those who jointly commit themselves to do something as a body can be said thereby to own each other's conforming actions, though not yet to possess them. Each therefore owes such actions to the others.

The plural subject theory of political obligation, then, both appeals to an established intuitive notion of directed obligation—in terms of owing, which is understood as grounding a special standing to make demands and so on—and deepens our understanding of that notion by revealing one clear context for its application.

In this connection it may be noted that plural subject theory meets well the subsidiary criterion of political bonds, according to which a maximally satisfactory theory would explain the tendency to speak of 'bonds', 'binding', and even 'bondage' in discussions of political obligation. First, it may be said that one who is obligated to another is bound to that other unless and until the obligation is discharged. If I owe you a future action of mine, I am in a sense 'in thrall' to you. Second, even disregarding the matter of obligation, a joint commitment in and of itself 'binds' the parties together, subsuming them, so to speak, under one and the same commitment. It binds the parties together in the sense of unifying them. Hence, both the idea of a 'bond' as something that unifies—often found in texts on social groups—and the idea of a 'bond' as something that confines or constrains—more in evidence in discussion of political obligation, but found in that other context as well—finds an explanation in the idea of a joint commitment which both unifies the parties and obligates one to another.

I turn now to the intelligible grounding criterion. According to this, the most satisfactory theory will show precisely how, given the carefully explicated, intuitive conceptions of these things invoked by the theory, membership in

---

[1] This approximates the proposal in Raz (1984).

a political society is such that members are obligated to uphold the society's political institutions. Plural subject theory meets this criterion: membership in a political society is conceived of as a matter of participation in a joint commitment of some kind, in consonance with a more general, intuitive idea of a social group. Participation in any joint commitment involves obligations. In this case, the obligations will be to uphold one or more rule of a special type. Using the set of labels for such rules introduced in Chapter 9, these may be governing rules, rules that engender a given instance of personal rule, or rules of governance (constitutional rules).

ii. The Interpretative Criteria   How likely is it that a given person's sense that they have political obligations can be interpreted in terms of participation in an appropriate joint commitment? At the end of the day, that must depend on who that person is. In general terms, however, a theory of political obligation that is likely to be interpretatively fruitful will invoke concepts that are, or correspond closely to, non-technical concepts of everyday life. The arguments presented in this book suggest that plural subject theory is of the right kind. The theory invokes a concept of political society that corresponds closely to a standard everyday notion. Whether or not a given person's sense that he is politically obligated involves that concept can be tested out in a variety of ways.

Thus, suppose Clare is a United States citizen whose language is English. Does she say that 'We are at war' when the United States is at war? Does she refer to United States laws as 'our laws'? Does she refer to 'our constitution' when she has in mind the Constitution of the United States? Suppose she does all of these things.

According to the plural subject account of such locutions as 'We are at war', Clare implies that she is party to a joint commitment that lies at the foundation of a certain collective agent—as she sees it, the United States is the collective agent in question. She may strongly disapprove of what 'we' are doing: but she understands herself to be 'one of us' nonetheless. Her use of the first-person plural pronoun in this context makes this clear. The same goes for the possibility that she plans some kind of protest action, with the hope of bringing to an end the war effort in question. She may have reasons to do this in spite of that fact that she is party to a joint commitment to espouse as a body that very war effort. Her being so committed is not refuted by her activism. She might say, precisely, 'I am marching because—*in my personal opinion*—the war in which we are engaged is unjust.'

In referring to United States laws and the United States constitution as 'ours', Clare may mean, once again, to allude to her participation in an underlying joint commitment to uphold the laws or the constitution in question. It is possible that she does not mean this. Perhaps by 'our laws' she means, for instance, 'those laws that I and other so-called Americans are coerced into following'. I take such a construal to be implausible unless Clare was using the qualifier 'our' in an 'inverted commas' sense, something that would need to be indicated by her tone. She would then imply that, in spite of her use of the qualifier 'our', she did not understand herself to be party to an appropriate joint commitment.

Some political theorists have indicated that they think it implausible that much information can be carried by the use of a single, indeed a very small word: 'we'.[2] Yet many people regard it as highly significant. Sometimes they have regarded it with distaste, sometimes not.[3]

Clare's speech is, in any case, not the only relevant consideration. How does she think, act, and feel in relation to the actions, laws, and so on, of the United States? Does she express or at least experience a kind of guilt over actions of the United States that she considers morally wrong? Does she feel pride in actions of the United States that she finds commendable? Does she take pride in its constitution or in laws or other political institutions she finds admirable? If she sees someone breaking the law, in her estimation inexcusably, does she have an inclination to object? If she does not think there is good reason for it, does she feel to some extent affronted by such law breaking? Critical of it as she may be herself, does she find herself reacting to hostile criticism of the United States *by outsiders* as an affront? Positive answers to these questions would all support a plural subject interpretation of her words, and the imputation to her of the understanding that she is part of a particular plural subject—a plural subject for which the standard label is 'the United States'. The phenomena referred to here are all, one might observe, associated with the phenomenon of subjective identification. I discuss the relationship of plural subject theory to subjective identification theory later in this chapter.

In addition, Clare herself might give voice to a sense that she is obligated to uphold the political institutions of the United States precisely because the United States is her country. She might not put things exactly thus, but this may be the gist of what she says. This is at least consistent with the hypothesis

---

[2] A related doubt has been raised about 'my'. See Wellman (2000). 'My' sometimes amounts to 'my, qua one of us', but not always, as in 'my sister', one of the types of cases at issue in Wellman's discussion.

[3] Albert Einstein apparently quoted with approval a verse expressing a negative attitude to 'that little word "we"', in a domestic context. (He also had occasion to speak more positively on its behalf. See Stern (1999).) Countless other examples might be cited.

that she is thinking of the United States as a political society whose political institutions she is jointly committed with the other citizens to uphold as a body.

That one or more people are thinking of a certain population (for instance, United States citizens) in plural subject terms can, then, be tested out. The tests in question include appropriate speech, action, and expressions of feeling and of obligation. When these all mesh appropriately there will be good grounds for attributing such thinking to the people in question. A given person may be conflicted, manifesting some but not all of these reactions. It may then be a matter of some delicacy to sort out what is going on, and properly to describe it. Be that as it may, a given person's sense of political obligation may well be easily and properly interpreted in terms of the plural subject theory of political obligation. One reason for this is that the concepts invoked by the theory closely track central everyday concepts of society and obligation.

One who has the plural subject conception of a political society is likely to understand how to tell whether those around them are operating in terms of that conception. Thus, if his beliefs and assumptions are at all sensitive to evidence, his belief or 'sense' that he is party to the relevant joint commitment is likely to have some foundation in terms of his experience. It may well, then, be reasonable.

There is more than one type of context in which this may be so. In one, the 'default reading' of the phrase 'our country' and related phrases such as 'our constitution' in the population is the plural subject reading. That is, 'our country' is understood to mean, roughly, 'that society whose political institutions we are jointly committed to uphold', and so on. Imagine, then, that it is common knowledge in the population at issue that in face-to-face conversations, letters, and so on everyone speaks without hesitation of 'our country', 'our constitution', 'our laws', and so on in relation to the population as a whole. They speak of what 'we' are doing in terms of both international relations and internal issues. They evince guilt, pride, and other such emotions over such things. And they give no indication that they do not wish the plural subject interpretation to be made. At this point the members of the population have good reason to suppose themselves to be party to the pertinent joint commitments. As is common knowledge in the population, they have all, in effect, intentionally expressed their readiness to be jointly committed in the relevant way. This may initially have been done through tendentious or initiatory or mistaken—though sincere—uses of 'our country' and so on, but once it is common knowledge that such readiness has been expressed in these ways, there is a foundation for everyone to use 'our country' and the rest straightforwardly, referring to what is understood to be an established plural subject.

Even if we do not assume that the plural subject interpretation of 'we' is the default interpretation, the idea that a widespread use of 'our country' and so on is generally intended in the plural subject sense may be supported by a variety of particular observations. That it is so supported may itself be common knowledge in a population. For example, one member of the population may say to another 'Hey! That's against the law!' He may do so in a way expressive of a complex of understandings including a sense that the speaker has been in some sense offended against, a sense of his own entitlement to intervene, and an understanding that the other will recognize this entitlement. These understandings suggest that the speaker takes there to be a corresponding joint commitment to which both members of the population are subject. The person addressed may accept what is expressed without demur, thereby suggesting that the assumption of a corresponding joint commitment is common ground. Such minute interactions—occurring on a large scale—will both confirm the plural subject interpretation of phrases and statements about 'our country' and so on, and count independently as expressions of readiness to be jointly committed in the relevant way. If, in the course of time, there comes to be common knowledge in the population that everyone has so expressed himself, any particular members of the population would have good reason to suppose themselves to be parties to a relevant joint commitment with other members of the population.

People will also be reasonable to believe themselves to be parties to a joint commitment if conditions approximating these obtain.[4] Whether they are reasonable to hold this belief in a given case is an empirical matter. Whether the belief is accurate in particular cases is also an empirical matter.

iii. Questions of Authority: The Standing to Command and to Punish Can some light be thrown on the question of political authority by the plural subject theory of political obligation? According to the theory, what is the relationship, if any, between political authority and political obligation? It will not be possible to present a full treatment of this topic. I hope to make clear, however, that the plural subject theory of political obligation can help to illuminate it. Some of the points made below will by now be familiar. Nonetheless, they bear repeating here.

I shall understand political authority as follows. Person or body A *has political authority in population P* if and only if, roughly, A has the standing to command members of P, as such, to do A's bidding with respect to the governance of P as a whole.

---

[4] See Ch. 8, above.

It is particularly important to be clear about what standing amounts to in the present context. To say that someone has the standing to command is another way of saying that they are in a position to command. For commanding is something you simply cannot do without the standing to do so. You can speak to someone in the imperative mood, you can yell at them, you can put a gun to their head while doing so—all possibilities in a modern 'state of nature' or, in Hobbesian terms, a modern war of all against all. None of that means you have the standing to command them.

Use of the term 'command'—in the sense at issue here—presupposes that the person in question has the right standing. In other terms, it presupposes that the person in question has the appropriate *authority*. Clearly, it is this sense of 'command' that is philosophically interesting. There is little that needs explanation about uttering imperatives, yelling at someone, putting a gun to their head, and so on. Before turning to political authority in particular, I first discuss this issue in general terms.

What is it to have the standing to command another person? What is the difference between issuing an imperative to them (with or without accompanying threats) and actually commanding them to do something? When is one in face of a genuine command, a command proper—in short, a command?

The first question is posed in terms of commanding another person to do something. It is helpful to separate this question from the question of issuing commands to oneself. I proceed in terms of the first question initially. It is not an easy question and there has been a fair amount of discussion of it by others.[5] None of these, to my knowledge, adopts precisely the position taken here. Not surprisingly, though, there are several points of contact.

Others have emphasized two features of commands proper that it is worth noting at the outset.[6] Indeed, they have sometimes proposed that a command be understood entirely in such terms. First, the status of a purported command as a command proper is not, as a matter of logic, a matter of its content. In a common phrase, it is *content-independent*. (In practice the status of a purported command can be extremely content-dependent: Saskia says to Rob, 'Tell me what to do and I'll do it—as long as it's not immoral, illegal, or contrary to

---

[5] e.g. Anscombe (1978) and Raz (1979, 1986); also R. P. Wolff (1970), in the context of his scepticism about the very possibility of commands. See also several articles in Edmunson ed. (1999) and Hampton (1997), the extensive first part of which focuses on the nature of political authority. Hampton ascribes authority (and the capacity to command, or rule) to those in respect to whose purported commands there is a (Lewis-style) convention of 'obedience' in a given society (1997: 80). Here 'obedience' seems to amount more or less to conformity.

[6] These are both emphasized by Raz.

my religion.' Saskia here sets fairly strict limits on what Rob may command her to do. Purported commands whose content lies outside the limits are not commands proper in this small political society. An even more extreme example: 'I'll not bow to anyone on anything—but tell me to sacrifice myself for the cause, and I will.') Second, commands have something *peremptory* about them: from the point of view of what reason requires the person commanded to do, they 'trump' at least some common considerations in favour of acting contrary to them.[7]

These points, though instructive, raise further questions. How are commands—as so far described—possible? How can it be that one person's saying 'Do this!' to another gives that other reason to do something irrespective of what the action is and in such a way that at least some existing reasons for action are properly discounted? What exactly *is* a command? How does one achieve the standing to issue one?

In approaching this last, crucial question, I first emphasize certain negative aspects of what it is to have the standing to command, as I understand this. To say, for instance, that Peggy has the standing to command Max is not to imply that there would be good consequences if he conformed to her imperatives. It is not, then, to suggest that the person with the standing has some kind of expertise (or is an authority, in that sense). More generally, it is not to suggest that the person with the standing has any good qualities in relation to any particular thing. Standing, here, is a matter of status or position rather than personal quality.

Thus I distinguish what one might refer to as *moral* standing from what I have in mind by *standing*, pure and simple. Suppose that, as far as Max is concerned, Peggy has the standing to command him to do anything she wishes. Fred, a concerned friend of Max's, says, 'You treat Peggy's word as law, but she has no moral authority whatsoever. She is, and is well known to be, cruel and unscrupulous.' This may well be true. Yet it may also be true that Peggy frequently tells Max what to do, where 'telling someone what to do' is tantamount to commanding them. Fred's words would most likely be intended to change that situation. However true they are, their meaning is not such as implicitly to deny its very existence.

When, then, does one have the standing to command? I propose that one can at least partially explicate this by reference to the *owing* relation.[8] That is, one can say something like this: if X has the standing to command Y to

---

[7] It is often argued that they do not trump all opposing considerations. See e.g. Hampton (1997: 4–5), representing the view of Raz: an authoritative political command might not trump reasons based on certain moral principles.

[8] R. P. Wolff (1970) has some inclination to see things this way.

do A, then, when X issues to Y the imperative 'Do A!' or does something that amounts to this, Y owes it to X to comply with this imperative.[9] Thus if Phyllis has the standing to command Marcelle to give her up to a thousand pounds, and says to Marcelle 'Give me five pounds!', Marcelle then owes it to Phyllis to give her five pounds. In addition, were Marcelle not to give her five pounds, Phyllis would have the standing to rebuke her for not doing so. For Marcelle will not have given Phyllis what she owed her; she will have withheld from Phyllis 'her thing'—something that is, in effect, hers.

I have just made a rough proposal as to a *necessary* condition for one's having the standing to command another person to do a certain thing. I propose further that it is at least close to a sufficient condition for this. That is, I propose that roughly the following is true: X *has the standing to command Y to do A* if and only if, when X issues to Y the imperative 'Do A!', or does something that amounts to this, Y owes it to X to do A. The next question is: how might this particular owing relationship arise? Given what has been said so far in this book, it is easy to provide an answer. The answer is: introduce an appropriate joint commitment of the parties.

Here, then, is one way to create such an owing relationship: X is party to a joint commitment with Y to uphold as a body the following rule: Y is to do as X says when X issues an imperative to Y, or to the members of some specified population of which Y is a member. Some limitations of context and content may of course be specified within such a rule. For instance: Y is to do what X says with respect to household management; otherwise Y need not do what X says. Y is to do what X says, provided X is acting in his capacity as chair of the department as opposed to his capacity as a private citizen. Y is to do what X says on their hike providing Y does not find it too frightening.

Once such a joint commitment is in place, and subject to whatever refinements, Y owes X conformity with the imperatives that X issues to Y. This is by virtue of the joint commitment. Any joint commitment to do something as a body makes it the case that the parties owe each other conformity with the commitment. In this particular case, conformity with the commitment requires that Y conform to X's imperatives. So Y owes X conformity to X's imperatives.

The following proposal, then, has something to recommend it: X has the standing to command Y, subject to conditions C, if and only if X and Y are subject to a joint commitment such that, in order to conform to it, Y must do what X says, subject to conditions C. For in that case Y owes it to X

---

[9] A command, I take it, need not be verbally expressed. There may be purely gestural commands.

to do what X says, and *it is not clear that there is any other way of bringing that situation about.* [10]

The condition stated conforms to points made earlier. It does not require that a commander have any special kind of expertise. Nor does his command have to have any particular content. At the same time, his command will have something peremptory about it: from the point of view of what reason requires the person commanded to do, it trumps at least considerations of personal inclination and self-interest, as such. He can't, then, effectively dismiss the command by saying 'I don't want to' or 'that won't do *me* any good'. Such peremptoriness is, of course, a function of the joint commitment that must be in place in order that someone has the standing to command. Whatever is true of any joint commitment applies here.

So as not to complicate the following discussion I shall assume that the condition stated is indeed a complete account of the basic case of one person's standing to issue commands, as opposed to mere imperatives, to another. (I say 'the basic case' since, as I shall argue, some cases plausibly thought to involve the standing to command do not have the same form as this case, but are derived from it.) This account of the basic case gives us an articulated basis for interrogating plural subject theory on the topic of political authority.

What of the case of commands to self? This seems to be less troublesome from the outset. Consider the contrast between the following two cases. First case: in a railway carriage, John turns to Angela, a stranger to him, and says, 'Shut the window!' She may well feel affronted. Even if she says nothing, she is liable to think, 'He has no right to order me about!' I construe this type of situation as follows. John struck her as attempting to give her an order. She denies that he has the standing to do so. Second case: John is sitting alone in the railway carriage, feeling cold. He is also lazy, and is finding it hard to bestir himself to get up and open the window. Finally he says to himself 'Get up and shut the window!' This strikes him—it is, indeed, intended—as an order. The thought that he has no right to order himself about is unlikely to occur to him. He may of course continue to resist getting up, thereby disobeying his self-addressed command. But he is unlikely to deny that it is indeed a command—an authoritative, self-addressed imperative. It seems, then, that one automatically has the standing to command oneself.[11]

Perhaps there should be a *ceteris paribus* clause here. Perhaps I could somehow deprive myself of that status. Be that as it may, there still appears to be a sharp

---

[10] Relevant here, once again, is the discussion in Ch. 7, above, arguing against the possibility of explicating the owing relationship in terms of moral requirements.

[11] I set aside here the possibilities inherent in e.g. multiple personality.

asymmetry between the case of self-commands and the case of commands to others. All else being equal (at least) one has the standing to command oneself. One does not, in other words, have initially to earn that standing by some 'special' relationship to oneself that one might have lacked. In contrast, all else being equal, one lacks the standing to command others. One has to earn that standing or, if 'earn' is not quite the right word, it has to be argued. This contrasts with the case of a self-command.

The issue may be obscured by the fact that human beings may have a natural instinct to react to all purported commands as if they were genuine. Someone calls out 'Stop!' and you freeze. If instinctual, such a reaction may be expected to play some kind of positive role along the lines evolutionary biology would posit. In more humdrum terms, it may be a prudent course, either in case the 'commander' is more powerful than you (and so may retaliate if you don't stop) or in case he knows something useful to you that you don't know (a car will drive right into you if you don't stop right now). It seems nonetheless that the stranger's capacity to command you—as opposed to helping you mightily by getting you to stop—can be properly questioned and, indeed, rebutted unless something more than the fact that he issued an imperative to you, with whatever intentions or consequences, can be cited.

Insofar as I can owe myself an action, my commanding myself to do so brings this about. In Chapter 7, I suggested that such owing is not the paradigm from the point of view of our everyday understandings. That is doubtless true of self-commands as well. Be that as it may, one does not have to earn the status of self-commander, such as it is.

Does one who has the standing to command automatically have the standing to punish those who do not comply with their commands? It can be argued that in the basic case—now assumed to involve joint commitment—they do.

This may be apparent from what I have said earlier, but it is worth drawing the threads together here. I have argued that those who are party to a joint commitment have the standing to rebuke those who violate the commitment, just as they have the standing to demand compliance when violation is threatened.[12] A rebuke, may be seen as an after-the-fact demand. Importantly for present purposes, one may rebuke another gently, but any rebuke has a sting, however mild, in its tail.[13]

What is punishment? A clear case of punishment in the standard sense intended here involves at least the following components. The first is some

---

[12] See Ch. 7, above.

[13] Someone who *purports* to rebuke will intend to have this effect. If the recipient is clear he lacks the necessary standing, this intention may not be satisfied. It may be satisfied if it catches the recipient unawares.

kind of negative treatment of one person (the person punished) by another (the one who punishes), in response to some action of the first person. Often some kind of pain, physical or mental, is involved. This may range from the emotional sting of a rebuke to the mental and physical agonies of torture. The imposition of a financial penalty or fine may not cross the pain threshold but obviously constitutes negative treatment. The second component is standing. Thus to disadvantage someone, even with good reason, is not necessarily to punish them.

Philosophical discussions of punishment tend to be surprisingly silent on the question of the standing to punish. Overwhelmingly, their focus is on the justification of punishment, where standing is either assumed or ignored. Thus the central question becomes: when is a person or body *justified* in imposing of negative treatment in response to some action?

Traditional answers, as is well known, appeal to a number of different factors, and are often considered to be in competition with one another. These answers appeal, among other things, to deterring the offender from committing further offences, to retribution, as in 'an eye for an eye', and to the denunciation of offenders.

An adequate theory of standing would surely be a useful adjunct to the discussion of justification. Since one does not have the *capacity* to punish without the appropriate standing, it has to be worth knowing what the source or sources of this standing are.

Focusing on the situation in which one person punishes another, I propose that the basic case is as follows. A has *the standing to punish* B if and only if A has not been given an action that was owed to him by B. A will actually *punish* B if, first, he has the standing to do so, as that was just characterized, and second, he inflicts some kind of negative treatment on B in response to B's failure to give him what B owed him. Precisely what kind of negative treatment, if any, would be appropriate in a given case will be a matter of judgement at least to some extent. Such treatment ranges, indeed, from a mild verbal rebuke to the taking of a person's life. To say one has the standing to punish is as yet to say nothing about what is appropriate, if anything, in a given case.

Does this understanding of punishment throw any light on the standard theories of the justification of punishment? From this perspective one would ask: what consideration or considerations would justify one who had been deprived of what he was owed in reacting negatively to the person who had so deprived him? Granted, he has the standing to do so. What would justify him in actually doing so?

Clearly, one might argue that negative action would be justified at least insofar as it deterred the offending person from once again failing to give one what he owed. Perhaps he owes one many things so many future failures are possible. One might also argue that negative action against this offender will send a discouraging message to all possible future offenders. Retribution might be invoked in the cause of returning the parties to a level playing field. The retributive punisher would be saying, in effect, 'You took my thing. I'd better take you down a peg—take this!' Denunciation also makes sense: 'Better speak out or he—and others—will think you are indifferent to what he has done to you.' In other words, as might have been expected, each of these common proposals has something to be said for them. This suggests that the standard justificatory theories are not really in competition. They are all explanations of how, given the standing to do so, one might with some reason act to the detriment of another. At the same time, it is unlikely that any of these justifications, or their combination, mandate such detrimental treatment irrespective of the circumstances.

The current proposal regarding the basic case of punishment is this: your negative treatment of another is not punishment—however justified the action is—unless you have the standing to punish him, and that means that he has not accorded you an action that he owed you. One who so construes punishment and the standing to punish need not endorse any particular practice of punishment, or even approve the general practice of punishment. His understanding concerns the nature of punishment rather than the justification of it as a practice particular or general.

Considering the basic case of the standing to command, it can be seen that the standing to punish as I have construed that goes hand in hand with it. I have the standing to command you to do something if, once I tell you to do it, you owe it to me to do it. Well, suppose I tell you to do something and you do not do it. I am now in the following position. You did not give me what you owed me; you did not give me what was mine. I therefore have the standing to punish you for this. It follows that, if I act to your detriment in light of your not giving me what was mine, I punish you.

The considerations adduced here suggest the following understanding of why there should be an *idea* of punishment. It is the precipitate of a sense that whether or not one has *reason* to act in a way detrimental to another, one may not be *entitled* to do so. In some cases, however, one's entitlement seems clear: who can more appropriately act negatively towards someone than one who has been deprived—knowingly and wilfully at least—by that person of something that was his? Perhaps, all things considered, he should not do so, but that is something else.

I have so far discussed what I have referred to as the basic cases of the standing to command and to punish. The question for plural subject theory is the question of what connection, if any, exists between political obligations as it explicates these and political authority. In order to discuss this with some care I now refer to the division among political societies that I introduced in Chapter 9.

Such societies, I proposed, could be divided into three distinct types. In my terminology, there are those characterized by governing rules, those characterized by the personal rule of some particular, specified person or body, and those characterized by rules of governance (or constitutional rules) that set criteria according to which a given person or body is deemed to have the standing, in effect, to create new governing rules for the population in question.

In the case of governing rules, there is no real issue about authority. I understand such rules as social rules according to the plural subject account of these. On that account there is a social rule in a population, P, when the members of P jointly accept a fiat of the form 'members of P are to do A in C'. What I called the group standard problem related to the case of an individual member of P who personally accepts a fiat of that form. That is, this individual accepts a fiat relating to what members of P are to do—all the members of P, not just himself. The question was: by what right does any one of them issue prescriptions for all of the members at once? Even if every member personally accepts such a fiat, the same question could be raised of each one. There does not seem to be authority in mere numbers. As argued earlier, this problem disappears if what is at issue is a social rule construed as above. No problem of authority arises. If the question of who issued this particular fiat is raised, the obvious answer is: the population as a whole. This surely has the standing to issue a fiat in relation to itself. Perhaps this is not always so; perhaps we can collectively give away our standing to issue commands to ourselves, perhaps by promising, as a body, to regard some particular person or body as the only agent authorized to issue fiats to us. Assuming that, in a given political society constituted by governing rules, nothing like this has happened, we can say that the population as a whole owes itself compliance to its own edicts. This translates to the following at the level of the individuals concerned: each owes each, as a member of the whole, conformity to the fiat in question. Each, as a member of the whole, has the standing to demand compliance, issue rebukes for non-compliance, and the like.

I turn next to the more complex case of a political society constituted by one or more rules of governance or constitutional rule, leaving the case of personal rule till last. In the former case, the authority of the population as a whole to issue fiats to itself is extended by fiat of the whole not to a given individual or collective body, but rather to individuals and bodies insofar as they fulfil the conditions specified in the constitutional rule. I shall refer to the authority one has by virtue of such an extension *delegated* authority. How does this work?

Suppose Regina is the monarch in population P, having succeeded to the throne by virtue of a constitutional rule of hereditary succession. She issues an edict relating to the resolution of conflicts. Does anyone owe her obedience? This is how things seem to stand. The members of P *owe one another* conformity to Regina's edicts. More, they owe it to one another to treat Regina as *one who is to be obeyed*. Insofar as she is one of them, they owe this to her, as one of them. Perhaps, though, she is not one of them. They have nonetheless given her delegated authority to rule in P.

It would hardly be practical were Regina not to understand the situation, so we can assume that she understands that the members of P owe one another obedience to her edicts. In other words, she understands herself to have delegated authority. This is a kind of stipulated authority. It is a matter, if you like, of the popular will. Thus, if Regina's standing to command is challenged, she may refer to the stipulation in question. In response to a member of P who says to her 'Who says you may boss me about?' She can say 'You (*inter alia*) do . . . you are party to a joint commitment to regard my edicts as authoritative.' *This is not quite to say*, 'You owe me'.

Though the standing or authority to command goes hand in hand, conceptually speaking, with the standing to punish, things could be different in the case where delegation is at issue. In a given society one person or body's authority could be explicitly or implicitly restricted to commanding rather than punishing. Perhaps it has been stipulated that Regina has standing to command and that her husband Rex, but not Regina, has the standing to punish. Once we are dealing with delegated authority things can become quite complex, as indeed they can, given special background understandings, in any case. Nonetheless, the default situation seems to be that one to whom the authority to command is delegated, *thereby* has delegated authority to punish.

I turn next to the case of personal rule. Similar things can be said of this case as can be said of the previous one. Here the population as a whole extends its authority over itself to a given individual or body by stipulation or fiat. Such an extension, also, may involve certain conditions. Thus the population may jointly commit to regarding Rex as having authority over them as long as his edicts continue to bring them good fortune. They may have no commitment with respect to any other person, however wise, but their commitment to regard Rex as authoritative is conditional on the continuing felicity of his rule.

In earlier discussion of personal rule it was clear that there are situations that behaviourally would look quite similar to the kind of case described, in which, indeed, there were mutual obligations of compliance with the edicts of a particular person or body, but where there was no stipulated authority. Thus one must be careful not to assume such authority even in a situation where people are obligated to one another to conform to the imperatives of a given ruler or body. The same goes for the case of constitutional rules: here too there could be mutual obligations of compliance without stipulation of authority.

I have not considered the possible case where there has been an agreement between Regina and the population as a whole, to the effect that given her fulfilment of whatever conditions the members of the population are to obey her commands. If and when this is the appropriate understanding of a given situation we have the clearest case of political authority insofar as it not a matter of stipulation. Here Regina can most clearly say 'You, as a member of the populace, *owe me* compliance with my edicts.'

In yet another kind of case, Regina is jointly committed with each member of a population individually so as to have the standing to command him. Here one might say that she rules each individual but not the population as a whole. The population constituting her and her various subjects may not constitute a society and hence a political society in the sense of this book.[14]

To sum up this brief discussion of questions of authority: I first discussed the standing to command and to punish, quite generally. I then argued that the plural subject theory of political obligation suggests a plausible conception of political authority, one that allows for useful distinctions among different kinds of political practice.

iv. Further Questions for a Theory of Political Obligation   I have so far tested the plural subject theory of political obligation against several of the desiderata for such a theory. It has done well in terms of all of these. An affirmative theory, it tests out well against the other core criteria. It also has merit in regard to the interpretative criteria and it has a specifiable relationship to the question of political authority.

What of the puzzle-solving criterion? This demands a response to three questions that are likely immediately to arise in face of the claim that there are political obligations in the sense of the membership problem.

First, there is the puzzle of how membership in a political society, something that looks like a natural fact, could involve obligations, which seem to have a different nature. The answer given by plural subject theory is a plausible one. It founds political obligations in joint commitment. Joint commitment

---

[14] Cf. the situation in early medieval Europe, e.g., where 'Every member of a kin–group or group of friends had a duty to every other member, but in the case of lordship, these obligations only existed between the lord and each of his men individually, not between the men themselves' Althoff (2000: 4).

is the product of expressions of readiness for joint commitment in conditions of common knowledge. Whether or not it qualifies as a natural fact on all possible conceptions, it is no more than the precipitate of the understandings and intentional expressions of human beings. At the same time it can be argued to involve obligations in a central sense of the term: the parties to a joint commitment owe each other actions that conform to it. Some may find this surprising. That it is so is clear enough.

Second, there is the puzzle that invokes evil laws and other malign political institutions. Can one be obligated to support such institutions if they are misguided, or worse? The question may arise as a practical one. It may also be spurred by a doubt that there can be such obligations. How could it be that one was obligated to obey an evil law? Assuming that such laws really are laws, how can the members of a political society be obligated to support and uphold its political institutions as such? How, in short, can there be political obligations?

The response of plural subject theory to such questions was indicated in Chapter 10, when actual contract theory was defended against the second no-obligation objection in light of a plural subject account of agreements. Similar things can be said about the more general plural subject theory proposed in this book, as for any theory of political obligation that appeals to obligations of joint commitment. Broadly speaking the puzzle is resolved by distinguishing between different types of obligation. The issue is of sufficient significance to be revisited here.

According to plural subject theory, the members of a political society have obligations of joint commitment to support and comply with its political institutions whatever they are. Thus if a given imperator has the standing to command them they have an obligation of this kind to do what it says. They may also have such an obligation to take the punishments it metes out.

In this connection it is important to emphasize that a joint commitment giving a particular imperator the standing to command and to punish the members of a given populace may incorporate certain conditions. It may be explicitly stated in a constitution, for instance, that those who determine these things must impose no 'cruel and unusual' punishments. Or there may be an unspoken rule to the effect that a particular imperator's commands are to be regarded as authoritative as long as they do not relate, for instance, to the religious observance of members of the population: his sphere of operations is strictly limited to the secular realm.

Are there any limits on the capacity to command that can be assumed in any political society as such? I shall not attempt to explore this question here. One reason for doubting that there is a positive answer is that the question concerns not what ought to be but what is. It concerns not only just or decent or sane political societies, but any political societies whatsoever.

There may yet be some such limits, since the political aspect of the political societies of plural subject theory is a matter of social rules constituted by joint commitments. It may be possible to argue that in all human populations a person's entry into such a joint commitment itself presupposes certain limits on the range of authoritative commands.[15]

Returning now to the puzzle at hand, one can say this. That one has obligations of joint commitment to do what a given imperator says constitutes an argument for so acting—an argument such that one's personal inclinations and self-interest, as such, are discounted. The joint commitment and its obligation, however, are only part of an argument with respect to what one ought to do, all things considered. That his orders are misguided, or worse, that the punishment is overly harsh, are considerations one can take into account in considering what, all things considered, one ought to do.

In some cases it is will surely be best not to obey a particular authoritative command if one can do so without undue risk to oneself—or even if one cannot. This is a matter of judgement. There may be little to say by way of proof, though plenty to say by way of argument. Cases must be presented and judgement elicited. It will be an important consideration that you owe your fellows a certain action. But there may be other considerations that override this in terms of what one ought to do, all things considered.

A famous case that is quite pertinent occurs at the beginning of Plato's dialogue *The Republic*. Your friend has left his weapons in your possession, so that you now owe him their return should he ask you to return them. Now something has caused him to go mad. He demands his weapons. Should you return them? The implication is that you should not, and the implicit argument for that conclusion goes like this. Clearly, in his present state your friend is likely to use his weapons for ill—he could kill or maim someone. Sure, he did not give them to you for yourself. They are his weapons, not yours, and you owe him their return. All else being equal, you ought to return them. But now all else is not equal. In these circumstances you should not return the weapons. That one owes another an action, therefore, does not necessarily determine how one should act, all things considered.

Evidently, on the plural subject construal, the assertion that there are political obligations is consistent with the claim that members of a political

---

[15] I return to this point in Sect. 11.4.

society should be prepared critically to evaluate the commands of their rulers.[16] That is not to say that it is necessary for people consciously to question every command with which they are faced. It is to say that no command closes the question of what one ought to do, all things considered.

The third puzzle that is likely initially to arise in relation to the very idea of political obligation can be introduced by reference to two different cases. On the one hand, to say that you may be politically obligated to do something at the cost of your own death suggests that this obligation is very significant indeed. On the other hand, consideration of the example of a stop sign on an empty desert road makes that idea look absurd. *Is* there really an obligation to stop and, if so, how significant can it be? The kind of obligation in question, if it exists, must somehow fit both of these cases and all others in between. How is that possible?

Plural subject theory has a clear answer to this last question: a member of a particular political society has an obligation of joint commitment to uphold a particular set of political institutions. This is something that has unvarying implications for what he ought to do when confronted with any relevant directives.

Consider the stop sign case. Suppose that Anne is party to a joint commitment that requires one to support and comply with a given set of directives, and that according to these she must stop at a certain type of sign in the road. She is driving on an empty road in the desert and comes across such a sign.

According to plural subject theory Anne has an obligation to stop—an obligation of joint commitment. This has the usual consequences: if there are no countervailing considerations, rationality requires that she stop; her contrary inclinations and self-interest as such do not suffice to change its dictates.

Given that it is not enough for Anne rationally to justify not stopping simply by reference to the fact that she does not feel like stopping, or that she would gain time by not stopping, then she must find other ways to do so. More precisely, she must find a way adversely to compare the value or rightness of fulfilling her obligation with the value or rightness of not doing so in the case at hand. Plural subject theory does not deny that she may be able to do this. I say something later in this chapter about the relative value of fulfilling one's joint commitments in general, and those quite special joint commitments that

---

[16] Cf. Lacey (1988: 122): 'women and men in political society should not be content unreflectively to obey the criminal law'. Lacey thinks this argues against the idea of an obligation to obey all the laws of a given political society. I argue here that it does not: one can agree with the quoted point, yet allow that members of a political society have such an obligation.

help to constitute a political society, a 'place' in which millions of people may live out their lives.

Now suppose that Anne is commanded to join the army when it is clear she will soon be sent to a dangerous combat zone. She is subject to a joint commitment to comply with this command and owes such compliance to her fellows.

Plural subject theory says similar things about this case also. This case is different from the previous one because, by hypothesis, Anne is likely to be seriously hurt, or worse, while in combat. As far as the case has been described so far, conformity with her obligations of joint commitment is very seriously in conflict with her self-interest. One's own death or serious hurt is about as far as one can go in that respect. In addition, she may well be fearful of going to war, and thus strongly inclined not to comply with the command. According to plural subject theory, as usual, Anne's own inclinations and self-interest, *as such*, do not suffice to override her obligation. That does not mean that there can be no considerations that do override it. All things considered, it may be that Anne ought not to comply with this order.

Considerations that would be relevant to Anne's defaulting on her obligation include the following. It may be that in joining the army and going out to the field of battle she will be playing a significant role in an unjust, aggressive war that has been undertaken by her political society. Or the way in which the war is being conducted may be unacceptable, though the war itself is just. It may be that lives, including Anne's, should not be sacrificed for such a cause. Nor will her country's political institutions generally crumble should the war be curtailed.[17] It may be that her only honourable course is to default on her obligation.

These matters are often none too easy to decide. One may feel, indeed, that one does not have the capacity to make such a decision. One may then fulfil one's political obligation since that is clear and the arguments against doing so are murky.

The difficulty of such decision is witnessed at the end of Plato's *Crito*. Socrates is strongly tending to conform to the agreements he believes himself to have made to abide by the laws of Athens and, hence, to accept the death penalty at their hands. The arguments that Crito has made against his doing so, however, are also in the air, buzzing around him, making it clear how difficult, in fact, this judgement is.

The plural subject theory of political obligation deals with the stop sign and conscription cases cited in a consistent manner. Political obligations are all of a

---

[17] On this particular type of consideration, see also Sect. 11.4, below.

piece. They are obligations of joint commitment, which always have the same, considerable impact on one's situation from a normative point of view. What one is to do in a given case, all things considered, is a matter of judgement. In principle things can go either way.

To anticipate a little, one thing that may be argued is that one or another political institution—a given law, a given command—is of little, or much, importance in the general scheme of things political in the country in question. Rulers will have their own understandings of these things. The difference in the sanctions they impose is likely to reflect such understandings. So is their use of the language of *treason,* which tends to be applied to actions that are apt to increase the vulnerability of society to the predations of forces outside it. I do not argue that rulers are always right as to which violations are most dangerous. Doubtless they are often wrong, and many people suffer grievously for their mistakes.

I have now set plural subject theory against the criteria mooted in Chapter 3 for a maximally satisfactory theory of political obligation. I conclude that it does well according to all of these criteria, and is therefore a maximally satisfactory theory. That does not mean that there are no other such theories. Perhaps there are some that invoke different intuitive understandings of what a political society is, or invoke a different species of obligation. Nor do I assume that my presentation of the theory so far will have forestalled all objections to it. I address several possible objections shortly.

11.2 Comparison with Three Related Theories

In this section, I compare plural subject theory to three other theories of political obligation that have something in common with it. In each case, I argue that plural subject theory is to be preferred to the other theory as an answer to the membership problem. The first two theories—identification theory and relationship theory—were introduced earlier. Both were argued to leave important matters unexplained. The third is an important theory proposed by H. L. A. Hart and modified by John Rawls and others: the theory of political obligations as obligations of fair play. This is a good time to introduce that theory and discuss its relationship with plural subject theory.

I have not included a discussion of actual contract theory here because it has already been discussed at length. Suffice it to say, in summary, that though in the version proposed actual contract theory has many of the virtues of plural subject theory, and has less to be said against it than has been thought, it is marred by its appeal to a narrow conception of a political society, a conception that is far from intuitive. In not requiring an agreement as the foundation of a political society, plural subject theory invokes a more intuitive conception. In doing so it may lose some of the moral or evaluative attractions of actual contract theory, but such attractions are beside the point in the context of analysis. The argument against actual contract theory from an analytical point of view is clear enough.

In the general form I shall discuss, identification theory argues that a person's membership in a particular political society is a matter of his identification with that society, which grounds obligations of the relevant type. There is significant common ground between identification theory and plural subject theory. Both take seriously linguistic phenomena such as references to 'our' actions, beliefs, laws, and so on, and emotions such as guilt over an action 'we' have done. Indeed, the prevalence of such references and emotions is understood to be a key mark of a given person's identification with a given political society.

There are at least two problems with identification theory from which plural subject theory is free. Most critical is the need for an argument from identification—the proposed source of political obligations—to those obligations themselves. A related problem with identification theory is its subjectivism. In its standard version, identification is a subjective phenomenon. As A. J. Simmons complains, one might identify with a certain political society without warrant—thinking of its actions as 'our' actions, say—just as someone might think he is Napoleon (thus 'identifying' with Napoleon) without warrant.[18] In short, identification is too subjective to constitute a person's membership in a society—or to generate obligations.

Taking the first point first, the identification theorist might respond that a given person's identification with the other members of a given population is a necessary but not sufficient condition of his societal membership: it is, if you like, the icing on the cake. He would then need to say more about the cake itself. The theorist may respond to this, or respond initially, that what is needed to supplement one's own subjective identification is that all or almost all of the people with whom one identifies must identify with one another (including oneself) as well.

There is still a problem: that each of us subjectively identifies with the population we comprise does not seem in itself to warrant that identification. Certainly if we all identify in private it seems hard to warrant our identification. And even if it is common knowledge that we all identify, that does not seem

---

[18] Simmons (1996).

to warrant our identification either. What we have is common knowledge of a set of subjective identifications that may, for all this says, be unwarranted.

Here plural subject theory provides a natural extension or supplementation for identification theory. Subjective identification with a given political society is warranted if it reflects one's participation in a joint commitment that constitutes that society. One's participation in this joint commitment both constitutes one as a member of the society and justifies one's subjective identification with it.

I now turn to the point that subjective identification cannot ground obligation. One way of arguing for a connection between identification and obligation is suggested in a passage from John Horton. He proposes that one's identification with a given political society is a particularly deep kind of identification. Thus a British woman may identify herself as a member of her tennis club without this identification going to the heart of who she takes herself to be. Her sense of herself as British, on the other hand, may be central to her understanding of who (or what) she is.[19]

Though Horton does not spell this out, it may be possible to argue from the existence of such 'deep' subjective identification to one's having sufficient reason to act in ways that conform to it. Perhaps one is even morally required so to act, all else being equal. But all else is unlikely to be equal in every case, given the possibility of identifying with an evil group. Thus whatever argument is in the wings here, it does not look promising with respect to the conclusion that membership in a political society in general morally requires or in *that* sense obligates one to uphold the political institutions in question. Nor does it look promising with respect to the conclusion that a kind of directed obligation is at issue. It is not clear, more generally, that this is an argument about *obligation* in an intuitive sense. That does not detract from its interest, which is considerable. It does detract from its adequacy as a solution to the membership problem, which is couched specifically in terms of obligation.

It may be observed that the argument just contemplated appears to work for subjective identification without reference to its justification. It depends only on the fact that a certain person views herself in a certain way, and that this way of viewing herself is particularly entrenched in her conception of herself. This may not prevent the argument having force; however, the more identification becomes detached from justificatory facts, the further it seems to go from something intuitively best referred to as *membership in a society*.

Once again, subjective identification is not a plausible account of membership; an account that appeals to something other than identification is

<hr>

[19] Horton (1992: 157)

therefore to be preferred. For this and other reasons, plural subject theory does better than identification theory as a solution to the membership problem. It might be regarded as a friendly, if quite far-reaching, amendment to identification theory: subjective identification may reflect one's participation in a society-constituting *joint commitment*, in which obligations can be shown to inhere.

Relationship theory argues that human relationships are a source of obligation. This is hard to doubt. It would be good, nonetheless, to see precisely how relationships give rise to obligations and to understand the nature of the obligations in question. There may, of course, be more than one way in which this happens, and more than one kind of obligation may be at issue. Plural subject theory cannot then be expected to have all the answers, but it can be argued to fill a significant gap. It makes explicit the way in which an important type of obligation is bound together with a central type of relationship or way of relating. This is the relationship of shared membership in a particular social group construed as membership in a particular plural subject. In conformity with the ideas of some relationship theorists, such as Hirschmann, plural subject theory allows that human relationships can involve obligations without being voluntary in any strong sense.

I turn now to what has come to be known as the fair play argument. This has appeared in the literature in more than one guise. One of the best-known discussions of it is that of H. L. A. Hart. It has generated considerable discussion, and continues to attract adherents. This is not the place to embark on a full consideration of the theory in its various forms. My purpose is to explain why I think plural subject theory is superior to the standard versions of fair play theory as a solution to the membership problem.

In Hart's version the argument runs as follows:

> [W]hen a number of persons conduct any joint enterprise according to rules and thus restrict their liberty, those who have submitted to these restrictions when required have a right to a similar submission from those who have benefited by their submission.[20]

Hart sees this as a quite general point that applies to political societies insofar as they can be regarded as joint enterprises with associated rules. Indeed, he proposes that we can best understand what he refers to as 'political obligation' in these terms.

Hart sees the right to which he alludes as a matter of fairness.[21] George Klosko elaborates the point thus: 'The sacrifices made by cooperators in order to produce benefits also benefit noncooperators, who do not make similar

---

[20] Hart (1955: 185).   [21] Hart (1955: 191).

sacrifices. According to the principle [of fairness], this situation is unfair.'[22] In other words, in the presence of a number of 'cooperators' it is morally wrong—in particular, unfair—to be a 'noncooperator'.[23]

For example, suppose there is a political society one of whose goals is ameliorating the conditions of life for its members generally. Accordingly it has various laws intended to help keep the air clean. Suppose further that many of the members of this society conform to these laws: they do not use certain cheap fuels for instance, but pay more for fuels that are less polluting. A member who has not yet used fuel of any kind will have benefited from their efforts: he will have enjoyed cleaner air. According to the principle, it would be unfair of this member to use cheap fuel himself, when the time comes, given that he has benefited from the sacrifices of the others.

Klosko writes 'On a more basic level, the principle expresses a general idea of fairness: similar individuals should be treated similarly. It is wrong for certain people to be exempt from burdens others must bear in the absence of morally relevant differences between them.'[24] Hart's own characterization of what is fundamental appeals not so much to treating similar individuals similarly as to 'maintaining an equal distribution of restrictions and so of freedom' among the people in question.[25] Such a distribution, in its turn, recognizes 'the equal right of all men to be free'.[26]

Whatever precise formulations or foundations they espouse, those who propose a version of Hart's fair play argument cite one or another moral principle that supposedly applies to all of those who find themselves in specified circumstances. These principles all crucially invoke the moral notion of (distributive) justice or fairness. I take it that this notion is or incorporates the evaluative idea of 'goodness in distribution'. All else being equal, it is understood that one is morally required to act fairly. One who does not so act does something morally wrong.

Hart's version of fair play theory has been criticized on the grounds that one can only infer a moral requirement to conform to the rules if the associated enterprise and its rules are themselves morally acceptable ones. Thus suppose some of the laws of a given political society are seriously unjust. Suppose, further, that one's fellow members have been following these laws to the letter and one has oneself personally benefited from this—for example, one has as a

---

[22] Klosko (1992: 34). Hart refers to the principle involved as 'mutuality of restrictions'.

[23] Other characterizations of the principle at issue in the fair play argument include that of two authors quoted by Klosko: Lyons (1965: 164) writes of 'the just distribution of benefits and burdens'; Rawls (1971: 112) says that 'We are not to gain from the cooperative labours of others without doing our fair share'. See also Simmons (1979: 102).

[24] Klosko (1992: 34).   [25] Hart (1955: 191).   [26] Ibid.

result acquired considerably more wealth than one would have acquired were the laws not so unjust. In such a case it may be morally incumbent upon one *not* to do as one's fellows have been doing.

Such judgements have led to explicitly qualified versions of Hart's fair play argument. Thus in his version of the argument John Rawls requires that the joint enterprise in question be a just one.[27] Such qualification makes the fair play argument less suited to solve the membership problem: it no longer argues for an obligation one has by virtue of membership in a political society as such.[28]

If my arguments regarding the obligations of joint commitment are right, plural subject theory is more suited to solve the membership problem than is fair play theory. Plural subject theory can allow that the members of a political society with seriously unjust laws may be morally required to do all they can to subvert them. It can allow that, at the same time, the members of this society have standing obligations that run in a contrary direction. These are obligations of joint commitment. They are the obligations of membership.[29]

In contrast, there may be no moral requirement or obligation in that sense to conform to seriously unjust laws. Though one can perhaps argue that it would be fair to the 'cooperators' that one also 'cooperate', this does not mean that, in the situation in question, one is morally required to conform to such laws. What plural subject theory achieves in contrast to fair play theory, is an account of obligations that are inevitable concommitants of membership as such.

Before concluding this discussion of the fair play argument, I return to Hart's model of a political society as a joint enterprise governed by (social) rules. In light of the discussion in this book one can see that an appeal to a moral principle of fair play is not necessary to an argument for the existence of obligations of membership given this model. Nor, indeed, is it necessary to refer to benefits received, or to posit the justice of the enterprise or its rules. For one can develop such an argument in plural subject terms as follows.

Suppose the following: a number of people are jointly committed to espouse a certain goal as a body. In words closer to Hart's, the goal of a joint enterprise

[27] Rawls (1958) and elsewhere.

[28] Dagger (2000) sees no problem for fair play theory here: the membership problem *has* no positive answer, given the possibility of unjust political societies. He plausibly argues contra Dworkin (1986: 186–216) (also Hardimon 1994) that 'true' political societies may be far from just. Dworkin's position is also criticized by Tamir (1993: 101–2).

[29] What of members (if such there are) who are themselves unjustly treated? Do they have obligations of membership? If they are party to the relevant joint commitment, the answer is: yes. See Sect. 11.4, below.

has been established among them. These people are also jointly committed to accept as a body certain rules for the conduct of their joint enterprise. Finally, a large number of them are doing what they can to further the joint enterprise while observing the rules as best they can. In other words, they are fulfilling the obligations associated with their joint commitments. In that case, each has a right to similar behaviour from the other parties. *This is a right they had through the joint commitment from the beginning.* In other words, the conforming participants have their initial rights of joint commitment and their initial basis for objection, should the others fail to conform. Had they themselves not conformed things might be different, depending on the circumstances. This would be a matter of whether or not the relevant joint commitments could still be considered to be in place. As things stand, the rights of the conforming participants and the correlative obligations of all are not in question. Perhaps one could call this the plural subject version of the fair play argument. It does not, however, refer to any moral principle of fairness.

Though this is so, there may be a connection between the idea of doing what is fair or of doing one's 'fair share' and joint commitment. The suggestion is something like this: a—if not the—canonical case of unfair action is action that is contrary to an obligation of joint commitment, without justification, when the other parties have fulfilled their own obligations or (perhaps) when there is every reason to expect them to do so. Not doing one's share, *in those circumstances*, is 'not fair'. Doing one's 'fair share' is doing one's share, in those circumstances.

It is not possible to pursue this line of thought here. Suffice it to say that if *conforming to a joint commitment* in the circumstances noted is a demand of fairness, that is, a *moral demand*, an appeal to fairness is one way of arguing that all else being equal, in those circumstances, one is morally required to abide by a given joint commitment. That is, it is a way of arguing that one is morally required—if all else is equal—to fulfil one's obligations of joint commitment in the circumstances in question.

11.3 Response to Objections

In the course of this book I have responded at various points to concerns that might arise regarding the plural subject theory of political obligation. In this section I address some objections that have been voiced by one commentator or another in response to earlier presentations of the theory.

In a well-known article critical of those who argue for the existence of 'associational obligations', John Simmons focuses, among other works, on my article 'Group Membership and Political Obligation'.[30] I there first set out in a relatively extended fashion my proposals about political obligation. Others, prompted by his article or independently, undoubtedly share some of Simmons's concerns.

Simmons describes my plural subject theory as a form of 'nonvoluntarist contract theory'.[31] He understands that joint commitments in my sense need not involve any datable act of commitment, but may, rather, result from a process that is considerably extended in time. His concerns do not relate to the idea of joint commitment or the idea that joint commitments obligate, but rather to the existence of obligating joint commitments in the political realm.

I should note at the outset that the presentation and defence of the plural subject theory of political obligation in the present work is both more extensive and somewhat different from that in the article Simmons addresses. As a result, some of his concerns may already seem less pertinent in this context.

Among other things, in this book I do not start from the statistical assumption that many people in the world today feel they have political obligations.[32] This was the starting point for Simmons's 1979 book, *Moral Principles and Political Obligations*, which reached the conclusion that the people in question are wrong. I took this assumption on board in 'Group Membership and Political Obligation', which was presented as a response to Simmons. I proposed that, in general, scepticism about the justifiability of a well-entrenched sense of things is more liable to provoke a search for justification than acceptance.[33] I then argued that given the plural subject understanding of political obligation there might well be as much political obligation in the world as there was thought to be. Contrary to what might be thought from Simmons's 1996 article, I did not and do not argue that every well-entrenched sense of things—even a sense of things common to all mankind—is in all probability right.[34]

As said, the present work does not assume a widespread sense of political obligation. There is little doubt that such feelings are relatively common. Their precise extent, however, is an empirical issue and hence a matter for social and political science rather than philosophy. That is not to say that philosophical results such as those of this book cannot help the sciences considerably in this

[30] Gilbert (1993c); Simmons (1996). Simmons also makes reference (1996: 256) to Gilbert (1993a). He discusses some theorists with related views including Dworkin (1986); Hardimon (1994); Horton (1992).

[31] Simmons (1996: 255–6).

[32] See Simmons (1996: 249) ('associative obligation' theorists appeal to 'shared moral experience').

[33] I still think this. See Ch. 3, above, here.

[34] See Simmons (1996: 249–50, 253) (associative obligation theorists take shared moral experience to be authoritative).

matter. Without a clear understanding of the structure of everyday concepts such research is liable to be seriously lacking.

The core of my plural subject theory of political obligation is an account of a political society sufficiently articulated to show how and in what sense membership in such a society involves political obligations. Given this account, one has a way of explaining how feelings of political obligation, *where they exist*, can be both reasonable and accurate.

The account also provides a new basis for exploring the actual extent of feelings of political obligation. It explains precisely what a feeling of political obligation might amount to, including the kind of obligation involved. It therefore gives empirical scientists something more to go on in exploring the question: do people generally feel obligated to uphold the political institutions of their country?[35]

Felt Obligations Versus Genuine Obligations

One of Simmons's concerns is that felt obligations, where they exist, not be confused with genuine obligations. I certainly agree that a 'sense of obligation' or a belief that I am obligated is not in itself enough to demonstrate the existence of the obligation. I think it will be agreed by all parties that obligations are not subjective—not in that way.

Simmons goes beyond this point about felt obligations, however, in this part of his discussion. 'The mere fact that individuals refer to "our" government and have a vague feeling of indebtedness to "our" country,' he avers, 'should not . . . lead us to believe that those individuals in fact have (or even really believe they have) political obligations.'[36]

On the topic of references to 'our' government and so on, I would of course allow that the mere utterance of uninterpreted *phrases* such as 'our government' is not enough to prove that people have obligations: not even if all openly use and are comfortable with the open use of such language in their communications, and all are well aware of this. As I argued earlier in this book, the case is different if such phrases, in the mouths of the people in question, are properly interpreted in plural subject terms (as might well be the case in standard circumstances). In other words, the case is different if by 'our government' people mean, roughly, 'that body I am jointly committed with the rest of us to regarding as having authority over us'. In the right conditions, this suffices for the existence of the relevant joint commitment and its associated obligations. Depending, then, on the proper interpretation

---

[35] See also Ch. 12, below.   [36] Simmons (1996: 257).

of these phrases in a given case, and the context in which they are used, one may be able reasonably to infer the existence of genuine as opposed to merely felt obligations in the face of widespread references to 'our government', 'our country', and so on.

How is one to decide what the best interpretation is? Though Simmons is right to claim that a feeling of obligation or indebtedness does not in and of itself suffice to prove the existence of an actual obligation, it would surely be wrong to deny that such feelings, where they occur, are an important clue to the way in which the people in question understand their references to 'our' government and so on. Their understanding these as references to a plural subject founded in a joint commitment would, after all, explain their feelings of obligation. Should they believe that these obligations are a function of the fact that a particular government, say, is 'their' government, the case for a plural subject interpretation becomes even stronger. This will be clear to all when these feelings and beliefs are widely expressed.

Acquiescence Versus Obligating Acts

Another of Simmons's concerns relates to a possible confusion between 'political acquiescence' and 'going along with arrangements' with 'positive, obligation-generating acts or relationships'.[37] He elaborates his point in terms of an example. 'My acquiescing to some pushy participant's efforts to organize our game (by, say, assigning team members and specifying rules) in no way commits me to accepting his further plans or pronouncements about the game or about anything else.'[38] I take it that by referring to a 'pushy' participant Simmons does not mean to import into this case an element of coercion but refers rather to a kind of a kind of overweening behaviour.

Simmons is surely correct to maintain that there are cases like the one he describes—in the small and in the large—in which no commitment of any kind to another's rule occurs. The fact that there are such cases, however, does not in itself cast doubt on the plural subject theory of political obligation. In particular, it does not show that people cannot in quite ordinary circumstances—in the small and in the large—become committed in this way.

Suppose six friends are gathered to play an informal game of volleyball and one of them, Joe, suddenly says in a commanding tone, 'Okay, guys. You, you, and you are on one side, and the rest are on the other. We'll go by these specific rules...'. The others do what he says. What does this mean?

Depending on further details, quite different things might be going on. One possible amplification—which may correspond to the situation Simmons

---

[37] Ibid.   [38] Ibid.

imagines—is this. Each friend might personally have decided to conform to the imperatives Joe has just issued, without intending to grant him the authority to command him either on this occasion or on any other. The situation may be such that it is clear to all that this is what is going on.

Here, as Simmons suggests, both of the following points may be made. First, each has merely 'gone along' with Joe's imperatives or 'acquiesced' in his 'efforts'. In other terms, he has *complied* with Joe's 'commands' not *obeyed* his *commands*. For no one has granted him the status of commander. Second, there is no commitment to doing what Joe says in the future—either as a matter of mere acquiescence or as a matter of obedience.

There are, of course, many other possibilities. For instance, by means of various verbal or non-verbal signals the friends might have collectively decided to conform to Joe's imperatives—on this occasion only. Perhaps one said, ruefully, 'Let's go along with him on this one!' and the others concurred. Or the friends might have collectively decided to regard Joe as having the standing to command them—once again, on this occasion only. Perhaps one said, without irony, 'He's the boss—on this one!' and the others spoke or gestured their concurrence.[39] Each of these decisions, personal or collective, might also have related to the indefinite future, as opposed to this one occasion. Thus it could be that when the original scenario is amplified it involves obligations both to comply with Joe's edicts on this occasion and to comply with them in the future.

So far we do not have much of an approximation to the case with which both Simmons and I are ultimately concerned. Populations of the kind with which a theory of political obligation deals have a history. Rather than a single occasion of conformity there will be what Hart refers to as a 'habit of obedience'—regular compliance with the edicts of a particular person or body of persons, or to people who satisfy certain specifiable conditions. Nor, as we have seen, is the evidence as to what people intend restricted to their conforming behaviour. There is plenty of time for evidence of their thoughts, feelings, and attitudes to emerge. Among other things, they may begin to talk in plural subject terms and act accordingly.

One can see the importance of an extended time frame on a small scale too. The original scenario with Joe and his friends may have had a history like the following. During earlier games, where Joe had behaved similarly, all conformed to his purported commands for their own reasons. After a few such

---

[39] Compare the distinctions made in Ch. 9, above, between *authority-stipulating* joint commitments, on the one hand, and both joint commitments to mere conformity (as opposed to obedience) and widespread personal conformity without joint commitment, on the other.

games a passing stranger asked 'Who's in charge here?' and the others pointed to Joe. On various occasions people ask Joe what to do, he issues a directive, and they comply. Sometimes one rebukes another for not doing what Joe said, on the grounds of his being 'the boss', and the rebuke is accepted, to the accompaniment of an excuse. All this is common knowledge.

Given such a background, the original scenario would look quite different. The players come to the situation jointly committed to accept that Joe has the standing to command them with respect to this and future games, until such time as their commitment is rescinded or is rendered obsolete—as when they cease to play together because all now live in different places. The players understand this by virtue of common knowledge of the history of their games, and their conforming behaviour is plausibly interpreted in light of it.

Simmons in effect suggests that the situation of the 'average political subject' is analogous to that of Joe's friends in the case where all that is involved is personal conformity on one occasion only. He sees that as a reason for denying that the average political subject has any obligation to future obedience to and support of an imperator.

It is an empirical question what the position of the average political subject is. Be that as it may, political subjects have ways of making it clear that they are ready jointly to commit with the relevant others to future obedience and support of the political community's government. They can thus become clear that they are jointly committed to regard that person or body as authoritative—until such time as they terminate the joint commitment.

I conclude that Simmons's concerns that a plural subject theory of political obligation may confuse felt with real obligations, or acquiescence with obligating acts, are unfounded. That is not to deny that he has focused attention on important distinctions.

Kant and the Housewives: Reasonable Expectations Versus Entitlements

I have yet to consider what Simmons takes to be 'the conclusive point' against plural subject theory.[40] This is introduced with his example of Kant and the Konigsberg housewives: Kant's regular walks create in them the reasonable expectation that they will be able to set their clocks by his passing. He, meanwhile, acquires no obligation to continue his walks. 'Only a much more direct, explicit, and personal agreement or understanding between Kant and the housewives . . . could transform reasonable expectations into legitimate entitlements.'[41] Kant may be personally committed to his daily walks but he

---

[40] Simmons (1996: 258).   [41] Ibid.

has not committed himself in any way productive of obligations. There is, in particular, no joint commitment here.

I am in complete agreement with Simmons that the creation of reasonable expectations in others falls short of making a promise or otherwise jointly committing oneself with others. What he says next, in criticism of the plural subject theory of political obligation, is less clearly correct.

According to Simmons the conclusive point against plural subject theory is this. *The relationship between fellow subjects in a large-scale political community* is more like the 'indirect, impersonal' relationship between Kant and the housewives than the direct and personal relationship of, say, a group of bridge-playing friends.

As to the friends, he allows that even without an explicit agreement at a given point in time, 'it may be reasonable for each of them to take the behaviour of the others to constitute a very loose, informal agreement, obligating each to continue to show up for the game on Friday evenings'. This, he suggests, is because there is 'more or less continuous, direct, personal contact between the friends, during which there have presumably been many opportunities to make genuine expressions of their joint commitment to the game (or to make clear just how their continued participation in the game should be understood)'.[42]

Simmons, suggests, then, that there is—and can be—nothing in the relationship between fellow subjects in a *large-scale* political community that allows for the constitution of a joint commitment. It should already be clear, however, that this is false.

As was argued earlier in this book, the processes involved in joint commitment formation in the large group case will be different from that in the small. In the large group case the individuals in question will not all know each other personally, even in the sense of having met and talked to each other. They may not, for that matter, have observed each other directly as the housewives observed Kant. Members of the large group must often extrapolate from a small sample, make use of reports rather than direct observations, and so on.[43] A difference of process, however, need not affect the identity of the product. More precisely, a difference of process does not rule out the production of a joint commitment. The same goes, as argued earlier, for the distinction between more and less benign precursors of a given individual's use of plural subject language.

---

[42] Both quotations in this paragraph from Simmons (1996: 257).

[43] Anderson (1983) emphasizes the role of the medium of print in the formation of a community of persons living far from one another. I take it to be significant that his book's title describes such communities as 'imagined' and not 'imaginary'.

Families Versus Political Associations: Vagueness Versus Clarity

Simmons has evinced a general concern in relation to those who propose to assimilate political obligation to obligations involved in other human associations such as families, friendships, and so on. He says that in these latter cases people are not usually very clear about the content of even their most central obligations. Whereas, in contrast, 'most people have quite a clear sense of at least the bulk of their political obligations. They feel that they must, in at least virtually all cases (i.e. where the law is not morally abhorrent) obey the laws of their country, the most central of which, at least, have a quite specific and widely known content.'[44] In relation to plural subject theory, it is unclear to me that Simmons has identified a serious objection to proposing both a plural subject account of say, living together as man and wife, on the one hand, and participating in a political society, on the other.

Political societies have political institutions that often take the form of a body of explicit laws whose existence—though not all of its specifics—is well enough known to the societies' members. Something analagous is true of many families, couples, and so on. Their members may explicitly agree on quite determinate rules and, indeed, rulers: the smaller social groups can have political institutions too. Even explicit laws and rules can, of course, be quite vague and require interpretation. At the same time, some inexplicit joint commitments within families, for instance, may be relatively determinate—enough to give rise to rebukes and offended stares, sometimes on the basis of fine discriminations among stimuli: how could you talk so loud, brag about your achievements, vote Republican?

Obligation and Strong Disapproval

What of the following objection to the plural subject theory of political obligation? Political obligations, it may be argued, have generally been understood as having a certain importance: one's failure to conform to such an obligation—if such there be—would always reasonably inspire strong disapproval. It may be less important to fulfil some such obligations than others, but their significance is always considerable and strong disapproval is always appropriate. Obligations of joint commitment, it may then be argued, are not such that failure to fulfil them is always a basis for strong disapproval. Thus to say that political obligations are obligations of joint commitment is to confuse a weighty kind of obligation with something less significant. In short, it is not to say anything

---

[44] Simmons (1996: 271).

about political obligations as they are generally conceived of in the literature on the subject.

The plural subject theorist can respond as follows. The literature may indeed conceive of what it refers to as 'political obligations' in the way described.[45] And those who contribute to it may only be interested in obligations that fit this conception. One can argue, however, that this is a mistake—irrespective of the truth of the claim the objection makes about the obligations of joint commitment.[46]

There is, after all, an important question that does not restrict itself in the way suggested: the membership problem. Are the members of a political society obligated to support the political institutions of that society by virtue of their membership? Obligations are here understood at least to be the kind of constraint on action characterized in Chapter 2. That is, they give one sufficient reason to act in a certain way, independently of one's inclinations or self-interest, and they are recalcitrant to one's own will. More may be required to produce what would intuitively count as an obligation, and in principle obligations may be of significantly different kinds. In any case *all* genuine obligations are of some consequence.

If the membership problem has an affirmative solution it is surely important to understand this is so and to be clear as to the nature of the obligations in question. Plural subject theory provides an affirmative solution to the membership problem in terms of genuine, directed obligation. Irrespective of whether strong disapproval—or any disapproval—is always appropriate when they are not fulfilled, such obligations are of undoubted practical relevance.

Obligations in the form of moral requirements may better fit the criterion of strong disapproval, and it may be that those who have written on political obligation are primarily interested in the existence or otherwise of moral requirements to support the political institutions of one's own country. That is of course a natural and important concern. It would be a great pity, however, if this led one simply to overlook obligations of joint commitment, whose practical importance is considerable.

That is in no way to decry an interest in moral requirements or in moral and evaluative questions generally. Indeed, once one recognizes the existence of obligations of joint commitment, many new evaluative and moral questions can be posed. I review some of these questions later.[47]

---

[45] Some theorists may, indeed, assume that it is a mark of obligation as such that it commonly elicits strong disapproval. Cf. Hart (1961) on 'rules of obligation'. For discussion see Sect. 11.4, below.

[46] I discuss this claim in Sect. 11.4, below.

[47] Sects. 11.4 and 12.2, below.

11.4 The Practical Import of Political Obligations

According to the plural subject theory of political obligation, membership in a political society involves the constraints inherent in any joint commitment. First, subject to whatever background understandings apply, one is constrained as by any commitment of the will. One has sufficient reason to act in conformity, reason that is independent of one's inclinations and self-interest as such. Second, one is unable to remove this constraint without the concurrence of the other parties to the joint commitment. Third, one owes these others conformity to it.

This aspect of the situation, this owing, is the one that most clearly stamps the situation as one of obligation. The obligations in this case are directed obligations, an important species of such obligations. There is an important element of obligation, also, in the second constraint.[48] It certainly resonates with the etymology of the English 'obligation' (and the Latin *Obligatio*) in *ligare*—to bind.

At the end of the day, what is most important here is the phenomenon in question, the total package, and the fact that one can argue, as I have done in this book, that membership in a political society—construed in plural subject terms—involves this triad of constraints. Given its practical importance, one can see why this particular package deserves singling out with a special label, albeit one that has come to be shared with at least one other, distinct phenomenon—moral requirement.

I argued earlier that one's owing another an action is a consideration that supersedes one's own inclinations and self-interest, as such, from the point of view of what rationality requires. This may be true, also, of one's being subject to any commitment of the will. In any case, assuming that it is true here, one's having an obligation of joint commitment is of great practical relevance. Given such an obligation, one's own inclinations or self-interest as such are not enough rationally to justify non-compliance.

The directed obligations of joint commitment, political or otherwise, are not only the business of the obligated person as he considers what he has reason to do. They are also the business of the other parties to the commitment, and their representatives, who have a special standing to demand compliance and to seek redress when there is non-compliance, and to issue appropriate rebukes.

Evaluating Obligations of Joint Commitment as Such

How important are the obligations of joint commitment in and of themselves? How bad is it not to fulfil such an obligation, when such non-fulfilment is

---

[48] This was emphasized in Gilbert (1993*a*). See also Gilbert (1999*a*).

considered apart from the content or circumstances of the obligation?[49] How important are political obligations construed as in plural subject theory? These are evaluative questions, and such questions are notoriously hard to answer to everyone's satisfaction. In short, this is an area in which reasonable people can disagree. These are, of course, crucial questions for those faced with a conflict between a political obligation and a consideration of a kind that appears to speak strongly against fulfilling it. It has not been my intention in this book to focus on such questions. Rather, the point has been to show that there is a positive solution to the membership problem that invokes the obligations of joint commitment. What follows is a brief, preliminary discussion of the important questions just posed.

As to the questions about the obligations of joint commitment in general, it will be best to consider a case of non-political obligation with the following two features. First, there are no considerations opposing the joint commitment at issue such that one need not conform, all things considered. Second, one has little reason to conform to it other than the bare fact that it exists: nothing much hangs on one's not performing the act in question. What if one fails to conform to one's joint commitment in such a case? How important is that? Here, then, is such an example. In developing it, and in what follows, I assume that an agreement is a matter of joint commitment, as I proposed in Chapter 10.

Greg has agreed to come to Meg's house on Tuesday to drop off a book he has borrowed. He knows that from her point of view he could just as well drop it off on Wednesday or even later. She is working hard on an unrelated project and will simply put the book back on her bookshelf when it arrives. Still, when she raised the matter he agreed to bring her the book on Tuesday. Meg expects him to do so, failing special circumstances, but she will not be disappointed if he does not, nor will she make any plans relating to Greg's bringing it back. All this is common knowledge between the parties. Suppose, now, that Greg does not show up. He remembered the agreement, and had no good reason not to fulfil it. He decided not to go to Meg's house because he did not feel like doing so. This feeling was nothing tremendous. He just wasn't in the mood to go. Nor did he make any attempt to square things with Meg.

I take it that Greg was in error, all things considered, in not taking the book back to Meg's in the circumstances. I take it, further, that his error is, essentially, his failure to conform to his agreement with Meg without adequate justification. With respect to the gravity of this error, people may disagree.

---

[49] Here I suppose one can meaningfully ask such questions without specifying a point of view from which they are asked.

I am inclined to judge that though strong disapproval is not in order, mild disapproval is.

This is both because of what Greg did, in and of itself, and because of some predictable consequences. These are often cited in connection with the breaking of agreements and promises, and with lying, and are appropriately mentioned in relation to joint commitments in general. They are consequences for Greg and Meg—he may find it easier, next time, to default on an obligation of joint commitment, she may find it harder to trust those who have created joint commitments with her—and for the valuable practices or activities of agreement-making, acting together, collectively endorsing social rules, and so on, which will be undermined if only slightly.[50] Some may say that strong disapproval is in order on either or both counts.

What of the position that there is nothing to disapprove of in an act of agreement breaking in and of itself? On this view, agreements are just 'cheap talk'. Greg has nothing to answer for. Meg is wrong to feel that she has been offended against. That is surely incorrect. Greg does have something to answer for: he failed to keep to his agreement, and he is answerable to Meg for this. There is something to disapprove: Greg failed to give Meg what he owed her—his bringing her book back that day—without reason sufficient to justify doing so. Agreements are not cheap talk. As do any joint commitment phenomena, they ground obligations, which limit what one is free to do rationally speaking.[51]

Even so, there is room for different evaluations in this area. One might put things this way: granted that fidelity to one's joint commitments is a virtue, *how* bad—if at all—is infidelity as such, irrespective of the content of the commitment and any consequences that might occur? It is not my ambition to make a definitive statement in this area, if such a statement can be made.

Often the important question in practice is of the form: is such-and-such significant enough to override the fact that I am jointly committed to do so-and-so? This assumes, correctly, that default on a joint commitment, as such, always leaves a case to be answered. In order that one can approve such default, the opposing considerations must be of a certain, restricted type—one's inclinations or self-interest as such are not of that type. I am not sure how best positively to characterize it, but for present purposes I shall describe the considerations in question as broadly speaking moral ones. And

---

[50] So one can see the *personal* impacting on the *political* even here.

[51] A standard context for 'cheap talk' talk about agreements is game or rational choice theory. That theory invokes a technical concept of rationality that differs from the more intuitive one I invoke here, and I make no attempt here to connect the present discussion with it.

it must be possible to argue that it is indeed justifiable not to give the other parties what one owes them given the consideration cited.

If some do, it is surely not the case that every opposing moral consideration overrides a given joint commitment from the point of view of what reason requires, all things considered. Thus suppose Kate is jointly committed with Ralph to work on his political campaign tonight. Now, she worked on Ralph's campaign the previous night and has not yet done anything for her equally good friend Carol, who is also a candidate. All else being equal it would be fairer for her to work on Carol's campaign tonight. Meanwhile, it is not at all clear that, in the circumstances, she ought to work on Carol's campaign tonight, all things considered. In other words, it is not at all clear that the unfairness of her working for Ralph tonight is capable of overriding her joint commitment as far as what she ought to do, all things considered, is concerned. Perhaps it would be best if she and Ralph rescinded their joint commitment. Perhaps, though, she is unable to contact Ralph. I find it plausible to judge that in that case she must be prepared to conform to their commitment rather than ignoring it and going to help Carol. Whatever precisely the merits or demerits of one's action, should one fail to fulfil an obligation of joint commitment, those to whom one owes its fulfilment have a powerful tool—as is any appeal to a violation of one's rights against another.[52]

Some observations on the rhetoric—as opposed to the substance—of contemporary international politics illustrate this point. The attack on Iraq in 2003 was frequently characterized by the leadership in both the United States and, in particular, the United Kingdom as a matter of enforcing compliance with an agreement. The rule *pacta sunt servanda*—agreements are to be kept—is a venerable tenet of just war theory. That is why, I presume, it was so frequently invoked.

The idea of humanitarian intervention, which was also mooted in the debates prior to the attack on Iraq, is a newer idea. That certain actions of certain governments are horrendous, that certain governmental policies are unspeakably awful, is not in doubt. Let us suppose that other nations are morally required to prevent the horror, irrespective of any agreements. Nonetheless it is best from a practical point of view that obligations like this be grounded in international conventions and agreements as well—as in the groundbreaking United Nations Convention on the Prevention and Punishment of Genocide of 1948. The existence of an agreement gives the parties the standing to insist on performance and to punish violations, as the parties will understand. Whether

---

[52] This is nicely illustrated by Joel Feinberg's story of Nowheresville, a town whose inhabitants never demand what is due to them from one another: Feinberg (1980).

such action is justified in a given case, and in what form it is justified, is another matter—one that is liable to occasion heated debate.

Evaluating Political Obligations

I now turn from obligations of joint commitment generally to political obligations construed as such. Three different types of political society have been described in this book: one of governing rules, one of personal rule, and one of rules of governance or constitutional rules. In all of these societies people have obligations of joint commitment to abide by certain rules and also, where relevant, to conform to certain commands. For the sake of simplicity I focus here on the case where there are constitutional rules. Similar things can be said, *mutatis mutandis*, for the other cases.

There is one particular argument that is likely to be made in relation to political obligations in particular. It runs roughly as follows. Almost any non-conforming action will have a tendency to undermine the whole edifice of rules and commands that organizes the life of the population in question. Insofar as the maintenance of this edifice, albeit problematic in parts, is superior—all things considered—to its demise, there is a weighty argument for compliance in almost every case. One might put things this way: the joint commitment in question is no humdrum everyday one, like a joint commitment one has with a friend to uphold the rule that you call each other for a chat on Saturday morning. This joint commitment has enormous significance. Those who fail to conform to the resulting obligations fail to treat it with the very special respect it deserves.[53]

This argument will be strongest for cases in which a particular act of non-compliance is most likely seriously to destabilize a central part of the mechanism of government. Victimless, unwitnessed violations of law like not stopping at a stop sign in an empty desert are not of that kind, though they may be argued necessarily to weaken the perpetrator's respect for the law, something that could lead to graver violations later on, and the co-opting of others to act in like manner. Escaping from prison while serving a sentence imposed by a court is an example more to the point, publicly suggesting a lack of respect for the law and those who stand behind its authority. Assassination of an established ruler would be even closer.

It clearly does not follow from this argument, as stated here, that one must always act so as to support and comply with the political institutions of one's political society. For one thing, the argument requires that the existence of the

---

[53] An extreme version of this point is found in Hegel (1977: 157), who writes of 'the absolutely divine principle of the state, together with its majesty and absolute authority'.

political system in question be preferable to its demise. This may generally be so, but it does not have to be so. Perhaps the existing system is deeply flawed and there is a saviour at the gates. Perhaps incorporation in a larger political entity is more desirable than the status quo. Perhaps a split into two or more distinct political entities is preferable to it. Perhaps the present system is so bad that the kind of anarchy that will result if it fails is actually to be preferred.

Again, it may be that the fact that not fulfilling one's obligation in a particular case will tend to undermine the political system can be countered by the argument that it will not lead to the demise of that system as a whole but only tend to change it in a good way.[54] It will not lead to anarchy with violence or to a worse regime. Political protest may not be allowed at present, but if there are enough protestors on a given issue, they may be allowed, after all, to make their point. Or they may be harassed, even shot, but provoke an international outcry that leads to badly needed improvements.

To say that political disobedience may be justified in particular cases is not to deny that the case for disobedience may need carefully to be argued. In plural subject terms, questions relating to the moral permissibility of political disobedience are matters of moral argument around a joint commitment and its obligations. In discussing them, specific cases will usefully be considered. Was Socrates morally required to submit to the death penalty, as he judges in Plato's dialogue? Was Antigone, as represented in Sophocles' play, morally required to obey the dictates of the ruler, Creon, or was it morally permissible for her to bury her brother contrary to those dictates, as she herself argued? [55] Such questions are part of an inquiry that goes beyond the essentially analytic framework developed in this book. Nonetheless, if my argument here is correct, it has provided tools essential for the purpose. The inquiry in question may be characterized in its broadest terms as the morality of politics.

The claim that one is not morally bound to conform to a joint commitment one was coerced into entering can be seen to belong here. The same goes for the claim that one is not morally required to fulfil one's side of a joint commitment whose satisfaction requires one to do something immoral.

In the context of political obligations, care will need to be taken as to when the conditions in which one entered a pertinent joint commitment allow one to ignore that commitment from a moral point of view. That one had little choice but to participate in a given political society may not be enough to allow one, morally speaking, to ignore the commitments one has thereby taken

---

[54] Compare here the Hart–Devlin controversy in the 1960s as expressed in Devlin (1965) and Hart (1963). Hart insisted that *change* and *destruction* were two different things.

[55] I return to these cases in Ch. 12, below.

upon oneself. One had little choice, but in becoming jointly committed one has invited and received the trust of others. Nor need anyone be culpable in regard to one's choice situation.[56]

Again, one may well have to take more into account than the fact that a particular law is unjust. A given system, though flawed, may be preferable to the alternatives, and one must weigh that in considering whether or not to conform to this particular law.

The injustice, other vices, and bad conduct of political societies can take various forms. They may have to do with a given political society's relations with other political societies, as when one invades another purely for the sake of self-aggrandizement. They can also be internal. A society's internal vices and bad conduct may directly affect every one of its members, as in a situation where there is no freedom of association in public places. Or one or more particular sub-populations may be most closely affected, as in a society where unfair distinctions are made on such grounds as race, gender, age, or economic class. Some classes of people may not be permitted an education, for instance, or may not be allowed into the professions.

In each case, a given individual who is jointly committed with his fellows to uphold the political institutions in question may wish personally to protest their injustice. He may wish to say, in effect, 'I personally think this is unjust!' I take such protest not to be ruled out by his joint commitment—unless the political institutions include an institution that forbids such protest. That is because it is put *in personal terms*.

There are many forms of protest in which one may engage. One may make a solitary personal protest, one may join one's personal voice to those of others, one may be part of an existing group that protests, or part of a group formed for the purpose—a protest group. All of these protests may be personal in that the protesters wish to say, in effect, either 'I personally think this is unjust!' or 'This group "personally" thinks this is unjust!'

The joint commitment in which one participates, meanwhile, need not require anything in terms of one's personal judgements. It requires the parties to it to espouse *as a body* one or more rules of a certain kind. When they say, in effect, 'I personally think', they mark the fact that they are not speaking as members of this body but in their own name. One who says in protest against a government action 'Not in my name...' marks the fact that, personally speaking, he strongly prefers that the government not act as they are doing. Meanwhile the government *is* acting in his name insofar as he is a member of

---

[56] Hume's famous analogy with one who has been kidnapped and impressed into service in a vessel obscures this fact. See Hume (1965: 263).

the political society whose government they are, and they are acting in the name of that society.

It is likely, of course, that there is more to a protester's agenda than the marking of his personal antipathy to, or adverse personal judgement on, a particular political institution. He wants things changed. His hope may be that those who are in a position to do so will take appropriate action: change the law, call off the war.

He may wish to foment a revolution: to overthrow the whole set of institutions, substituting a theocracy for a democracy, or vice versa. His protesting voice may be intended as a rallying cry, calling on the other members of the political society jointly to rescind the joint commitment that sustains it in its present form.

I am assuming that someone can be jointly committed with others to uphold as a body an unjust or otherwise oppressive institution, when he is himself one of the oppressed, either in person or as the member of a particular class of persons. Injustice can, of course, range from what is relatively minor to what is extremely severe. Thus it may be that though unjustly treated in certain respects the individuals in question can still be said to have the possibility of living reasonably good lives. Or this may not be the case. At the extreme, we have the case of genocidal laws mandating the destruction of a particular class or particular classes of persons. This is indeed an extreme case, though in terms of world history to date, it is a depressingly realistic one.

This raises a question that was touched on earlier.[57] Are there any limits on what political institutions one can be jointly committed with others to uphold? This is an important question to which I cannot give a full treatment here. Some pertinent points are as follows.

The question is not whether there are joint commitments one would be reasonable to avoid, or, indeed, that one ought to avoid, given the chance. Nor is it the question whether there are joint commitments one should attempt to free oneself from, given the chance. These, which can easily be answered in the affirmative, are not questions about joint commitment as such. This *is* a question about joint commitment as such—an essentially conceptual question.[58] There is one way of putting it that is liable to obscure its nature, as I explain.

What if one was jointly committed with certain others to uphold a certain set of quite reasonable political institutions, but through a quirk of fate a duly instituted leader driven by personal hatreds began to issue genocidal edicts

---

[57] Sect. 7.2 above.

[58] That is neither to say, nor deny, that moral considerations may be germane to it.

in a way that was somehow consistent with the laws already existing in that political society?[59] Could one's joint commitment entail that one is obligated to support—and hence comply with—this law? What if one is oneself a member of the targeted group? Could one still be obligated to support this law?[60]

These questions are posed in terms of obligation. As I have argued quite strenuously in this book, there are different kinds of obligation. I have distinguished in particular moral obligations in the sense of context-sensitive moral requirements, and obligations of joint commitment. The first thing to emphasize, in response, then, is that it is consistent with plural subject theory to argue that in the situation envisaged neither the members of the targeted group nor the other members of the political society in question are obligated to support the genocidal edicts—where obligation is a matter of moral requirement. It can easily allow that no one is morally required to commit suicide, to hand himself in to be killed, to hand others over to be killed, or whatever these genocidal injunctions require. It can allow, indeed, that in this situation one ought to do all that is in one's power to thwart the implementation of these evil injunctions, whether one is the target of them or not.

For practical purposes this may suffice to allay any morally based concerns about the case in question. What, though, of obligations of joint commitment? Since one cannot have such obligations without a joint commitment that supports them, and since every joint commitment supports obligations of conformity, the question about the obligations of the targets of a genocidal injunction, for instance, is the question about whether they, in particular, can be *subject to a joint commitment* to (among other things) support this injunction.

This returns us to the original question—in a particularly stark form. To put it in simple terms: what if your country turns on you? This way of putting things makes it clear that your situation is different from the usual case of a soldier commanded to do something that risks his life to further the course of a war, or of someone who, in normal circumstances, has been assigned the death penalty for a crime committed.[61] I shall not attempt to decide this question here but note some pertinent considerations.

---

[59] Some may argue that this cannot be, since the moral law is always an integral part of the law of any political society. Pursuit of the question requires that one either reject or at least set aside this assumption. Such phrases as 'One nation, under God' suggest a different conception—they imply that God's laws limit those of the nation.

[60] Samuel Wheeler III and Stephen Schiffer, at least, have raised this in discussion.

[61] In real life such cases have sometimes been tainted by the kind of malign intent at issue here. I take such circumstances not to be 'normal'. In any case they can be set aside.

In this connection several people have informally proposed something along these lines: it is understood that I entered the initial joint commitment *for the sake of my self-preservation*, so I can have no political obligation to comply with a command to die or allow myself to be killed. The most difficult problem with this is that it is not always apposite to talk of *the reasons for which a given person entered into the joint commitment*. One may simply have fallen into it as one went about one's life. One may, indeed, have had reasons, but a variety of kinds of reasons are possible. Pleasing one's parents is one. Staying in one place is another.

Another problem for the self-preservation view is that it has trouble accounting for those who volunteer to join the army in dangerous times and those, like Socrates, who 'patiently submit' to a statutory penalty of death. In fact it tends to be assumed and is often publicly stated that one's political obligations may extend to risking death, or dying, either in combat or by imposition of a death penalty. Thus the Roman poet Horace famously wrote: 'Dulce et decorum est pro patria mori.'[62] For those who accept this position, it is hard to argue for the primacy of self-preservation. A motive more nuanced than self-preservation may then be proposed, but will not take care of the first problem.

It is possible that either of two other lines of questioning may lead to a negative answer. The first is interpretative. It concerns the act or acts by means of which a person becomes jointly committed. Can those who express their readiness to enter a joint commitment to accept certain rules of governance ever properly be interpreted as ready to accept ensuing rules that target themselves in the way envisaged? Unfortunately, there is some reason to think that they can. People may explicitly offer their fanatic support to a would-be leader whose wisdom they do not and will not doubt, *whatever* he enjoins. In spite of this unpleasant possibility, one may be able to argue for a negative answer in situations not involving such fanaticism. It may be hard, though, to insist that there are specific implicit provisos to the general case of entry into a joint commitment just as it is hard to insist on the existence of a certain motive for entry. Both this and the self-preservation view may at base be moral positions as to when one is morally entitled to say 'No' to one's country, something that does not speak precisely to the present issue.

A further line of inquiry allows that there may be cases in which one did jointly commit with one's fellows to regard all of the edicts of a certain person as authoritative, whatever they might be. It may take as an example the fanatics

---

[62] Horace (1969: 33 Bk III, ode 2, l. 1). In translation, very roughly: 'It is a sweet and proper thing to die for one's country.' Horace's words were later quoted with heavy irony by the British poet Wilfrid Owen.

mentioned above. It seeks out considerations that would allow that in these special circumstances one may now be free of one's erstwhile commitment or that the option of concluding it is now in one's own hands.[63]

The overall situation in the special circumstances that are under discussion, and in many others less stark as well, is hardly moot. It is not the case that one ought, all things considered, to connive in the wanton destruction of one's person. Accordingly, if his government has turned on him in this way, one who *does* still take himself to be jointly committed with his fellows to uphold its authority is not likely to feel conflicted about violating this joint commitment if he can. In a less extreme, less cut and dried situation, a standing joint commitment is likely to be more important in practical terms.

In every case where there is a joint commitment, one has the corresponding obligation. One owes conforming actions to the other parties. In at least some cases where there are strong moral reasons for deviating from the commitment one may retain a strong sense of this obligation. It may be felt even when one recognizes these moral reasons. It may then contribute to a felt sense of dilemma. Letting down those who trust one, in whatever way, is liable not to feel quite right, however right it is all things considered.

Pertinent here are well-known social psychology experiments of Stanley Milgram and his associates, in which some experimental subjects struggled mightily when faced with orders from a supposed scientific experimenter that went against their sense of what it was morally appropriate to do. Many went the way of the experimenter in spite of believing they were inflicting grave damage on another human being. (In fact, they were not.) Milgram himself had expected to find that most people would not do this.[64]

Depending on whether or not one focuses on just or unjust political societies, one is likely to see political obligations of joint commitment as a good thing or its opposite.[65] These obligations constitute a significant constraint on action. In a wholly admirable political society, therefore, they will help to keep members' behaviour within reasonable bounds. Members will not be unduly hampered by the praiseworthy political institutions they are obligated to obey. They will have a basis for trusting others to support these impeccable institutions, and an entitlement to stand up against one who is failing to uphold them. In a

[63] Ch. 7, above, discussed a variety of general considerations on how one might be freed from a joint commitment in which one has participated, including considerations on how a joint commitment may be terminated.

[64] See e.g. Milgram (1983).

[65] The extreme anarchist who sees all non-self-imposed constraints as an evil will not go for them at all. But then he will not consistently approve of doing things with other people, entering agreements, or establishing rules of any kind. All these things have disadvantages, indeed, but we can hardly live human lives without them.

society that is far from admirable, political obligations will help to shore up an unfortunate status quo. Failing a strong moral sense in its members, there will be nothing to counterbalance these obligations. This is something on which unscrupulous leaders can trade. Naturally, in such a society, as in any, there may well be other elements that shore up its political institutions as well. In particular the threat of force may play a significant role in keeping at least some people's behaviour in check. This is true even when what we are faced with is not a political society at all, in the terms of plural subject theory. Political obligations, meanwhile, offer practical support to tyranny, as they do to any given form of political society.

It is not my brief to raise a paean of praise to political obligations. Nor is it to denigrate them. It is to explain how they are possible.

12

Summary and Prospect

In this concluding chapter I summarize the argument of this book. I briefly explore the consonance of the theory proposed with two famous situations of crisis: Socrates in his prison cell awaiting his punishment of death, and Antigone in her conflict with Creon, the ruler of her political society. Finally, I note some avenues for further investigation, including both empirical inquiry and moral reflection, given the theory of political obligation sketched here.

12.1 Summary

This book has addressed the membership problem: does membership in a political society, in and of itself, involve obligations to uphold that society's political institutions? In short, are there political obligations? It has offered a fine-grained account of a political society and has concluded on this basis that members of a political society in the sense in question are obligated to one another to uphold its political institutions. This has consequences not only for the world as it is, but for the world as it might be.

It may be helpful at this point to run through the main steps in the argument. I first distinguished the membership problem from several other problems that have concerned political philosophers. In my formulation the membership problem is not limited in its concerns to obligations qualified as *moral*. It has to do with a broader class of so-called obligations, those I characterized as *genuine* obligations. These were distinguished from *imputed* obligations. If one has a genuine obligation, one then has sufficient reason to fulfil it.

I then gave a partial characterization of those obligations on the genuine side of the divide. This derived from a number of intuitive judgements on obligation. It allowed for the possibility that there might be importantly different types of genuine obligation.

There is a recognized class of genuine obligations that have a special feature—directedness—that I interpreted in terms of *owing*, following

H. L. A. Hart and others. If I have a directed obligation towards you I owe you an action. In other terms, I am obligated *to* you to perform that action. Precisely how one could come to owe another person an action remained to be seen.

Having formulated the criteria I felt a maximally successful solution to the membership problem would satisfy, I explored the credentials of a classical theory that is in some ways the most promising solution to date: actual contract theory. An important difficulty for this theory from the point of view of the membership problem is that it invokes a conception of membership in a political society that is artificially narrow. Some quite promising alternative contemporary proposals still fell short of a maximally adequate solution to the problem.

What would be a more intuitive conception of a political society? Societies in general are commonly conceived of as social groups in a relatively narrow sense. It is understood that such groups can be very large or extremely small. What, though, does this idea of a social group amount to? In exploring this question I first focused on a—relatively!—manageable small-scale case: two people out on a walk together. I then proposed a general account of what it is to do something with another person. Centrally, one must be jointly committed with them to endorse as a body a certain goal, and you must both be acting in light of that goal. I explained what joint commitment was and made the key argument that joint commitments obligate the parties to one another, their obligations being to act in conformity with the joint commitment.

I refer to those who are jointly committed in some way or other as constituting a plural subject. Having made the connection between joint commitment and those who constitute a social group by acting together, I defended an account of social groups generally as plural subjects. I explained how plural subjects could be inclusive, anonymous, and hierarchical, characteristics often associated with societies as opposed to social groups in general. I explained also how their borders could to some extent be 'fuzzy'. I construed a political society as one with political institutions or, in other terms, institutions of governance. In plural subject terms, people constitute a political society if they are jointly committed to uphold as a body a particular set of institutions of governance. I distinguished three broad types of political society, where each type was characterized by a particular set of social rules: governing rules, rules stipulating some person or body's ruling capacity, and rules of governance or constitutional rule. These rules constitute the most basic political institutions of the society. The members of that society can appropriately refer to these institutions as *theirs* collectively. A plural subject account of social rules was defended as an alternative to the classic account of H. L. A. Hart.

In sum, I have argued that given intuitive interpretations of the relevant terms, which I explained, the members of a political society are obligated to uphold its political institutions by virtue of their membership in that society. That membership is a matter of participation in a joint commitment to accept together with the other members the political institutions in question.

This argument constitutes the theory I have labelled the plural subject theory of political obligation. Rather than simply stating, as some do, that there is an integral connection between membership and obligation—or 'we'-thoughts and obligation—I have made that connection out by carefully articulating the senses in which the key terms of the argument are to be understood. Perhaps most important, I have clarified the nature of the obligations in question and shown that such obligations are an inevitable concomitant of membership in a social group as that has been construed here.

This theory was brought up against the several desiderata specified for a theory of political obligation proposed in the third chapter and, as I explained, it does well in terms of these. In this respect, also, it does well in comparison with several theories that are somewhat close to it, both classical and contemporary.

I have argued that actual contract theory is a special case of plural subject theory. Any agreement, I propose, brings a joint commitment into being. The more general plural subject theory does not appeal to agreements but rather to joint commitments, which can be formed in contexts other than an agreement, as in the gradual development of a social rule. It can allow, of course, that it is possible to found a political society by agreement.

Important aspects of my discussion of agreements as joint commitment phenomena apply, *mutatis mutandis*, to joint commitments generally, including those that sustain a society's political institutions. Thus neither coercive circumstances nor immoral content prevents a joint commitment from obligating the parties in the usual way. I have made it clear that this position does not imply that from a rational point of view one must always act in ways supportive of the political institutions of one's society. This accords with a general consensus that one may have an obligation that one need not fulfil, *all things considered*. Though an obligation of joint commitment need not always be acted upon, the other parties can invoke it as long as the joint commitment stands. It will therefore always be of practical relevance to those involved, and of predictive relevance to any observers.

The plural subject theory of political obligation clearly surmounts the problem of group character: how can membership in an evil society obligate and, if it cannot, how can membership in a political society always obligate?

The answer is that membership in a society always obligates, but members are not always required to support its institutions, all things considered.

My theory has been cited as a form of 'nonvoluntarist contract theory'.[1] It does not in fact appeal to contracts or agreements, but it is in an important sense 'non-voluntarist'. According to the theory, an understanding of joint commitment and a readiness to be jointly committed are necessary if one is to accrue political obligations, as is common knowledge of these in the population in question. One can, however, fulfil these conditions without prior deliberation or decision, and if one has deliberated, one may have had little choice but to incur them.

A major aim of this book has been to argue for and draw attention to the obligations of joint commitment, and to recommend to those interested in obligation in the context of political life that they take account of this particular form of obligation. If this book helps to put obligations of joint commitment—and joint commitment itself—on the map of this part of contemporary political philosophy that will, in my view, be an important advance. Whatever one's final conclusion as to the obligations in play in any actual situation, one needs to be aware of all the possibilities.

The following quotation from H. L. A. Hart, sits well, on the face of it, with the plural subject theory of political obligation. This assumes, rightly or wrongly, that the legal obligation of which he speaks is a species of political obligation in my sense. Hart first refers to

the views which I have always held and which most of my critics reject that the concept of legal obligation is morally neutral, and that legal and moral obligation are conceptually distinct...

He goes on:

A morally neutral conception of legal obligation serves to mark off the points at which the law itself restricts or permits the restriction of individual freedom. Whether laws are morally good or evil, just or unjust, these are focal points demanding attention as of supreme importance to human beings constituted as they are.[2]

One might argue, in any case, that the political obligations of plural subject theory are, indeed, focal points demanding attention, whether the political institutions they help to sustain are morally good or evil, just or unjust.

This book started with the laws of Athens talking. It will be good to return at this point to that conversation—to Socrates awaiting the death penalty in an Athenian prison. He imagines what the laws would say to him, to

---

[1] Simmons (1996). [2] Hart (1998), quoted in Lacey (2004: 354).

counterbalance Crito's plea that he escape, with Crito's help, to another place, outside the bounds of Athens's laws. To repeat part of the quotation given earlier, they say

if you cannot persuade your country, you must do whatever it orders, and patiently submit to any punishment that it imposes ...

In the rest of their speech, they detail several reasons why this is true of Socrates in particular. At the same time the quotation suggests something quite stark: you must do what your country orders, because it is your country ... unless you can persuade it otherwise. Others have thought as much, whether or not the author of the *Crito* meant to imply it. Is it true? How can that be? What is the force of the 'must'?

This book suggests an answer. It may or may not apply to the historical Socrates, though there is reason to think it did. So thinking, the laws might have put things like this: 'Your country is a political society of which you are a member. As we understand it, this means that you are jointly committed to uphold with your fellow members its political institutions. From this it follows that you have obligations of joint commitment to uphold those institutions—that is the sense in which you "must" uphold them. They include the courts and processes of trial, and punishments imposed through the courts according to those processes. If you are fully to uphold these institutions, then, you must submit to the punishment that has been imposed on you. You are obligated to your fellow members of this political society to do so.

'You may try to argue that you never committed yourself to die at our hands. We respond that in the course of your life among them, you committed yourself, with your compatriots, to uphold these institutions, and we are aware of no proviso to that commitment of the kind you suggest.

'Perhaps you can persuade us that we are in error in punishing you, in particular, in this way. Or perhaps you can persuade us that it is morally wrong to punish anyone in this way—with the death penalty. Or perhaps, if you cannot persuade us, you can persuade your fellows to do away with us, rescinding together those joint commitments that make us yours, and start afresh with new political institutions. Unless and until any of these things happen, our order stands, and your obligation stands as well. What it means, in terms of what you are rationally required to do, has been explained in this book'—here the laws gesture to an advance copy of the book you are reading.

'Though it is not, perhaps, in our interest to say it, you may not be rationally required to submit to this punishment, all things considered. Your desire for self-preservation, though, is not enough, in and of itself, to permit your escape.

You need to find some higher law, if you like to call it that, which mandates or at least permits your escape from a rational point of view.

'In seeking for this higher law, remember that you owe your submission to your compatriots, as a matter of the joint commitment in which you participate. You will betray them if you flee, and they will understand this. Though, as laws, we are not experts in morality, we also caution this: there is some virtue in fidelity. It is hard to put a definite price on it, as all such judgements are hard.

'We wish you well with your deliberations. For though we can command, and even compel you with force, we are not in a position to determine what is rationally required or permitted. That will have to be left to your judgement, unless there is someone else's judgement—human or divine—that you wish to rely on.'

The historical Socrates did not escape, but died as commanded by drinking hemlock. If he had listened to this imaginary speech, we might be tempted to infer he judged that there was no higher law to override the laws' commands on this occasion.[3]

In contrast, in Sophocles' play about her, Antigone explicitly appeals to such a law. King Creon has forbidden anyone to bury his nephew Polyneices, on pain of death. Polyneices had fallen in battle after bringing an army to fight against the city ruled by Creon, the city of which Antigone is a citizen. Polyneices is Antigone's brother, and she is determined to bury him. Antigone and Creon confront each other. Cleon argues that for her not to follow his order would be for her to undermine the political society that is the framework within which everything she values is possible. Without that society there would be no place for the peaceful progress of family life or of friendship. Antigone argues that a higher law, one that existed well before his edict, compels her to bury her brother:

nor deemed I that thy decrees were of such force, that a mortal could override the unwritten and unfailing statutes of heaven.[4]

Neither will back down, Antigone buries her brother, and Creon punishes her with a death sentence.

These are just two of the often tragic cases, from literature and from life, which might be cited in connection with the topic of political obligation.

---

[3] In Plato's *Apology* (1978*b*: 28d; also 38a), Socrates says that even were the laws to forbid him to do so, he would follow a higher command that directed him to philosophize as long as he lived, saying that he owes a greater obedience to God than to them. (Thanks to David Conway, personal communication, 2005.)

[4] Sophocles (1962: 89–90, ll. 453–5).

Taken together, and interpreted in plural subject terms, these two cases suggest something I have argued in the course of this book. In reckoning what one is to do, all things considered, there are at least three distinct types of consideration that may need to be set against each other: one's inclinations and, more broadly, one's self-interest, one's commitments including the joint commitments to which one is a party, and the dictates of morality or, in a similar role, of a deity or deities. As to the relationship of these considerations, I have suggested that obligations of joint commitment trump one's inclinations and self-interest as such. Hence, depending on the case, even one's interest in continuing to live may be trumped by a lawful command. Yet it may be that one need not, all things considered, obey that command. One may, indeed, be morally required *not* to do so—for a variety of reasons. As the cases of Socrates, Antigone, and many others make clear, there is room for judgement here, and for disagreement. The more one can understand the nature of these different considerations, then, and their relationship, the better.

12.2 Prospect

This book has advanced a novel theory of political obligation. The theory is distinctive in several ways. In particular, the type of obligation to which I appeal has no explicit role in other contemporary theories of political obligation. My energies in writing the book have therefore been focused on explaining how and why one might take membership in a political society to involve obligations of that type. This has led me to articulate a conception of a political society that allows for many different kinds of constitution—both beautiful and ugly. As I have argued, there is reason to take this to be one of the central conceptions of a political society that inhabits human minds.

I have here almost totally eschewed references to the findings of historians, and social scientific findings. That is largely because my primary aim has been the exploration and clarification—to some degree at least—of a number of interlinked concepts. In pursuit of this aim it has often seemed best to stick to hypothetical cases and examples. The results of conceptual investigations of the sort on which this book engages, meanwhile, are well suited to be an integral part of empirical inquiry.

The articulation of the plural subject conception of a political society suggests new questions for political scientists. With this conception in mind they can ask of the members of various populations, particularly those geographically defined, how precisely they view the purported commands of a given imperator in whose territory they reside. They may not love that imperator, or admire it, or they may. Do they, in any case, understand themselves to be jointly committed with all or some other residents in its territory to regard its edicts as authoritative? Are they rather jointly committed simply to comply with these edicts as long as that seems to be a practical necessity? Is there no sense of joint commitment at all? Naturally one will have to find a way to investigate these matters from an empirical standpoint. It is not an easy matter to elicit useful answers to direct questions on such matters, and one can hardly invoke the technical term 'joint commitment' in one's questioning.

A number of informal suggestions are implicit in this book. Evidence that people think in terms of 'our' government, 'our' constitution, and so on, is clearly helpful. It is not definitive, but it is an important start. If someone talks, rather, of 'their' government we know this person is *not* thinking of himself as jointly committed with 'them' to uphold the political institution in question. Among other things, one can also test for such things as the presence or absence of pride, guilt, and so on, in relation to the actions of a given imperator. If people express strong discontent with a particular imperator or a particular set of political institutions, one may have to probe to see if they are best characterized as 'uncommitted' or as discontented, perhaps vociferously discontented, parties to a joint commitment. Is emotional alienation accompanied with a sense of participation? Does the language of 'us' persist?

There are others better equipped than I carefully to formulate empirical tests for the presence of joint commitment thinking and, indeed, joint commitment, in a given population. This is in any case not the place to investigate such matters. I urge, simply, that one should not ignore the possibility that joint commitment thinking is more or less widespread in a given population.

One reason for not ignoring it is that one who understands himself to be jointly committed with others understands himself to be subject, therefore, to an important constraint. Many of his thoughts, feelings, and actions—including his sense of crisis on occasion—may be explicable in these terms. He may act so as to conform to the commitment without pausing for reflection. He may do this because his participation in the joint commitment is what is most salient to him at the moment. Or he may believe, through personal deliberation or as a result of external pressure, that such conformity—or such conformity in a given case—is the strongest demand of morality. The plural subject theory of political obligation is highly pertinent, then, to questions of motivation in the political realm.

Contemporary discussions of political obligation tend to be presented as moral arguments—or as contestations of moral arguments. They proceed in terms of such moral concepts as justice and fairness, and in terms of moral obligation in the sense of moral requirement. Either specific duties such as duties of gratitude, reciprocation, or fair play are invoked, or the presence of an otherwise unqualified moral requirement is posited. The argument of this book is not in that sense a moral one, nor are its primary aims either moral or political in a practical sense. Its aim has been, rather, to show that if we restrict ourselves to the standard approach to political obligation in terms of moral requirement we stand to lose sight of an enormously consequential fact: the existence of a distinct realm of obligation.

That is of course not to say that we should cease to ask moral questions or cease to evaluate the different aspects of the human situation as they are in themselves, and in relation to one another. Indeed, if it is granted that this situation involves joint commitments of a variety of kinds, a range of new evaluative and moral questions arise. Perhaps it is best not to say that they are all new. If my argument in this book is right, some are old questions. Now, however, they can be formulated in a relatively precise fashion.

Some of these evaluative questions have already been mooted. They include the following. What is the value, if any, of the existence of a joint commitment as such? In other words, how valuable in itself is this particular form of human connection? What are its positive aspects and what its negative? What, if anything, can be said about the value of fulfilling such a commitment, in general, and its relation to other kinds of considerations, such as justice and care? What of those joint commitments that sustain particular political societies in being? Can some value be put on conformity to such commitments as such? How and in what way does the character of the political society affect the importance of conformity? Under what circumstances is nonconformity allowable or even required? When should one push for rescission? When should one do what one can to escape the scene? What is the truth, if there is one, about particular cases? Was Socrates right to take his punishment? Was Antigone right to bury her brother in spite of Creon's orders? Should Creon have ordered and punished as he did?

What if one is faced with two conflicting joint commitments? Suppose that, retaining one's membership in the political society in whose confines one was born, one later joined another, making a solemn pledge. These countries face each other, war is in the air. How is one to proceed? Is the order in which one entered the joint commitments determinative of which one is to follow, and if so, how, and why? Should one factor in benefits received? How, then, is one's education in one society to be weighed against the opportunities for advancement one has enjoyed in the other? How relevant are the moral properties of these countries—the freedom they represent, the justice of their political institutions, their compassionate character—and how are they to be weighed against each other, and against the benefits one has received?

What of those who live among those jointly committed to uphold a particular set of political institutions, yet are not themselves party to the joint commitment? It may not in all circumstances be easy to maintain this position, given the encouragement or pressure of others to join one's voice to theirs, and those who avow it may do so without proper warrant. They may deny that they are parties yet otherwise speak and act as if they are.[5] Suppose, in any case, that the population of those living on a certain island—the 'residents'—contains some individuals who are self-styled anarchists—the 'hold-outs'. The residents who are not hold-outs are party to a joint commitment to support certain political institutions. The hold-outs refuse to become parties to the joint commitment. Perhaps each lives reclusively in a particular part of the island, and each has explicitly rejected the residents' invitation to join them in their joint commitment. This is not because there is anything especially immoral about these institutions in particular. The hold-outs simply do not wish to be bound to uphold them. A number of moral questions arise.

What, if anything, is morally required of these hold-outs, in relation to the political institutions in question? Are they required to become parties to the sustaining joint commitment, albeit reluctantly, if they will thereby help to support a valuable set of institutions? Are they at least morally required not to do anything to undermine the institutions in question—a question that applies equally to those travelling through a given territory? Again, how may the rest treat the hold-outs, morally speaking?[6] Is it morally permissible to pain the hold-outs for acting contrary to the dictates of the residents' political institutions, given that they remain hold-outs? Deciding such questions is an important role for moral inquiry in the context of a plural subject model of political societies. The parties to the joint commitment cannot allege that they have a right of joint commitment to a hold-out's conformity to it. They must find a moral argument that entitles them to pressure him to act accordingly.

Other moral questions: when are members of a given population morally required jointly to decide to set up and support a system of political institutions? Are they morally required to set up a particular type of system, for instance a democratic one? If so, should this be a liberal democracy and, if so, of what stripe? What of the relationship of one political society founded on a joint

---

[5] Cf. Horton (1992: 159–60).

[6] Jonathan Wolff once urged this question in discussion. His own perspective is developed in Wolff (1995, 2000). See also Horton (1992: 160).

commitment with another such society? Is every such society sacrosanct in some way—so that whatever its problems, outsiders are morally required not to intervene in its affairs? Or does this depend on the society's character? When may outsiders intervene in such a society's affairs?[7]

Evidently the plural subject theory of political obligation raises many significant evaluative and moral questions, some of which have been referred to as 'problems of political obligation'. At the same time, its purview needs to be distinguished from them. This theory is essentially an analytic theory. Its primary purpose is to explain that and how there can be political obligations in the sense of this book. In setting out this theory, I have not tried to settle all of the many questions it raises, empirical, moral, or indeed, conceptual. Rather, my ambition has been to set such questions in motion.

---

[7] On this last group of questions, Walzer (1977) is a classic text. Walzer places a high value on the common life that people make together—a life that will include their political institutions but not be restricted to these.

Bibliography

Altham, James E. J. (1985), 'Wicked Promises', in Ian Hacking (ed.), *Exercises in Analysis* (Cambridge: Cambridge University Press).

Althoff, Gerd (2000), *Family, Friends and Followers: Political and Social Bonds in Early Medieval Europe* (Cambridge: Cambridge University Press).

American Restatement of the Law of Contracts (First), vol. i (1932) (St Paul: American Law Institute Publishers).

Anderson, Benedict (1983), *Imagined Communities: Reflections on the Origin and Spread of Nationalism* (London: Verso).

Anscombe, G. E. M. (1978), 'On the Source of the Authority of the State', *Ratio*, 20.

—— (1981), 'On Promising and its Justice, and Whether it Need be Respected *in Foro Interno*', in her *Ethics, Religion, and Politics: Collected Philosophical Papers*, vol. iii (Minneapolis: University of Minnesota Press).

Atiyah, Patrick (1981), *Promises, Morals, and the Law* (New York: Oxford University Press).

Aumann, Robert (1976), 'Agreeing to Disagree', *Annals of Statistics*, 4.

Bach, Kent (1995), 'Terms of Agreement', *Ethics*, 105/3.

Bacharach, Michael (2005), 'Foreword: Teamwork', in N. Gold (ed.), *Teamwork: Interdisciplinary Perspectives* (Basingstoke: Palgrave MacMillan).

Baier, Annette (1997), *The Commons of the Mind* (Peru, Ill.: Open Court Publishing).

Balzer, Ulrich (2002), 'Joint Action in Large Groups', in Meggle ed. (2002).

Bayles, Michael (1992), *Hart's Legal Philosophy: An Examination*, Law and Philosophy Library 17 (Dordrecht: Kluwer).

Becker, L. C. (1981), 'Hard Choices Are Not Enough', *Virginia Law Review*, 67.

Ben-Menachem, Hanina (1987), 'Comment', in Gavison ed. (1987).

Beran, Harry (1977), 'In Defense of the Consent Theory of Political Obligation and Authority', *Ethics*, 87.

—— (1987), *The Consent Theory of Political Obligation* (Croom Helm: London).

Bittner, Rudiger (2002), 'An Action for Two', in Meggle ed. (2002).

Boucher, David, and Kelly, Paul eds. (1994), *The Social Contract from Hobbes to Rawls* (London: Routledge).

Brandt, Richard (1964), 'The Concepts of Obligation and Duty', *Mind*, 73.

Bratman, Michael (1993*a*), 'Shared Intention', *Ethics*, 104; repr. in Bratman (1999).

—— (1993*b*), 'Shared Intention and Mutual Obligation', *Cahiers d'épistemologie*, 9319; repr. in revised form in Bratman (1999).

—— (1999), *Faces of Intention* (Cambridge: Cambridge University Press).

Broad, C. D. (1915–16), 'On the Function of False Hypotheses in Ethics', *International Journal of Ethics*, 26.

Broome, John (2001), 'Are Intentions Reasons? And How Should We Cope with Incommensurable Values?', in C. W. Morris and A. Ripstein (eds.), *Practical Rationality and Preference: Essays for David Gauthier* (Cambridge: Cambridge University Press).

Card, Claudia (1988), 'Gratitude and Obligation', *American Philosophical Quarterly*, 25.

Cook, Michael (2001), *Commanding Right and Forbidding Wrong in Islamic Thought* (Cambridge: Cambridge University Press).

Cotterell, Roger (1995), *Law's Community: Legal Theory in Sociological Perspective* (Oxford: Oxford University Press).

Dagger, Richard (2000), 'Membership, Fair Play, and Political Obligation', *Political Studies*, 48.

Davidson, Donald (1969), 'How is Weakness of the Will Possible?', in J. Feinberg (ed.), *Moral Concepts* (London: Oxford University Press).

Dawson, Francis (1975), 'Fundamental Breach of Contract', *Law Quarterly Review*, 91.

Devlin, Lord Patrick (1965), *The Enforcement of Morals* (Oxford: Oxford University Press).

Durkheim, Émile (1951), *Suicide: A Study in Sociology*, trans. J. A. Spaulding and G. Simpson (New York: Free Press) (1st pub. 1897).

—— (1968), *Les Règles de la méthode sociologique* (Paris: Presse universitaire de France) (1st pub. 1895).

—— (1982), *The Rules of Sociological Method*, trans. W. D. Halls (New York: Free Press) (trans. of Durkheim 1968).

Dworkin, Ronald (1977), *Taking Rights Seriously* (Cambridge, Mass.: Harvard University Press).

—— (1986), *Law's Empire* (Cambridge, Mass.: Harvard University Press).

—— (1989*a*), 'The Original Position', in Norman Daniels (ed.), *Reading Rawls* (Stanford, Calif.: Stanford University Press).

—— (1989*b*), 'Liberal Community', *California Law Review*, 77.

Edmunson, William ed. (1999), *The Duty to Obey the Law* (Lanham, Md.: Rowman and Littlefield).

Elias, Norbert (1978), *The Civilizing Process*, trans. Edmund Jephcott (New York: Urizen Books).

Ewing, A. C. (1947), *The Individual, the State, and World Government* (New York: Macmillan).

—— (1953), 'What Would Happen if Everyone Acted Like Me?', *Philosophy*, 28.

Farley, Margaret (1990), *Personal Commitments: Beginning, Keeping, Changing* (San Francisco: Harper).

Feinberg, Joel (1980), *Rights, Justice and the Bounds of Liberty: Essays in Social Philosophy* (Princeton: Princeton University Press).

Finnis, John (1987), 'Comment', in Gavison ed. (1987).

Frank, Robert (1988), *Passions within Reason: The Strategic Role of the Emotions* (New York: W. W. Norton).

Gans, Chaim (1992), *Philosophical Anarchism and Political Disobedience* (Cambridge: Cambridge University Press).

Gavison, Ruth ed. (1987), *Issues in Contemporary Legal Philosophy: The Influence of H. L. A. Hart* (Oxford: Clarendon Press).

Gibbs, J. P. (1965), 'Norms: The Problem of Definition and Classification', *American Journal of Sociology*, 70.

Gilbert, Margaret (1981), 'Game Theory and *Convention*', *Synthese*, 46; repr. in Gilbert (1996).

——(1983), 'Notes on the Concept of a Social Convention', *New Literary History*, 14; repr. in Gilbert (1996).

——(1987), 'Modeling Collective Belief', *Synthese*, 73; repr. in Gilbert (1996).

——(1989), *On Social Facts* (London: Routledge; repr. 1992, Princeton: Princeton University Press).

——(1990a), 'Fusion: Sketch of a "Contractual" Model', in R. C. L. Moffat, J. Grcic, and M. Bayles (eds.), *Perspectives on the Family* (Lewiston, NY: Edwin Mellen Press); repr. in Gilbert (1996).

——(1990b), 'Rationality, Coordination, and Convention', *Synthese*, 84; repr. in Gilbert (1996).

——(1990c), 'Walking Together: A Paradigmatic Social Phenomenon', in P. A. French, T. E. Uehling, Jr., and H. K. Wettstein (eds.), *MidWest Studies in Philosophy*, vol. xv. *The Philosophy of the Human Sciences*; repr. in Gilbert (1996).

——(1991), Review of M. Robins, *Promising, Intending and Moral Autonomy*, *Philosophical Review*, 100.

——(1993a), 'Agreements, Coercion, and Obligation', *Ethics*, 103; repr. in Gilbert (1996).

——(1993b), 'Is an Agreement an Exchange of Promises?', *Journal of Philosophy*, 90; repr. in Gilbert (1996).

——(1993c), 'Group Membership and Political Obligation', *The Monist*, 76; repr. in Gilbert (1996).

——(1996), *Living Together: Rationality, Sociality, and Obligation* (Lanham, Md.: Rowman and Littlefield).

——(1997a), 'Group Wrongs and Guilt Feelings', *Journal of Ethics*, 1.

——(1997b), 'What Is It for *Us* to Intend?', in G. Holmstrom-Hintikka and R. Tuomela (eds.), *Contemporary Action Theory*, vol. ii (Dordrecht: D. Reidel).

——(1998a), 'In Search of Sociality', *Philosophical Explorations*, 1.

——(1998b), Review of R. Tuomela, *The Importance of Us*, *Ethics*, 108.

——(1998c), 'Social Norms', in *Routledge Encyclopedia of Philosophy* (London: Routledge).

——(1998d), Review of R. Hardin, *One For All*, *Philosophical Review*, 108.

——(1999a), 'Obligation and Joint Commitment', *Utilitas*, 11.

——(1999b), 'Reconsidering the "Actual Contract" Theory of Political Obligation', *Ethics*, 109.

—— (1999c), 'Social Rules: Some Problems with Hart's Account and an Alternative Proposal', *Law and Philosophy*, 18.

—— (2000), *Sociality and Responsibility: New Essays in Plural Subject Theory* (Lanham, Md: Rowman and Littlefield).

—— (2001a), 'Sociality, Unity, Objectivity', *Proceedings of the 1998 World Congress of Philosophy*, 11. *Social and Political Philosophy*, ed. D. Rasmussen (Charlottesville, Va.: Philosophy Documentation Center).

—— (2001b), 'Joint Action', in *Elsevier Encyclopedia of the Social and Behavioral Sciences*, vol. xii (Amsterdam: Elsevier Publishing).

—— (2002a), 'Aspects of Joint Commitment: Responses to Various Comments', in Meggle ed. (2002).

—— (2002b), 'Acting Together', in Meggle ed. (2002).

—— (2002c), 'Collective Wrongdoing: Moral and Legal Responses', *Social Theory and Practice*, 28.

—— (2002d), 'Belief and Acceptance as Features of Groups', *Protosociology*, www.protosociology.de

—— (2003), 'The Structure of the Social Atom: Joint Commitment as the Foundation of Human Social Behavior', in Frederick Schmitt (ed.), *Social Metaphysics* (Lanham, Md.: Rowman and Littlefield).

—— (2004a), 'Scanlon on Promissory Obligation: The Problem of Promisees' Rights', *Journal of Philosophy*, 101.

—— (2004b), Review of K. Graham, *Practical Reasoning in a Social World*, *Philosophical Review*, 113.

—— (2005a), 'Shared Values, Social Unity, and Liberty', *Public Affairs Quarterly*, 19.

—— (2005b), 'Towards a Theory of Commitments of the Will: On the Nature and Normativity of Intentions and Decisions', in Wlodek Rabinowicz and Toni Ronnow-Rasmussen (eds.), *Patterns of Value II* (Lund: Lund University Press).

—— (2005c), 'A Theoretical Framework for the Understanding of Teams', in Natalie Gold (ed.), *Teamwork: Multidisciplinary Perspectives* (Basingstoke: Palgrave Macmillan).

—— (2005d), 'Three Dogmas about Promising', paper delivered at a symposium on promising, American Philosophical Association, Pacific Division.

—— (forthcoming), *Rights Reconsidered* (Oxford: Oxford University Press).

Graham, Keith (2002), *Practical Reasoning in a Social World: How We Act Together* (Cambridge: Cambridge University Press).

Green, Leslie (1990), *The Authority of The State* (Oxford: Oxford University Press).

—— (1996), 'Who Believes in Political Obligation?', in J. Narveson and J. T. Sanders (eds.), *For and Against the State* (Lanham, Md.: Rowman and Littlefield).

Grice, H. P., and Strawson, P. (1956), 'In Defense of a Dogma', *Philosophical Review*, 65.

Guest, A. G. ed. (1984), *Anson's Law of Contracts* (26th edn., Oxford: Clarendon Press).

Hampton, Jean (1980), 'Contracts and Choices: Does Rawls Have a Social Contract Theory?', *Journal of Philosophy*, 77.

Hampton, Jean (1997), *Political Philosophy* (Boulder, Colo.: Westview Press).

Hardimon, M. O. (1994), 'Role Obligations', *Journal of Philosophy*, 91: 333–63.

Hardin, Russell (1995), *One for All: The Logic of Group Conflict* (Princeton: Princeton University Press).

Hare, R. M. (1989), 'Political Obligation', in *Essays in Political Morality* (Oxford: Oxford University Press).

Hart, H. L. A. (1955), 'Are There Any Natural Rights?', *Philosophical Review*, 64.

——— (1961), *The Concept of Law* (Oxford: Clarendon Press).

——— (1963), *Law, Liberty, and Morality* (Stanford, Calif.: Stanford University Press).

——— (1982), *Essays on Bentham: Jurisprudence and Political Theory* (Oxford: Oxford University Press).

——— (1994), *The Concept of Law* (2nd edn., Oxford: Clarendon Press).

——— (1998), 'Entrevista a H. L. A. Hart' (interview with Juan Ramón de Páramo, trans. into Spanish), *Doxa*, 5.

Heal, Jane (1978), 'Common Knowledge', *Philosophical Quarterly*, 28.

Hegel, G. W. F. (1977), *The Philosophy of Right*, ed. T. M. Knox (Oxford: Clarendon Press) (1st pub. 1821).

Hirschmann, Nancy (1989), 'Freedom, Recognition, and Obligation: A Feminist Approach to Political Theory', *American Political Science Review*, 83.

——— (1992), *Rethinking Obligation: A Feminist Method for Political Theory* (Ithaca, NY: Cornell University Press).

Hobbes, Thomas (1982), *Leviathan* (Harmondsworth: Penguin) (1st pub. 1651).

Hohfeld, Wesley Newcombe (1914), 'Some Fundamental Legal Conceptions', *Yale Law Journal*, 23.

Hollis, Martin, and Sugden, Robert (1993), 'Rationality in Action', *Mind*, 102.

Homans, George Caspar (1974), *Social Behavior: Its Elementary Forms* (rev. edn., New York: Harcourt Brace Jovanovich).

Honderich, Ted (1976), *Political Violence* (Ithaca, NY: Cornell University Press).

Horace (1969), *The Third Book of Horace's Odes*, trans. Gordon Williams (Oxford: Clarendon Press).

Horton, John (1992), *Political Obligation* (London: MacMillan).

Hume, David (1965), 'Of the Original Contract', in *David Hume's Political Essays*, ed. C. W. Hendel (Indianapolis: Bobbs-Merrill) (1st pub. 1742).

——— (1978), *A Treatise of Human Nature* (London: Oxford University Press) (1st pub. 1739).

Ibbetson, D. J. (2000), *A Historical Introduction to the Law of Obligations* (Oxford: Oxford University Press).

Jamieson, Dale (1975), 'David Lewis on Convention', *Canadian Journal of Philosophy*, 5.

Jaspers, Karl (1947), *The Question of German Guilt*, trans. E. B. Ashton (New York: Capricorn Books).

Kagan, Shelly (1989), *The Limits of Morality* (Oxford: Clarendon Press).

Kamm, Frances (2002), 'Owing, Justifying, Rejecting', *Mind*, 111.

Kant, Immanuel (1991), *The Metaphysics of Morals* (Cambridge: Cambridge University Press) (1st pub. 1785).

Kavka, Gregory (1983), 'Rule by Fear', *Nous*, 17.

——— (1986), *Hobbesian Moral and Political Theory* (Princeton: Princeton University Press).

Klosko, George (1992), *The Principle of Fairness and Political Obligation* (Lanham, Md.: Rowman and Littlefield).

Kramer, Matthew H. (1999), 'Requirements, Reasons, and Raz: Legal Positivism and Legal Duties', *Ethics*, 109/2: 375–407.

Kripke, Saul A. (1972), *Naming and Necessity* (Cambridge, Mass.: Harvard University Press).

Kutz, Christopher (2000), *Complicity: Ethics and Law for a Collective Age* (Cambridge: Cambridge University Press).

Kymlicka, Will (1995), *Multicultural Citizenship: A Liberal Theory of Minority Rights* (Oxford: Clarendon Press).

Lacey, Nicola (1988), *State Punishment: Political Principles and Community Values* (London: Routledge).

——— (2004), *A Life of H. L. A Hart: The Nightmare and the Noble Dream* (Oxford: Oxford University Press).

Ladd, John (1970), 'Legal and Moral Obligation', in J. R. Pennock and J. W. Chapman (eds.), *Nomos XII: Political and Legal Obligation* (New York: Atherton Press).

Levine, Donald ed. (1980), *Georg Simmel: On Individuality and Social Forms* (Chicago: Chicago University Press).

Lewis, David K. (1969), *Convention: A Philosophical Study* (Cambridge, Mass.: Harvard University Press).

Locke, John (1980), *Second Treatise of Government*, ed. C. B. MacPherson (Indianapolis: Hackett Publishing Co.) (1st pub. 1690).

Lyons, David (1965), *Forms and Limits of Utilitarianism* (Oxford: Oxford University Press).

MacCormick, Neil (1978), *Legal Reasoning and Legal Theory* (Oxford: Clarendon Press).

——— (1981), *H. L. A. Hart* (Stanford, Calif.: Stanford University Press).

MacDonald, Margaret (1951), 'The Language of Political Theory', in A. G. N. Flew (ed.), *Logic and Language*, 1st se. (Oxford: Basil Blackwell).

Mackie, John (1977), *Ethics: Inventing Right and Wrong* (Harmondsworth: Penguin).

McPherson, Thomas (1967), *Political Obligation* (London: Routledge and Kegan Paul).

Martin, Michael (1987), *The Legal Philosophy of H. L. A. Hart: A Critical Appraisal* (Philadelphia: Temple University Press).

Marx, Karl, and Engels, Friedrich (1977), *The Communist Manifesto*, in *Karl Marx: Selected Writings*, ed. D. McClennan (Oxford: Oxford University Press) (1st pub. 1850).

Mason, Andrew (2000), *Community, Solidarity and Belonging* (Cambridge: Cambridge University Press).

Medina, Vicente (1990), *Social Contract Theories: Political Obligation or Anarchy?* (Savage, Md.: Rowman and Littlefield).

Meggle, Georg ed. (2002), *Social Facts and Collective Intentionality* (Frankfurt: Dr. Hänsel-Hohenhausen AG).

Milgram, Stanley (1983), *Obedience to Authority: An Experimental View* (New York: HarperCollins).

Mill, John Stuart (1979), *Utilitarianism* (Indianapolis: Hackett Publishing) (1st pub. 1861).

Miller, Seamus (1992), 'On Conventions', *Australasian Journal of Philosophy*.

——— (2001), *Social Action: A Teleological Account* (New York: Cambridge University Press).

Moore, G. E. (1968). *Principia Ethica* (Cambridge: Cambridge University Press).

Pateman, Carole (1979), *The Problem of Political Obligation: A Critical Analysis of Liberal Theory* (Chichester: John Wiley).

——— (1992), 'Political Obligation, Freedom and Feminism', *American Political Science Review*, 86: 179–82.

Pink, Thomas (1996), *The Psychology of Freedom* (Cambridge: Cambridge University Press).

Pitkin, Hannah (1966), 'Obligation and Consent, II', *American Political Science Review*, 60.

Plato (1974), *Republic*, trans. G. M. A. Grube (Indianapolis: Hackett) (original *c*.380 BC).

——— (1978*a*), *Crito*, in *The Collected Dialogues*, ed., E. Hamilton and H. Cairns (Princeton: Princeton University Press) (original *c*.360 BC).

——— (1978*b*), *Apology*, in *The Collected Dialogues*, ed., E. Hamilton and H. Cairns (Princeton: Princeton University Press) (original *c*.360 BC).

Pothier, Robert Joseph (1802), *A Treaties on Obligations Considered in a Moral or Legal View*, trans. Francis-Xavier Martin (Newburn, NC: Martin and Ogden) (1st pub. 1791).

Postema, Gerald (1982), 'Coordination and Convention at the Foundations of Law', *Journal of Legal Studies*, 11.

Prichard, H. A. (1949), 'Exchanging', in Prichard (1968).

——— (1968), *Moral Obligation and Duty and Interest* (Oxford: Oxford University Press).

Quine, W. V. O. (1951), 'Two Dogmas of Empiricism', *Philosophical Review*, 60.

Rawls, John (1958), 'Justice as Fairness', *Philosophical Review*, 68.

——— (1971), *A Theory of Justice* (Cambridge, Mass.: Harvard University Press).

Raz, Joseph (1975), *Practical Reason and Norms* (Princeton: Princeton University Press).

——— (1979), *The Authority of Law* (Oxford: Clarendon Press).

——— (1984), 'On the Nature of Rights', *Mind*, 92.

——— (1986), *The Morality of Freedom* (Oxford: Clarendon Press).

——— (1999), 'The Obligation to Obey: Revision and Tradition' in Edmunson ed. (1999).

——— (2001), *Value, Respect and Attachment* (Cambridge: Cambridge University Press).

Robins, Michael (1984), *Promising, Intending, and Moral Autonomy* (Cambridge: Cambridge University Press).

Ross, W. D. (1965), *The Right and the Good* (Oxford: Clarendon Press).

Rousseau, Jean-Jacques (1983), *On the Social Contract and Discourses*, trans. D. A. Cress (Indianapolis: Hackett Publishing Company) (1st pub. 1792).

Sartorius, Rolf (1966), 'The Concept of Law', *Archives for Philosophy of Law and Social Philosophy*, 52.

—— (1987), 'Positivism and the Foundations of Legal Authority', in R. Gavison (ed.), *Issues in Contemporary Legal Philosophy: The Influence of H. L. A. Hart* (Oxford: Clarendon Press).

—— (1999), 'Political Authority and Political Obligation' in Edmunson ed. (1999).

Scanlon, Thomas (1990), 'Promises and Practices', *Philosophy and Public Affairs*, 19.

—— (1995), 'Moral Theory: Understanding and Disagreement', *Philosophy and Phenomenological Research*, 55.

—— (1998), *What We Owe to Each Other* (Cambridge, Mass.: Harvard University Press).

—— (2001), 'Promises and Contracts', in Peter Benson (ed.), *The Theory of Contract Law: New Essays* (Cambridge: Cambridge University Press).

—— (2003), 'Thickness and Theory', *Journal of Philosophy*, 100.

Scheffler, Samuel (1997), 'Liberalism, Nationalism, and Egalitarianism', in Robert McKim and Jeff McMahan (eds.), *The Morality of Nationalism* (New York: Oxford University Press).

Schelling, Thomas (1960), *The Strategy of Conflict* (Oxford: Oxford University Press).

Schiffer, Stephen (1972), *Meaning* (Oxford: Oxford University Press).

Schutz, Alfred (1970), *On Phenomenology and Social Relations*, ed. Helmut R. Wagner (Chicago and London: University of Chicago Press).

Searle, John (1990), 'Collective Intentions and Actions' in P. R. Cohen, J. Morgan, and M. E. Pollack (eds.), *Intentions in Communication* (Cambridge, Mass.: MIT Press).

—— (1995), *The Construction of Social Reality* (New York: Free Press).

Sen, Amartya (1977), 'Rational Fools: A Critique of the Behavioral Foundations of Economic Theory', *Philosophy and Public Affairs*, 6.

Sesonske, Alexander (1964), *Value and Obligation* (Oxford: Oxford University Press).

Shockley, Kenneth (2004), 'The Conundrum of Collective Commitment', *Social Theory and Practice*, 30.

Simmel, Georg (1971), 'How is Society Possible?', in *Georg Simmel: On Individuality and Social Forms*, ed. D. N. Levine (Chicago: University of Chicago Press) (1st pub. 1908).

Simmons, A. John (1979), *Moral Principles and Political Obligations* (Princeton: Princeton University Press).

—— (1984), 'Consent, Free Choice, and Democratic Government', *Georgia Law Review*, 18.

—— (1996), 'Associative Political Obligations', *Ethics*, 106.

Singer, Peter (1973), *Democracy and Disobedience* (London: Routledge).

Smith, M. B. E. (1973), 'Is There a Prima Facie Obligation to Obey the Law?', *Yale Law Journal*, 82.

Sophocles (1962), *The Plays and Fragments, Part III. The Antigone*, trans. R. C. Jebb (Amsterdam: Servio Publishers).

Stern, Fritz (1999), *Einstein's German World* (Princeton: Princeton University Press).

Stocker, Michael (1970), 'Moral Duties, Institutions, and Natural Facts', *Monist*, 54.

Sumner, Wayne (1987), *The Moral Foundation of Rights* (Oxford: Clarendon Press).

Tamir, Yael (1993), *Liberal Nationalism* (Princeton: Princeton University Press).

Thomson, Judith Jarvis (1990), *The Realm of Rights* (Cambridge, Mass.: Harvard University Press).

Tuomela, Raimo (1984), *A Theory of Social Action* (Dordrecht: Reidel).

—— (1995), *The Importance of Us* (Stanford, Calif.: Stanford University Press).

Tussman, Joseph (1960), *Obligation and the Body Politic* (New York: Oxford University Press).

Upton, Hugh (2000), 'Right-Based Morality and Hohfeld's Relations', *Journal of Ethics*, 4.

Vitek, William (1993), *Promising* (Philadelphia: Temple University Press).

Walzer, Michael (1970), *Obligations: Essays on Disobedience, War, and Citizenship* (Cambridge, Mass.: Harvard University Press).

—— (1977), *Just and Unjust Wars: A Moral Argument with Historical Illustrations* (New York: Basic Books).

Weber, Max (1964), *The Theory of Social and Economic Organization*, trans. T. Parsons and A. M. Henderson (Glencoe, Ill.: Free Press) (1st pub. 1915).

Wellman, Christopher (2000), 'Relational Facts in Liberal Political Theory: Is there Magic in the Pronoun "My"?', *Ethics*, 110.

Wolff, Jonathan (1995), 'Political Obligation, Fairness, and Independence', *Ratio*, 8.

—— (2000), 'Pluralistic Models of Political Obligation', in M. Baghramian and A. Ingram (eds.), *Pluralism* (London: Routledge).

Wolff, Robert P. (1970), *In Defense of Anarchism* (New York: Harper Torchbooks).

Woozley, A. D. (1967), 'The Existence of Rules', *Nous*, 1.

—— (1979), *Law and Obedience: The Arguments of Plato's Crito* (Chapel Hill, NC: University of North Carolina Press).

Wordsworth, William (1982), *The Borderers*, ed. R. Osborn (Ithaca, NY: Cornell University Press) (1st pub. 1842).

Index

Compiled with the help of Karl Stocker.

Technical terms defined in this work are printed in bold type as is the number of the page where they are defined